D0982580

Before Pastoral

BEFORE PASTORAL:
Theocritus and the Ancient Tradition of Bucolic Poetry

DAVID M. HALPERIN

YALE UNIVERSITY PRESS

NEW HAVEN AND LONDON

Published with assistance from
the Mary Cady Tew Memorial Fund

Excerpt from Wallace Stevens' poem "Of Modern
Poetry" from *The Collected Poems of Wallace Stevens,*
copyright © 1954 by Wallace Stevens, Alfred A.
Knopf, Inc. is reprinted with permission.

Designed by James J. Johnson
and set in Bembo Roman by
The Composing Room of Michigan, Inc.
Printed in the United States of America by
Halliday Lithograph, West Hanover, Mass.

Library of Congress Cataloging in Publication Data

Halperin, David M., 1952–
    Before pastoral, Theocritus and the ancient tradition
of bucolic poetry.

    Bibliography: p.
    Includes index.
    1. Theocritus—Criticism and interpretation.
2. Pastoral poetry, Greek—History and criticism.
I. Title.
PA4444.H33 1983   884'.01   82–10879
ISBN 0–300–02582–3

10 9 8 7 6 5 4 3 2 1

IN MEMORIAM
S. WILLIAM HALPERIN
11.I.1905–15.IV.1979

Contents

Preface

What kind of expectations should a modern reader bring to an encounter with the text of Theocritus? All too often the answer to this question has been automatic and, it would appear, self-evident: in Theocritus a modern reader may expect to discover the first true pastoral poet in Western literature. So strong is the force of this interpretative habit, so crisply defined the placed assigned to Theocritus in the pageant of classical literary tradition, that the poet's numerous deviations from what is normally expected of him have not been able to check the prevailing critical tendency. It is the purpose of this book to demonstrate the inadequacy of the pastoralist interpretation of Theocritus and to offer a new theoretical perspective from which his poetry can be viewed with greater coherency and historical precision.

The poetry of Theocritus, or a certain portion of it at any rate, possessed in antiquity a distinctive literary character. Ancient readers of Theocritus accordingly tended to group some of his works together and to treat them as members of a single class. The literary category to which these poems were thought to belong was called *bucolic,* a term invented by the poet himself and employed in his text to refer to several of his own compositions (or to parts of them). The meaning of this term and the nature of the literary category it once served to designate are obscure, despite the survival of the word in the modern European languages. Any attempt at a fresh and accurate historical understanding of Theocritus must begin with an investigation into the ancient significance of *bucolic* and the original meaning of the category represented by it. This task requires little new research: most of the sources on which my work is based have long been familiar to students of Hellenistic poetry. Rather, I offer this study as a kind of conceptual housecleaning intended to sweep aside the network of false expectations which have impeded a more profound appreciation and critical understanding of Theocritus and his imitators.

There is no clear evidence that Theocritus understood the word *bucolic* and its derivatives in a formal, generic sense. It is possible that he employed the word merely as an occasional or descriptive term appropriate to contexts featuring cowherds or other pastoral figures. (Such, in fact, is the implied consensus of the Greek scholia.) Perhaps Theocritus did not even conceive himself to have invented a new kind of poetry—perhaps he regarded his own oeuvre more informally, leaving it to subsequent generations to discover in aspects of his various and multifaceted work a unified artistic achievement. The search for the ancient meaning of *bucolic* may ultimately unearth a literary concept devised by Theocritus' followers, and the results of this investigation may tell us more about the way Virgil read Theocritus than about how Theocritus viewed his own poetry.

The justification for the strategy outlined above is twofold. Regardless of his specific (and by now unfathomable) intentions, Theocritus somehow endowed a portion of his work with a sufficiently distinctive literary profile to impress its unique qualities on later generations of readers. It is legitimate to inquire into the nature of those qualities. Second, even if Theocritus was content to leave nameless the class or classes comprising his most brilliant and innovative poetic experiments, we still need a means of referring to them under their common aspect, and *bucolic* need stand for nothing more than the peculiar set of characteristics which distinguished some fraction of Theocritus' work from the literary productions of his contemporaries as well as from the monuments of the past. Whether or not bucolic poetry as such was a deliberate and conscious invention of Theocritus, as I believe it was, is a question which every reader of this volume is entitled to answer in his or her own fashion.

Ancient bucolic poetry is a field of study in which one is counted lucky to have convinced oneself, and successful if one is able to persuade one's friends, of the essential rightness of any particular hypothesis. No wider agreement is to be hoped for. I am aware that many of the arguments employed in my discussion could be made to demonstrate the opposite point if they were to be wielded by someone hostile to my approach—one need only glance at the first fifty-odd pages of E. A. Schmidt's *Poetische Reflexion* (1972) or at Susanne Wofford's 1980 Yale dissertation, "The Choice of Achilles: The Epic Counterplot in Homer, Virgil, and Spenser," for a ready illustration. I feel no compulsion to insist that the definition of bucolic poetry offered here is the only possible or correct one, simply that it is plausible and can account for the evidence as well as or better than the currently prevailing critical concept.

I have for the most part refrained from engaging in scholarly controversy in the text and have confined detailed consideration of technical matters to the notes and appendix. I have tried to restrict the scholarly apparatus so as not to distract the historical student of literature, to whom this book is addressed, from the general argument, and I have often presented what I take to be the current state of knowledge in classical studies without attempting to credit all the scholars responsible for it; to them and to others whose views I may have unwittingly incorporated in my own exposition I offer thanks and apologies. Specialists who find a favorite conjecture, hypothesis, or line of argument passed over in silence or summarily dismissed are invited to consult my 1979 Stanford dissertation, "Theocritus and the

Ancient Definition of Bucolic Poetry," on which this book is closely based, before taxing me with simple neglect. Having insisted on the distinction between *bucolic* and *pastoral* with such pedantic consistency, I have freely tolerated impurities of terminology elsewhere: both the Idylls of Theocritus and the Eclogues of Virgil were known in antiquity as *Bucolics;* it is for the sake of clarity rather than of historical accuracy that I have occasionally reverted to the modern nomenclature. Finally, in citing Greek and Latin authors, I have relied on authoritative English translations whenever possible; in framing my own translations I have often borrowed a felicitous phrase from one of my more able predecessors without acknowledgment. In rendering Theocritus I have benefited particularly from the English versions of A. S. F. Gow (Cambridge, 1952) and Anna Rist (Chapel Hill, 1978).

I have also been extremely fortunate in my teachers and colleagues. I was introduced to classical studies by James J. Helm, Nathan A. Greenberg, and Charles T. Murphy of Oberlin College, for whose intellectual leadership and personal example I shall remain ever grateful. My interest in ancient bucolic poetry was nurtured by three extraordinary, and very different, men: John Van Sickle, under whose tutelage I first encountered Virgil's bucolic poetry at the Intercollegiate Center for Classical Studies in Rome; William Berg, with whom I studied during my first year at Stanford; and Edward W. Spofford, who supervised my early work on Theocritus and later directed my dissertation. The earliest formulation of the ideas elaborated here was presented at an undergraduate seminar on Hellenistic poetry conducted at Stanford by Phillip W. Damon, who graciously consented to serve on my dissertation committee after his return to the University of California at Berkeley. N. Gregson Davis and George H. Brown kindly agreed to serve on that committee as well. Edwin Good provided valuable extramural assistance with the interpretation of ancient Near Eastern source materials and commented on relevant sections of the manuscript. Portions of the finished dissertation were read by Charles Segal of Brown University and Martha A. Morrison of Brandeis University. John Van Sickle of Brooklyn College and Leo Marx of the Massachusetts Institute of Technology commented on the dissertation in its entirety; the latter also supplied unfailing encouragement and reliable advice throughout the composition of the final draft. In short, my teachers and colleagues have exhibited a generosity that far exceeds the demands of professional obligation and is more akin to the manifestations of friendship. They have saved me from numerous errors of omission and commission; nonetheless, I am under no illusion that they share my views or endorse the thesis of this book.

Some of the work contained in the early chapters was begun with the aid of a Fellowship granted by the American Academy in Rome. The Department of Humanities at M.I.T. provided financial assistance with the typing of the dissertation and the indexing of the book. I particularly wish to thank Deborah Kurimay for her meticulous and sympathetic help in preparing the final manuscript. The staff of Yale University Press have proved the most diligent and pleasant of collaborators; the reader, as well as the author, has much to thank them for.

A less tangible, but no less real, debt of gratitude is owed to my family, to my fellow graduate students at Stanford—victims and survivors—to my colleagues in the Literature Section at M.I.T., and, most inclusively, to my friends. Without their support I could have neither begun nor completed this book.

Abbreviations

AC	*L'Antiquité classique*
AJP	*American Journal of Philology*
ANRW	H. Temporini et al., eds., *Aufstieg und Niedergang der römischen Welt. Geschichte und Kultur Roms im Spiegel der neueren Forschung* (Berlin, 1972–)
AUMLA	*Journal of the Australasian Universities Language and Literature Association*
BICS	*Bulletin,* Institute of Classical Studies, University of London
CP	*Classical Philology*
CQ	*Classical Quarterly*
CR	*Classical Review*
CSCA	*California Studies in Classical Antiquity*
D-K	H. Diels and W. Kranz, eds., *Die Fragmente der Vorsokratiker,* 10th ed. (Berlin, 1960–61)
ELH	*English Literary History*
FGrHist	F. Jacoby et al., eds., *Die Fragmente der griechischen Historiker* (Berlin and Leiden, 1923–)
Gow-Page	A. S. F. Gow and D. L. Page, eds., *The Greek Anthology: Hellenistic Epigrams,* 2 vols. (Cambridge, 1965)
GRBS	*Greek Roman and Byzantine Studies*
Hagen	H. Hagen, ed., *Appendix Serviana ceteros praeter Servium et scholia bernensia Vergilii commentatores continens* (Leipzig, 1902) = Thilo, vol. 3, pt. 2
HSCP	*Harvard Studies in Classical Philology*
JHS	*Journal of Hellenic Studies*
JRS	*Journal of Roman Studies*
Kaibel	G. Kaibel, ed., *Comicorum graecorum fragmenta,* vol. 1, pt. 1 (Berlin, 1889)
Keil	H. Keil, ed., *Grammatici latini,* 7 vols. (Leipzig, 1855–80)
MH	*Museum Helveticum*
M-W	R. Merkelbach and M. L. West, eds., *Fragmenta Hesiodea* (Oxford, 1967)
MPhL	*Museum Philologum Londiniense*
N^2	A. Nauck, ed., *Tragicorum Graecorum Fragmenta,* 2d ed., reprinted with suppl. by B. Snell (Hildesheim, 1964)

NJbb	*Neue Jahrbücher für Philologie und Paedagogik = Jahrbücher für classische Philologie,* ed. M. J. C. Jahn, R. Dietsch, A. Fleckeisen et al.
NJbb. klass. Altert.	*Neue Jahrbücher für das klassische Altertum, Geschichte und deutsche Literatur und für Pädagogik = Neue Jahrbücher für Pädagogik,* ed. J. Ilberg
NLH	*New Literary History*
OCD²	N. G. L. Hammond and H. H. Scullard, eds., *The Oxford Classical Dictionary,* 2d ed. (Oxford, 1970)
OED	*The Oxford English Dictionary,* 12 vols. (Oxford, 1933)
OLD	*Oxford Latin Dictionary* (Oxford, 1968–)
Page	D. L. Page, ed., *Epigrammata Graeca* (Oxford, 1975)
Pfeiffer	R. Pfeiffer, ed., *Callimachus,* 2 vols. (Oxford, 1949–53)
PMG	D. L. Page, ed., *Poetae Melici Graeci* (Oxford, 1962)
PMLA	*Proceedings of the Modern Language Association*
Powell	J. U. Powell, ed., *Collectanea Alexandrina* (Oxford, 1925)
QUCC	*Quaderni Urbinati di cultura classica*
Rabe	H. Rabe, ed., *Hermogenis opera* (Leipzig, 1913)
RE	A. Pauly and G. Wissowa, eds., *Real-Encyclopädie der classischen Altertumswissenschaft* (Stuttgart, 1894–)
RhM	*Rheinisches Museum für Philologie*
Σ	scholia
SIFC	*Studi italiani di filologia classica*
TAPA	*Transactions of the American Philological Association*
Thilo	G. Thilo, ed., *Servii Grammatici qui feruntur in Vergilii carmina commentarii,* vol. 3, pt. 1: *In Bucolica et Georgica commentarii* (Leipzig, 1887)
TrGF	B. Snell, ed., *Tragicorum Graecorum Fragmenta,* vol. 1: *Didascaliae Tragicae, Catalogi Tragicorum et Tragoediarum· Testimonia et Fragmenta Tragicorum Minorum* (Göttingen, 1971)
UCalPublClPh	*University of California Publications in Classical Philology*
Wendel	C. Wendel, ed., *Scholia in Theocritum vetera* (Leipzig, 1914)
WS	*Wiener Studien*
YCS	*Yale Classical Studies*

INTRODUCTION

Bucolic Poetry and Pastoral Poetry

A work of art is "timeless" only in the sense that, if preserved, it has some fundamental structure of identity since its creation, but it is "historical" too. It has a development which can be described. This development is nothing but the series of concretizations of a given work of art in the course of history which we may, to a certain extent, reconstruct from the reports of critics and readers about their experiences and judgements and the effect of a given work of art on other works. . . . One can speak of the "life" of a work of art in history in exactly the same sense in which one can speak of an animal or a human being remaining the same individual while constantly changing in the course of a lifetime. . . . [T]here is a substantial identity of "structure" which has remained the same throughout the ages. This structure, however, is dynamic: it changes throughout the process of history while passing through the minds of its readers, critics, and fellow artists.[1]

The Idylls of Theocritus have undergone precisely this kind of dynamic transformation during the two and a quarter millennia since their creator first delivered them into the interpretative custody of the educated public. The story of this transformation, especially in its latter stages, has been told often and well; it provides an index to the cultural changes and literary developments which have taken place in the West over the intervening centuries and reveals the range of meanings which the text of Theocritus is capable of sustaining. The literary historian of classical antiquity, however, is concerned principally with neither of these aspects of Theocritean survivals, interesting as they are, but is called upon rather to chart the actual process of transformation in order to distinguish, insofar as possible, the original identity of the artistic achievement and the character of its earliest metamorphoses. If, indeed, one accepts the doctrine that the "controlling principle in meaning [is] the idea of will"—the will of the author as it is embodied in a text—one might even go so far as to claim, with E. D. Hirsch, Jr., that "in ethical terms, original meaning is the 'best meaning.'"[2]

1. Wellek and Warren (1962?), 155, citing L. Teeter, "Scholarship and the Art of Criticism," *ELH,* 5 (1938), 173–93; cf. also Wellek and Warren, 254–55.
2. E. D. Hirsch, Jr., "Three Dimensions of Hermeneutics," *NLH,* 3 (1972), 261; for Hirsch's earlier statement about the controlling principle in meaning, see his *Validity in Interpretation* (New Haven, 1967), 101. These passages are discussed by S. Suleiman, "Interpreting Ironies," *Diacritics,* 6, no. 2 (Summer 1976), 15–21.

Theocritus is generally regarded as the inventor of pastoral poetry by classical scholars and modern literary critics alike.[3] Yet he owes this title less to his own virtues and attainments than to his historical role in Graeco-Roman literary tradition: he furnished Virgil with a model, thereby becoming the ultimate (if indirect) "cause" of a major European poetic form. Like the holder of an honorary degree, Theocritus continues to enjoy his reputation in recognition of his services to Virgil. "The position of Theocritus thus resembles in some respects that of Homer. He is the acknowledged classic of pastoral poetry"—as Homer is the acknowledged classic of epic poetry—"though his influence upon the tradition is less direct and in the long run less formative than that of Virgil."[4] In this assessment by Frank Kermode all modern authorities on pastoral from W. W. Greg to Leo Marx concur.[5] To agree with them is not to underestimate the direct impact of Theocritus on the later tradition: it was more extensive than is often credited. The scholars and artists of the Italian Renaissance, starting with Petrarch and Boccaccio, knew the reputation of Theocritus, and Sannazaro was well acquainted with the Greek text. By 1531 the translation of Theocritus into Latin hexameters by Elius Eobanus of Hesse had made the poet accessible to those who could not read him in the original and had assured his influence on the neo-Latin literary productions of the Humanists. After 1545 Theocritus was a required author in the Greek curriculum at the University of Wittenberg.[6] His name was familiar to English scholars from the beginning of the sixteenth century; the first English translation of Theocritus appeared in 1588 contemporaneously with Abraham Fleming's rendering of Virgil's *Eclogues* and the composition of Shakespeare's *Venus and Adonis*.[7] Michael Drayton, who categorically proclaimed in 1619 that "The *Greek* Pastorals of THEOCRITUS, have the chiefe praise," was perhaps the first Englishman to voice such an opinion,[8] and his verdict was later echoed by Gessner.[9] Theocritus' stock has continued to rise and fall with changes in literary fashion. His popularity has been generally on the increase since the turn of the nineteenth century and the success of the Romantic movement: he was greatly admired by Hugh Blair, by Coleridge (who read him in school), and by Tennyson; he was selectively imitated by almost every

---

3. E. g., Murley (1940), 283; Coleman (1969), 100; idem (1977), 1; Segal (1963), 53, n. 36; idem (1975), 126–27; Barrell and Bull (1974), 4; Poggioli (1975), 3.

4. Kermode (1952), 22.

5. See Hieatt (1972), 6: "that Vergil is the more formative and influential of the two [classical pastoral poets] is one of the rare observations on which critical opinion agrees."

6. Grant (1965), 66.

7. Kerlin (1910), 2, 27–29.

8. Congleton (1952), 49.

9. Fritzsche-Hiller (1881), 26; Levrault (1914), 21.

major Romantic poet.[10] Recently, Thomas G. Rosenmeyer has attempted to demonstrate the prefiguration in Theocritus of the generic concept of the European pastoral lyric, but he has been unable to dislodge Virgil from preeminence.[11]

The dominant position of Virgil in the pastoral tradition is the result, then, not of any unchallenged authority or permanent and unvarying favor among his readers throughout the centuries, but of his overpowering influence and prestige during three specific periods of great formative significance in the history of pastoral taste. Accidents of transmission play their part in this story as much as cultural preferences and coincidences of temperament. The first of these periods is the era of later antiquity, in which Virgil stood out as the classic model among all the ancient poets. The most substantial imitations of Virgil produced during this period, the poetry of Calpurnius Siculus and Nemesianus, depend for their literary effects on an intricate reworking of Virgilian themes. "In the *Eclogues,* as in his other poetry, Virgil had succeeded in suggesting the intellectual complexities in his relation to tradition through a delicately controlled allusiveness, through personal emphases achieved within borrowed phrases, figures, and images. Calpurnius Siculus and Nemesianus, by revising the master's sylvan scene in the interest of their own more pragmatic themes, demonstrate how thorough their apprenticeship in his school has been."[12] In other words, the later Roman poets did not find it necessary to reach beyond Virgil to his sources because their manipulation of inherited themes and images required no other background than Virgil's own highly original synthesis. Pre-Virgilian sources were effaced by this practice. The influence of the Greek bucolic poets on Calpurnius and Nemesianus is at all events negligible;[13] the arguments recently advanced for dating Calpurnius to the early reign of Severus Alexander in the third century, a scant two generations before Nemesianus, make this indifference to Greek sources all the more understandable.[14] Calpurnius and Nemesianus continued to be read during the Middle Ages and the Renaissance, and their poetry (along with Virgil's) contributed to later European notions of what pastoral was and ought to be.[15]

10. Kerlin (1910), 81–103.

11. Rosenmeyer (1969); *contra,* Muecke (1975). On the influence of Theocritus, see Walker (1980), 133–49.

12. Damon (1961), 298.

13. *Pace* L. Castagna, "Le fonti greche dei 'Bucolica' di Nemesiano," *Aevum,* 44 (1970), 415–43.

14. E. J. Champlin, "The Life and Times of Calpurnius Siculus," *JRS,* 68 (1978), 95–110; but see now G. B. Townend, "Calpurnius Siculus and the *Munus Neronis,*" *JRS,* 70 (1980), 166–74, and R. Mayer, "Calpurnius Siculus: Technique and Date," *JRS,* 70 (1980), 175–76.

15. See W. P. Mustard, "Later Echoes of Calpurnius and Nemesianus," *AJP,* 37 (1916), 73–83; Grant (1965), 74, 112, 371–72.

The second formative period in the European pastoral tradition is the early Italian Renaissance. Here once again Virgil's influence dominated literary production. Dante, Petrarch, and Boccaccio all wrote Latin eclogues in imitation of Virgil, and their authoritative innovations triggered a fashion. "Events conspired to make Vergil the model for later writers. The fame of the poet was a potent cause among many. . . . Accidental conditions, too, told in favour of the Roman poet. During the middle ages Latin was a universal language among the lettered classes, while the knowledge of Greek, though at no time so completely lost as is sometimes supposed, was a far rarer accomplishment, and was restricted for the most part to a few linguistic scholars. Thus before the revival of learning had made Greek a possible source of literary inspiration, the Vergilian tradition, through the instrumentality of Petrarch and Boccaccio, had already made itself supreme in pastoral."[16] Theocritus had no direct imitators in this period; later, when increasing numbers of Humanists made his acquaintance, the Greek poet tended to suffer from comparison with the Roman. To be sure, many Renaissance critics made no sharp distinction between the merits of Virgil and Theocritus, stressing instead their common qualities. Nevertheless, the foundations of the subsequent Virgil cult were already being laid by the enthusiasm expressed in Politian's *Sylvae* (1489) and Vida's *De Arte Poetica* (1527).[17]

The third period of critical significance for the shaping of the pastoral tradition is the age of Neo-Classicism. Virgil's influence was decisive throughout. Julius Caesar Scaliger, who had proclaimed Aristotle the permanent lawgiver of poetry (a doctrine whose authority would be confirmed by the Council of Trent as well as by the aesthetic theory of the following century), also argued in his *Poetices Libri Septem* (1561) that each kind of literature has its own standard of perfection—"Est in omni rerum genere unum primum ac rectum ad cuius tum normam, tum rationem cætera dirigenda sunt"—and recommended Virgil's pastoral poetry as the embodiment of such a standard; to depart from him was to court poetic disaster, for Virgil "[does] not seem to have been taught by nature, but to have vied with it, or even better to have given it laws. . . . We have not been able to get from nature a single pattern such as the *ideas* of Virgil can furnish us."[18] With the publication in 1659 of René Rapin's *Dissertatio de Carmine*

---

16. Greg (1906), 17–18; cf. Gerhardt (1950), 67–68. See also Grant (1965), 77–115; G. Martellotti, "La riscoperta dello stile bucolico," in *Dante e la cultura Veneta*, ed. V. Branca and G. Padoan (Florence, 1966), 335–46.

17. Congleton (1952), 16–17, 297.

18. Spingarn (1908), 141–42; 149–50; Congleton (1952), 17. Scaliger devoted book 5, chapter 5 to an extended comparison of Virgil and Theocritus.

Pastorali the Neo-Classical doctrine of pastoral poetry received its definitive formulation. Rapin often praises Theocritus and Virgil, "those Fathers of *Pastoral*," in the same breath and commends them both as models: "For all the Rules that are to be given of any Art, are to be given of it as excellent, and perfect, and therefore ought to be taken from them in whom it is so." But whenever Rapin finds that "our Guides, *Virgil,* and *Theocritus,* do not very well agree," he tends to favor the former (who, unlike Theocritus, is "never faulty"). Rapin's critic Fontenelle, in his *Discours sur la nature de l'églogue* (1688), did not dissent from his adversary's judgment on this one point; he went beyond him in attacking the "Clownishness" of Theocritus and protested against the pedantry of scholarly historians who "have resolv'd to dubb him Prince of the Bucolick Poets."[19] The essays of both Rapin and Fontenelle were extremely influential in eighteenth-century England, and quite apart from their specific doctrines are expressive of the taste of the age. A typical and authoritative representative of that taste is Alexander Pope. Although Pope allows that in "nature and simplicity" Theocritus "excells all others" and concedes that his "Dialect alone has a secret charm in it which no other could ever attain," he asserts his opinion that "Virgil refines upon his original: and in all points where Judgement has the principal part, is much superior to his master" ("A Discourse on Pastoral Poetry," 1717). Even Samuel Johnson, who found a great deal of Neo-Classical theory objectionable, was unwilling to abandon Virgil as a standard of poetic excellence. All in all, critics of this period agree on the respective merits of the two poets. They maintain that Virgil "has improved upon *Theocritus*" (Edward Manwaring; 1737), observing that "Theocritus is like a rich mine, in which there is plenty of ore: but a skillful hand is required to separate the dross from the pure metal" (John Martyn; 1749).[20] The tastes and preferences of these critics, who were responsible for the most complete and authoritarian definition of pastoral poetry, have shaped all subsequent thinking on the topic.

The role played by Virgil's *Eclogues* in molding and defining the European pastoral tradition presents an instructive example of how the personality of a great artist will at times impress itself so deeply upon a literary form that the two cannot thereafter be dissociated without difficulty; even if the literary form in question is already the product of a long and eventful prehistory, its origins tend to be eclipsed by the brilliant course of its subsequent evolution. Such a fate has indeed overtaken Theocritus and his Greek imitators. But the dominance and authority exercised by Virgil over

19. Congleton (1952), 54, 61, 66 (quoting from contemporary translations).
20. Ibid., 82, 305; cf. Kerlin (1910), 48.

the European pastoral tradition have not only bedeviled most efforts to
arrive at an unmediated understanding of Theocritus; they have also, paradoxically, impeded an accurate appreciation of Virgil himself by obscuring
the sources of his inspiration and the literary context of his own far-reaching
experiments. In losing sight of the Greek bucolic tradition, scholars have
allowed their thinking about the *Eclogues* to be conditioned by more recent
commonplaces about the nature of pastoral; they have preferred to approach
Virgil by an oblique path leading back to antiquity by way of Pope and
Shakespeare.[21] But Virgil, emerging as he did from the Hellenistic tradition, may have had something altogether different in mind when he set out
to compose his *liber bucolicon,* and in blurring over the Greek background of
his poetry we forfeit the possibility of understanding what Virgilian pastoral actually was and instead reduce it to what it later became. The influence of genre theory has been blamed for such a telescoping of historical
phenomena, for anachronisms in the focus of scholarly studies and a lack of
attention to "the irreducible, atypical singularity of the ancient poems."[22]
But however serious the critical lapses it has occasioned, the application of
generic archetypes derived from post-Theocritean or even from postclassi-
cal pastoral to the works of Theocritus and Virgil should be viewed as only
one aspect of the more general "Virgilianizing" tendency which has affected
our entire historical understanding of ancient bucolic poetry. If the task of
interpreting Theocritus is complicated as a result, Virgil cannot be said to
have benefited correspondingly. On the contrary: "One of our difficulties
in dealing with the *Eclogues,*" writes a recent commentator on the history of
pastoral attitudes, "has been that we have not known what to make of
Theocritus. He is usually praised for seasoning his idealization of rustic life
with humor and realism, but such praise simply confirms the tendency to
regard his pastoralism as whimsical and unreal."[23] An undistorted evaluation of Theocritus and of the historical significance of his achievement is
therefore essential to a clearer assessment of two major figures in classical
literature.

    The ancient tradition of bucolic poetry took a new turn with Virgil.
His role was pivotal: it is possible—indeed it is imperative—to distinguish
pre-Virgilian from post-Virgilian varieties of bucolic poetry.[24] There is
need for a historical study of the relatively obscure literary tradition before

    21. E. g., Coleman (1977), 1.
    22. A. J. Boyle, introduction to *Ancient Pastoral* (= *Ramus,* 4. no. 2 [1975]), 85; cf. Van
Sickle (1976), 18.
    23. Alpers (1972), 356; cf. Segal (1975), 115; Hieatt (1972), 24: "neither the poems of
Theocritus nor of Vergil answer to the orthodox notions of pastoral"; Weingarth (1967),
185–89.
    24. Cf. Rohde (1932), 73.

Virgil, and that need is not altered by a consideration of the possible generic relationships between the Idylls of Theocritus, the Eclogues of Virgil, and the poetic corpus of the later pastoral tradition. Even if it could be shown that the Idylls of Theocritus belong to what has been held at certain times in the evolution of European literary theory to be the fixed and determinate genre of pastoral poetry, such proof (which for the majority of the Idylls, in any case, will not be forthcoming) would affect neither the motives behind this inquiry nor its historical purpose and methodology: so long as the character of the pre-Virgilian tradition remains to be identified, no intellectual advantage can be gained by applying to the poetry of Theocritus the generic title or the concept of pastoral.[25] For "literary genres are human inventions which have concrete histories rather than an ideal absolute existence. They develop first in practice and only gradually are theorized; their definitions change and evolve according to the interests, tastes, and needs of successive poets, audiences, and critics."[26] Generic considerations, far from obviating the need for historical analysis of literary developments, intensify it: "One reason why a historical study of genre makes most sense theoretically is that the range of literary possibilities does not remain the same for all time, but is subject to modification." In the case of pastoral, a historical investigation reveals that Virgil "was responsible for either reinforcing or changing expectations about the nature of the genre, and thus creating the norms for his successors."[27] The impetus to uncover the distinctive nature of the pre-Virgilian bucolic tradition and to elucidate the practice of Theocritus and his Greek imitators remains.

If no work on Theocritus can avoid grappling with the effects of Virgil's influence on the later tradition, scholarly as well as poetic, it is not sufficient merely to acknowledge or lament this state of affairs. Rather, the precise extent and significance of Virgil's influence on current thinking about ancient bucolic poetry must be determined. One aspect in particular of Virgil's impact on the presuppositions of modern criticism will provide a point of departure for this study: the pervasive assumption that Theocritus and his Greek successors represent a primitive but nonetheless identifiable version of pastoral and can therefore be adequately interpreted within the conceptual framework provided by the generic definition of pastoral poet-

25. Cf. W. Allen, Jr., "The Epyllion: A Chapter in the History of Literary Criticism," *TAPA*, 71 (1940), 1–26: "It is also folly to talk of authors writing in a definite literary form before it is known that there was such a form and that they believed themselves to be writing in that form" (p. 4).

26. Van Sickle (1975), 49; cf. idem (1976), 18.

27. Muecke (1975), 170; cf. Hieatt (1972). For a discussion of the relation between generic criticism and literary history, see Schmidt (1972), 10–14, who offers some objections to the procedure outlined here.

ry—a definition derived, *pace* Rosenmeyer, from a literary tradition subsequent to Theocritus and alien to his artistic objectives. The distortionary effects on Theocritean criticism brought about by the habit of treating the Idylls as early specimens of pastoral poetry have been quite severe, and they continue to be felt. The current interpretative prejudice has led to the isolation of certain portions of Theocritus' many-faceted oeuvre from their context in the whole and to an emphasis on a single thematic aspect of his work at the expense of other (equally typical) themes.[28] It is time once and for all to demonstrate the limitations imposed on our understanding of Theocritus by the prevailing practice of viewing his poetic idiom through the prism of the post-Virgilian pastoral tradition.

Theocritus, of course, had never heard of pastoral poetry. He did have a name for his own brand of poetic specialization, however: he called it "bucolic." Unfortunately, we no longer know exactly what he meant. The word itself is not sufficiently informative. Herodotus terms one of the excavated channels in the Nile delta "bucolic" (τὸ Βουκολικὸν στόμα: 2.17) without further comment.[29] The precise literary significance of *bucolic* in its original sense is even more obscure, for the word has been overlaid during the intervening centuries with an accretion of new meanings, while the literary category to which it once referred has been concealed, as we have seen, by a series of subsequent and influential artistic developments. *Bucolic* is of course a perfectly decent English word—it means "of shepherds, pastoral, rustic," according to the sixth edition of *The Concise Oxford Dictionary* (1976).[30] The synonymous English meanings of *bucolic* and *pastoral* conspire with the pastoral qualities of much ancient bucolic poetry (both Greek and Latin) to encourage the assumption that the literary categories represented by these terms can also be equated. After all, both words are names of a literary form and refer to works of poetry belonging to the same literary tradition. Moreover, their semantic identity appears to rest on an etymological foundation: *bucolic* is probably derived from the Greek word for cowherd, and *pastoral* comes from the Latin word for herdsman or shepherd. As such, the two adjectives are often treated as ancient equiv-

28. Effe (1978), 48; cf. Stark (1963), 380–83. That the pastoralist interpretation of Theocritus is inadequate will be argued at greater length in part II, chapter 7.

29. Cited by Segal (1974a), 133, who remarks, "For us 'bucolic' has the romantic associations conferred upon it by centuries of literary tradition. 'Bucolic' is itself a literary word in our vocabulary. But for Theocritus, who stands at the beginning of that tradition, the word evokes still the toil of the countryman and the smell of his beasts."

30. According to Marinelli (1971), 8, the word *bucolic* today "frequently takes on a comic aspect as suggesting a rural lack of sophistication, a comic clumsiness that works to the detriment of the idealistic qualities of both eclogue and idyll."

alents and are enrolled among the many instances of paired terms in the technical vocabularies of antiquity (along with *hypostasis* and *substantia, persona* and *prosopopeia* in theology, for example). Bolstered by this etymological support, scholars and literary critics employ the two words interchangeably, never doubting the appropriateness of applying what is in fact a modern usage to the realities of poetic practice in the ancient world.[31]

But the two words are not ancient equivalents. *Boukolikos* is not a synonym of *pastoralis,* nor does *pastoralis* mean precisely what *pastoral* does in English. It is well to heed the caution lately expressed in another context "against easy equation of the critical terminology of different languages, particularly when they are separated by significant intervals of time. Ancient terminology certainly forms the basis for that of all subsequent literary criticism. This does not mean, however, that because we continually speak, for instance, of 'metaphor and simile' we should assume without hesitation that the ancients did the same. Such facile assumptions have led, at best, to lack of precision among modern scholars in their understanding . . . and, at worst, to real inaccuracies and misinformation to which even careful scholars have fallen prey."[32] In the case of the terminological difficulties surrounding *pastoral* and *bucolic,* it should be recalled that two "significant intervals of time" have elapsed, each accompanied by transpositions of critical vocabulary from one language to another. The first of these intervals occurred between the composition of the Idylls and the literary commentaries of late antiquity (thus coinciding with a shift from Greek to Latin); the second occurred between late antiquity and the Renaissance (with a corresponding shift from Latin to the various modern European languages). The problem of terminology is more acute in English, in which both *pastoral* and *bucolic* are commonly used and therefore easily conflated, but it also exists on the Continent. There, however, linguistic continuities with the past (especially in the case of Romance languages and languages influenced by them) have favored the use of *bucolic.* In European countries, then, the problem is not so much to distinguish the ancient meaning of *bucolic* from

31. One example will have to do service for many, since they are too numerous to list. Renato Poggioli's *The Oaten Flute* is subtitled "Essays on Pastoral Poetry and the Pastoral Ideal"; yet, in an earlier note, Poggioli said he would try to "reinterpret the bucolic ideal as presented in the idyllic or quasi-idyllic literature of the past," and went on to talk about "the modern bucolic tradition, from the early Renaissance to the seventeenth and eighteenth century neoclassicism and preromanticism, from Sannazaro to Rousseau, . . . [and] conscious or unconscious survivals of the bucolic attitude in the literature of our times" (v).

32. M. H. McCall, Jr., *Ancient Rhetorical Theories of Simile and Comparison* (Cambridge, Mass., 1969), x; cf. B. Effe, *Die Genese einer literarischen Gattung: Die Bukolik,* Konstanzer Universitätsreden, 95 (Constance, 1977). For a discussion of similar "verbal revolutions," see E. W. Tayler, *Nature and Art in Renaissance Literature* (New York, 1964), 1–10.

the contemporary meaning of *pastoral* as it is to distinguish between the various meanings which *bucolic* has acquired over time.

There is no foundation for believing that the two words functioned interchangeably in antiquity: *boukolikos* appears to be a technical literary term—it refers to a specific type of poetic composition and can be employed as a title—whereas *pastoralis* is wholly descriptive, denoting (in particular) a relation to animal husbandry. To be sure, the distinction between the technical term and a purely descriptive one is not always perfect or complete, especially when writers are able to characterize varieties of literature descriptively, by subject, as well as by a proper generic designation. But the patterns of usage in antiquity are sufficiently distinct to warrant making a sharp division between the ancient senses of *boukolikos* and *pastoralis,* adjectives which are never equated.[33]

The language of the ancient commentaries on Theocritus and Virgil, the lists of titles contained in the Byzantine *Suda* and elsewhere, and an abundance of references scattered throughout the works of other ancient and medieval grammarians all plainly demonstrate that *bucolic* represented in antiquity a discrete type of poetic enterprise with a recognizable profile of its own. It will be sufficient to recall the well-known epigram in the *Palatine Anthology* (9.205) ostensibly prefixed to the collection of bucolic poetry compiled in the first century B.C. by Artemidorus of Tarsus.

> Βουκολικαὶ Μοῖσαι σποράδες ποκά, νῦν δ' ἅμα πᾶσαι
> ἐντὶ μιᾶς μάνδρας, ἐντὶ μιᾶς ἀγέλας.

The Bucolic Muses were once scattered, but are now all united in one fold, in one flock. [trans. Gow]

Unless it was possible to recognize the distinguishing features of bucolic poetry and to identify accordingly a bucolic poem or poet that had strayed outside the corpus, the epigram of Artemidorus makes no sense. Clearly, then, the ancients could differentiate bucolic from other varieties of literary expression. Athenaeus and Hesychius even go so far as to call *boukoliasmos* an *eidos,* a form of genre, of poetry.[34]

By contrast, the word *pastoral* was very late in acquiring a technical literary dimension. The basic meaning of *pastoralis* in classical Latin (and of its synonyms *pastoricius* and *pastorius*) is, according to Lewis and Short, "of

---

33. A possible exception is Terentianus Maurus (2123–26), who wrote two centuries after the composition of Virgil's *Bucolics.* The passage is discussed below, p. 12.

34. Cf. Rossi (1971a), especially 82–83. That *boukoliasmos,* the term employed by these two authorities, had become equivalent to *boukolikon* is illustrated by the linguistic practice of the mid-fourth-century grammarian Diomedes, who uses *bucolismus* synonymously with *bucolicon* (Keil, I, 486). In any case, *boukoliasmos* is a late form derived from the verb *boukoliasdesthai,* an original coinage of Theocritus.

or belonging to herdsmen or shepherds"; the new *Oxford Latin Dictionary* properly gives the word a more general sense: "of or connected with animal husbandry" (both dictionaries include the English word *pastoral* in their definitions). Already in the classical period *pastoralis* tends to refer to shepherds in particular more often than to any other kind of herdsman because the Romans seemed to prefer the more general word *pastor* to the technically exact *opilio*.[35] The word *pastoralis* could, of course, be used to characterize individual works of literature pertaining to animal husbandry, but unlike *boukolikos* it never achieved a specifically literary point of reference.

This observation can be substantiated by an examination of the two passages which seem most directly to contradict it. Quintilian writes (10.1.55): "admirabilis in suo genere Theocritus, sed musa illa rustica et pastoralis non forum modo verum ipsam etiam urbem reformidat." There is a temptation to translate this sentence (which is cited by neither Lewis and Short nor the *OLD*) as follows: "Theocritus is much to be admired as an example of his genre, but that rustic and pastoral poetry of his shuns not only the marketplace and politics, but even the very City itself."[36] Quintilian, however, has not been using the word *genus* rigorously. In praising Homer, a few sentences before his verdict on Theocritus, he remarks (10.1.51): "verum hic omnes sine dubio et in omni genere eloquentiae procul a se reliquit" ("Homer has left all others far behind in every branch [*genus*] of eloquence"). Whereas it might be possible, then, to read *pastoralis* here in a specifically generic sense, this would be to view Quintilian in the light of subsequent literary experience. It is more logical to understand *pastoralis* according to its customary usage, and indeed the context of Quintilian's judgment on Theocritus favors such a method; for Quintilian has been discussing different varieties of epic poetry and commenting on their style and subject. In the preceding sentence he takes Aratus to task for his choice of subject matter ("Arati materia motu caret, ut in qua nulla varietas . . . sit"); his appraisal of Theocritus seems to be based on the same grounds, and an alternate translation therefore recommends itself: "Theocritus is worthy of admiration in his way, but the subject of his poetry—the life of the countryside and of herdsmen or shepherds—shies away from politics," and so on.

35. Most occurrences of *opilio* are poetic; even so, Quintilian translates Homer's ποιμένα λαῶν as *pastorem populi* (*Inst.* 8.5.18). Note, however, that the meaning of ποιμήν was broadened with the passage of time: see the passage from Dio Chrys. 56.2, cited by Gow (1952), II, 184, *ad* Theoc. 8.92. For the similarly extended meaning of βουκόλος, see Dover (1971), liv–lv; Giangrande (1968), 509–11; Hom. *Il.* 6.23–25.

36. Compare the version offered by Russell and Winterbottom (1972), 388: "Theocritus in his genre is wonderful; but that rustic and pastoral muse of his fights shy even of the city—let alone the law-courts."

A more ambiguous passage can be found in the long verse treatise on metrics by the grammarian Terentianus Maurus, who wrote at the end of the second century A.D. It occurs in a section on the dactylic tetrameter and the use of what came to be called the bucolic diaeresis.

> pastorale volet cum quis componere carmen,
> tetrametrum absolvat, cui portio demitur ima,
> quae solido a verbo poterit conectere versum,
> bucolicon siquidem talem voluere vocari.

$$[2123-26]$$

Let whosoever wishes to construct a poem about herdsmen round off a unit of four feet, separating it from the final part [of the verse] which, starting from a whole [intact, unbroken] word, will be able to unify the line—which some have wished to term *bucolic*.[37]

On the strength of this passage alone the *Oxford Latin Dictionary* establishes a secondary meaning for *pastoralis:* "(of a type of poetry), pastoral, bucolic." Indeed, the usage of Terentianus is an index of the change in perspective which Virgil's *Bucolics* and its subsequent imitations had effected in the poetic and scholarly traditions. Terentianus is searching for Latin terminology (a few lines below he translates the first two verses of Theocritus' First Idyll into Latin in order, he says, to avoid introducing Greek citations into his text) and he seems hesitant about using the term *bucolic*. He is consequently obliged to resort to a periphrasis, and because the subject matter of bucolic poetry had been conventionally pastoral since Virgil, Terentianus can describe bucolic poetry by alluding to its content.[38] In this he does not differ from Quintilian, who had similarly used *pastoralis* to signify the proper subject matter of bucolic poetry as he understood it. But Quintilian did not invoke *pastoralis* to designate a literary class. Terentianus, however, writing at a time when it was beginning to be possible for theoreticians and critics to categorize works of literature descriptively, according to subject, is tempted to employ *pastoralis* as the generic name of a literary phenomenon. Even so, when he requires a technical term for the specific metrical feature under discussion, only *bucolic* will do—and Terentianus' informal use of *pastoralis* acquires whatever critical rigor it has only from its close association with the traditional literary term.

The earliest usage of *pastoral* in a specifically literary sense is difficult to

37. I wish to thank Professor Robert A. Kaster of the University of Chicago for help in elucidating this passage.

38. On the practice of alluding to genres by referring to their traditional content, see Berg (1974), 145, 148; Bettini (1972), 273–76. Servius calls the technique of indicating generic titles through allusion to poetic content "periphrasis" (Prooim. in *Georg.*, p. 128.9 Thilo).

determine. At the close of the *Georgics* Virgil had glancingly referred to his bucolic poetry as "carmina . . . pastorum" and this, together with the famous judgment of Quintilian already quoted, provided Italian Humanists with sufficent justification for pressing the Latin *pastoralis* into service as a literary term in the vernacular.[39] It quickly gained currency in English. In a verse prologue to his collection entitled *Certayne Egloges* (c. 1514), Alexander Barclay proclaimed:

> In this saide maner the famous Theocrite
> First in Siracuse attempted for to write
> Certayne Egloges or speeches pastorall,
> Inducing Shepherdes, men homely and rurall.
> Which in playne language, according to their name,
> Had sundry talking, sometime of mirth and game,
> Sometime of thinges more like to grauitie,
> And not exceeding their small capacitie.
> Most noble Uirgill after him longe while
> Wrote also Egloges after like maner stile.
> His wittes prouing in matters pastorall,
> Or he durst venture to stile heroicall.
>
> [19–30]

The context here does not of necessity impose a literary sense on "pastorall," although it makes such a meaning likely. Later, Barclay confronts the challenge that his labor has been

> vayne and reprouable,
> Because it maketh onely relation
> Of Shepherdes maner and disputation.
> If any suche reade my treatise to the ende
> He shall well perceyue, if he thereto intende,
> That it conteyneth both laudes of vertue,
> And man infourmeth misliuing to eschue,
> With diuers bourdes and sentences morall,
> Closed in shadow of speeches pastorall. . . .
>
> [92–100][40]

Although Barclay may signify no more by "speeches pastorall" than "Shepherdes disputation," his use of the word borrows a certain literary flavor from its context.

By 1544, with the publication of "The Preface of Ludovicus Vives to his Glosse upon Virgils Æglogues," the word *pastoral* has achieved its technical status as a generic label. Vives contends that Virgil would never have

---

39. For this and much of what follows, see Congleton (1952), 6–10.
40. White (1928), 1–3.

been so "infinitely delighted, with such kindes of light matter as Pastoralls, had they not afforded some hidden meaning and sense of higher nature";[41] here, perhaps for the first time in English (although the casual introduction of the term makes that seem unlikely), *pastoral* refers to a distinct species of literature. George Puttenham, author of *The Arte of English Poesie* (1589), employs the word in a similar sense: "Some be of opinion, and the chiefe of those who haue written in this Art among the Latines, that the pastorall Poesie . . . should be the first of any other. . . ." Although "pastorall" in this sentence may still be largely descriptive rather than technical—as the chapter heading which precedes it seems to suggest: "OF THE SHEPHEARDS OR PASTORALL POESIE CALLED EGLOGUE, AND TO WHAT PURPOSE IT WAS FIRST INUENTED AND VSED"—Puttenham's example shows that the word could also function in the Elizabethan period as a literary label.[42]

Puttenham is perhaps the first critic to equate the meaning of *pastoral* explicitly with that of *bucolic*. In the passage already quoted he mentions "the pastorall Poesie which we commonly call by the name of *Eglogue* and *Bucolick*, a tearme brought in by the Sicilian Poets." The tendency to identify the meanings of *pastoral* and *bucolic* was indeed common in Puttenham's day: the same year that saw the publication of his essay also witnessed the appearance of Fleming's *The Bvcoliks of Pvblivs Virgilivs Maro, . . . otherwise called his Pastoralls, or Shepherds Meetings* (note the merging of both the technical and descriptive dimensions of *pastoral* in Fleming's usage).[43] The relation of the modern to the ancient term was clarified by Hobbes in 1650. Having divided poetry according to "the three Regions of mankinde" in which "Poets . . . have lodg'd themselves" (Court, City, and Country) and "the manner of Representation" (narrative or dramatic), Hobbes declared, "The Pastorall narrative is called simply Pastorall, anciently Bucolique."[44] Hobbes at least was careful not to mistake his own term *Pastorall,* for an ancient literary formula. Succeeding generations have been less fastidious. To be sure, occasional protests have been made about the promiscuous confusion of technical vocabulary. Rapin pointed out the problem of tangled nomenclature in the mid-seventeenth century;[45] at the turn of the twentieth Martha Hale Shackford lamented the "confusion of form with subject-matter" in pastoral definitions and inveighed against the loose use of such literary terms as *pastoral* and *bucolic.*[46] But because no one has been able

---

41. Congleton (1952), 39.
42. Smith (1904), II, 39.
43. *OED*, s.v. "pastoral," B.I.3.
44. Behrens (1940), 126.
45. Congleton (1952), 62.
46. Shackford (1904), 583–85; cf. Cholmeley (1919), 58.

to distinguish precisely the meaning of the ancient term *bucolic* from that of its modern usurpers, these protests have been ineffective.

To argue that the word *pastoral* represents a modern critical notion is not to claim that no pastoral literature was composed before the Renaissance or that the ancients did not have a concept of pastoral. It is important not to confound the history of the word with the mode of existence of the literary category. The criteria which contemporary critics use today to identify works of pastoral literature in all times and places were simply not perceived in antiquity as constituting a basis for literary groupings.[47] At the time when Theocritus was composing the Idylls, and in the intellectual community for which he was writing, it was the custom to classify poetry chiefly according to metrical criteria, and so the hexameter poems of Theocritus and Virgil were included in the ancient genre called *epos*. Thematic considerations, which are highly pertinent to the modern concept of pastoral, were subordinated to metrical ones and did not figure prominently in any ancient scheme of literary classification from the Hellenistic period until the second century A.D. It was only the multiplication of forms, conventions, and topoi *within* the traditional generic categories, for which the Hellenistic and Roman poets were principally responsible, that led the classifiers of late antiquity to revert to the Platonic and Aristotelian categories, or to a jumbled amalgamation of them with earlier schemes.[48] In short, the tendency of most ancient literary theorists to insist on the primacy of purely formal criteria in the enterprise of poetic division and classification by genre prohibited them from regarding the presence of pastoral qualities in a specific work as distinguishing it from other works which lacked such qualities but were composed in a similar meter. Hence, no body of pastoral literature was recognized as such in antiquity.

This lack of critical recognition does not alter the fact that many artistic products of the ancient world, in both the literary and the visual media, both before and after Theocritus, exhibit pastoral features; a good number of them fully satisfy the requirements of the modern definitions of pastoral. The confusion between what Theocritus meant by *bucolic* and what we mean by *pastoral* could not, of course, have arisen but for the prominence of pastoral elements in much ancient bucolic poetry. Many of the bucolic Idylls, and possibly all of Virgil's Eclogues, can be thought of as pastorals in

---

47. According to Coleman (1975), 140, the anonymous *Lament for Bion* provides "the one firm testimony we have that a specific pastoral genre was recognized in the Hellenistic world." But the title of bucolic poet, conferred on Bion in the *Lament*, does not depend on the alleged pastoral qualities of his verse (see part IV, chapter 11). Against Coleman's belief in an ancient pastoral genre one can invoke the authority of Rohde (1932), 81, and Curtius (1953), 187.

48. Steinmetz (1964), 459–63; cf. Curtius (1953), 436–43; Gallavotti (1928).

the current sense (Virgil's closer adherence to pastoral conventions bespeaks his greater responsibility for producing them).

Furthermore, although the ancients neither possessed a single term signifying *pastoral* as we understand it nor regarded the presence of pastoral elements in a poem as determining that poem's generic identity, their writings do testify to the existence of a concept of pastoral (or a close approximation to it). If a recent audacious interpretation of Bacchylides 10.35–45 is correct, the notion of a kind of poetry associated with country life could date from as far back as the early fifth century B.C., although the relevant line of Bacchylides, οἱ δ' ἐπ' ἔργοισίν τε καὶ ἀμφὶ βοῶν ἀ[γ]έλαις / θυμὸν αὔξουσιν ("some rejoice in labor and in herds of cattle"), suggests by its choice of vocabulary a Hesiodic rather than a pastoral subject.[49] Later, when Clearchus wished to refer to the song of one who guarded flocks, he did not have to look very far for a natural Greek expression, according to Athenaeus (14.619c): νόμιον καλεῖσθαί τινά φησιν ᾠδήν—"he says there's something called a herdsman's song" (*nomios ōdē*).[50] But when Athenaeus speaks of an *eidos* or genre of poetry, only a few sentences earlier, his vocabulary changes significantly (14.619ab): ἦν δὲ καὶ τοῖς ἡγουμένοις τῶν βοσκημάτων ὁ βουκολιασμὸς καλούμενος. Δίομος δ' ἦν βουκόλος Σικελιώτης ὁ πρῶτος εὑρὼν τὸ εἶδος—"those in charge of herds had what's called the *boukoliasmos*. It was Diomos, a Sicilian cowherd [*boukolos*], who first discovered the form [*eidos*]." In a similar fashion, Hesychius glosses *boukoliasmos*: μελοποιίας τινὸς εἶδος καὶ ὀρχήσεως—"a kind [*eidos*] of music and dance."[51] Whereas a purely descriptive word like *nomios*, then, could be applied to certain kinds of poetry (no less than *pastoralis* in Latin), it did not serve to identify a specific genre and did not acquire a technical literary meaning; *bucolic*, in contrast, could represent the name of a particular *eidos* of poetic composition. Clearly, the ancients did not avail themselves of such a concept of pastoral as they had in their efforts to differentiate literary genres, and they endowed *bucolic* with a specific (and, as yet, mysterious) significance of its own.

Nonetheless, the pastoralist interpretation of bucolic poetry is not an altogether modern phenomenon. Already in the latter half of the third

---

49. D. Pinte, "Un classement des genres poétiques par Bacchylide," *AC*, 35 (1966), 459–67, especially 465. Observe that these lines of Bacchylides seem to have been imitated by Theocritus, 16.55–56: καὶ βουσὶ Φιλοίτιος ἀμφ' ἀγελαίαις/ἔργον ἔχων. For some persuasive objections to Pinte's thesis, see Calame (1974), 124n.

50. Cf. Athenaeus 619d: τὸ καλούμενον νόμιον (apparently a love song addressed to a herdsman). Donatus actually translates Nomius, a cult epithet of Apollo, into Latin by rendering it *pastoralis;* see p. 18.10 Wendel. On the ancient usages of *nomios* and *bukolikos*, see Welcker (1844), 409–11.

51. Welcker (1844), 410; Legrand (1898), 420n.

century B.C., perhaps even in Theocritus' own lifetime,[52] readers began to place a disproportionate emphasis on the rustic setting of certain Idylls and to reduce the multiplicity of bucolic themes to a set of pastoral conventions.[53] The earliest critical responses to Theocritus took the form, according to a long-established literary custom, of attempts to emulate him in verse. These poetic imitations, which loudly proclaim their bucolic identity in programmatic utterances and strive to reproduce (or, occasionally, to correct and amplify) the master's characteristic practice, reveal what later generations considered typical of the bucolic style. The first such experiment in post-Theocritean bucolic mannerism, Idyll 8 (probably composed by a near-contemporary of Theocritus),[54] contains a polished but highly schematized depiction of a rustic singing match; the second, Idyll 9, elaborates on the contest in Idyll 8 by retaining the names of the participants but altering the outcome.[55] Both poems implicitly associate the bucolic category with the portrayal of a rustic locale and cast of characters, and they seem to treat the theme of poetic competition among herdsmen as the distinctive bucolic subject. The tendency to select and stress the pastoral qualities of Theocritean poetry to the exclusion of other thematic elements was carried further by the author of the *Lament for Bion*—a late Hellenistic work formerly ascribed to Moschus—who boasts (in lines 93–97) of continuing the bucolic tradition as it was handed down to him, but whose own contribution largely consists of infusing the literary convention of the funeral elegy with pastoral color. Finally, the epigram of Artemidorus (quoted earlier) celebrates his new collection of bucolic poetry "in a metaphor drawn from the matter": the Bucolic Muses, who first appear by name in the closing invocation of Idyll 9, are now said to have been penned, like cattle, in a single fold. With the publication of Artemidorus' distich, the rustic subject of bucolic poetry "becomes a token of the literary design."[56]

In the light of these developments within the post-Theocritean Greek tradition, Virgil's subsequent "pastoralization" of bucolic poetry may be seen not as a rupture but rather as the continuation (highly original, to be sure) of a previously established interpretative tendency. Even a superficial reading of the *Eclogues* reveals Virgil's thorough indebtedness to Idylls 8 and 9 and possibly to the late bucolic elegies as well; his conception of bucolic was undoubtedly affected by the post-Theocritean critical tradition. The Byzantine commentators on Theocritus, at any rate, did not derive their

---

52. Cf. Effe (1978), 48.
53. Van Sickle (1976), 25.
54. Rossi (1971b); see, generally, W. Arland, *Nachtheokritische Bukolik bis an die Schwelle der lateinischen Bukolik,* diss. Leipzig (1937).
55. Van Sickle (1976), 25–27.
56. Ibid., 27.

pastoralist reading of the Idylls from Latin sources: if they considered the essence of bucolic poetry to be the realistic depiction of rural life, their outlook must be based on an interpretative heritage innocent of all Virgilian influence—on the same heritage, in fact, bequeathed to Virgil by his Greek predecessors and attested several centuries later by Hermogenes (περὶ ἰδεῶν 2.305–06, pp. 322–24 Rabe). Moreover, the manuscripts of Theocritus circulating in the Renaissance included excerpts from the Byzantine scholia, and later pastoral theorists such as Scaliger and Rapin relied on the testimony of these scholia in formulating their own rules for the pastoral genre. Thus, it would be inaccurate to attribute European concepts of pastoral to the influence of Virgil alone, for the pastoralist interpretation of Theocritus was already well established and influential when Virgil made it the canonical interpretation of bucolic poetry in the Western, Latin-speaking world. Although pastoral poetry as we know it remains principally Virgil's creation, the pastoral qualities of bucolic poetry had been singled out for emphasis long before Virgil's own practice called attention to them, and an awareness of those qualities continued to shape the European pastoral tradition.

What distinguishes critical readings of bucolic poetry up to and through the time of Virgil from later misconceptions of the form is an unwillingness on the part of the earlier imitators to lose sight of the relation between bucolic and the genre (called *epos*) to which it belonged; even the *Lament for Bion* testifies to the connection.[57] So long as bucolic was regarded as a species of *epos,* no amount of emphasis on its rustic locale could obliterate its formal identity or sever its thematic links with earlier works in the same generic category. Theocritus' followers surely considered the pastoral features of his poetry the most interesting, original, and arresting aspect of his art; they did not, however, go so far as to define the category to which his Idylls together with their own efforts belonged by the presence of such features. Only in late antiquity, when thematic criteria began to play a greater role in generic differentiation than they had hitherto, did the pastoralist interpretation of bucolic poetry start to affect its literary classification. In the West, Virgil's example had already wedded bucolic poetry to a rural setting—Quintilian is an early witness to this union—and as the impact of Virgil's innovative synthesis was felt ever more deeply by Roman readers, bucolic poetry came to be defined as a picture or expression of rustic folk culture. Although this interpretative tendency, which John Van

---

57. See below (part IV, chapter 11; and conclusion). The introduction of elegiac distichs into Idyll 8 constitutes the only possible departure from the generic conventions of *epos* in the bucolic poetry of this period; but see Schmidt (1972), 38, 282, on the lack of generic distinction between elegy and *epos.*

Sickle has termed "the simple mimetic conception of bucolic genre,"[58] is fully and explicitly articulated only in the Byzantine scholia on Theocritus, it can be seen to underlie the late antique commentaries on Virgil by Donatus, Servius, and pseudo-Probus (as well as the earlier passages from Quintilian and Terentianus previously quoted), in which bucolic poetry is characteristically associated with a rustic subject. In the introduction to his commentary on Virgil's *Bucolics,* for example, Servius implies that when a poem ceases to be purely pastoral ("merus rusticus") it also diverges from the norms of the bucolic genre ("a bucolico carmine . . . discessit"). The simple mimetic conception of bucolic poetry is also attested by Diomedes, who remarks, "Bucolica dicuntur poemata secundum carmen pastorale conposita" (Keil, I, 486)—"bucolics are poems made in the manner of a herdsman's song."[59]

But neither Servius nor Diomedes ventures to suggest that differences in subject matter or in details of scenery can provide a basis for classifying kinds of literature. Servius' term *rusticus* is not employed in the enterprise of generic differentiation. To be sure, the word *humilis* (which Servius also applies to bucolic poetry) is so used, but *humilis,* though perfectly appropriate to pastoral poetry in the modern world as well as to bucolic poetry in the ancient, is a rhetorical term: it belongs to the vocabulary designed to articulate the hierarchy of styles (high, low, and intermediate). As such, *humilis* is as relevant to levels of diction in oratory as it is to degrees of grandeur in poetry; it is not an essentially thematic concept and does not involve a specific notion of pastoral.[60] Similarly, the apparent equivalency between *bucolic* and *pastoral* implied by the passage from Diomedes is an illusion created by the modern habit of mind: in Diomedes' usage, *bucolicon* remains the technical term requiring a gloss, whereas *pastoralis* supplies the needed explanatory information.

Thus, even when the ancients finally began to consider the presence of pastoral themes a characteristic feature of bucolic poetry, they still declined to create a literary category defined exclusively by the portrayal of a rustic subject. The pastoralist interpretation of bucolic poetry established itself long before a separate word had been devised to refer to a type of poetry distinguished by the representation of rural life. The only literary term that

58. Van Sickle (1976), 25.

59. Cf. Donatus: "unde igitur magis decuit pastorali carmini nomen imponi nisi ab eo gradu, qui fere apud pastores excellentissimus invenitur?" (repeated by Iunius Philargyrius). Cf. also Isidore of Seville: "Bucolicum, id est pastorale carmen." Pp. 17.26–28, 19.16–18, 21.28 Wendel.

60. The Greek equivalent of *humilis*—or, rather, one of the Greek equivalents (for ἰσχνός should not be ignored)—seems to be ἀφελής ("simple"), which applies to both bucolic poetry and comedy in Hermogenes' classification; see Patterson (1970), 59.

could refer specifically to the Idylls of Theocritus, the Eclogues of Virgil, and all the various subsequent efforts in the eclogue-form throughout both the ancient and medieval periods was *bucolic*. The meaning of the word continued to be redefined and transvalued, but the name remained unchanged. Furthermore, the literary theoreticians of the late antique and medieval eras consistently followed the practice of their classical predecessors in refusing to treat "bucolic" poetry as an independent and autonomous branch of literature: rather, the breakdown in the traditional understanding of that poetic category can be measured by the tendency to subsume bucolic under more than one generic heading.

In late antiquity, the replacement of conventional Hellenistic methods of literary classification by the newly revived Platonic and Aristotelian schemes provided the impetus behind the fragmentation of the bucolic category. In the introduction to his commentary on the Third Eclogue, Servius adapts Plato's distinctions (*Rep.* 394bc) to suit his own purposes:

We know that there are three manners of composing—namely, one in which only the poet speaks (as in the first three books of the *Georgics*); a second, the dramatic, in which the poet never speaks (as in comedies and tragedies); and a third, the mixed (as in the *Aeneid*), in which both the poet and his characters speak. It is fitting that bucolic poetry contain all three, as this book [of Virgil's] shows.[61]

Servius does not, however, make these three *characteres dicendi* a basis for generic differentiation; they refer rather to the compositional form of a poem and provide a way of analyzing its manner of representation. The classification of poetry according to speaker was left to Diomedes, who seems to have substituted modality of representation for metrics as the fundamental determinant of genre.[62] In the third book of his *Ars grammatica* Diomedes divides literature into a *genus activum* (also called *imitativum* in Latin, *dramatikon* or *mimētikon* in Greek), in which the poet speaks through characters of his own creating; a *genus enarrativum (enuntiativum, exēgētikon* or *apaggeltikon*), in which the poet speaks in his own person, and a third, *genus commune (mixtum, koinon* or *mikton), combined of the other two. As one might predict from Servius' analysis, bucolic poetry does not fit comfortably into this scheme. Diomedes cites Virgil's Third Eclogue as an example of his first (dramatic) category, but he seems to place bucolic poetry in general in his third (mixed) division. In fact, Diomedes positions his discussion of bucolic poetry last in a survey of the poetic varieties of the *genus commune* and moves on directly to a consideration of the first two genera which he had postponed treating up to that point—perhaps because

---

61. The Byzantine *Anecdoton Estense* III, 6 (p. 11. 11–18 Wendel) testifies to the Greek source of Servius' formulation.

62. See note 48, above.

he believed that the last item in his "mixed" category, namely bucolic, could provide a transition to his remarks on "drama" (the first of the two remaining classes to be discussed). In any case, Diomedes shows that the ancient metrical classification of bucolic poetry as a species of *epos* had been forgotten, and his treatise prepares the way for medieval efforts to include bucolic in one or another of the literary categories that survived.

With the passage of time the confusion surrounding the proper classification of what continued to be called bucolic poetry increased. Horace had failed to use the term *epos* in his *Ars poetica,* preferring more elegant periphrases instead; as a result, the word virtually disappears from the technical vocabulary of literary critics for centuries and does not recover its original meaning for a thousand years.[63] The silence of Proclus, Tzetzes, and Hugh of St. Victor on the subject of classifying bucolic poetry has been taken to signify their fidelity to the traditional inclusion of bucolic in the more general category of *epos;*[64] their silence may be ascribed more plausibly, however, to the effects of the widespread confusion surrounding the proper classification of bucolic at the end of antiquity rather than considered a sign of adherence to a long-outmoded theory of formal literary relationships which seems to have been completely abandoned.

During the Middle Ages, "bucolic" was absorbed by a variety of other poetic categories which themselves underwent many shifts of meaning. Thus, whereas Photius in the East used the word *dramatikon* to signify the Greek Romance, a twelfth-century Latin commentator on Priscian defines drama as follows: "'Dragma, atis' tertie declinationis, quod est interrogatio. Unde dragmaticum genus loquendi dicitur quasi interrogativum, quod fit per interrogationem et responsionem." Thus, the Aristotelian concept of drama as a kind of poetry in which the author speaks entirely through characters rather than in his own person and thereby imitates human action, subsequently reduced by Diomedes to mere dialogue, is gradually altered until by the twelfth century it has been assimilated in the West into the form of a rhetorical disputation. Drama has become a *genus loquendi,* no longer a branch of poetry *per se,* and is characterized by an exchange of questions and answers in the manner of a philosophical dialogue or formal disputation, while the quarrel poem in dialogue form is called an *Altercatio, Conflictus,* or *Causa* and is no longer considered a part of drama.[65] The theory of bucolic poetry suffers a double distortion in the medieval period: it is assigned to literary categories to which it did not

63. Behrens (1940), 35, 68.

64. Rosenmeyer (1969), 5; see Behrens (1940), 31, 41, 44, for references to these medieval authors.

65. Behrens (1940), 38, 45, 50. For an interesting discussion of the ambivalent attitudes toward "bucolic" in the Middle Ages, see Krauss (1938), 143–44.

traditionally belong while those very categories are reinterpreted in the light of contemporary interests and concerns.

Bede, following closely the scheme of Diomedes in chapter 25 of his own *De Arte Metrica,* adduces as examples of drama the specific Eclogues cited by Diomedes together with the Song of Songs (because it is a dialogue between Christ and the Church). No further mention is made of bucolic in Bede's classification. Papias, the Italian author of a Latin encyclopedia composed about 1050, continues to include the eclogue in the dramatic genus but uses a telling choice of vocabulary: "Aegloga dicitur interlocutio dramatica." In the twelfth century, Hugh of St. Victor quotes from Virgil's *Eclogues* but does not mention bucolic in his list of poetic genres; Matthew of Vendôme uses the term *bucolic* in his text, chiefly when citing Virgil, but does not include it among the personifications of poetry which appear to him in a vision in the second part of his *Ars Versificatoria* (before 1175). At the turn of the thirteenth century, Eberhard of Béthune treats *bucolicon* as an example of the genus *dragmaticon,* one of three "sermonum genera." A bit later John of Garland subsumes bucolic under the branch of narrative he calls *Hystoricum* (defined as "res gesta ab etatis nostre memoria remota"), although elegy, another member of the same branch, is made to include "amabeum quod aliquando est in altercacione personarum et in certamine amantum, ut in Theodolo et in Bucolicis." Only with Dante does bucolic poetry begin to acquire a certain independence. Virgil is called " 'l cantor de' buccolici carmi" in *Purgatorio* 22.57 (the episode relates Statius' conversion to Christianity through the mediation of the Fourth Eclogue), and in a letter to Can Grande, Dante mentions bucolic along with comedy, tragedy, elegy, and satire as "genera narrationum," although he is not attempting to propose a systematic division of poetry. In accord with his tendency to esteem bucolic more highly than his contemporaries are inclined to do, and in opposition to the customary medieval scheme, Dante chooses elegy instead of bucolic as his example of the "stilus humilis" in his treatise *De Vulgari Eloquentia.* Bucolic poetry seems to recover an integrity and autonomy of its own for the first time only in Boccaccio's commentary on the *Divine Comedy:* "A notizia della qual cosa è da sapere che le poetiche narrazioni sono di più e varie maniere, si come è tragedia, satira, e commedia, buccolica, elegia, lirica ed altre."[66] It is obvious that the literary form which has recovered its independent identity in this passage has little or nothing to do with the species of poetry invented by Theocritus in the third century B.C.[67]

Boccaccio is also the author of a famous historical survey of bucolic

---

66. Behrens (1940), 36–64.

67. Cf. H. Bénac, "Humanité de la pastorale," *Lettres d'humanité* (Assoc. G. Budé), 5 (1946), 235–57, especially 236–37, on the "modernity" of pastoral.

poetry in which he admits that he values the example of the ancients mainly because it provides him with the means of satisfying his own literary objectives.

Theocritus, a Syracusan Poet, according to the ancient tradition, was the first to devise the bucolic style in Greek poetry, but he meant nothing more than the mere bark of his words makes show of. After him, Virgil wrote in Latin, but he concealed some of his meanings under the bark, because he did not always wish us to understand something under the names of his characters. After him there were many other poets, but they're worthless and one need take no notice of them, except for my famous Teacher Francesco Petrarca, who raised the style a bit above the ordinary and, in accordance with the matter of his Eclogues, always made the name of his characters mean something. Among these poets I have followed Virgil, because I did not care to conceal my meaning behind all the names of my characters.[68]

This thoroughgoing allegorical emphasis, though not new, was to become a hallmark of the Renaissance attitude. It is at this point that bucolic poetry begins to be explicitly identified with at least one aspect of what we understand by pastoral, namely, the use of a rustic locale and cast of characters as a vehicle for political commentary or ecclesiastical satire. "Bucolic" is employed by Renaissance pastoral poets to describe their practice of reinterpreting the works of Virgil and (to a lesser degree) Theocritus in conformity with their own concerns and in their own idiom. Although the designation "bucolic" comes to signify an increasingly important branch of literature, it no longer refers to the realities of poetic composition in the ancient world. For the modern reader of Theocritus, the original meaning of bucolic remains to be discovered.

68. "Theocritus Syracusanus Poeta, ut ab antiquis accepimus, primus fuit, qui Graeco Carmine Bucolicum escogitavit stylum, verum nil sensit, praeter quod cortex verborum demonstrat. Post hunc Latine scripsit Virgilius, sed sub cortice nonnullos abscondit sensus, esto non semper voluerit sub nominibus colloquentium aliquid sentiremus. Post hunc autem scripserunt et alii, sed ignobiles, de quibus nil curandum est, excepto inclyto Praeceptore meo Francisco Petrarca qui stylum praeter solitum paululum sublimavit et secundum Eclogarum suarum materias continue collocutorum nomina aliquid significantia posuit. Ex his ego Virgilium secutus sum quapropter non curavi in omnibus colloquentium nominibus sensum abscondere."

PART I

The Evolution of Pastoral Theory

CHAPTER ONE

The Problem of Definition

If the original significance of the term *bucolic* must remain obscure, at least for the moment, it should certainly be possible to clarify what contemporary critics and literary historians mean when they use the word *pastoral*. Unfortunately, this task is not an appreciably easier one, and the student of literature who is confronted by it may well experience the sort of perplexity Augustine felt when he wanted to define time: "Is there any more common or familiar topic in our daily speech? We certainly understand what we mean by it when we use it in conversation; we also understand when we hear it mentioned by someone else. What is it, then? So long as no one asks me, I know what it is—but as soon as I am asked to explain it, for all my willingness I cannot" (*Confessions* 11.14). Substitute "literary terminology" for "daily speech" in Augustine's declaration, and the result will be a fair sample of the sort of apology that prefaces most contemporary studies of pastoral.

The apologetic tradition in pastoral criticism has a long history of its own and has even produced something of a *topos* in scholarly writing. W. W. Greg, whose monumental study of pastoral poetry and drama laid the groundwork for modern scholarship in the field, opened his investigation with the following remarks:

In approaching a subject of literary inquiry we are often able to fix upon some essential feature or condition which may serve as an Ariadne's thread through the maze of historical and aesthetic development, or to distinguish some cardinal point affording a fixed centre from which to survey or in reference to which to order and dispose the phenomena that present themselves to us. It is the disadvantage of such an artificial form of literature as that which bears the name of pastoral that no such *a priori* guidance is available. . . . [L]ittle would be gained by attempting beforehand to give any strict account of what is meant by "pastoral" in literature. Any definition sufficiently elastic to include the protean forms assumed by what we call the "pastoral ideal" could hardly have sufficient intension to be of any real value.[1]

Greg's Augustinian bewilderment has continued to be echoed by his successors, and more than sixty years later Thomas G. Rosenmeyer inaugurated his book-length attempt to identify the defining characteristics of the pastoral genre with a similar confession: "In all probability a tidy definition of what is pastoral about the pastoral tradition is beyond our reach. . . . A definition of the genre and its limits is likely to run counter to much accumulated experience."[2] Similarly, the editors of the recent *Penguin Book of English Pastoral Verse* assert: "The main problem which confronts anyone attempting to make an anthology such as this is one of definition."[3] Clearly, the problem is twofold, and involves difficulty of both a particular and a general kind: there is uncertainty about exactly what *pastoral* refers to (that is, to which literary works the label may properly be applied) and about what sort of distinction is implicit in the use of the term (what kind of category it is, what other categories it includes or excludes). The causes of this confusion require some exploration.

First of all, pastoral has been known to trespass freely on the territory of the major literary genres. It is all very well to say that pastoral, whatever its form, "must be reduced to the common denominator of the lyrical mode," or to claim a certain core of identity for the pastoral lyric despite the frequent admixture of pastoral in the more clearly defined of literary categories.[4] But it is more usual for critics to describe pastoral as "invasive" or "expansionist."[5] A recent scholar elaborates on this theme and speaks of pastoral's "capacity to devour elegies, lyrics, plays, fairy tales, masques, odes, and . . . to gnaw ambitiously at romances, epics, and novels."[6] Even modern opera began under the auspices of pastoral.[7] As George Sand declared in her preface to *François le Champi,* "La musique, la peinture, l'architecture, la littérature sous toutes ses formes: théâtre, poème, roman, églogue, chanson; les modes, les jardins, les costumes même, tout a subi l'engouement du rêve pastoral."[8] In fact, the fluid boundaries of the pastoral

---

1. Greg (1906), 1–2.
2. Rosenmeyer (1969), 3, 6.
3. Barrell and Bull (1974), 7; see also Marinelli (1971), 5; Hieatt (1972), especially 1–6; Alpers (1981/2), especially 437–48; *contra,* Gerhardt (1950), 21–22, 29.
4. Poggioli (1975), 39; Rosenmeyer (1969), 9–20; cf. Marinelli (1971), 73–74; Hieatt (1972), 16–19.
5. Cf. Chambers (1895), xxviii; Rosenmeyer (1969), 7.
6. Toliver (1971), vii.
7. Behrens (1940), 151–53; see now E. Harris, *Handel and the Pastoral Tradition* (London, 1980), 1–141.
8. Quoted by Levrault (1914), 6.

form represent something of a historical legacy from antiquity. Theocritus and Virgil furnished examples of pastoral poetry in both narrative and dramatic arrangements; pastoral epigrams and funeral elegies were produced in relative abundance; and the later Roman Empire actually saw the rise of the pastoral romance or prose fiction. Pastoral themes were also treated in the visual arts. The multiplicity of forms assumed by the pastoral impulse, then, was already characteristic at an early date and may be thought essential to its nature.[9] The diversity of ancient manifestations, further expanded in the Renaissance, conspired with a wealth of learned Humanist commentary to spawn the variety of modern forms—not completely differentiated from one another—all of which can be comprehended to some extent under the category of pastoral: the idyll, the *egloga* or eclogue, the pastoral or *pastorale,* the bucolic, *bergerie, pastourelle, Hirtengedicht, Schäferspiel,* and even the romance.

In response to this multiplication of forms within pastoral literature, critics have taken refuge in the notion that specific kinds of subject matter can provide distinguishing marks of the genre. As one editor of Theocritus maintains, "Strictly understood pastoral poetry must be defined not by its *form* so much as by its *contents.* It is a comedy of rustic character and speech, brief, written to please not to instruct, in dialogue or monologue drawn from the life."[10] Quite apart from this confusing jumble of formal and thematic criteria, the tendency to define pastoral by its contents raises a whole new set of difficulties. For a second cause of modern perplexity about the meaning of pastoral can be found in its variable subject matter and in the flexibility and adaptability of its component forms to a multitude of themes. "What is called 'Pastoral' in 1580 is not at first sight much like what is called 'Pastoral' in 1770, and yet the reader is left with a firm impression of a shared tradition, of a common body of material being worked over."[11] Profiting from a rather free interpretation of this poetic tradition, Swift developed the town eclogue, Ramsay the native eclogue, Collins the exotic eclogue, Walter Savage Landor the railroad eclogue, and Coleridge composed a poem entitled "Fire, Famine, and Slaughter: A War Eclogue."[12] While critics attempting to find a coherent pattern of development amid this spontaneous profusion often appeal to notions of tradition, imitation, and continuity of artistic purpose, they complain no less frequently of the lati-

---

9. Rohde (1932), 81; see Reitzenstein (1893), 279–84, on the plastic arts.

10. Cholmeley (1919), 58, selecting Idylls 3, 4, 5, and 10 as typical examples of pastoral.

11. Barrell and Bull (1974), 7–8; cf. Marinelli (1971), 4–9.

12. Rosenmeyer (1969), 7, citing R. F. Jones, "Eclogue Types in English Poetry of the Eighteenth Century," *Journal of English and Germanic Philology,* 24 (1925), 33–60. Rosenmeyer quotes Coleridge as saying, "Do not let us introduce an Act of Uniformity against poets" (6).

tude which poets in their practices and theorists in their pronouncements have allowed themselves in manipulating the boundaries of the genre. Wordsworth, for example, is taken to task for referring to Tennyson's "Dora" as a pastoral—but Wordsworth had been guilty of more egregious excesses: in a preface of 1815 he defined "idyllium" so as to include "the processes and appearances of external nature," "characters, manners, and sentiments" (either alone or "in conjunction with the appearances of Nature"), "the Epitaph, the Inscription, the Sonnet, most of the epistles of poets writing in their own persons, and all loco-descriptive poetry."[13]

Finally, recent changes in literary theory have made the enterprise of defining pastoral even more problematic. Benedetto Croce's attack, in the early part of this century, on the usefulness and meaning of the doctrine of literary genres touched off a controversy over the proper methods of classifying works of literature which has since called into question the validity of all formal literary definitions.[14] By its very intractability—its resistance to being worked into a coherent scheme of formal literary relationships—pastoral has been partly responsible for continuing and extending this controversy. Nonetheless, because pastoral, despite its tendency to invade the province of other well-established literary categories, had traditionally been assigned a discrete place in the literary taxonomies of the past, its status has been left in considerable uncertainty by the current flux of critical theory.

It was during the Renaissance that pastoral was numbered for the first time among the genres or "kinds" of literature—categories which the Humanists adopted from the literary theorists of classical antiquity. Although the practice of generic composition almost certainly predates Greek literature itself, the idea of the separateness and fixity of the various genres was first set forth by Plato and Aristotle and was not fully articulated until the Roman period. Cicero, Horace, and Quintilian taught that each branch of literature or oratory requires what is uniquely appropriate to it; in accordance with this notion, which must have been quite widespread, the literary classes were set apart from one another in antiquity by clear, formal boundaries.[15] Pastoral did not figure among these divisions, as we have seen.

13. Rosenmeyer (1969), 3–6; W. M. Merchant, ed., *Wordsworth: Poetry and Prose* (Cambridge, Mass., 1967), 244; cf. Lindenberger (1972), 346.

14. Cf. Hack (1916); C. E. Whitmore, "The Validity of Literary Definitions," *PMLA*, 39 (1924), 722–36; K. Viëtor, "Die Geschichte literarischer Gattungen," *Geist und Form* (Bern, 1952), 292–309; M. Fubini, "Genesi e storia dei generi letterari," *Critica e poesia* (Bari, 1956), 143–274; C. Guillén, "On the Uses of Literary Genre," *Literature as System* (Princeton, 1971), 107–34; Hernadi (1972); Todorov (1976/77); J. P. Strelka, ed., *Theories of Literary Genre*, Yearbook of Comparative Criticism, 8 (University Park, Pa., 1978).

15. For a detailed discussion of the ancient texts relating to genre theory, see part IV, chapter 10.

When in the period following Boccaccio works of pastoral literature began to be produced in ever-growing abundance, Humanist scholarship consequently found itself at liberty to exercise a good deal of ingenuity in classifying them.[16]

Pastoral came to acquire more substantial generic outlines in the minds of literary theorists at the start of the sixteenth century, when its popularity had reached a new height. A category called *Bucolicum* accompanies epic, lyric, elegy, satire, comedy, tragedy, and epigram in the eightfold division of poetry proposed by Joachim Vadianus in his *De Poetica et Carminis Ratione Liber* (Vienna, 1518) under a section entitled "De Multiplici Genere Poetarum et Speciebus Poematis Variis." Vadianus was followed closely by the German Foedericus Nausea, whose *Ars Poetica* appeared in Venice in 1522, and by Benedetto Varchi, a mid-sixteenth-century commentator who repeats the same eight categories.[17] With the substitution of "iambic" for "epigram," this eightfold division of literature would achieve at times (as in the Elizabethan period) an almost canonical status. Although many literary theorists of the Renaissance failed to mention pastoral in their schemes for dividing and classifying literature, or did not treat it as a genre of equal rank with tragedy or lyric, it never lost the independent identity and distinction with which Boccaccio had invested it. The continually increasing production of pastoral literature is probably responsible for the survival of its generic identity.

The first authority to discuss the pastoral "genus" explicitly was Marco Girolamo Vida, whose *De Arte Poetica* (1527) transmits the traditional doctrine that pastoral is the lowest and most humble of the poetic genres.[18] The form, subject matter, rank, and literary classification of pastoral poetry continued to be discussed in Italy by such men as Bernardino Daniello, who, although he does not mention pastoral by name, alludes to its content ("i campi, le selve, gli armenti, le gregge, et le capanne") in a survey of the subjects of the various genres in his *Poetica* (1536); by Claudio Tolomei, in his introduction to an anthology of poems composed in classical forms but written in the Tuscan dialect (1539); by Mario Equicola, in a treatise of 1541; by Trissino, who, following Vida, ranks the "Egloga pastorale" at the bottom of the hierarchy of genres (the fifth and sixth parts of Trissino's *Poetica* were completed about 1549 but were published posthumously in 1563); by G. P. Capriano, who claims in *Della vera poetica* (1555) that "quelli

16. Cf. Krauss (1938), 140; Nichols (1969), 96–97.
17. Behrens (1940), 68–70, 81–82.
18. See Congleton (1952), 16–17; Nichols (1969), 104–06, and generally 97–104, for a detailed discussion of the older critical tradition concerning the rank of "bucolic" in the hierarchy of styles.

che imitano attioni intiere di misurata grandezza . . . come fanno Comici, Traggici, et Heroyci sono piu perfetti di quelli che imitano queste cose se non in parte, come Elegiaci, Eglogici o simili . . .''; and by Minturno, who in his *De Poeta* (1559) incorporates ''bucolic'' verses into a new system for subdividing the epic genre.[19] But formal criticism of the genre as such began in France with a short passage on ''L'églogue''in *L'Art poétique fran-çoys* (1548) by Thomas Sebillet, who includes pastoral among the classical genres and introduces the doctrine of decorum. It was Scaliger, however, who made the theory of genres the central doctrine of his *Poetice* (1561); as we have seen, Scaliger argued for the first time in the modern period that each genre had its own standard of perfection which can be determined by reason, and devoted considerable effort to formulating a theory of pastoral as a genre.[20]

The autonomy of the pastoral genre was well established in England by the late sixteenth century. In his *Apologie for Poetrie* (written c. 1583 and published in 1595), Sir Philip Sidney carved out a place for pastoral—last in order of importance—in his subdivision of poets ''into sundry more speciall denominations,'' namely, ''*Heroick, Lirick, Tragick, Comick, Satirick, Iambick, Elegiack, Pastorall,* and certaine others, some of these being termed according to the matter they deale with, some by the sorts of verses they liked best to write in.'' William Webbe, in *A Discourse of English Poetrie* (1586), mentions ''the compyling *Eglogues*'' as ''an other kinde of poetical writing, which might notwithstanding for the variablenesse of the argument therein vsually handled bee comprehended in those kindes before declared.'' Sir John Harington listed ''the Pastorall'' in a rather heterodox account of ''all the kindes of Poesie'' in the preface to his translation of *Orlando Furioso* (1591); and seven years later the pastoral poet is again ranked at the bottom of the ''eight notable severall kindes'' by Francis Meres, repeating the roll call of genres from Sidney.[21] The powerful influence of genre theory is evident in Drayton's insistence that ''Pastorals'' are ''a *Species* of Poesie'' and in his emphasis (echoing the sentiments of Cicero's *Orator*) that ''the chiefe Law of Pastorals is the same which is of all Poesie, and of all wise carriage, to wit, Decorum. . . .''[22] It is hardly cause for wonder that modern commentators on the Elizabethan period tend with equal insistence to class pastoral among the various generic divisions of literature.

19. Behrens (1940), 72–89; Nichols (1969), 107–10.
20. Congleton (1952), 17–25; Spingarn (1908), 150.
21. Smith (1904), I, 159, 262; II, 209, 319. See Behrens (1940), 119–23; Congleton (1952), 42–46.
22. Congleton (1952), 48–49; Barrell and Bull (1974), 88.

The systematic theory of literary genres properly belongs to the age of Neo-Classicism, which produced in the field of pastoral poetics such definitive treatises as René Rapin's *Dissertatio de Carmine Pastorali* (1659) and Alexander Pope's "A Discourse on Pastoral Poetry" (1717).[23] Contemporary genre theory differs from the traditional version only in being "descriptive rather than prescriptive, tentative rather than dogmatic, . . . philosophical rather than historical," and pluralistic rather than absolutist.[24] The nature of the criteria employed in generic differentiation has remained the same: genres continue to be distinguished "by specifically literary types of organization or structure,"[25] that is, by a variety of formal characteristics. According to a typical current definition, "Genre should be conceived . . . as a grouping of literary works based, theoretically, upon both outer form (specific metre or structure) and also upon inner form (attitude, tone, purpose—more crudely, subject and audience)."[26] The critical distinction between outer and inner form in this definition suggests misleadingly that both "structure" and "attitude" are equally formal characteristics, whereas the latter is more closely allied to the *subject* of a work, the former to those "specifically literary types of organization" previously invoked as legitimate determinants of genre. The clarity of formal criteria is indeed essential to a smoothly functioning theory of genres. Although such a generic system, in order to be flexible, should take into account attitude, subject matter, *Kunstwollen* or aesthetic intent, and so forth, it must lay greater stress on those features of literature which admit of formal definition: "In general, our conception of genre should lean to the formalistic side. . . . [W]e are thinking of 'literary' kinds, not such subject-matter classifications as might equally be made for non-fiction."[27] The concept of "inner form," then, is something of a mystification, designed to convert certain aspects of literature that lack formal value into coherent criteria for generic differentiation.

Pastoral presents a special problem for genre theory because its distinguishing features belong almost exclusively to the category of "inner form." The doctrine of genres admits of classification according to tone or purpose in certain special cases (satire is another example), "but the critical problem will then be to find the *other* dimension," the specific literary

23. Congleton (1952), 82; on the natural connection between Neo-Classicism as an ideal critical type and the doctrine of literary genres, see P. Goodman, "Neo-Classicism, Platonism, and Romanticism," *Journal of Philosophy*, 31 (1934), 148–63, especially 148–49.

24. Hernadi (1972), 7–8; Wellek and Warren (1962?), 233–35.

25. Wellek and Warren (1962?), 226, citing A. Thibaudet, *Physiologie de la critique* (Paris, 1930), 184ff.

26. Wellek and Warren (1962?), 231.

27. Ibid., 233.

structure or structures appropriate to the expression of a specific attitude, in order "to complete the diagram."[28] Except for the continued use of the dactylic hexameter line in medieval eclogues and the neo-Latin pastoral poetry of the Renaissance,[29] the search for an "outer form" corresponding to the attitudes displayed by pastoral has turned up everything and nothing. Accordingly, the tendency in recent literary theory—and not only in scholarship on pastoral—has been to champion inner form against outer form and to seek for new categories which can encompass matters of attitude or tone without losing clarity and rigor as instruments of classification.

The recent trend in criticism has therefore emphasized literary manners or means instead of kinds: it has tended to substitute the literary *mode* for the literary *genre*. The most influential agent in this movement has been Northrop Frye, who declared in the introduction to his pioneering *Anatomy of Criticism:*

> [T]he critical theory of genres is stuck precisely where Aristotle left it. The very word "genre" sticks out in an English sentence as the unpronounceable and alien thing it is. Most critical efforts to handle such generic terms as "epic" and "novel" are chiefly interesting as examples of the psychology of rumor. Thanks to the Greeks, we can distinguish tragedy from comedy in drama. . . . When we come to deal with such forms as the masque . . . we find ourselves in the position of the Renaissance doctors who refused to treat syphilis because Galen said nothing about it.[30]

The usefulness of generic criticism, according to Frye, has nothing to do with the business of literary differentiation. "The purpose of criticism by genres is not so much to classify as to clarify . . . traditions and affinities, thereby bringing out a large number of literary relationships that would not be noticed as long as there were no context established for them."[31] Frye offers instead his now well-known classification of literature by mode, symbol, and *mythos*. Modern critics are often hesitant to place much interpretative importance on the genre to which a work belongs or could at one time be identified as belonging. This trend has been particularly welcome to students of pastoral. "We are accustomed to consider tragic and comic elements in works that are neither tragedy nor comedy and to recog-

---

28. Ibid., 231.

29. Rosenmeyer (1969), 14.

30. Frye (1957), 13. Frye does reserve a place for genres in his scheme, but it is a subsidiary one and has to do with what he calls the "radical of presentation. Words may be acted in front of a spectator; they may be spoken in front of a listener; they may be sung or chanted; or they may be written for a reader. . . . The basis of generic criticism is in any case rhetorical, in the sense that the genre is determined by the conditions established between the poet and his public" (246–47).

31. Ibid., 247–48.

nize that they shape and distinguish a work as significantly as form or structure can do. Modern criticism seeks inner distinctions based on the view of life, or the view of truth, that the work strives to present"; according to this approach, the criteria which distinguish pastoral "from other genres . . . ultimately rest on a view of life or a way of representing it."[32] Contemporary experts in several fields refer to pastoral quite matter-of-factly as a "mode."[33] But a system of literary modes has yet to displace the method of classification by formal genres.

The expansionist tendency of pastoral, the dynamic nature of its historical development, its variable subject matter, the differing attitudes of its practitioners and critics, and, finally, the difficulties surrounding its literary classification all contribute to the problem of defining it. That problem must now be confronted. It should be stressed at the outset that even a good definition of pastoral can provide only a very limited description of the literary form. Rapin, for example, discussed in detail eleven themes relating to the rules of the pastoral genre (origin, purpose, scene, characters, matter, fable, form, verse, language, style, qualities);[34] no account of pastoral can be complete without doing the same. Yet the purpose of this investigation is not to offer a complete description but to arrive at a set of criteria which will allow the reader to determine whether or not a literary work under consideration can qualify for the designation of *pastoral* as that term is currently understood by modern literary critics. For in order to gauge the usefulness of pastoral criticism as a tool for analysis of ancient bucolic poetry, it is necessary first to understand the attitudes and assumptions bound up with the application of pastoral concepts. The philological argument that *pastoral* cannot signify whatever Theocritus intended by *bucolic* does not, after all, invalidate the pastoralist interpretation of bucolic poetry. Alterations of nomenclature and taxonomic schemes, however drastic and long-standing, merely reflect the changing expectations which successive generations of readers have brought to their encounter with the ancient texts. It remains to show that modern expectations are inappropriate—are actually detrimental—to an accurate assessment of the historical phenomenon. In short, the operation of testing the value of pastoral criticism against the evidence of the ancient literary record must await an investigation into the nature and development of pastoral theory.

32. Lincoln (1969), 1–2.

33. E.g., Marx (1964), 3, 7, 10, and elsewhere; Alpers (1972), 352; Cooper (1977), 2; A. M. Kettering, "Rembrandt's *Flute Player:* A Unique Treatment of Pastoral," *Simiolus,* 9 (1977), 20.

34. Congleton (1952), 17, 54. Scaliger was even more exhaustive.

CHAPTER TWO

Early Modern Concepts of Pastoral

The history of critical efforts to define the meaning of pastoral is a branch of modern history. No such efforts were made during the ancient and medieval periods because pastoral did not then constitute a discrete literary category. This is not to claim that there was a hiatus in the composition of pastoral literature between the third century A.D. and the Renaissance. To be sure, the thousand years separating Longus from Boccaccio did not witness the creation of a single pastoral romance. But the tradition of the Latin eclogue was rather more persistent. The writings of Endelechius in the fifth century, Theodulus before the tenth, Alcuin and his school during the Carolingian era, and Metellus about 1160 are marked by a dependence on Virgil and an increasing use of the pastoral convention for the purposes of allegory.[35] Other traces of pastoral in the literature of the medieval period are visible to the eye of modern criticism. Nonetheless, it was only with the significant literary achievement represented by the Latin eclogues of Dante, Petrarch, and Boccaccio that the composition of pastoral poetry

35. Congleton (1952), 296–97; Rosenmeyer (1969), 4–5; Greg (1906), 18–19. The later Greek bucolic tradition, represented by such authors as Messalla, who wrote bucolics before Virgil, and Olybrius, a patron of Claudian, should not be ignored: see Knaack (1903), cols. 260–61; Schmidt (1964), cols. 965–66. On the medieval and Byzantine traditions, see Knaack (1897), cols. 1009–10, 1012; W. Schmid, "Tityrus Christianus. Probleme religiöser Hirtendichtung an der Wende vom vierten zum fünften Jahrhundert," *RhM*, 96 (1953), 101–65; P. C. Jacobsen, *Die Quirinalien des Metellus von Tegernsee. Untersuchungen zur Dichtkunst und kritische Textausgabe* (Leiden, 1965); W. Bühler, "Theodulus' *Ecloga* and *Mythographus Vaticanus 1*," *CSCA*, 1 (1968), 65–71; T. Alimonti, *Struttura, ideologia ed imitazione virgiliana nel "De Mortibus boum" di Endelechio* (Turin, 1976); A. Ebenbauer, "Nasos Ekloge," *Mittellateinisches Jahrbuch*, 11 (1976), 13–27; D. Korzeniewski, ed., *Hirtengedichte aus spätrömischer und karolingischer Zeit,* Texte zu Forschung, 26 (Darmstadt, 1976); Cooper (1977), 8–46. For other aspects of pastoral poetry in the Middle Ages, see Gerhardt (1950), 31–66; generally, Cooper (1977).

in the West received a fresh impetus; this achievement coincided, naturally enough, with the emergence of the pastoral form as a distinct, identifiable, and independent literary entity. Thus, the meaning or purpose of pastoral became a conscious literary issue only after the revival of classical learning in the West. For our purposes the modern era may be separated into two epochs, conveniently divided by the year 1800. That year saw the publication of Friedrich Schiller's final version of his essays on naive and sentimental poets (in the second volume of his *Kleinere prosaische Schriften*), essays which laid the foundation for all recent thinking about pastoral.[36] The critical efforts of the period before 1800 can be grouped together because of their lesser relevance to current ideas and because of the tenacity with which the earlier critics clung, despite their many disagreements, to a continuous interpretative tradition.

Boccaccio's *Ameto,* the first modern example of a pastoral romance, was composed in 1341. The first pastoral drama, Politian's *Favola d'Orfeo,* was performed in 1471; ten years later appeared the first collection of eclogues in the vernacular, appended to an Italian translation of Virgil— eloquent testimony to pastoral's growing popularity, and harbinger of an explosion of pastoral literature. Mantuan's Latin eclogues were published in 1498; a collection of works by thirty-eight Latin pastoralists was printed at Basel in 1546. This anthology included the piscatory eclogues of Sannazaro, who had completed publication of his *Arcadia,* a vernacular pastoral romance, in 1504. Two years after the completion of Sannazaro's *Arcadia,* Castiglione, himself the author of several Latin pastorals, and Cesare Gonzaga recited an *ecloga rappresentativa* to the ducal court at Urbino. Eclogue writing came to attract such diverse temperaments as Machiavelli and Ariosto, while Lorenzo de' Medici introduced rustic dialects into vernacular pastoral verse.[37] The many differences among the varieties of pastoral being composed in this period—between, for example, the allegorical strain extending from Virgil through the Middle Ages to Mantuan on the one hand and the more sentimental, escapist version of Sannazaro and his ilk on the other—must have intensified the pressure on Humanist scholars to fit pastoral into a coherent anatomy of literature. Although Sicco Polentone, writing about 1437, had little to say concerning the "buccolici," and Politian did not address himself definitively to pastoral theory, while Mantuan left no criticism of pastoral poetry,[38] the general drift of scholarship on

36. Marinelli (1971), 4, also treats 1800 as a watershed by reason of the publication of Wordsworth's "Michael," a work that in his view marks the transition from the classical to the modern pastoral.

37. Greg (1906), 30–33; Gerhardt (1950), 82–86 and 93–94, distinguishes *le "genre rustique" florentin* from pastoral proper.

38. Behrens (1940), 65–66; Congleton (1952), 16.

pastoral in *quattrocento* and *cinquecento* Italy is fairly clear despite its fragmentary nature:

> [T]he critics make use of the doctrines of decorum and verisimilitude and study the pastorals of Theocritus and Virgil. There is a tendency to deduce the subject matter from the classical pastoral, but some critics insist that there is no reason why the pastoral may not develop beyond the bounds set by Theocritus and Virgil. . . . What the critics had to say about the form of the pastoral seems to have been derived directly from the works of Theocritus and Virgil.[39]

When the pastoral form was first recovered from obscurity in something like its original splendor, its usefulness was perceived to lie chiefly in satire or allegory. Pastoral afforded a vehicle for veiled comment on ecclesiastical or political matters. The allegorical exploitation of pastoral, a legacy of the late antique and medieval scholiastic tradition, was considerably expanded during the Renaissance. Consequently, the allegorical tendency in pastoral criticism is important from the very start, as Boccaccio's comments on Petrarch's Latin eclogues illustrate. Allegorical criticism of pastoral poetry reaches from Boccaccio through Mantuan to Barclay (c. 1514), Vives (1544)—who even translates Boccaccio's contemptuous remark that Theocritus had nothing more in mind "than the very barke of the words makes shew of"—Spenser, and the Elizabethan essayists Sidney and Puttenham, whose words about the hidden but lofty import of pastoral are so often invoked by current interpreters of Virgil. Sebillet also took a narrowly allegorical view of pastoral. "To vnfold great matter of argument couertly" is the task of pastoral according to "E. K.," Spenser's mysterious critic, and Renaissance scholars therefore had little to say about the specific subject matter of pastoral, although Scaliger deemed love an appropriate theme. Scaliger is unusual in pointing out that gods and heroes often took charge of flocks in antiquity; the vast majority of Renaissance critics viewed pastoral characters as simple men, ranked pastoral below the other genres, and, applying the law of decorum, taught that its style should be "base and humble."[40] It was also thought that pastoral could be identified with a dramatic or dialogue form; this belief, which originates in late antique commentaries on bucolic poetry, remained in currency as late as Diderot's *Encyclopédie* of 1778, and it cannot yet be presumed to have died out completely.[41] Although it is quite possible to form a coherent impression about the nature of the Humanist outlook on pastoral from what has been said above, no scholar during the Renaissance undertook to provide an explicit definition of the literary concept.[42]

39. Congleton (1952), 22–23.
40. Ibid., 23–25, 39, 298.
41. Ibid., 249; Behrens (1940), 174.
42. Congleton (1952), 297.

Before and after the turn of the seventeenth century there occurred a period of innovation in the classical pastoral, marked chiefly by the Mannerist or Baroque experiments of Tasso and Guarini in Italy; Vauquelin, D'Urfé, Laudun d'Aigaliers, Chapelain, and Saint-Amant in France; and Fletcher and Chapman in England. A preliminary summing up of pastoral theory was provided by the Dutch scholar Gerrit J. Vossius, who published the first Latin work devoted entirely to the subject of pastoral: *De Bucolico Carmine: Poeticarum Institutionum Libri Tres* (1647). Soon afterward the Neo-Classical reaction set in. It was fueled in part by the first separately printed vernacular study of pastoral poetry, a work undertaken by a French *académicien*, Guillaume Colletet, who published in 1657 his *Discours du poëme bucolique, Où il est traité, de l'églogue, de l'idyle, et de la bergerie.*[43] The same year witnessed the appearance of Gilles Boileau's *Avis à Monsieur Ménage sur son eglogue intitulée Christine,* a criticism of a contemporary poem on the ground of its lack of conformity to the rules derived from the practice and dicta of the ancients. Two years later came Rapin's *Dissertatio,* and the Neo-Classical doctrine concerning pastoral was established.

Like the classification of literature by genres and the composition of aesthetic laws, the definition of pastoral poetry belongs to Neo-Classical criticism. Explicit attempts to formulate the literary concept of pastoral are thus hardly more than three hundred years old. Rapin is the first critic of any importance—and perhaps the first critic ever—to define pastoral poetry.[44] He begins by complaining of the difficulty of the task and adds, "I have no guide, neither *Aristotle* nor *Horace* to direct me. . . . And I am of the opinion that none can treat well and clearly of any kind of *Poetry* if he hath no help from these two." Rapin's strategy is to extract a definition of the genre from the observed practice of its acknowledged masters (in this case, Theocritus and Virgil) and to cast it in traditional conceptual language. The resulting definition is naively pseudo-Aristotelian: "It is the imitation of the Action of a Sheapard, or of one taken under that Character." (By this means Rapin seeks to disqualify the baroque compositions of his own day.) Citing "the old *Scholiast* on *Theocritus*" together with Scaliger and Heinsius, Rapin asserts that the form of a pastoral may be narrative, dramatic, or mixed, but adds, "'tis very manifest that the manner of *Imitation* which is proper to *Pastorals* is the mixt: for in other kinds of Poetry 'tis one and simple, at least not so manifold."[45]

Rapin's definition was widely influential. The definitions of Chetwood (1697) and Pope (1717) follow it almost word for word; Charles Gildon

43. Nichols (1969), 113; Congleton (1952), 31–34.
44. Congleton (1952), 301.
45. Ibid., 53–57, 157, 250–51.

(1718) echoes them, and even Thomas Purney (1717), for all his dislike of Neo-Classicism, could not avoid the Aristotelian term *imitation*.[46]

It is in the writings of Rapin's adversary Fontenelle and his rationalist followers that we first begin to glimpse pastoral breaking away from a formalistic definition and starting to acquire as its hallmark a set of distinctive attitudes or moods which constitute its "inner form" and frustrate attempts at literary classification by genre. In composing his *Discours* (1688) Fontenelle apparently intended to enter the Battle of the Books and to confront the authoritarian standard set by the practice of classical writers with "the Natural Light of Reason." Although in matters of taste he is not far removed from Rapin, his approach is entirely different. Fontenelle analyzes pastoral in terms of the human psychological impulse from which it springs (in his view, a twin desire for laziness and for an activity that somehow does not violate it—namely, love) and he advocates the kind of deceitful presentation that does not disturb our dream of wish-fulfillment.[47] Concluding that the "Idea is all in all," Fontenelle declares, "The Illusion and at the same time the pleasingness of pastoral therefore consists in exposing to the Eye only the Tranquility of a Shepherd's Life, and in dissembling or concealing its meanness, as also in showing only its Innocence and hiding its Miseries."[48] The importance of Fontenelle's analysis lies in its implication that pastoral presupposes or expresses an inborn quality of human consciousness and should conform itself to that rather than to objective laws deduced from the practice of the Ancients.

Pope, despite his general adherence to the tenets of Neo-Classicism, felt a need to "reconcile" the views of Rapin's adversary with his own. His definition of pastoral in the "Discourse" begins in an orthodox manner, but in subsequent paragraphs Pope moves on to consider broader issues.

A Pastoral is an imitation of the action of a shepherd; the form of this imitation is dramatic, or narrative, or mix'd of both; the fable simple, the manners not too polite nor too rustic. . . . If we would copy Nature, it may be useful to take this consideration along with us, that pastoral is an image of what they call the Golden age. So that we are not to describe our shepherds as shepherds at this day really are, but as they may be conceiv'd then to have been; when a notion of quality was annex'd to that name, and the best of men followed the employment. . . . For what is inviting in this sort of poetry (as *Fontenelle* observes) proceeds not so much from the Idea of a country life itself, as from that of its Tranquillity. We must therefore use some illusion to render a Pastoral delightful; and this consists in exposing the best side only of a shepherd's life, and in concealing its miseries.[49]

46. Ibid., 157–58.

47. Cf. Poggioli (1975), who identifies the "psychological root" of pastoral with "wishful thought" and "sentimental or aesthetic illusion."

48. Congleton (1952), 65–67.

49. N. Ault, ed., *The Prose Works of Alexander Pope* (Oxford, 1936), I, 297–99.

But Fontenelle found a somewhat more enthusiastic disciple in the Abbot Fraguier, whose writings on pastoral were excerpted and translated into English by the Huguenot Michael de la Roche in 1710.

Poetry is an Imitation. The Design of *Bucolick* Poetry is to imitate what is said and transacted among Shepherds. But it must not be confin'd to the bare Representation of real Truth, which would seldom please: It ought to rise as far as Ideal Truth, which embellishes Nature, and carries Poetry, as well as Painting, to the highest Perfection. Pastoral Poetry is like a Landskip, which is seldom drawn from a particular Place; but its Beauty results from the Union of several Pieces placed in their true Light; in the same manner as beautiful Anticks have been generally copied, not from a particular object, but from the Idea of the Artist, or from several beautiful Parts of different Bodies, reunited in one subject.[50]

Fraguier seems to anticipate Schiller in stressing the ideal mode of presentation necessary to pastoral at the expense of an emphasis on the value of formal structures in pastoral composition.

A second forward-looking trend can be observed in the same period: a chafing at the narrowness of Neo-Classical rules and an attempt to widen the permissible subject matter of pastoral. There is a hint of a broadening of restrictions even in the definition of such a staunch Neo-Classicist as Gildon: "Poetry in all its Parts is an *Imitation,* and *Pastoral Poetry* is an Imitation of the Lives and Conversations of *Shepherds,* or rather of *rural Actions.*" But for the most part this trend was manifest among pastoral's rationalist critics, inspired by Fontenelle and led by Thomas Tickell and Samuel Johnson in England. Tickell added two new psychological motives to Fontenelle's account, human approbation of goodness in others (perhaps the first time natural goodness is associated with pastoral characters) and love of the country; further, he advocated the creation of an indigenous British pastoral inspired by local color rather than by the example of the ancients. Tickell was followed by Thomas Purney, chaplain at Newgate Prison, who wrote perhaps the longest essay on the subject ever published, *A Full Enquiry into the True Nature of Pastoral* (1717), in which he called for, among other things, an enlargement in the cast of pastoral characters. (Purney was undeterred by—presumably ignorant of—Swift's rumblings against the anglicized pastoral and his suggestions to Pope, voiced as early as 1716, about the need for "a set of quaker pastorals" and even "a Newgate pastoral, among whores and thieves there.") The clearest break with the Neo-Classical doctrine of genres was made by Dr. Johnson in his *Rambler* essays on pastoral poetry, published in 1750. Attempting to reconcile the rationalist theory that the rules of art and the natural principles on which they rest can be sought directly in the mind with the more traditional notion that they must be derived directly from the study of artistic masterpieces (whose very greatness is a sign of conformity to

50. Congleton (1952), 158.

them), Johnson framed his own criteria for excellence in pastoral by taking into account both subjective and objective criteria: "If we search the writings of Virgil, for the true definition of a pastoral, it will be found a poem in which any action or passion is represented by its effects upon a country life. Whatsoever, therefore, may, according to the common course of things, happen in the country, may afford a subject for a pastoral poet." Although Johnson's abandonment of the principles of Neo-Classicism is based on rationalist and empiricist premises, he refuses to jettison the authority and aesthetic standard set by the perfection of his beloved Virgil; his position, therefore, can be seen to represent a logical compromise between the Neo-Classicism of Rapin and Chetwood and the Romanticism of Blair and Drake which was to follow. Johnson's idea was taken a step further by the anonymous author of an essay on pastoral in the *Mirror* (no. 79 [1780]), who maintained that those who treat pastoral poetry as the province of shepherds "have considered that as primary which was merely an accidental circumstance. . . . May we not be permitted to ask why a species of poetry should be appropriated to one particular profession or occupation, in contradistinction to all others? What is there in the life of a shepherd to distinguish it from that of the other inhabitants of the country, or to mark the peculiar style and character of those verses which are employed in describing it?"[51] In acquiring as its distinguishing feature a wholly thematic element, pastoral evades forever the formal bounds set by discrete literary genres.

The Romantic critics of the late eighteenth century in England left no definitions with an intellectual profile corresponding to the distinct changes of attitude which they brought to bear on pastoral criticism. They were content to stress the importance of proper feelings and direct, empirical observation of nature. Nathan Drake stipulated in 1798 that "simplicity in diction and sentiment, a happy choice of rural imagery, such incidents and circumstances as may even *now* occur in the country, with interlocutors equally removed from vulgarity or considerable refinement, are all that are essential to success."[52] The importance of the Romantics for the modern view of pastoral lies in their outlook on the relations between man and nature which the pastoral impulse implies (to be discussed below in its place).

In 1795 and 1796 Friedrich Schiller published three essays in his journal *Die Horen*. The first, "Ueber das Naive," appeared in the eleventh issue of 1795, followed in succession by "Die sentimentalischen Dichter" and "Be-

51. All of the information and ideas and much of the language in this paragraph are derived from Congleton (1952), 9, 84–94, 101–08, 157–59.

52. Ibid., 159–60, on the relation between Romantic and rationalist definitions of pastoral.

schluss der Abhandlung über naive und sentimentalische Dichter, nebst einigen Bemerkungen einen charakteristischen Unterschied unter den Menschen betreffend." These pieces, originally designed to form a Kantian triad, were later combined by the author into a single work entitled *Ueber naive und sentimentalische Dichtung* (Thomas Mann called it "the greatest of all German essays"). Schiller's work constitutes the intellectual foundation for all modern approaches to pastoral. Even when Schiller is given only a nod of recognition by recent critics such as Frye and Poggioli or is passed over in silence by classical scholars such as Adam Parry,[53] his influence on them is obvious to anyone familiar with his thought. What makes *On Naive and Sentimental Poetry* a seminal work is Schiller's analysis of literature according to the modality of the relations between man and nature expressed in it. This has two important implications for pastoral criticism. First, Schiller regards all art (whether poetry or politics) as a free exercise of human creativity aimed at fashioning a rational harmony out of the natural environment; hence, the degree of intimacy or distance between the individual artist and nature will determine both the character and outcome of the creative impulse. That the artist's proximity to or alienation from nature dictates his manner of representing the world has proved a fertile notion for subsequent pastoral criticism. Second, Schiller's attempt to identify and enumerate the various *Empfindungsweisen* (ways of feeling or modes of perception) in works of art corresponding to the limited range of possible responses to nature available to the artist generates an entire typology of literature which, although it is not intended to provide an alternate basis for literary classification, nonetheless gives rise to a new set of categories that cut across all traditional generic boundaries.

Schiller begins with a discussion of the "naive." This term refers to the triumph of good, natural instincts over the morally false, repressive codes of society. Not every violation of artifice is naive in the proper sense, for "nature must be in the right where art is in the wrong"; only if the "affect" which triumphs is morally superior to the art which inhibits it, is the expression truly naive. Naiveté in art is the direct, spontaneous, and simple portrayal of nature as it is, without an intervening moral consciousness or elaborate aesthetic convention. It is found in all art in all periods but is characteristic of art in the earliest developmental stages of human society. Homer is the supreme example of the naive poet; because "to be naive it is necessary that nature be victorious over art," however, Schiller stresses that the naive is not what the Greeks themselves felt but what we feel for them. The modern age is characterized by a loss of innocence and by alienation

53. Frye (1957), 35; Poggioli (1975), 4; Parry (1957), 3–29.

from nature, whereas for the Greeks nature was an object of knowledge—
something to be understood, not an object of moral feeling: they did not
cling to nature "with fervor, with sentimentality, with sweet melancholy,
as we moderns do." "As long as we were children of nature merely, we
enjoyed happiness and perfection; we became free, and lost both. Thence
arises a dual and very unequal longing for nature, a longing for her *happiness,* a longing for her *perfection.*"[54] Compare Poggioli: "As civilization
becomes more complex and sophisticated . . . the artistic and literary mind
is made aware of cultural demands and psychological needs hardly felt
before." In the case of pastoral, Poggioli has already defined these needs as
"a double longing after innocence and happiness"; and his use of "innocence" interchangeably with "moral truth"[55] makes it an exact equivalent
of Schiller's *Vollkommenheit* (for the German concept always carries with it
in Schiller the sense of *moral* perfection).

The modern man, then, is drawn to nature as to a lost childhood, and
the modern poet characteristically regards nature with sentimental longing.
Why, Schiller asks, are we so different from the Greeks?

Because for us nature has disappeared from humanity and we encounter her again in
her true aspect only outside of it, in the inanimate world. It is not our greater *accord
with nature* but, quite the contrary, the *unnaturalness* of our relations, conditions, and
manners that drives us to procure a satisfaction in the physical world—since none is
to be hoped for in the moral—for the incipient impulse to truth and simplicity
which, like the moral tendency whence it flows, lies incorruptible and ineradicable
in every human heart.[56]

Schiller gives a psychological account of the origins of the modern sensibility similar to the rationalist explanation of the origins of pastoral: the
fulfillment and satisfaction in a spiritual realm of a longing which cannot be
realized in life. When he goes on to speak of sentimental art restoring to us
in ideal form the harmony with nature we have lost within ourselves,
Schiller's notion seems reminiscent of Fraguier's. But the underlying sense
of alienation from nature which distinguishes the sentimental type of poetry
from the naive evokes most vividly the Romantic analysis of pastoral.
Whereas Neo-Classical authorities, bolstered by the testimony of the scholia on Theocritus, had seen the origin of pastoral in an imitation of shepherds and held pastoral poetry to be a reflection of the pastoral life (as it
existed either in primitive society or, as Rapin preferred, in the Golden
Age), and the rationalists had reacted by claiming pastoral to be a late form

54. Schiller (1966), 89–91, 100, 102, 105.
55. Poggioli (1975), 1–4.
56. Schiller (1966), 103. (I have taken the liberty of altering the published translation to
conform with my understanding of the German text.)

produced by a sophisticated urban society,[57] the Romantics went a step further and commented on the loss of innocent feeling entailed by the growth of an urban civilization. In the latter part of the eighteenth century, Hugh Blair wrote:

Though I begin with the consideration of Pastoral Poetry, it is not because I consider it as one of the earliest forms of Poetical Composition. On the contrary, I am of the opinion that it was not cultivated as a distinct species, or subject of Writing, until Society had advanced in refinement. . . . [The early Bards] did not think of chusing for their Theme, the tranquillity and pleasures of the country, *as long as these were daily and familiar objects to them.* It was not till man had begun to be assembled in great cities, after the distinctions of rank and station were formed, and the bustle of Courts and large Societies was known, that Pastoral Poetry assumed its present form. Men then began to look back upon the more simple and innocent life, which their forefathers led, or which, at least, they fancied them to have led: they looked back upon it with pleasure; and in those rural scenes and pastoral occupations, imagining a degree of felicity to take place, superior to what they now enjoyed, conceived the idea of celebrating it in Poetry.[58]

Schiller goes beyond this evolutionary description, however. According to him, poets are "the *guardians* of nature," not of crude nature, to be sure, but of nature understood as "a balance of sense and reason."[59] When they cannot quite fulfill this role and have experienced the destructive influence of "arbitrary and artificial forms," they become "the *witnesses* and *avengers* of nature. They will either *be* nature, or they will *seek* lost nature." From these alternatives arise the two possible modes of poetry, the naive and the sentimental.[60] It is instructive to compare Schiller's typology with that of Adam Parry, who maintains that

there are two modes of use of natural scenes in poetry, and these modes seem to belong generally, one to the earlier and one to the later stages of a culture. In the first, a natural phenomenon is made directly a simile of something human. . . . the poets of early Greece did not look to nature for something different from themselves. . . . Interest in landscape, or nature, *for its own sake* could be best understood as applying to that literary art wherein man looks to nature for something which he has not within himself or which exists in an imperfect and adulterated manner in his daily life. This means a significantly different use of nature in poetry from what we described as the first mode. Nature no longer tells us what we are: it tells us what we are not but yearn to be. . . . An evident feature of such an attitude is that nature as a whole now becomes a complex metaphor.[61]

---

57. Congleton (1952), 160–72.
58. Ibid., 171 (italics added).
59. Schiller (1966), 24 (explication by Elias, the translator, of the concept of pure nature).
60. Ibid., 106.
61. Parry (1957), 3–8.

Schiller anticipated Parry's conclusion, formulating it in a more univer-
salized and abstract fashion: "Just as nature began gradually to disappear
from human life as *experience* and as the (active and perceiving) *subject,* so we
see her arise in the world of poetry as *idea* and *object.*"[62]

Schiller's investigation into the consequences of this development for
the possibilities of artistic expression reveals a second reason for his importance, a reason already implicit in Parry's telling choice of the term *mode.* If a
shift in man's aesthetic psychology is responsible for causing a corresponding change in his creative response to the world, then the differing types of
artistic production which result can be distinguished according to the expressive function peculiar to each of them.

So long as man remains pure . . . nature, he behaves as an undivided sensuous unity
and as a harmonizing whole. Sense and reason, receptive and active faculties, have
not yet split into their separate functions, still less do they stand in conflict with one
another. . . . Once man has passed into the state of civilization [*Kultur*] and art has
laid her hand upon him, that *sensuous* harmony in him is withdrawn [*aufgehoben*],
and he can now express himself only as a *moral* unity, i.e., as striving after unity.
The agreement between feeling and thinking, which in his first condition *actually*
took place, exists now only *ideally;* it is no longer in him but outside of him, as a
thought still to be realized, no longer as a fact of his life. If one now applies the
notion of poetry, which is nothing but *giving mankind its most complete possible expression,* to both conditions, the result is that in the condition of natural simplicity it
is the completest possible *imitation of actuality* . . . whereas here in the condition of
civilization, where that harmonious cooperation of man's whole nature is merely an
idea, it is the elevation of actuality to the ideal or (what amounts to the same thing)
the *representation of the ideal* that can make the poet.[63]

The alienation of the civilized artist from nature is expressed in his work by
an "ideal" treatment of the world: the character of his creative response
distinguishes the sentimental mode of poetry. When compared with the
rationalist "Illusionism" of Fontenelle or with the Platonism of Fraguier,
Schiller's formulation reveals its originality in an insistence that "ideality" is
a spiritual equivalent to the actuality of nature, as real and necessary to man
as the natural harmony he has lost. Schiller imparts to the problematic
notion of "the idealization of nature" at once a more solid and a more
precise meaning. Contemporary criticism almost invariably associates pastoral with an "idealized landscape," but it provides little in the way of
guidance to help differentiate in practice between the accurate depiction of
natural beauty and the beautification of an ordinary scene. Furthermore, a
certain degree of "idealization" seems inherent in the process of "reduc-

62. Schiller (1966), 105.
63. Ibid., 111–12 (translation somewhat altered).

tion," which is a necessary precondition of all mimetic art.[64] If any artistic rendering of nature lends it some kind of human meaning,[65] how can a landscape fail to be idealized? What special quality distinguishes pastoral landscapes in particular from other specimens? Schiller's discussion suggests that idealization does not consist either in the falsification of reality according to a mental construct or in an artificial means of representing human experience but in a tendency to portray the world in conformity with an idea of rational harmony implicit in it, though yet to be achieved.

The naive and sentimental modes of poetry, as Schiller defines them, do not respect the boundaries of the traditional genres. "Since the naive poet only follows simple nature and feeling, and limits himself solely to imitation of actuality, he can have only a single relationship to his subject and in *this* respect there is for him no choice in his treatment. The varied impression of naive poetry depends . . . solely upon the various degrees of one and the same mode of feeling. . . . The form may be lyric or epic, dramatic or narrative. . . . Our feeling is uniformly the same . . . for just this pure unity of its origin and of its effect is a characteristic of naive poetry."[66] Because the sentimental poet, however, does not imitate a single actuality but stands back from nature and reflects on his own varied experience of it, he enjoys the possibility of choosing among a plurality of attitudes: he may emphasize the limitations of actual experience or the infinitude and freedom to be found in an ideal transcendence of it. Once again, Schiller's method ignores generic classes and emphasizes instead the fundamental perception of the artist and the dominant feeling expressed in his work.[67]

Schiller accordingly divides sentimental poetry into the sub-modes of satire and elegy. Every sentimental artist is either satiric (if the limitations of actuality cause him to react with antipathy) or elegiac (if the infinitude of the ideal attracts him by arousing his sympathy). Elegy can be further subdivided: "Either nature and the ideal are an object of sadness if the first is treated as lost and the second as unattained. Or both are an object of joy represented as actual."[68] The former condition produces elegy proper, the latter creates the pastoral or the "idyllic" sub-mode, as Schiller calls it.[69]

64. For the term *reduction* see C. Lévi-Strauss, *La Pensée sauvage* (Paris, 1962), 34, cited by Redfield (1975), 54, who emphasizes its relevance to theories of imitation.
65. Cf. Parry (1957), 3.
66. Schiller (1966), 115–16.
67. Ibid., 116.
68. Ibid., 116–17, 125.
69. Schiller's choice of the word *idyll* was no doubt influenced by the poems of Gessner as well as by Herder's commentary on them; see Rosenmeyer (1969), 9.

(One might compare the scheme of Frye, who sees elegy and idyll as tragic and comic versions, respectively, of the "romantic" mode of fiction.) At this point Schiller appends a long note explaining exactly what he means by *mode*:

That I employ the terms satire, elegy, and idyll in a wider sense than is customary, I will hardly have to explain to readers who penetrate deeper into the matter. My intention in doing so is by no means to disrupt the boundaries which have been set for good reasons by usage hitherto for satire and elegy as well as for idyll; I look merely to the *modes of perception* predominant in these poetic categories, and it is sufficiently well known that these cannot be accommodated at all within those narrow limits. We are not moved elegiacally solely by the elegy which is exclusively so called: the dramatic and epic poets can also move us in the elegiac manner. . . . Finally, I would still observe that the division attempted here, for the very reason that it is simply based on the distinction of mode of perception, should by no means whatever determine the division of poetry itself nor the derivation of poetic genres; since the poet is in no way bound, even in a single work, to the same mode of perception, the division by genre therefore cannot depend on it, but must be taken from the form of the presentation.[70]

Again, Schiller's formulation recalls Frye: "Once we have learned to distinguish the modes, however, we must then learn to recombine them. For while one mode constitutes the underlying tonality of a work of fiction, any or all of the other four may be simultaneously present."[71] But Schiller's influence was also felt immediately: his interest in "the processes of consciousness which govern a literary genre" made way for Hegel's treatment of pastoral as "a mode of thought—above all, one that exists in relation to other modes of thought rather than as a static form, or setting, or type of imagery."[72] Would it be too improbable to suggest that William Empson's characterization of pastoral as a "trick of thought" is indebted to this same tradition? The notion is at all events so familiar today that it is with something like a shock of recognition that one finds it so clearly and freshly set forth by Schiller. Later in the essay, again in a note, Schiller makes it clear that the sub-modes of sentimental poetry are related to what Wellek and Warren have called the "inner form" of a work, that is, the attitude displayed in it, rather than to its outer form, which has traditionally been considered a more important determinant of genre.

I must repeat once again that satire, elegy, and idyll, as they are here laid down as the only three possible species of sentimental poetry, have nothing in common with the three particular genres of poem which are known by these names, other than the

70. Schiller (1966), 125–26 (translation somewhat altered). Schiller's caution was not universally heeded; the German traditions of Romanticism and Idealism often featured expressive concepts of genre; see Hernadi (1972), 10–37.

71. Frye (1957), 50.

72. Lindenberger (1972), 346.

modes of perception which are proper to the former as well as to the latter. . . . [One must recall] the mood into which the poetic genres known by these names place the mind, and [abstract it] from the means by which they achieve it.[73]

Subsequent pastoral criticism has adhered almost unswervingly to Schiller's precept: although the modern concept of pastoral derives its very name from a formal literary genre, it shares with that genre chiefly the "mood"— the *Gemüt*—or the mode of perception predominant in it. The mood has been fully abstracted from the traditional literary means once used to evoke it.

There is not sufficient space to discuss Schiller's interesting critique of the pastoral mode, but his principal points may be sketched in briefly. Schiller agrees with Poggioli that the representation of human innocence and happiness (*Unschuld* and *Glück*) is the "universal concept" of pastoral. The pleasance and the rest of pastoral's literary machinery should be understood only as an inessential means to the portrayal of man in a condition of harmony and peace. (Thus, Schiller fully anticipates the current distinction between pastoral as convention and pastoral as theme.) Since such a condition should be the goal of civilization—for otherwise no one would willingly put up with its encumbrances—pastoral's *raison d'être* is "to render that idea palpable to intuition and to realize it in individual cases."[74] Unlike Poggioli, then, Schiller sees the proper function of pastoral not as the invitation to a retreat from civilization but rather as a summons to purify civilization and make it conform more closely to a reasoned and natural harmony.[75] The danger of pastoral lies in its potential for being turned against the ideal it ought to promote. A representation of the goal of civilization as yet to be achieved may become the destructive criticism of civilization as presently constituted. In Schiller's view, pastoral has an unfortunate tendency to place that goal of harmony in the irretrievable past instead of in the future; hence it "cannot unify, only assuage. This shortcoming grounded in the essence of the pastoral idyll has been beyond the art of the poets to correct." The tension in pastoral between the real and the ideal admits of no completely satisfactory resolution. Pastoral is "so far ideal that thereby the representation loses in individual truth, yet again . . . so far individual that the ideal content suffers thereby."[76] This trenchant criticism continues to be echoed by contemporary writers.[77]

73. Schiller (1966), 145–46.
74. Schiller (1966), 148.
75. For an interesting discussion of how the concept of a "militant pastoral" recurs in Schiller's thought, both in his theoretical writings and in his poetry, see Rüdiger (1959), especially 15–20.
76. Schiller (1966), 149, 151.
77. Cf. Parry (1957), 29.

CHAPTER THREE

Pastoral Theory since Schiller

The empirical tendency of the Romantics and their impatience with elaborate literary conventions combined to discourage both the practice and the theoretical investigation of pastoral in the nineteenth century. Even "during the eighteenth century the quantity of pastoral criticism is disproportionate to the quality of pastoral poetry. So great was the difference between the value of pastoral poetry and the plethora of pastoral criticism that a number of the critics of the time . . . were aware of and commented on the discrepancy."[78] Poggioli identifies four cultural trends which made themselves felt toward the end of the eighteenth century and which, as they gathered momentum, delivered the *coup de grâce* to an already moribund form: "the humanitarian outlook, the idea of material progress, the scientific spirit, and artistic realism."[79] Only in the final quarter of the nineteenth century, when historical criticism began to deal with all aspects of past culture, did an interest in pastoral poetry revive; that interest has continued to grow ever since, reaching alarming proportions in the last fifteen years, and may still not have passed its peak. As a consequence, the recent scholarly bibliography on pastoral is immense; only the most important and typical examples of recent critical thinking can be considered here.

In his preface to an anthology of English pastoral poetry published in 1895, E. K. Chambers offered no more than a guarded and cautious account of the form of an eclogue: "Sometimes descriptive, it was more often dramatic or pseudo-dramatic in its setting, the dialogue or monologue, generally interspersed with songs, of imagined shepherds." Chambers goes on to emphasize that pastoral does not constitute the poetry of country life

78. Congleton (1952), 295.
79. Poggioli (1975), 31.

but rather the poetry of a townsman's dream of country life; he considers its highest function that of depicting "an imaginary and not a real life." Finally, Chambers turns to the inner form of pastoral and isolates three characteristic thematic features. "One is this exaltation of content, connecting itself on the one side with the longing for renewed simplicity of manners, on the other with a vivid sense of the uncertainty of all human advantages"; the second is love, mainly of simplicity and of simple girls; the third is a "note of delight in, and refreshment from, natural beauty." Nature is a thing to be felt, not studied, and provides a sense of joy, though Chambers does not omit to discuss the theme of pastoral melancholy.[80]

Shortly after the turn of the century, Martha Hale Shackford vigorously denounced the loose use of critical terms as well as the tendency to give "the word pastoral as wide a signification as possible and let it stand for anything rural and unconventional." In her view, attempts to arrive at a coherent definition of pastoral have been plagued by such abuses. Shackford confesses that the idyll, though a species of pastoral, is now impossible to define and is known chiefly by the *mood* it awakens: it is "a brief poem or story where some simple sort of happiness is dramatically presented, where no tragic elements enter. Idyllic means free from dissatisfaction" and the purpose of idyllic literature is to make us love life as we would wish it to be.[81] Not content with the unscientific nature of this description, Shackford goes on to offer her own definition in more traditionally formal terms:

A pastoral idyll is a dramatic presentation of some characteristic scene in the joyous life of herdsmen. It is dramatic in that it represents the movement and speech of the actors *in propria persona,* but it has neither the action nor the unity of movement necessary to true drama. The subject appeals to the eye and the ear . . . the emphasis is placed . . . upon emotion and appreciation. The descriptions of nature, the stories of love . . . are all part of a lyric mood. . . . Uniting in composite fashion the elements of two generic divisions, the pastoral idyll cannot be placed in one category or the other, but must be defined, in general, as lyric in intention and dramatic in execution.[82]

The inadequacy, or rather the limitations of this definition, admirable as it may be in a formal sense, betray the shortcomings of the "scientist" (for whom "looseness of terms is not permissible in a just appreciation of values") in the arena of pastoral definition.

W. W. Greg's approach is more sophisticated. He begins frankly by admitting the inadequacy of formal definitions and goes on to remark that if

---

80. Chambers (1895), xxvii, xxxviii–xliii. The theme of pastoral "anti-realism" will be developed by Gerhardt (1950), Leach (1974), and Barrell and Bull (1974).

81. Shackford (1904), 583–87.

82. Ibid., 591–92; cf. Hieatt (1972), 19.

one insists on the representation of actual shepherd life as the essential ingredient of pastoral, nine-tenths of the literature traditionally associated with that name would fail to qualify. Instead, pastoral refers to a grouping of literary phenomena "related among themselves in form, spirit, and aim" which express certain "instincts and impulses deep-rooted in the nature of humanity." What these instincts or impulses are and how they have endowed the pastoral form with its "strange vitality" are questions Greg declines to answer immediately. He prefers to take a more oblique approach: pastoral is not a document of the humble life, nor is it an exercise in primitivism, agricultural instruction, or anthropology; "the quality of pastoralism is not determined by the fortuitous occurrence of certain characters, but by the fact of the pieces in question being based . . . upon a philosophical conception" that retains signs of an organic unity despite its constant modification over the years. In attempting to articulate this philosophical conception, Greg isolates an important and abiding feature of pastoral—a feature repeatedly emphasized in different ways by modern critics ever since: "What does appear to be a constant element in the pastoral as known to literature is the recognition of a contrast, implicit or expressed, between pastoral life and some more complex type of civilization." Thus, while ruling out of consideration primitive folk songs concerned with shepherds on the ground that "no common feature of a kind to form the basis of a scientific classification can be traced" in them, Greg allows that the poetry of early agricultural and herding communities became distinctively pastoral only when it ceased "to be the outcome of unalloyed pastoral conditions." The idea of the Golden Age arises from this contrast between complexity and simplicity and "comes perhaps as near being universal in pastoral as any," but its significance lies in its being connected to pastoral "by a common spring in emotion and constant literary association."[83]

Greg comments on the escapist nature of pastoral but does not dwell on it. He sees the "disseverance from actuality which haunted the pastoral throughout its many transformations" in somewhat broader terms. "The pastoral, whatever its form, always needed and assumed some external circumstance to give point to its actual content. The interest seldom arises from the narrative itself. . . . [T]he content *per se* may be said to be a matter of indifference; it receives meaning in relation to some ulterior intention of the author."[84] One might compare Poggioli's statement that "all pastoral poetry is allegorical, because it deals only rarely with shepherds in the literal sense of the term: in the main it uses the shepherd's disguise to give an idealized representation . . . of the man for whom private life is the highest

83. Greg (1906), 2–5.
84. Ibid., 66–67.

value on earth"; even more general is Herbert Lindenberger's notion that pastoral is defined by the tensions it creates with aspects of reality ostensibly excluded from it.[85] Greg's eloquent refusal to consider pastoral strictly as a formal genre and his probing search for an underlying principle or philosophical conception make his work a landmark in the history of modern pastoral criticism.

William Empson's *Some Versions of Pastoral,* first published in 1935, completed Greg's inquiry in an altogether unexpected fashion. The historical/critical role of Empson's famous book has been to divorce the concept of pastoral entirely from any kind of formal or generic definition. "Most critics who have dealt with pastoral theoretically since Empson's *Some Versions of Pastoral . . .* have extended the principles of the old shepherd poem freely to literature that abandons many of its conventions while illustrating its themes and attitudes."[86] Empson's work represents, then, the triumph of inner form over outer form in critical definitions and the predominance of pastoral as theme over pastoral as convention. Empson of course was well aware that pastoral had once been perceived as a poetic "kind"; indeed, he provides a lively description of this "version": "The essential trick of the old pastoral, which was felt to imply a beautiful relation between rich and poor, was to make simple people express strong feelings (felt as the most universal subject, something fundamentally true about everybody) in learned and fashionable language (so that you wrote about the best subject in the best way)." Thus, the author/reader combined and mirrored "in himself more completely the effective elements of the society he lived in," and this attempt at comprehensiveness was reflected by a firmly unconscious clash between style and theme.[87] Empson's analysis of the social value of the old pastoral carries over to his general description:

The poetic statements of human waste and limitation, whose function is to give strength to see life clearly and so to adopt a fuller attitude to it, usually bring in, or leave room for the reader to bring in, the whole set of pastoral ideas. For such crucial literary achievements are likely to attempt to reconcile some conflict between the parts of society; literature is a social process, and also an attempt to reconcile the conflicts of an individual in whom those of society will be mirrored. . . . So "fundamentally true" goes to "true about people in all parts of society, even those you wouldn't expect," and this implies the tone of humility proper to pastoral. "I now abandon my specialised feelings because I am trying to find better ones, so I must balance myself for a moment by imagining the feelings of the simple person. . . . I must imagine his way of feeling because the refined thing must be judged by the fundamental thing. . . ."[88]

85. Poggioli (1975), 121–22; Lindenberger (1972), 345.
86. Toliver (1971), viii.
87. Empson (1974), 11–12.
88. Ibid., 19.

Later, Empson elaborates on his thesis about the latency of pastoral ideas in statements of waste and limitation, apropos of Shakespeare's Sonnet 94:

The feeling that life is essentially inadequate to the human spirit, and yet that a good life must avoid saying so, is naturally at home with most versions of pastoral; in pastoral you take a limited life and pretend it is the full and normal one, and a suggestion that one must do this with all life, because the normal is itself limited, is easily put into the trick though not necessary to its power. Conversely an expression of the idea that all life is limited may be regarded as only a trick of pastoral, chiefly intended to hold all our attention and sympathy for some limited life. . . . It is clear at any rate that this grand notion of the inadequacy of life, so various in its means of expression, so reliable a bass note in the arts, needs to be counted as a possible territory of pastoral.[89]

For Empson pastoral is essentially a "trick of thought," not a genre or literary form. His tactic is to follow "the same trick of thought, taking very different forms," through a historical series. Empson is well aware of the danger of such an approach ("taken widely the formula might include all literature, and taken narrowly much of the material is irrelevant"), but he is confident of his ability to identify the content of this "trick" with some precision. Broadly expressed, it is the "process of putting the complex into the simple,"[90] but its features can be characterized more specifically. They include a certain distance between an author and his characters with a con- comitant sense of "I am both better and not so good" as they; a false pretense of humility which takes the form of treating the simple man as superior to the refined man and capable of criticizing him (in a "pathetically charming" manner); the clash of style and theme already mentioned; a penchant for imitating strong and real feelings in an artificial manner; and, finally, a tendency to be inclusive, to use the device of "pantification" ("treating the symbol as everything that it symbolises, which turns out to be everything") in order to enable the refined man to say "the simple man is every man, especially me." Empson's use of his term is itself something of a conceit. His study is not designed to throw light on our understanding of the pastoral genre or of pastoral literature as traditionally defined; rather, he uses *pastoral* in a somewhat figurative sense to identify or name the "trick of thought" he wishes to examine.[91] One may note by way of analogy that Empson readily confessed, in his *Seven Types of Ambiguity,* to regarding

89. Ibid., 114–15. Cf. Alpers (1972), 359, who maintains that Virgil's "sense of con- tingency and limitation are ways of facing the world," not of escaping from it.

90. Empson (1974), 22–23.

91. It is a measure of Empson's influence that his figurative use of the word *pastoral* has evolved into a new definition—a complete inversion of what Empson intended! Cf. Marinelli (1971), 3: "In the modern sense, pastoral is a very broad and very general term far removed from the more specific and distinct meaning attributed to it in earlier times. . . . For us it has come to mean any literature which deals with the complexities of human life against a back- ground of simplicity."

ambiguity not as a single, unified, and profound quality of great literature so much as a useful rubric which could provide him with the means of exemplifying certain techniques of literary analysis and of discussing whatever poems he liked. Nonetheless, many readers will feel that Empson has succeeded in adumbrating what Greg called the "philosophical conception" underlying most versions of pastoral. Empson established that pastoral is a literary mode for expressing a view of life equal in scope to that conveyed by tragedy, comedy, and other primary modes.

Subsequent critics, though hesitant to abandon Empson's vastly expanded conception of pastoral, have felt a need to defend the more traditional, less extended sense of the term and have looked for rigorous means to do so. Kermode, for example, while calling "perfectly justifiable" the use of "the term 'Pastoral' to describe any work which concerns itself with the contrast between simple and complicated ways of living" and which exalts the naturalness of the simple man at the expense of the complicated, nonetheless feels obliged to add a cautionary remark: "[O]ur historical inquiry must be directed, not only upon the general situation which produces significant contrasts between the natural and the cultivated, but upon the tradition of literary Pastoral which is carried on by one poet's imitating another." The nature of Kermode's historical inquiry imposes certain limits on the sorts of pastoral literature he is willing to consider, as a parenthetical remark indicates: ". . . here I limit the meaning of the word [*Pastoral*] to literature which deals with rural life, and exclude other 'versions' of Pastoral. . . ." The distinguishing features of pastoral, as they can be deduced from the literary tradition, are indissolubly linked to the convention of portraying rural life.

Kermode agrees with Greg that "the first condition of pastoral poetry" is a sharp contrast or differentiation between the rustic and the urban ways of life and with both Greg and Chambers that pastoral is an urban product. Particularly interesting is his endorsement of Greg's opinion that primitive poetry can become pastoral only when it ceases to be a reflection of primitive society: "This idea that the world has been a better place and that men have degenerated is remarkably widespread, and a regular feature of pastoral poetry. . . . All such ideas are more ancient than the pastoral convention, but they naturally become attached to it in the course of time. They occur in primitive poetry as well as in the poetry of the cultivated, but this should not deceive us into thinking that there can be primitive Pastoral." Nonetheless, Kermode admits that pastoral's "primary impulse, human resentment at the conditions and struggles of life, . . . establishes its kinship with similar primitive myths."[92]

92. Kermode (1952), 13–15.

Kermode notes pastoral's pretense of humility and then makes an interesting observation which seems to anticipate E. W. Leach's view of pastoral as embodying the oscillations of a divided consciousness. He observes that "the simplest kind of pastoral poetry assumes that the quiet wildness of the country is better than the cultivated and complex life" of the city or court, but he senses that "always at the back of this literary attitude to Nature is the shadow of its opposite; the knowledge that Nature is rough, and the natural life in fact rather an animal affair." This tendency to tease the mind with a sense of the undesirable aspects of its own desires or with the impossibility of their satisfaction does not figure, however, in Kermode's final formulation: "Pastoral depends upon an opposition between the simple, or the natural, and the cultivated. Although this opposition can be complex, the bulk of pastoral poetry treats it quite simply, and assumes that natural men are purer and less vicious than cultivated men, and that there exists between them and Nature a special sympathy."[93]

Renato Poggioli was the first critic to chart all the potential expressions of the pastoral impulse. The impulse springs, in his view, from a "double longing after innocence and happiness," a longing which can be fulfilled only through retreat from the strife of society and the ordeal of human fellowship. This retreat can take the form of a momentary flight, a temporary withdrawal, or permanent escape. Pastoral is an urban phenomenon, for it is the metropolis which reveals, paradoxically, the private side of life and awakens a yearning for greener pastures, moral relaxation, and emotional release from the restrictions of a complex civilization. Pastoral thus supports an ideal of self-sufficiency, simple pleasures without luxury, freedom from work, want, and pressure: a Golden Age where there is no gold.[94] The shepherd is a figure of *homo artifex,* and pastoral poetry recovers the ancient function of art as charm or enchantment, but it accomplishes its object through a sentimental or aesthetic illusion, the pure exercise of the imagination. Poggioli agrees with Kermode in assigning a small role to irony and the double consciousness: "Even in the land of innocence and happiness . . . there lurk evil and ill. Yet the bucolic imagination tends to banish evil without its borders. . . . As for ill, it simply pretends it does not exist." Even death is somehow harmonized into a "principle that rules both world and self." The "real function" of the classical funeral elegy is "to sublimate one's coming death through compassion for the recent death of a dear one. . . . This explains why the pastoral of death must also be . . . a pastoral of friendship."[95] In moving gracefully from one manifestation of

93. Ibid., 17–19.
94. Poggioli (1975), 1–8.
95. Ibid., 64, 78.

pastoral to another, Poggioli does not feel the need to specify what he considers basic or essential to the literary works he is studying and does not offer a more explicit definition of pastoral than what has been suggested here.

That may be just as well, for according to Northrop Frye there can be no formal laws of art that are true; to employ a fixed criterion of excellence—such as unity of action in drama—means either to exclude some works of proven effectiveness or to adapt the requirements of the definition to literary practice until it becomes a tautology (as Greg saw), a technical way of saying "all good art must be good art."[96] Frye prefers to classify literature descriptively: he identifies five modes of fiction, based on the relation of the quality of the characters to that of their "audience," and four pre-generic narrative categories called *mythoi* or generic plots. Pastoral belongs to the romantic mode and the romantic *mythos*:

> If superior in *degree* to other men and to his environment, the hero is the typical hero of *romance,* whose actions are marvellous but who is himself identified as a human being. The hero of romance moves in a world in which the ordinary laws of nature are slightly suspended. . . . In romance the suspension of natural law and the individualizing of the hero's exploits reduce nature largely to the animal and vegetable world. Much of the hero's life is spent with animals. . . . The hero's death or isolation thus has the effect of a spirit passing out of nature, and evokes a mood best described as elegiac. The elegiac presents a heroism unspoiled by irony.[97]

Frye is describing in this passage the tragic version of the romantic mode. He identifies it as elegiac, significantly enough, by the "mood" into which it puts the audience. In describing the comic version, Frye seems once again to recall Schiller's typology in his choice of vocabulary:

> The theme of the comic is the integration of society, which usually takes the form of incorporating a central character into it. . . . The mode of romantic comedy corresponding to the elegiac is best described as idyllic, and its chief vehicle is the pastoral. Because of the social interest of comedy, the idyllic cannot equal the introversion of the elegiac, but it preserves the theme of escape from society to the extent of idealizing a simplified life in the country or on the frontier (the pastoral of popular modern literature is the Western story). The close association with animal and vegetable life that we noted in the elegiac recurs in the sheep and pleasant pastures (or the cattle and ranches) of the idyllic and the same easy connection with myth recurs in the fact that such imagery is often used, as it is in the Bible, for the theme of salvation.[98]

By selecting as the typical episodic theme of romantic fiction "the boundary of consciousness, the sense of the poetic mind as passing from one world to

96. Frye (1957), 26.
97. Ibid., 33, 36.
98. Ibid., 43.

another, or as simultaneously aware of both," Frye endeavors to account for the oppositions or double consciousness latent in pastoral. Yet the romantic *mythos,* the generic plot concerned with the ideal, is opposed to the *mythos* of irony, concerned as it is with the actual; the romance is "nearest of all literary forms to the wish-fulfilment dream" and evokes a world of innocence rather than one of experience.[99] The inelasticity of Frye's scheme should not, however, obscure its important function of liberating pastoral from formal bounds—not only in critical practice (Empson's achievement), but in critical theory as well.

Literary critics have generally prized the freedom of interpretation won by Empson, Poggioli, and Frye, but some have reacted against it out of a desire to be able to specify more precisely what pastoral is and is not. After criticizing the exclusive definitions of Scaliger and the Neo-Classicists, Rosenmeyer remarks, "In our day the pendulum may be said to have swung too far in the opposite direction," and complains that the term pastoral has become "uninformative."[100] Rosenmeyer sets out to show that the practice of some of the most typical exponents of pastoral is conformable with the practice of Theocritus and to use the ancient poet as a major "fix" from which to "triangulate" a definition of pastoral as a genre. Rosenmeyer's general concern about the lack of precision in current critical usage is shared by Laurence Lerner, although the latter has no interest in recovering a generic definition of pastoral. Lerner's insistence on the need to respect literary history seems to echo Kermode: "For us to set what pastoral really is against what it was thought to be is to tamper with history; and since without literary history we would not have the concept of pastoral in the first place, we could be said to be knocking away the scaffold we are standing on."[101]

Most critics, however, have been comfortable with an extended meaning of pastoral. Some have moved beyond Empson in the direction of orthodox Marxism: "[T]he pastoral vision is, at base, a false vision, positing a simplistic, unhistorical relationship between the ruling, land-owning class—the poet's patrons and often the poet himself—and the workers on the land; as such its function is to mystify and to obscure the harshness of actual social and economic organization." Although it may seem curious to treat the Golden Age as "an idealized form of modern society, one which reflects its structure without its complexities," it can hardly be doubted that "the availability of the pastoral myth, to describe quite different sorts of changes in social organization [throughout history], is one of the most

99. Ibid., 57, 162, 182, 186.
100. Rosenmeyer (1969), 5–6.
101. Lerner (1972), 39.

important reasons for its perpetuation long after the passing of the particular circumstances which had first called it into existence."[102] This approach has been carried to its logical conclusion by Leo Marx, who defines pastoral as "the literary mode *par excellence* for recording man's ambivalent response to rapid social change." It is clear that by "rapid social change" Marx intends us to think of the innovations in social organization and human relations accompanying technological progress, and he traces the origins of pastoral to the invention of agriculture and urban settlement.[103]

Different critical outlooks have given rise to different definitions of pastoral. "In its widest sense pastoral becomes a figure for the contemplative life, a withdrawal from action that affords a perspective upon battlefield and market place. . . . The essentials that shape the pastoral are withdrawal to a place apart and from that place a perspective of what man has made of man. . . . The pastoral genre then seems best defined as a figure for a condition in which the characters understand life in relation not to man's activity but to the fundamental patterns of the created world."[104] From the fundamental patterns of the created world to the fundamental patterns of consciousness: Eleanor Winsor Leach forcefully articulates the Jungian interpretation of pastoral as a vehicle for expressing innate conflicts of human identity.

The desire to enter the pastoral world—to recreate in imagination the infancy of mankind—is the expression of a longing for rebirth, for the awakening of some freer, hitherto unrealized self whose potential has been repressed by the limitations of mortal nature or everyday life. . . . The continual tension between the pastoral impulse and the need to preserve a known identity in the face of the overwhelming power of nature gives rise to conflict and complexity in pastoral. . . . What we study in this literature may be called a displacement of simple gratification, a turning aside of the original pastoral impulse into some more demanding form of intellectual or emotional activity, inspired by proximity to nature, yet based upon recognition of the futility of the pastoral ideal.[105]

Herbert Lindenberger puts it more succinctly: "The most significant manifestation of pastoral . . . reveals itself . . . in a particular stage of reality which achieves its meaning through its relationship to and its tension with other stages. . . . Pastoral defines itself, one might say, through the forces

102. Barrell and Bull (1974), 4–5; for a more sophisticated approach, see Williams (1973). A vulgarized adaptation of this kind of historical perspective to the views of Kermode and Poggioli can be found in Coleman (1969), 101.

103. Marx (1978).

104. Lincoln (1969), 2–3.

105. Leach (1974), 31–32, 35–36. Cf. Marx (1964), 8 (on the Freudian approach); 11–19, especially 16–17 (on the "sense of dislocation, conflict, and anxiety" inherent in pastoral); and 24–27 (on the meaning of "counterforce").

with which it sets up tensions."[106] These forces are further elaborated by Harold E. Toliver, who identifies four sets of basic contrasts—each with its subcategories of potential contrasts, varying with the historical period—which emerge from and define pastoral: Nature/Society, Nature/Art, Idyllic Nature/Antipastoral Nature, and Nature/Celestial Paradise. "Such contrasts permeate the pastoral tradition from Theocritus to the eighteenth century and create similar tensive structures in pastorals with less definite conventions thereafter."[107]

106. Lindenberger (1972), 343, 345. Cf. Williams (1973), 18: "[E]ven in these developments, of classical pastoral and other rural literature, which inaugurate tones and images of an ideal kind, there is almost invariably a tension with other kinds of experience. . . ." Williams discusses some examples on 22–26.

107. Toliver (1971), 3.

CHAPTER FOUR

The Modern Concept of Pastoral

In offering the following definition of pastoral, as promised at the outset, I aim neither to reconcile the views of the various authorities cited here nor to forge from their disagreements a new and original definition of my own. I am not interested in the composition of formal rules and stipulative criteria on the basis of which to praise some poems as true pastorals and reject others. My purpose in defining pastoral is, first, to provide a *description* of a certain type of literature (and an amalgam of those elements common to different critical definitions of pastoral can form the starting point for such a description); second, to furnish a *guide* (supported by whatever critical consensus can be established) for determining whether any given piece of literature would be considered pastoral according to the norms of current literary criticism—and this will be useful in surveying examples of pastoral poetry before Theocritus as well as isolating the pastoral components of his Idylls; finally, to arrive at a fairly clear, if general, understanding of the individual qualities and distinctive identity of pastoral as it is viewed today in order to distinguish it from the ancient concept of bucolic, which will be explored in the final two parts of this book. The definition is composed of four points, each of which requires some elaboration.

1. Pastoral is the name commonly given to literature about or pertaining to herdsmen and their activities in a country setting; these activities are conventionally assumed to be three in number: caring for the animals under their charge, singing or playing musical instruments, and making love.[108]

---

108. Cf. van Groningen (1958), 294; Weingarth (1967), 187; Marinelli (1971), 5; Dover (1971), liv; G. Highet, *The Classical Tradition* (Oxford, 1949), 162: "*Pastoral poetry and drama* (seldom plain prose) evoke the happy life of shepherds, cowboys, and goatherds on farms in the country. Ploughmen and field workers are not introduced, because their life is too la-

It should be remarked that point 1 alone of my definition could probably satisfy the requirements of most definitions of pastoral before Schiller. It is very close to the mid–eighteenth-century definitions offered by the so-called rationalist school of pastoral critics; compare Batteux: "Pastoral poetry may be defined an imitation of rural life represented with every possible attraction"; Goldsmith: "This poem takes its name from the *Latin* word *Pastor, a Shepherd;* the subject of it being something in the Pastoral or rural life; and the persons, or interlocutors, introduced in it, either shepherds or other rusticks"; Formey: "Pastoral poetry, is an imitation of rural life, represented with all its possible charms."[109] When these definitions are supplemented by the formulation of Dr. Johnson, already quoted, about the effects of any action or passion on a country life, the result approximates the first entry under "pastoral" in *The Concise Oxford Dictionary:* "Of shepherds; relating to flocks and herds; (of land) used for pasturage; (of poem, picture, etc.) portraying country life, whence ~ISM."

I have had to amplify the standard definition. The Latin root of *pastoral* indicates that the subject may pertain to any person whose occupation is the care of grazing animals, and pastoral poets have traditionally included cowherds and goatherds in their works. The pastoral profession places its members in a country setting and brings them into contact with other inhabitants of the countryside who may not be similarly occupied. The herdsman's job, then, though not constituting an exclusive topic, is central; it provides an orientation, a locality, and a way of life that are significant.[110] Although a

---

borious and sordid. Nymphs, satyrs and other flora and fauna also appear, to express the intense and beautiful aliveness of wild nature. Pastoral life is characterized by: simple love-making, folk-music (especially singing and piping), purity of morals, simplicity of manners, healthy diet, plain clothing, and an unspoilt way of living, in strong contrast to the anxiety and corruption of existence in great cities and royal courts. The coarseness of country life is neither emphasized nor concealed, but is offset by its essential purity."

109. Congleton (1952), 159.

110. Curtius (1953), 187, in describing the tradition of the *locus amoenus,* reverses the process of signification: it is the landscape which expresses a value and requires the pastoral economy to populate it. "To write poetry under trees, on the grass, by a spring—in the Hellenistic period, this came to rank as a poetical motif in itself. But it demands a sociological framework: an occupation which obliges him who follows it to live outdoors, or at least in the country, far from towns. He must have time and occasion for composing poetry, and must possess some sort of primitive musical instrument. The shepherd has all of these at his disposition. He has ample leisure. . . . The shepherd's life is found everywhere and at all periods. It is a basic form of human experience; and through the story of the Nativity in Luke's gospel it made its way into the Christian tradition too." This emphasis on the primacy of the landscape betrays vestiges of a romantic sensibility. Curtius does not explain *why* the theme of poetic composition alfresco was featured in the Hellenistic period for the first time. Moreover, by stressing the shepherd's qualifications to inhabit the very landscape devised around him by the poets, Curtius can be convicted of undertaking a targeted search: that is, he ingenuously states the requirements for the job with an eye to the specific candidate he has already selected. I shall

herdsman must be minimally alert in order to look after his flock, he is not often required to perform any very strenuous or absorbing activity. His guardianship implies a "watchful ease." In the words of one commentator, "Pastoral nature is more ceremonial than useful; it has no need of planting, cultivation, or harvest, and its periodic renewal is less economic than symbolic or miraculous."[111] Meliboee makes the same point to Sir Calidore in Book Six of Spenser's *Faerie Queene* (9.21):

> The litle that I have growes dayly more
> Without my care, but onely to attend it;
> My lambes doe every yeare increase their score,
> And my flockes father daily doth amend it.
> What have I, but to praise th'Almighty that doth send it!

This ease and simplicity of life were made into a figure for the classical mean, for moderation of character and station. Meliboee's confession elevates the pastoral economy to the definition of the good life. "It consists of four elements: (1) being content with what you have, however small it is—this is the way taught by nature . . . (2) enjoying freedom from envy of others and from excessive care for your own possessions . . . (3) avoiding the dangers of pride and ambition and also the insomnia that plagues those who hold positions of responsibility . . . (4) doing what you like."[112] Thus, there is an intimate connection between the structure of the pastoral economy and the values or associations cherished by pastoral literature: "The shepherd in particular leads a deliciously idle life and whiles away the time playing a pipe. He became the type of the natural life, uncomplicated, contemplative, and in sympathy with Nature."[113]

A slightly different perspective on the herdsman's life, emphasizing its importance as a crossroads between nature and civilization, is useful in distinguishing pastoralism from primitivism. In his commentary on Virgil's First Eclogue, Leo Marx notes that Tityrus' "ideal pasture has two vulnerable borders: one separates it from Rome, the other from the encroaching marshland. . . . Although he [Tityrus] is free of the repressions entailed by a complex civilization, he is not prey to the violent uncertainties of nature. His mind is cultivated and his instincts are gratified. Living in an oasis of

---

argue in part II, chapter 6 that the herdsman is primary to the historical evolution of pastoral literature and the landscape secondary; for a different argument to the same effect, see Alpers (1981/82), especially 457–60.

111. Toliver (1971), 4.

112. Smith (1952), 11.

113. Kermode (1952), 16. On the value of *otium* in pastoral literature, see Smith (1952), 2–9; Rosenmeyer (1969), 65–129; M. O'Loughlin, *The Garlands of Repose: The Literary Celebration of Civic and Retired Leisure* (Chicago, 1978), especially 11–154.

rural pleasure, he enjoys the best of both worlds—the sophisticated order of art and the simple spontaneity of nature."[114] But the distinction between pastoralism and primitivism may not always be so sharp as it is in Virgil; in proportion as the artist affords glimpses of the crude realities of the pastoral economy, the retreat into nature takes on something of the roughness associated with rural manners.

Singing and composing music are both natural occupations for a person of leisure; herdsmen can be observed, empirically, to practice them.[115] Such activities also facilitate the identification of the shepherd with the poet, a theme as old as pastoral itself and as essential to its vitality. The shepherd is thereby able to represent not only human freedom, but the free exercise of the mind's highest faculty, and he stands in an intimate and privileged relation to his creator: *ludere quae vellem calamo permisit agresti* (Virgil *Buc.* 1.10: "he has allowed me to play whatever I wish on my rustic pipe").[116] Next, love satisfies Fontenelle's requirement for a pastoral activity that does not disrupt a person's lazy enjoyment of freedom; yet in this "private masculine world, where woman is not a person but a sexual archetype," the "utopian projection of the hedonistic instinct" must be disappointed, must become elegiac, because successful eroticism is not consistent with moderation, and love cannot burn forever without fuel. Hence, according to Poggioli, the erotic act centrally featured in this literature is the kiss: "the pastoral insists on the preliminaries of love rather than on its final consummation. . . . From the viewpoint of its psychological significance, the imagery of kissing may . . . symbolize man's wistful desire to enjoy the pleasures of the flesh without being threatened by . . . the burden of a future family and the duty of raising the children."[117] Rosenmeyer agrees that orgies "are not conducive to the pastoral vision."[118] The issue is disputed, however, and it seems likely that this aspect of the pastoral vision varies somewhat with the attitudes of the different European nationalities.[119] But the importance of love among pastoral themes is beyond doubt.

Although I have stressed the centrality of the pastoral occupation, too great an emphasis on a literal shepherd in a literal landscape would confer a privileged status on a specific literary convention and validate the authority of traditional generic definitions. The herdsman's role has been taken over in the last two centuries by a variety of other figures—from Jefferson's

114. Marx (1964), 22.
115. Duchemin (1960), 87–126; Maxwell (1960), 47–50.
116. Cf. Berg (1974), 1–25; Coleman (1969), 108; Hieatt (1972), 20–24; Poggioli (1975), 23–24, 40–41, 121–22; Rosenmeyer (1969), 145–67; Toliver (1971), 12.
117. Poggioli (1975), 16, 54. Cf. Gerhardt (1950), 296.
118. Rosenmeyer (1969), 72; on the pastoral kiss, 77–82.
119. Smith (1952), 15–18; Lerner (1972), 81–104.

yeoman farmer to Fitzgerald's naive midwesterners.[120] The programme of extending the pastoral profession metaphorically to embrace a new cast of characters is at times articulated explicitly: James Fenimore Cooper likens Natty Bumppo to a "shepherd of the forest."[121] In other cases, the burden of showing that a new personage has in fact displaced the herdsman in his central figurative capacity rests on the individual critic.[122] Moreover, once post-industrial literature begins to fall within the province of pastoral, those attributes of the countryside featured in more traditional versions of the form can be transferred to a highly synthetic manmade environment so long as it continues to evoke a contrast with still less "natural" areas of urban blight. In short, the terms *herdsmen* and *country setting* in point 1 of my definition should not be construed too literally.

Many indeed are the advantages of a country life. But not just any country life makes for pastoral. Rosenmeyer deplores the critical attitude which assumes "that we are dealing with a pastoral whenever a poem shows an interest in the countryside, no matter whether the subject is cattle or olive groves, highland rocks or greensward; or whether the mood is lyrical or anthropological."[123] It should be evident, at all events, that pastoral is not an attempt to see the countryside solely for what it *is* but for what it *means*. Lerner accordingly opens his discussion of pastoral by illustrating the useful distinction between viewing nature for its own sake "and seeing it mainly as the opposite to something else, between a direct and a mediated vision."[124] Hence, the second point of my definition:

2. Pastoral achieves significance by oppositions, by the set of contrasts, express or implied, which the values embodied in its world create with other ways of life.

120. Cf. H. B. Parkes, "Metamorphoses of Leatherstocking," in *Literature in America,* ed. P. Rahv (Cleveland, 1957), 431–45. Parkes does not connect the Leatherstocking figure with the pastoral tradition, however.

121. For this piece of information and for the ideas in this paragraph generally, I am indebted to Leo Marx.

122. E.g., L. E. Taylor, *Pastoral and Anti-Pastoral Patterns in John Updike's Fiction* (Carbondale, Ill., 1971); L. Marx, "Susan Sontag's 'New Left' Pastoral: Notes on Revolutionary Pastoralism in America," *TriQuarterly,* 23/24 (1972), 552–75; M. Squires, *The Pastoral Novel: Studies in George Eliot, Thomas Hardy, and D. H. Lawrence* (Charlottesville, Va., 1974); R. A. Bone, *Down Home: The Pastoral Impulse in Afro-American Short Fiction* (New York, 1975); L. P. Simpson, *The Dispossessed Garden: Pastoral and History in Southern Literature* (Athens, Ga., 1975); H. D. Peck, *A World by Itself: The Pastoral Moment in Cooper's Fiction* (New Haven, 1977).

123. Rosenmeyer (1969), 3. Cf. Barrell and Bull (1974), 8: "But it is not sufficient to point to the subject matter which these . . . versions of Pastoral have in common, the description of life in the country, for by no means all the poems about life in the country justify the name of Pastoral, or would have been thought to do so when they were written." One recalls the earlier protest of Shackford (1904) against allowing *pastoral* to signify "anything rural and unconventional" (585).

124. Lerner (1972), 18.

Let us consider contrasting social worlds before moving on to personal ones. According to Anthony Holden, "Pastoral is unavoidably a yardstick for other kinds of society; this is what distinguishes it from simple nature poetry."[125] The alternative pastoral society is constructed with a critical purpose: it is designed to highlight certain features of conventional human society too often taken for granted or assumed to be inevitable defects of civilization. Pastoral does not have to create a utopia in order to suggest an effective counter-cultural alternative—any harmonious solution to the problems of society takes on the aspect of a golden age. As Toliver puts it, "where the pastoral contrasts between a golden age and the normative world are not exploited, we do not have the dialectical, tensive structure characteristic of all worthwhile pastoral. Such a structure is not in itself difficult to isolate as an abiding feature of pastoral, but it operates on many levels and changes significantly in the evolution of pastoral forms."[126] One common denominator throughout these transformations of pastoral is the founding of social contrasts on contrasts of scale: *sic paruis componere magna solebam* (Virgil *Buc.* 1.23: "So I used to compare great things with small"). Point 2 of my definition therefore continues:

> The most traditional contrast is between the little world of natural simplicity and the great world of civilization, power, statecraft, ordered society, established codes of behavior, and artifice in general.

Unlike the subjects specified in point 1, the contrasts enumerated in point 2 have not always been explicitly recognized as essential to pastoral. The importance of opposed values in defining the identity of pastoral seems to have been emphasized for the first time in English scholarship by Greg.[127] Speaking of the contrast between town and country, Greg says, "It would be an interesting task to trace how far this contrast is the source of the various subsidiary types [of pastoral literature]—of the ideal where it breeds desire for a return to simplicity, of the realistic where the humour of it touches the imagination, and of the allegorical where it suggests satire upon the corruption of an artificial civilization."[128] In other words, the opposition between the pastoral world and the great world is basic to the form but

---

125. Holden (1974), 26.

126. Toliver (1971), 5.

127. For earlier hints of a similar approach, compare Thomas Purney's notion that pastoral must describe a "State, or Life" which we would "willingly exchange our present State for. . . . [T]here are but two States of Life . . . particularly pleasant to the Mind of Man; the busy, great, or pompous; and the retir'd, soft, or easy" (quoted by Congleton [1952], 91). Centuries before, Conrad of Hirschau had claimed the task of pastoral poetry was "privati ruris et urbis differentiam ostendere" (quoted by Krauss [1938], 143).

128. Greg (1906), 7. See Marx (1964), 9–10, for several more examples of such contrasts.

can create different versions of pastoral according to its specific points of reference.

Thus, if the great world is seen in terms of political and ecclesiastical authority, the pastoral alternative will produce the allegories of Mantuan and other Renaissance practitioners and theorists. If the great world is seen as exemplifying the corruption of a decadent civilization, a contrast can be furnished by the "green world" pastorals of Shakespeare or the golden age fantasies of other writers. "The identification of the pastoral life with the conditions of the Golden Age was natural enough. One was a criticism of life by means of adopting the point of view of its simplest and purest elements; the other was a criticism of the present way of life by describing an ideal past."[129] Civilized society may represent to some the tyranny of sexual inhibitions; pastoral opposes to it the ethic of free love so beautifully articulated in the first chorus of Tasso's *Aminta*. Or the great world may signify ambitious striving for wealth, privilege, and honor in society or at court; pastoral portrays in contrast the tranquillity of Spenser's Meliboe. If the great world is identified with the ruthless drive of material progress, its antithesis will celebrate the spiritualized poverty of Baucis and Philemon in the second part of *Faust*.[130] Or society may require of each individual the subordination of his instincts to the demands of a bounded and defined personal identity; Nietzsche's notion of a Dionysiac abandonment of self to the "Will"of savage nature can be considered a pastoral alternative.[131] If the great world evokes not so much the corruption of society but merely its expanded use of artifice, pastoral provides for discussion about the merits of grafting flowers and fruit which can be found in *The Winter's Tale* and Marvell's "The Mower against Gardens." Finally, if the great world is seen as a place of practical achievement, action, and concrete accomplishment, the natural world portrayed by pastoral will acquire value as an expression of human feelings and dreams. This is the "spiritual landscape" of pastoral identified by Bruno Snell, which offers an "escape from life, escape into the realm of feeling and pathos." Snell's description of this "world of pure feeling" fits the concept of a pastoral alternative, but it is a personal rather than a social one and has far-ranging implications: "Myth and reality intrude upon each other; concrete existence gives way before significance. . . . Each image acquires a metaphorical meaning . . . and literature is transformed into a kingdom of symbols."[132]

129. Smith (1952), 14.
130. Poggioli (1975), 194–219.
131. On Nietzsche and pastoral generally, see Krauss (1938), 162–64.
132. Snell (1953), 297, 306.

Such a definition of the pastoral landscape can be applied to a great deal of literature. Francis Bacon characterized poetry in *The Advancement of Learning* (1605) as "submitting the shows of things to the desires of the mind."[133] In W. H. Auden's view, "Every good poem is very nearly a Utopia," an idyllic "community of substances forced to yield their disagreements for the sake of the poem," and therefore "an attempt to present an analogy to that paradisal state in which Freedom and Law, System and Order are united in harmony."[134] The status of this attempt will be evaluated according to one's assumptions about the world: either it represents the falsification of reality in conformity with a wish-fulfillment dream (in the case of pastoral, "a way of *not* looking at the country, at least as much as a way of looking at it")[135] or it is a process of making the objects of sense meaningful through imaginative interpretation. Whatever view is taken of the role of the imagination, the pastoral mode would seem a fitting vehicle for expressing the interpretative activity of the mind. This dimension of pastoral suggests the third point of my definition:

3. A different kind of contrast equally intimate to pastoral's manner of representation is that between a confused or conflict-ridden reality and the artistic depiction of it as comprehensible, meaningful, or harmonious.

The frequent occurrence of this contrast in other kinds of literature need not obscure its special relevance to pastoral. "A related theme in many pastorals is the contrast between reality and the poem itself, as a fictional construction—as its own kind of transforming locality capable of reshaping nature in art (to make 'poetic' is in part to 'pastoralize'), and one of the important threads in the evolution of pastoral is the shifting relationship between the poetic enclosure and the exterior world."[136] Hence Lerner, following Empson with some caution, insists on the distinction between pastoral as convention and pastoral as theme. The prior two points of my definition mainly describe the *convention* of pastoral in which characters are dressed up as shepherds or placed in a landscape opposed to a more familiar reality in order that other themes, such as politics or morality, can be treated. A change in the pastoral disguise or setting might, depending on the work, change only the form, not the theme. With point 3 of my definition we leave the conventional aspects of pastoral behind and approach more closely

133. Cited by Poggioli (1975), 40–41.

134. Toliver (1971), 13, citing Auden, *The Dyer's Hand* (New York, 1962), 71. A canceled passage in Shelley's *A Defence of Poetry* reads: "The words which Poets build are paradise-islands amid the waves of life"; see E. R. Wasserman, *Shelley: A Critical Reading* (Baltimore, 1971), 441n.

135. Barrell and Bull (1974), 4; cf. Gerhardt (1950), 22, 285, 297–302.

136. Toliver (1971), 11–12.

its thematic content. Lerner examines Milton's line, "Batt'ning our flocks with the fresh dews of night," for the presence of authentic pastoral themes: "If we are meant to notice the effect of this terminology on the subject-matter, if we are meant to remember that reading is *not* driving sheep, and that to call it so is to see it differently, then we have pastoral as theme."

Although for Lerner pastoral as theme is "explicitly concerned with the nature of country life," he adds the proviso that pastoral must treat country life as an illusion in the Freudian sense. The Freudian concept of illusion can perhaps help us find a middle ground between the view of pastoral as a falsification of reality and the view of pastoral as the classical example of an imaginative response to the problem of interpreting the world or giving it a human meaning. Lerner quotes Freud as saying, "An illusion is not the same as an error, it is indeed not necessarily an error." Rather, it is a belief in which "wish-fulfilment is a prominent factor in its motivation."[137] The "desire of the mind" which such an illusion satisfies does not have to be specified. The Freudian concept of illusion allows for a wide variety of possible motives. Freud's own example of an illusion is Columbus' belief that he had discovered a new sea route to India, obviously involving a complicated and high-level sort of "wish." Lerner concludes by emphasizing the psychological orientation peculiar to pastoral: "[I]f pastoral is an illusion there is a book to be written on it in a way that there is not, for instance, a book to be written on nature poetry. . . . [T]o write on nature poetry, unless one is to stick to descriptive literary history, is to write on nature. . . . To write on pastoral, however, is to enter [a] region of the mind."[138] According to this line of reasoning, it is the mental faculty responsible for fostering the growth of illusions (in particular, illusions of meaning or harmony) that generates the true themes of pastoral.

Leach, like Lerner, seeks to enter the region of the mind identified with pastoral, but she accounts differently for the presence of pastoral illusions:

References to Eden, to Arethusa, to the magical realm of the nymphs, warn us that the landscapes are unreal. But the unreality is not in any poetic misrepresentation of nature, which often shows itself profuse and seductive to human eyes. . . . The mind of the beholder has created the unreality. While he remains in restless exclusion from his vision, he confesses his bondage to another, harsher environment. . . . At the very point of losing himself amidst nature's spontaneous profusion, he hesitates, doubtful that her influence can effect a desirable transformation of self. . . . The landscape of an ideal world with its abundant fertility, eternal greenness or unusual tranquillity contains intimations of a new beginning. . . . Yet . . . the myth that embodies these promises would never exist if its garden of innocence were not

137. Lerner (1972), 19–29.
138. Ibid., 40.

irrevocably lost to mankind. Pastoral fantasies lure us with the impossibility of their fulfillment.[139]

Leach's treatment of pastoral as a myth suggests alternate possibilities of interpretation. The "attempt to quiet discord and produce a pastoral harmony and transformation"[140] may aim at more, after all, than the creation of illusions: it may produce a teaching myth in which the world's basic oppositions are distilled. Paul Alpers finds support for this view in a return to the origins of pastoral. "The eclogue tradition shows us that the pastoral is not merely, or even primarily, a matter of projecting worlds, real or imaginary, golden or savage. At the center of the pastoral is the shepherd-singer. The great pastoral poets are directly concerned with the extent to which song that gives present pleasures can confront, and if not transform and celebrate, then accept and reconcile man to the stress and realities of his situation."[141]

The fourth and final point:

4. A work which satisfies the requirements of any two of the three preceding points has fulfilled the necessary and sufficient conditions of pastoral.

It is evident that none of the three points is sufficient by itself. An account of the pastoral economy and the customs of herdsmen, informed by no sense of opposition or colored by no mediating idea, is not in itself pastoral—as a glance at the work of Gavin Maxwell or Gavino Ledda on these subjects indicates.[142] Nor is a contrast between natural simplicity and the complexities of civilization sufficient: if it were, *Heart of Darkness,* Aristophanes' *Birds,* or the *Mimiambi* of Herodas could qualify. Finally, the imaginative reordering of reality into a vision of harmony or meaning is too widespread a feature of art to distinguish pastoral in and of itself; when applied to a rustic setting or used to sharpen the contrast between nature and civilization, it produces a pastoral effect. To repeat the entire definition:

1. Pastoral is the name commonly given to literature about or pertaining to herdsmen and their activities in a country setting; these activities are conventionally assumed to be three in number: caring for the animals under their charge, singing or playing musical instruments, and making love.
2. Pastoral achieves significance by oppositions, by the set of contrasts, expressed or implied, which the values embodied in its world create with other ways of life.

139. Leach (1974), 30–32. For a completely different approach to pastoral illusions, see B. Wormbs, *Ueber den Umgang mit Natur. Landschaft zwischen Illusion und Ideal* (Munich, 1976), 11–57.

140. Toliver (1971), 13.

141. Alpers (1972), 353.

142. Maxwell (1960), 45–53; G. Ledda, *Padre padrone: l'educazione di un pastore,* 6th ed. (Milan, 1975).

The most traditional contrast is between the little world of natural simplicity and the great world of civilization, power, statecraft, ordered society, established codes of behavior, and artifice in general.

3. A different kind of contrast equally intimate to pastoral's manner of representation is that between a confused or conflict-ridden reality and the artistic depiction of it as comprehensible, meaningful, or harmonious.

4. A work which satisfies the requirements of any two of the three preceding points has fulfilled the necessary and sufficient conditions of pastoral.[143]

The concept of *pastoral,* as that term is currently used and understood, comprises a variety of critical ideas, some of them more traditional and better established than others. The preceding chapters have endeavored to isolate the intellectual components of modern pastoral theory, to trace the origins of each, and to document their comparatively recent amalgamation. The critical concept which emerges from this survey is a powerful and highly versatile one. Only a purist or a pedant would willingly forfeit the convenience of applying it to any work of art likely to benefit from being viewed as a version of pastoral. Nonetheless, it is necessary to be aware of the implications of any chosen critical method and to acknowledge that the use of the pastoral category to classify works of ancient literature imports alien values and literary associations into the cultural context of these works. To impose pastoral theory on the ancient texts without a proper regard for its relatively late genesis is to be guilty of an unconscious anachronism in critical thinking. How effective such an anachronistic method can be is evident from the numerous studies which have analyzed the pastoral qualities of ancient literature; how dangerously our understanding of ancient writers may be impaired when this method is employed without a corresponding awareness of its historical ramifications is, unfortunately, no less obvious from the interpretative difficulties which have arisen in the criticism of Theocritus and Virgil as a result. Even Rosenmeyer was unable to avoid the pitfalls: though admitting at the outset that his attempt to extract a definition of the pastoral lyric from a comparison of the practices of Theocritus, Virgil, Spenser, Sidney, Drayton, and Milton, among others, constitutes a "simulated synchronism," Rosenmeyer persists in regarding Theocritus as the first and truest pastoralist in this company, not only a "fellow worker" but also "a standard that imposes certain obligations," and therefore Rosenmeyer's attempt "to generate the criteria for an understanding of pastoral poetry from Theocritus" rather than from later "competitors" has the effect (perhaps desired) of projecting onto Theocritus many characteristics of the later poetic tradition.[144] More serious than this is the pressure Rosenmeyer consequently

143. For a different attempt at definition, see now Alpers (1981/82).
144. Rosenmeyer (1969), viii, 13, 29–30.

feels to select examples of Theocritus' art according to critical imperatives dictated by later developments in pastoral and to stress or ignore specific features of his poetry accordingly. All in all, the effect is to distort our historical picture of Theocritus, to create distinctions between portions or aspects of his work which the poet did not himself keep separate, and to jeopardize our sense of the wholeness and integrity of his artistic vision.[145] At the turn of this century Eduard Schwartz observed that the concept of pastoral was derivative, unhistorical, and that it only rendered more difficult the already arduous task of interpreting Theocritus.[146] The need to free our historical understanding of Theocritus from modern preconceptions about the nature of pastoral poetry is no less urgent today. The remainder of this study will attempt to view Theocritus from the perspective of the traditions out of which he emerged—instead of the traditions he created.

145. Cf. Effe (1978), 48–49.
146. E. Schwartz, *Charakterköpfe aus der antiken Literatur,* 2d ed. (Leipzig, 1911), II, 52; the passage is cited by Rosenmeyer (1969), 286, n. 8.

PART II

The Originality of Theocritus

CHAPTER FIVE

The Invention of Bucolic Poetry

An inquiry into the ancient meaning of bucolic poetry presents difficulties quite unlike those encountered in the search for a definition of pastoral. The distinguishing features of bucolic and pastoral are not merely diverse; they are different in kind. The two terms represent thoroughly dissimilar categories. *Pastoral* does not pertain exclusively to literature; as it is understood today, it can apply to music, fashions in dress, and the visual arts, among other things. *Bucolic,* as the word was used in antiquity, referred only to poetry; it would have been impossible for an ancient writer to qualify a prose narrative, a painting, or an outlook on the world as bucolic. Furthermore, what differentiates pastoral in the view of many modern critics is not a way of ordering verbal structures or combining particular themes—not, in short, a mode of literary discourse—but a set of attitudes which, to be sure, are expressed *par excellence* in the formal productions of Renaissance and Neo-Classical pastoral but which can nonetheless be shown to antedate the creation of the pastoral convention in antiquity and to have survived the death of the genre in the late eighteenth century. This persistent habit of mind cannot be traced to the authorship or influence of any one individual; its origins seem to be as old as civilization itself. Bucolic poetry, however, was invented by a historical personage at a specific point in time. Pastoral, in its verbal manifestation, constitutes a major and autonomous division of literature, broad in its contours if rather vague in its boundaries, whereas bucolic grew out of preexisting literary forms and, in order to be distinguished from them, had to possess a coherent, clearly defined identity. The various artistic vehicles for expressing pastoral attitudes have undergone many changes at many hands in different periods. Bucolic poetry, by contrast, was created and sustained by a brief series of poets whose con-

sciousness of working in a common literary territory is attested by an
unusual frequency of references and allusions to earlier members of the
tradition by later ones. For all these reasons, critical definitions must hover
tentatively about pastoral, whereas bucolic poetry can be firmly and precisely circumscribed.

Quite apart, then, from the semantic problem of distinguishing
boukolikos and *pastoralis* from their modern cognates and each other, or the
critical problem of disentangling the ancient concept of bucolic from current notions of pastoral, there remains the methodological problem of determining the mode of analysis most appropriate to each category. The
difficulty of comprehending pastoral is that of seizing upon the essence of
any living cultural phenomenon, any form of expression which has evolved
over the centuries and spanned vast changes in society. Critics are justifiably
unsure whether to locate the identity of pastoral in certain enduring literary
norms and conventions, or in a specific (if perennial) subject, or in some
continuity of feeling, attitude, "philosophical conception," or mode of consciousness which informs the literary imagination but originates outside it.
An investigation into the primary meaning of pastoral would resemble an
investigation into the nature of tragedy, insofar as both terms refer at once
to a set of conventions, a cluster of themes, and also to some general
outlook on the world of an extra-literary kind. No approach to pastoral can
lay claim to adequacy if it ignores any one of these three elements. Bucolic
poetry, instead, poses the same problems of understanding as the detective
story or *Bildungsroman:* it lacks the autonomy of an independent mode or
genre yet remains distinct from the literary traditions to which it is most
closely allied. An attempt to recover the ancient identity of bucolic poetry
must therefore begin by taking a historical approach—that is, it must concern itself centrally with the evolution of literary forms and critical theories—and finish by elucidating the criteria which in the eyes of the ancients
differentiated bucolic poetry from its numerous antecedents as well as from
the contemporary productions of Hellenistic writers.

That bucolic poetry was indeed recognized in antiquity as a distinct
kind of poetic expression has already been suggested.[1] Athenaeus and
Hesychius, as we have seen, called bucolic an *eidos,* a form or genre of
poetry. Their testimony would be of greater moment were it not so far
removed in time from the composition of the texts to which it refers, or,
more important, could one demonstrate that ancient critics were inclined to
be rigorous and consistent in their use of critical vocabulary (in fact, the
reverse appears to have been the case). If by *eidos* Athenaeus and Hesychius

---

1. Cf. van Groningen (1958), 296: "Le terme est d'un usage beaucoup plus large.
Puisqu'il existe et doit avoir un sens, il désigne un type de poésie qu'il s'agira de définir."

mean only "a discrete variety of poetic endeavor," they tell us nothing about bucolic poetry that cannot be more aptly surmised from a glance at the language of the Ninth Idyll, the *Lament for Bion,* and the epigram ascribed to Artemidorus of Tarsus. To determine the formal status and dimensions of bucolic poetry in antiquity requires considerably more precision than the testimony of Athenaeus and Hesychius can provide. The issue is complicated by a recent tendency among classical scholars to call any formal or thematic convention of literature "generic." In what sense, then, or subject to what kind of qualifications, can bucolic poetry be described as a genre?

If the ancients did in fact regard bucolic as a kind of poetry, they must have been able to acknowledge its unique identity without reckoning it a separate branch of literature. The classical genres—the autonomous, distinct, self-contained divisions of literature current in the Hellenistic and Roman periods (until well into the second century A.D.)—were few in number, and bucolic did not figure among them. Luigi Enrico Rossi has warned against the modern practice of conferring generic autonomy upon what the ancients may have considered merely a subspecies of an authentic, more inclusive genre; the status of bucolic poetry is likely to have been inflated by such a practice.[2] Nonetheless, we need a way of talking about that set of literary characteristics which distinguished bucolic poetry in antiquity from compositions perceived as belonging to other classes. It is legitimate to call the distinctive qualities or attributes of bucolic poetry "generic" if we abandon the purely formal criteria of genre employed by the ancient categorists and adopt instead the current view of genre as "a system of conventions, or literary norms, which determine the form, content, style and diction of a work . . . [and] function as a code according to which the work is to be read and through which it becomes meaningful."[3] This notion of "genre" (accompanied by quotation marks) will be invoked consistently here in discussing the distinguishing features of ancient bucolic poetry; it should be confounded neither with the historical meanings of *eidos* and *genos,* nor with the "classifications of literature in terms of content"— the rhetorical conventions and *topoi*—enumerated by Francis Cairns,[4] nor with the thematic conventions and compositional structures identified in the Greek epinician ode by Elroy L. Bundy.[5] Rather, my inquiry into the

---

2. Rossi (1971a), 82; 92, n. 67; cf., generally, Gallavotti (1928).

3. Muecke (1975), 170, citing J. Culler, *Structuralist Poetics* (London, 1975), 145–48.

4. Cairns (1972), 6; cf. the objections of Calame (1974), 115, n. 6, and Rossi (1972), 279n., to Cairns's use of "genre."

5. Bundy himself maintains the distinction between *genre* and *convention* throughout his writings: "Studia Pindarica I: The Eleventh Olympian Ode," "Studia Pindarica II: The First Isthmian Ode," *UCalPublClPh,* 18, nos. 1–2 (1962), 1–92, especially 1–4, 35–36, and 92.

"generic" qualities of bucolic poetry will be directed at the principle or conception controlling the peculiar combination of literary elements (subject, structure, language, style, and meter)[6] which endowed bucolic poetry with a distinctive and recognizable identity. Although such a formulation of "genre" was not shared by the ancients, the analysis based on it will be historical in that it will aim to reveal what caused the ancients to differentiate bucolic from other kinds of poetry.

Theocritus invented bucolic poetry early in the second quarter of the third century B.C. On this point virtually all modern scholars are agreed although, curiously, their consensus does not rest on the testimony of a single ancient source. To be sure, bucolic poetry was frequently associated with Theocritus in antiquity—and with no other name more often than with his[7]—while some mention of Theocritus tended to crop up whenever bucolic poetry was under discussion.[8] But despite the closeness of the ancient connection between Theocritus and bucolic poetry, no one in antiquity explicitly credited him with having invented it. "From our viewpoint, the bucolic genre begins with Theocritus, though ancient critics considered him not the founder but the best in a class."[9] Such is the only estimate to be found in the scholia on those rare occasions when consideration is given to the question of Theocritus' historical role.[10]

Nonetheless, the modern view of the matter can be upheld; for once, it is almost certainly correct. First of all, the word *boukolikos* is not attested in a literary sense before Theocritus, who would therefore seem to have coined

6. Cf. Rossi (1971a), 71, 75.

7. *TrGF*, CAT A5b.1: Θεόκριτος ὁ τὰ βουκολικὰ γράψας (p. 55); ps.-Longin. περὶ ὕψους, 33.4: κἂν τοῖς βουκολικοῖς . . . ὁ Θεόκριτος ἐπιτυχέστατος; Hermog. περὶ ἰδεῶν 2.305: Θεοκρίτου ἐν τοῖς βουκολικοῖς (p. 322.17 Rabe); Serv., Prooim. in *Buc.*: "Theocritum Syracusanum, meliorem Moscho et ceteris qui bucolica scripserunt" (p. 2.15–16 Thilo); ibid., Prooim. in *Georg.*: "Theocritum in bucolicis" (p. 128.3 Thilo); Σ in Theoc., Prol. A.a.: περὶ δὲ τὴν τῶν βουκολικῶν ποίησιν εὐφυὴς γενόμενος πολλῆς δόξης ἐπέτυχε (p. 1.11–13 Wendel); *Anec. Est.* 3.3: Θεόκριτος ὁ τῶν τὰ βουκολικὰ συγγραψάντων ἄριστος (p. 9.6–7 Wendel); Σ ad A. R., *Arg.* 1.1234–39b.: Θεόκριτος ἐν τοῖς Βουκολικοῖς (cited by Gow [1952], I, lxi n.); *Suda*, s.v. Θεόκριτος: οὗτος ἔγραψε τὰ καλούμενα Βουκολικὰ ἔπη (ibid., xv).

8. E.g., Σ ad Hermog. περὶ ἰδεῶν, 2.375: τοὺς τὰ βουκολικὰ ποιήσαντας ποιήματα . . . ὡς ὁ Θεόκριτος (cited by Legrand [1898], 423n.); Diomedes: "putant autem quidam hoc genus carminis primum Daphnin composuisse, deinde alios complures, inter quos Theocritum Syracusanum" (p. 17.14–16 Wendel); Donatus: "restat ut, quae causa voluntatem adtulerit poetae bucolica potissimum conscribendi considerare debeamus. aut enim dulcedine carminis Theocritei ad imitationem eius inlectus est . . ." (p. 18.19–22 Wendel).

9. Van Sickle (1976), 18; cf. idem (1975), 67–68.

10. In addition to the passages cited above (ps.-Longin. 33.4; Serv., p. 2.15–16 Thilo; *Anec. Est.* 3.3, p. 9.6–7 Wendel), note the insertion by a later hand of the words τοὺς πάντας νικήσας σχεδὸν, possibly from an early source, into a version of the scholiastic prolegomena in a fourteenth-century manuscript (*app. crit. ad* Σ in Theoc., Prol. A.a. p. 1.11 Wendel).

it. Perhaps it is because *bucolic* in its literary application is an invented term, and consequently lacks a semantic history before Theocritus, that its precise meaning in the Idylls is now so unclear. Although *boukolikos* must signify something like "of or pertaining to a cowherd or cowherds," its usage in the Idylls appears to deny the relevance of its literal meaning to Theocritean poetics: the word can bear its literal sense only in the First Idyll, where it has been construed to mean "about Daphnis, the cowherd."[11] Related to *boukolikos* is the verbal form *boukoliasdesthai,* featured in Idylls 7 and 5 and found infrequently elsewhere in the bucolic corpus; another apparent coinage of Theocritus, *boukoliasdesthai* suggests by morphological analogy with other verbs of speaking the utterance characteristic of cowherds[12]—a meaning it cannot actually possess in the contexts of either Idyll 7 or Idyll 5. The reasons behind Theocritus' specific choice of vocabulary are difficult to fathom: why should he have called his poetry bucolic rather than *poemenic* (cf. Idyll 1.23),[13] *aepolic* (cf. Idyll 1.56), or *nomic,* if he wished to call attention to his programme of portraying the lives of herdsmen? A survey of the various solutions to this conundrum which have been proposed since ancient times produces little consensus. "It is best to acknowledge that at this point we do not know why Theocritus' poems about herdsmen came to be called bucolics, or why Theocritus uses *boukoliasdesthai.*"[14]

At all events, no known poet or historical figure of any kind is credited with composing bucolic poetry before Theocritus. The sole exception is the archaic Greek lyric poet Stesichorus, who, according to Aelian eight hundred years later (*V.H.* 10.18), produced an ode about Daphnis—the actual inventor of bucolic poetry, in Aelian's view (τὰ βουκολικὰ μέλη πρῶτον ἤισθη: *PMG* 279 p. 138)—and so inherited (ὑπάρξασθαι) that form of composition from his subject. K. J. Dover, noting that the scholia make no mention of Stesichorus in their accounts of the origin of bucolic poetry, concludes that "the reason for this may be very simple: Stesichoros can have told the story, or part of the story, of Daphnis in a lyric poem, but need not have represented Daphnis as composing songs, nor need the lyric poem

11. Cf. Van Sickle (1975), 56–58, and (1976), 22–23, who argues that Theocritus, subsequently reflecting on the nature of his accomplishment in Idyll 1, extended the originally literal sense of *bucolic* to form the basis of a new generic terminology. Among the ancient interpreters of Theocritus, Diodorus Siculus seems to have read *boukolikos* in Idyll 1 in a similar way (the passage is discussed below). But even in Idyll 1.20 a narrowly literal interpretation of *boukolikos* is not fully adequate to the context (although Theocritus does appear to be playing on the word's literal dimension).

12. Dover (1971), lv.

13. According to Trencsényi-Waldapfel (1966), 2n., a passage in Pollux's *Onomasticon,* 4.56, indicates that Epicharmus mentioned a ποιμενικόν τι μέλος; the reading ποιμενικόν, however, is conjectural.

14. Rosenmeyer (1969), 36.

have been presented as the utterance of a herdsman."[15] The association of
Daphnis with bucolic poetry as well as the particular habit of ascribing the
discovery of bucolic poetry to Daphnis[16] seem in fact to result from Theocritus' influence: neither tendency makes its appearance before the time of
Diodorus Siculus (at the turn of the first century A.D.), who wrote:

> In Sicily, so the story goes, was born one by the name of Daphnis, a son of Hermes
> and a Nymph, who got his name from the quantity and density of the bay [*daphnē*]
> which grew in that region. He was raised by the Nymphs, and he took such diligent
> care of the numerous herds of cattle he possessed that he was called for that reason
> the Cowherd [*Boukolos*]. Equipped by nature with a particularly good facility for
> singing, he discovered the bucolic poem and song. . . . He hunted with Artemis,
> rendering the goddess acceptable service, and he pleased her exceedingly by playing
> on his syrinx and singing bucolic songs. [4.84.2–4]

Diodorus' aetiological tale can itself command little credence, but it illustrates the impact of Theocritus on the mythological tradition. Diodorus'
narrative seems to be shaped in part by an unspoken question: "How did
the sort of poetry exemplified by the First Idyll come about and how did it
get its name?" His response takes the form of a "Just-So" story, an account
devised to explain the nature of a current phenomenon by projecting its
origin into a mythical past. To be sure, Diodorus may have drawn some of
his notions about Daphnis from Timaeus, a Sicilian historian and older
contemporary of Theocritus, on whom Diodorus is accustomed to rely for
much of his information about Western Greek myths. We know that Timaeus recounted the story of Daphnis, because Parthenius cites him as a
source for the legend; certain details in Parthenius' version (*Narr. am.* 29)
coincide with the account provided by Diodorus (4.84.4), indicating perhaps that both authors derived their material from a common source, now
lost, in Timaeus. Nonetheless, the sole point of agreement between Diodorus and Parthenius which bears on the connection between Daphnis and
bucolic poetry is their mention of his aptitude for the syrinx—and the
association of the syrinx with herdsmen[17] is more ancient than either Theocritus or Timaeus (see Hom. *Il.* 18.525–26; Soph. *Ph.* 213–14; Eur. *Iph.
Aul.* 574–76 and *Rhesus* 551–53; Mnasalces 16 [Gow-Page] = *A.P.* 9.324).
For the rest, a comparison of the two surviving sources demonstrates that
Timaeus was not concerned with Daphnis' musical or poetic abilities (even
the detail about the syrinx may have been added independently by Par-

---

15. Dover (1971), lxv. Della Valle (1927), 9–22, and Snell (1953), 285, accept Aelian's
testimony; Gow (1952), II, 1, is more skeptical.

16. Daphnis is regarded as the founder of bucolic poetry by Diodorus 4.84.2–4; Aelian
V.H. 10.18; an anonymous tradition mentioned by Diomedes (p. 17.14–15 Wendel); and a
scholiast commenting on Idyll 1.141 (p. 74.10 Wendel).

17. See Duchemin (1960), especially 19–56.

thenius in the first century B.C.), still less with expounding the origin of bucolic poetry; he seems simply to have retold the Daphnis myth.[18] The need to combine the story of Daphnis with an explanation of how he came to be the protagonist of bucolic poetry arose only after Theocritus published the First Idyll. No traces of an interest in bucolic poetry can be found before the birth of Theocritus or can be dated to a period earlier than the acme of his career.

Daphnis is not the only mythological figure credited with the invention of bucolic poetry. According to Athenaeus, a Sicilian cowherd named Diomus was the first to discover the *eidos* of bucolic poetry. Like Daphnis, Diomus is one of the legendary characters of Sicilian folklore; he is said to have been mentioned in two works of Epicharmus, a Sicilian comic poet who wrote in the fifth century B.C. Hence, Athenaeus may have judged Diomus the most appropriate source for the herdsmen's work-song he calls the *boukoliasmos* (14.619ab).[19] Whatever the logic behind the ingenious speculations of Aelian, Diodorus, Athenaeus, and the others, their claim on our belief is at best a feeble one. It is absurd to ascribe to either Daphnis or Diomus the invention of what is plainly a Hellenistic literary *jeu d'esprit.* Such aetiological stories about the origin of bucolic poetry are most plausibly viewed in the context of the Greek habit of searching out mythological precedents for all existing social and literary institutions, a habit whose effects begin to be felt at a very early date in Greek culture.[20] The tendency to attribute the discovery of bucolic poetry to such improbable figures as Daphnis and Diomus may be taken as an index of the increased pressure on ancient scholiasts and mythographers to devise a legendary origin for what was all too obviously and embarrassingly a recent, influential literary invention. And the selection of a fictitious *herdsman* to play the role of mythical founder conforms to the simple mimetic conception of bucolic poetry prevalent in later antiquity.

A second class of theories about the origin of bucolic poetry seems to have been more widely espoused in the ancient world than were the mythological explanations previously discussed and may be thought to comprehend them. These theories locate the origin of bucolic poetry in the indigenous folk cultures of Sicily and the Peloponnese. The scholia relate three or four different aetiological stories designed to explain how a verse

18. F. Jacoby's opposing view (*FGrHist* 566, fr. 83), anticipated by Reitzenstein (1893), 202, is persuasively refuted by Legrand (1898), 144–45.

19. Dover (1971), lxv.

20. See A. Kleingünther, ΠΡΩΤΟΣ ΕΥΡΕΤΗΣ. *Untersuchungen zur Geschichte einer Fragestellung,* Philologus Supplbd., 26.1 (Leipzig, 1933), 1–155; also the discussion in W. K. C. Guthrie, *A History of Greek Philosophy III: The Fifth-Century Enlightenment* (Cambridge, 1969), 301–02, of Critias' elegiac catalogue of inventors.

form characteristic of rustic cult practices was introduced into the high literary tradition of the cities. According to one account, bucolic poetry was invented in Lacedaemonia (the area around Sparta) during the Persian Wars when the virgins who customarily celebrated the festival of Artemis Caryatis could not be induced to emerge from hiding and were replaced by some countrymen of the region who sang rustic hymns to the goddess in their own uncouth fashion.[21] A second version asserts that when Orestes brought to Sicily the cult statue of Artemis from Tauris in Scythia the local inhabitants of Tyndaris welcomed the goddess with their own provincial hymns and so gave rise to bucolic poetry, or, alternately, that Orestes imported some rustic celebrants of the cult with him from Scythia.[22] A third account maintains that when civic strife had ended in Syracuse, Artemis was deemed author of the peace and was honored with gifts and rustic songs by local countrymen.[23] Connected with this story but often mentioned independently of it is the tradition that companies of rustics wearing antlers and other rural emblems competed in Syracuse with hymns to Artemis (because, depending on the version, she had either ended civic strife or lifted a plague) and so created bucolic poetry.[24] Finally, a number of Latin sources claim that bucolic poetry is derived from ritual hymns offered by rustics to one of several gods—either Apollo, Dionysus, Hermes, Pan, Silenus, or Silvanus and the Nymphs, Fauns, and Satyrs.[25] Theocritean poetry seems to invite such speculation by its exploitation of certain formal and stylistic devices of folk poetry as well as by its keen observation of rural life. The likelihood that Theocritus' verb *boukoliasdesthai* was or could have been construed in antiquity to mean the speech of herdsmen supplies an additional motive for the multiplication of attempts to elucidate the connection between bucolic poetry and traditional folkloric themes or modes of expression. Modern scholars have added new conjectures to the ancient literature on this subject.[26]

21. Σ in Theoc., Prol. B.a. (p.2.5–12 Wendel); *Anec. Est.* 3.2 (p. 8.15–22 Wendel); Donatus (pp. 17–18 Wendel); Diomedes (p. 16.15–27 Wendel); Servius (p. 20.23–28 Wendel); ps.-Probus (pp. 13–14 Wendel); Iunius Philargyrius (p. 19.20–28 Wendel); Isidore of Seville (pp. 21–22 Wendel). See A. Meineke, *Analecta Alexandrina* (Berlin, 1843), 360–63; Rosenmeyer (1969), 293, n. 18.

22. Σ in Theoc., Prol. B.a. (p. 2.13–20 Wendel); *Anec. Est.* 3.2 (p. 8.23–30 Wendel); Donatus (p. 18.3–9 Wendel); Servius (p. 20.29–33 Wendel); ps.-Probus (pp. 14–15 Wendel); Iunius Philargyrius (echoing Donatus: pp. 19–20 Wendel).

23. Σ in Theoc., Prol. B.a. (pp. 2–3 Wendel); cf. *Anec. Est.* 3.1 (p. 8.2–4 Wendel); *Anec. Est.* 3.2 (pp. 8–9 Wendel).

24. Σ in Theoc., Prol. B.b. (p. 3.2–15 Wendel); *Anec. Est.* 3.1 (pp. 7–8 Wendel); Diomedes (pp. 16–17 Wendel); ps.-Probus (p. 14.16–30 Wendel).

25. Donatus (p. 18.10–18 Wendel); Diomedes (p. 17.10–13 Wendel); Servius (p. 21.1–4 Wendel); Iunius Philargyrius (p. 20.6–12 Wendel).

26. See, generally, Rosenmeyer (1969), 31–36; Dover (1971), lix–lxv. Cf. also C. C. Fauriel, *Chants populaires de la Grèce moderne,* 2 vols. (Paris, 1824–25); Welcker (1844); J. A.

Both sets of ancient theories about the origin of bucolic poetry rest on a basic fallacy. As Dover has pointed out, the ancient scholars and critics who devised these explanations were "quite reasonably looking not for songs *about* countrymen but for songs *by* countrymen."[27] Hence the belief in a legendary herdsman who invented bucolic poetry or in the derivation of bucolic poetry from primitive rural cults, religious festivals, or other aspects of folk culture. It is easy to see how the presence of rustic speakers in so many of the Idylls, the verb *boukoliasdesthai*, and the variety of stylistic and formal borrowings from folk songs would have encouraged such speculation once the actual literary origin of bucolic poetry—its invention by Theocritus—had receded into the remote past. For both sets of theories minimize the historical role of Theocritus; perhaps they were intended to do so. Now that modern scholars have begun to recognize the existence of pastoral attitudes in Greece before Theocritus[28] and have also succeeded somewhat at clarifying the relation of his poetry to preexisting folk traditions, it is increasingly clear that the learned and highly allusive, consum-

---

Hartung, ed., *Theokrit, Bion und Moschus* (Leipzig, 1858), xxxv–xliv; A. Lang, trans., *Theocritus Bion and Moschus* (London, 1880), xviii–xxi; Reitzenstein (1893), 193–228; E. Hoffmann, "Die Bukoliasten," *RhM*, 52 (1897), 99–104; Knaack (1897), cols. 998–1003; Legrand (1898), 159–72; M. C. Sutphen, "Magic in Theokritos and Vergil," in *Studies in Honor of Basil Gildersleeve* (Baltimore, 1902), 315–27; Knaack (1903), col. 260; E. Riess, "Studies in Superstition," *AJP*, 24 (1903), 423–40, especially 430–40; Della Valle (1927), 38–72; C. Di Mino, "Il folklore siciliano di Teocrito," *Folklore italiano*, 6 (1931), 217–59; T. A. Krasotkina, "Fol'klorno-bytovye korni bukolicheskogo sostiazaniia," *Vestnik drevnei istorii*, 24, no. 2 (1948), 208–12; R. Mandra, "Theocritean Resemblances," *Revue Belge de philologie et d'histoire*, 28 (1950), 5–28; R. Merkelbach, "ΒΟΥΚΟΛΙΑΣΤΑΙ," *RhM*, 99 (1956), 97–133; Cremonesi (1958); D. Petropoulos, "Θεοκρίτου Εἰδύλλια ὑπὸ λαογραφικὴν ἔποψιν ἑρμηνευόμενα," Λαογραφία, 18 (1959), 5–93; B. A. van Groningen, "Quelques problèmes de la poésie bucolique grecque" (II), *Mnemosyne* 4th ser., 12 (1959), 24–53; Duchemin (1960), 87–126; Maxwell (1960), 47–50; R. Y. Hathorn, "The Ritural Origin of Pastoral," *TAPA*, 92 (1961), 228–38; Ławińska (1963); Schmidt (1964), col. 964; Trencsényi-Waldapfel (1966); J. Horowski, "Le folklore dans les idylles de Théocrite," *Eos*, 61 (1973), 187–212; A. D. Pagliaro, "Amoebaean Song in Ancient Greece," *AUMLA*, 44 (1975), 189–93; G. Cipolla, "Folk Elements in the Pastoral of Theocritus and Vergil," *Journal of the University of Durban–Westville*, 3, no. 2 (1979), 113–21; Walker (1980), 56–57, 127–28.

27. Dover (1971), lx; for a different, and equally persuasive, objection to the scholiastic account, see Cremonesi (1958).

28. Egger (1862); Couat (1882), 76–77, 82–83; Reitzenstein (1893), 123–36; Knaack (1897), cols. 1003–05; Legrand (1898), 154–58; Levrault (1914), 12; Della Valle (1927), 7–37; A. A. Day, *The Origins of Latin Love-Elegy* (Oxford, 1938), 19n., 20; Murley (1940); Curtius (1953), 185–90; Parry (1957); Duchemin (1960); G. Schönbeck, *Der Locus Amoenus von Homer bis Horaz*, diss. Heidelberg (1962); H. Parry, "Ovid's *Metamorphoses*: Violence in a Pastoral Landscape," *TAPA*, 95 (1964), 268–82, especially 280–81; Schmidt (1964), col. 964; Trencsényi-Waldapfel (1966); Coleman (1969), 101–03; Rosenmeyer (1969), 37–44; E. A. Barber and C. A. Trypanis, "Pastoral (or Bucolic) Poetry, Greek," *OCD²* (1970), 786–87; Berg (1974), 1–6, 12–22; W. Elliger, *Die Darstellung der Landschaft in der griechischen Dichtung*, Untersuchungen zur antiken Literatur und Geschichte, 15 (Berlin, 1975); Walker (1980), 115–20.

mately refined strain of poetic composition called bucolic—whatever it may
owe to earlier pastorals or to folk songs—is the historical creation of Theocritus.[29] But what exactly did Theocritus invent? If bucolic poetry was so
closely connected with previous pastoral art and with folk customs, what
served to distinguish it, to lend it an identity so unmistakable as to emerge
from the work of Theocritus' Greek and Latin imitators with undiminished
clarity? Before proceeding with the positive task of elucidating the historical
achievement of Theocritus, it may be helpful to prolong the negative argument far enough to show, by an investigation of pastoral origins, that the
originality of Theocritus and of his contribution to Greek literature will
never be understood so long as bucolic poetry is seen merely as an offshoot
of the rustic ballads produced by the early pastoral and agricultural communities.

29. The judgment of Welcker (1844), 408–09, is still worth quoting: "Es ist vollkom-
men klar, dass die Erklärungen der Alten über den Ursprung der bukolischen Poesie aus den
Festen der Artemis, sowohl aus den dabey von Hirten gesungnen Hymnen als aus dem
Liedchen beym Erheben von Gaben, die eigentliche Frage ganz vorbeygehn und ohne alle
Kenntniss der Natur der Sache geschrieben sind. . . . Alles, was wir von dem Sicilischen
Hirtengesang wissen können, ist daher aus einzelnen Zügen der kunstreichen, aber auf scharfe
Beobachtung des Hirtenstandes und gute Kenntniss seiner Sangesart gegründeten Nachah-
mung desselben durch Theokrit, den ersten und einzigen eigentlichen Bukoliker der Griechen,
zu erschliessen." Cf. M. Haupt, "Ueber eine stelle des Callimachus und eine des Hermesianax," *Opuscula,* ed. U. von Wilamowitz-Moellendorff (1875; rt. Hildesheim, 1967), I,
252–62, especially 252–53; O. Ribbeck, "Die Idyllen des Theokrit," *Preussische Jahrbücher,* 32
(1873), 59–98, especially 59–64.

CHAPTER SIX

Pastoral Origins and the Ancient Near East

Toute question sur les origines est obscure, dans l'histoire littéraire comme dans l'histoire politique. Quand, pour la première fois, on s'avise d'écrire l'histoire d'une institution, il n'est plus temps, d'ordinaire, d'en retrouver les commencements à travers l'obscurité du passé. Il en est de même pour les divers genres de compositions littéraires; mais aucun n'a soulevé à cet égard plus de débats que le genre pastoral.[30]

These words are as true today as they were when Émile Egger uttered them at the annual meeting of the Académie des Inscriptions in Paris on 2 December 1859. Egger is perhaps the first authority among modern classical scholars to distinguish clearly what Theocritus actually invented from what is currently understood by the "idyllic" mode; bucolic poetry was the product of an individual artistic genius, Egger notes, whereas pastoral has existed from time immemorial—it was not invented. Already in the mid-nineteenth century Egger could point to a sizable body of scholarly literature which attempted to derive the pastoral inspiration of Theocritus from a continuous poetic tradition originating in the ancient Near East and transmitted to Sicily by the Phoenician colony at Carthage.[31] Rightly dismissing such speculation as improbable, Egger instead was forced to appeal rather vaguely to the Indo-European ancestry of the Greeks, who, as descendants of the Aryan race, had a share in the cultural heritage of the civilization responsible for producing the Vedas, so rich in allusions to the pastoral economy.[32] We need no longer resort to such desperate expedients, howev-

30. Egger (1862), 242. On the general difficulty of all inquiry into origins, see the passages from Aristotle cited by Rosenmeyer (1969), 31, 292, n. 1.
31. See Rosenmeyer (1969), 31, on "the Orientalizing theory" of pastoral origins.
32. Egger (1862), 243–44.

er: the decipherment of cuneiform writing, still incomplete when Egger was composing his essay, the lexical progress achieved in the study of Akkadian (as the dialects of ancient Babylonia and Assyria are now called) and other languages of the ancient Near East, the amazing contributions of archaeology, and the discovery of Sumer have provided a vast quantity of new and precise information about the cultural life of the earliest literate peoples.

As the frontier of historical understanding recedes, the search for the origins of pastoral is correspondingly extended. Far from being a late and peripheral development, pastoral is beginning to be considered one of the oldest and most characteristic forms of man's spiritual expression.[33] Hence the question arises how far back in human history one must look for the genesis of pastoral. In accordance with his theory that "pastoral is the literary mode *par excellence* for recording man's ambivalent response to rapid social change," Leo Marx has attempted to trace the origins of pastoral to the birth of technology itself, specifically to the technical and social innovations which accompanied the Neolithic age: the development of agriculture and permanent settlements.[34] This approach, taken seriously, might well place the origins of pastoral far beyond the reach of the historical scholar. "It is a not improbable conjecture that the feeling that humanity was becoming over-civilized, that life was getting too complicated and over-refined, dates from the time when the cave-man first became such. It can hardly be supposed—if cave-men were at all like their descendants—that none among them discoursed with contempt upon the cowardly effeminacy of living under shelter or upon the exasperating inconvenience of constantly returning for food and sleep to the same place instead of being free to roam at large in the wide-open spaces."[35] In short, the methodological implications of treating pastoral as a reflection of the conflicts produced by socio-economic process effectively bar further inquiry into its origins.

Such, of course, was not Marx's intention. He was simply trying to

33. See Rüdiger (1959), 7; Berg (1974), 14–15: "From religious texts of the ancient Near East, and from the earliest of Greek literature, emerges the figure of the first shepherd-poet, a singer of hymns and oracles. . . . His song is the ultimate theme of all poetry."

34. Marx (1978). Marx has since modified his views; see "American Literary Culture and the Fatalistic View of Technology," *Alternative Futures: The Journal of Utopian Studies,* 3, no. 2 (Spring 1980), 45–70: "The original devices of the pastoral, after all, figure forth a retrospective idealization of the unconstrained ways of herdsmen, a fact which suggests that when the mode first came into existence . . . it involved a degree of nostalgia generated by the changes attendant upon the first great technological revolution: the invention and subsequent triumph of settled agriculture and cities" (53). For purposes of argument, however, I continue to refer to Marx's earlier, more extreme formulation.

35. A. O. Lovejoy and G. Boas, *Primitivism and Related Ideas in Antiquity,* A Documentary History of Primitivism and Related Ideas, 1 (Baltimore, 1935), 7.

extend his analysis of more recent examples of pastoral literature to what he considered the earliest identifiable representatives of that tradition—the rural scenes depicted on the shield of Achilles in book 18 of Homer's *Iliad* and the story of Cain and Abel in the fourth chapter of Genesis. These he ascribed to the social ramifications of the invention of agriculture: the displacement of the shepherd by the farmer, the transition from nomadic wandering to settlement in permanent communities, the consequent tensions in society, and the consciousness of social change. But if the origins of pastoral (in its literary formulation and expression) are related in some way to the momentous developments of the Neolithic period, why look no further for evidence of this relation than the documents of the early first millennium B.C.? The quest for pastoral origins can now legitimately be pushed back in time as far as the invention of literature itself. By adopting as a *terminus post quem* for the expression of pastoral attitudes the historical boundary marked by the earliest use of writing in southern Mesopotamia around 3100 B.C., one can test Marx's hypothesis and intensify the search for pastoral origins.

The pastoral economy was without doubt a crucially important component of the material base of Neolithic cultures in the Near East and it contributed prominently to the subjects, images, and language of the earliest literature. In fact, the very development of the techniques which made possible the "Neolithic Revolution" in scattered areas of the Near East depended on "adequate rainfall and the presence of the six wild plant and animal species that were to be domesticated—namely, emmer wheat, barley, goats, sheep, pigs, and the ancestor of the cow"; these were "the two necessary and sufficient conditions" of progress, according to one authority.[36] Thus, the pastoral opportunities afforded by the ancient Near East proved central to the evolution of human society there. Although in many areas the domestication of plants took place roughly in tandem with the domestication of animals—followed in turn by the move from temporary to permanent settlements—the little evidence supplied by the archaeological record concerning the relative chronology of each development tends to invalidate Marx's hypothesis that pastoral may derive from the original displacement of the shepherd by the farmer. It is clear that the domestication of plants preceded the domestication of animals at Jericho and at other sites of the proto-Neolithic Natufian culture in Palestine; indications that the order of development elsewhere was reversed may be an illusion caused by the incompleteness of archaeological evidence. At Jarmo, where full evidence of agriculture is available from an early period, only the goat and

36. Hallo and Simpson (1971), 11–14; cf. Mellaart (1965), 13–14, and Oppenheim (1977), 33, 45–46 (with references, 349–50).

perhaps the dog were domesticated; pigs, sheep, gazelles, and wild cattle continued to be hunted.[37] Thus, intensified food-gathering may well have evolved into agriculture *before* the techniques of animal husbandry were mastered. (Such techniques, it should be recalled, never were mastered by Native Americans before the arrival of Europeans on the continent.) If later cultures, then, seem to view the shepherd as a predecessor of the farmer, their attitude must reflect a subsequent age's comparative assessment of the two economies or some similar retrospective deduction from the structure of contemporary societies, for it cannot be held to represent the accurately preserved memory of an earlier stage of social evolution.

The villages of the early Neolithic eventually gave way to the great river valley civilizations separated from them by a qualitative gap which, in the words of one scholar, "we are as yet unable to bridge with theories or narrow with new information."[38] The intervening millennia had witnessed the spread of agriculture (after 7000), the increased use of ceramics and the movement of permanent settlements to lower altitudes within easier reach of the necessary clays (after 6000), the consequent use of groundwater for irrigation (rainfall in the lowlands being inadequate), the earliest experiments with metal, and the beginnings of monumental architecture.[39] Needless to say, the pastoral economy remained a basic condition of social organization. The earliest pictographic texts—as yet imperfectly understood—which begin to make their appearance after 3100 (or about five hundred years into the Bronze Age) seem to be records of "the number and nature of grazing animals entrusted by their owners to specified herdsmen."[40] It is generally agreed that writing was first exploited, if not invented, by the Sumerians in southern Mesopotamia who left behind them a sizable literature in an agglutinative tongue which has yet to be related, even remotely, to any other language or linguistic group. But the Sumerian language is understood sufficiently well to allow scholars to identify, however tentatively, a number of pre-Sumerian or substrate words embedded in its vocabulary and in the neighboring vocabularies of Akkadian and (less often) Hittite. These words are presumed to represent a linguistic heritage from earlier periods, a sampling of the languages spoken during the Neolithic or prehistoric age. The earliest group of such words is composed of kinship terms, the next group refers to various stone weapons, and the third group, finally, comprises the oldest identifiable professional names, including "plowman," "miller," and "shepherd-boy" (observe that farming and hus-

37. Mellaart (1965), 23, 32, 49–50.
38. Oppenheim (1977), 32.
39. Cf. Hallo and Simpson (1971), 15–17.
40. Ibid., 33.

bandry are accorded parity of mention). The more specialized words for baker, fuller, leatherworker, herdsman, yoke, sheaf, and sickle appear only slightly later.[41] The Sumerian language (as it has come down to us) contains two hundred words for different types and varieties of sheep, although the nuances of meaning which once distinguished them from one another are mostly lost.[42]

Before embarking on a survey of pastoralism in Sumerian literature, it is necessary to make a fundamental distinction which is often ignored or insufficiently appreciated by laymen writing on this topic—the distinction between a shepherd or herdsman, who is part of the economic enterprise of a city-state and lives in the countryside at a certain remove from the town, and a pastoral nomad, who drives his flocks through uninhabited areas in the company of his fellow tribesmen and does not practice agriculture. A similar distinction can be found implicitly in the Cainite genealogy in Genesis 4, which separates Cain and Abel in the second human generation from Jabal, Jubal, and Tubal-cain in the eighth: Cain and Abel illustrate the contrast between farmer and shepherd, whereas their three descendants represent the trades of pastoral nomad, musician, and smith. Pastoral nomads have existed along side the more developed societies of the Near East down to the present day; this startling cultural juxtaposition has been a perennial source of social tension and (in the case of the settled communities) of literary inspiration. A similar state of affairs already existed in the Neolithic era; one archaeologist, commenting on aspects of regional variation during that period, remarks: "[N]owhere was the contrast between settled farmers and pastoral nomads as strongly developed as in Asia."[43] The threat of marauding nomads continued to challenge, and often to menace, the settled communities throughout historical times.

Sumerian literary documents reflect the fear evoked in cities and townships by nomadic tribesmen—fear compounded by a sense of contempt for their primitive stage of social evolution. When the eponymous god of the Martu (the name given to the Semitic nomads, usually called Bedu, dwelling to the west and southwest of Sumer) decides to marry, according to a Sumerian myth, the bride's female companions warn her against consorting with such a barbarian:

> A tent-dweller [buffeted(?)] by wind and rain, [he knows not(?)] prayers,
> With the weapon he [makes(?)] the mountain his habitation,
> Contentious to excess, he turns(?) against the lands, knows not to bend the knee,

41. Ibid., 17–19; cf. Oppenheim (1977), 33–34, 49–50.
42. Kramer (1963a), 110; on substrate words, 41.
43. Mellaart (1965), 15.

Eats uncooked meat,
Has no house in his lifetime,
Is not brought to burial when he dies.[44]

Somewhat the same attitude is conveyed by a Sumerian proverb which
reads, "Wheat is prepared with(?) *gu-nunuz*-grain as a confection; the Martu
eat it but know not what it contains."[45] An example of more friendly
condescension can be found in the casual reference to the gifts brought by
the Martu to the goddess Inanna at the Akkadian capital of Agade, in a
Sumerian poem composed c. 2000 B.C. and entitled by its translator "The
Curse of Agade, or The Ekur Avenged":

The Martu, (the people of) the lord that knows not grain,
Brought her perfect oxen, perfect sheep.

[46–47][46]

Another Sumerian poem, "Enki and the World Order," depicts the Martu
as receiving cattle, their distinctive source of livelihood, from the god of
wisdom and contrivance:

To him who has no city, to him who has no horse,
The Martu—Enki pre[se]nted cattle as a gift. . . .[47]

Otherwise, the destructive talents of the Martu are revealed by such works
as "Lugalbanda and Enmerkar," a Sumerian epic tale which refers to the
ravages perpetrated by the Martu throughout both Sumer and Uri, culmi-
nating in their siege of Uruk (biblical Erech). It has even been suggested that
a measure of Sumerian antagonism can be found in the possible derivation
of *arad,* the word for slave, from *(m)art(u)*—compare the English word
slav(e)—although the term has been variously etymologized.[48] At all
events, these attitudes bear out the hypothesis that the source of the frequent
contrast between farmer and wandering herdsman should not be located in
the socioeconomic displacement of the latter by the former, but rather in the
effect made upon city dwellers by contact with a contemporary culture so
visibly lacking the attainments of an advanced civilization.[49]

    The Sumerians, instead, took a positive pride in their urban achieve-
ments: one poetic text asserts "that even a native of Marhaši—a mountain

44. Kramer (1963a), 253; also, 164.
45. Ibid., 287; Kramer connects this passage with the one cited on 253.
46. Pritchard (1969), 648.
47. Kramer (1963a), 176.
48. Ibid., 273, 287; cf. Hallo and Simpson (1971), 24.
49. According to "The Eridu Genesis," a Sumerian text, civilized life began when man
was turned from nomadic camping by Nintur and taught to inhabit cities; see Jacobsen (1976),
114, and Albright (1935), 425.

region of Elam—becomes civilized when living in Ur."[50] They do not seem to have fallen prey to that infatuation with the primitive which underlies much of the pastoral impulse. In this, the Sumerians and later Semitic inhabitants of Mesopotamia concur with the Egyptians (in contrast to the ancient Israelites) and share with them a steady confidence in the value of civilized life as well as a temperamental disinclination to seek for avenues of escape. If times are getting worse or things do not conform themselves to one's desires, the only alternatives are suicide or (more frequently) hedonism. The outlook familiar to us from the Bible and especially from prophetic literature is quite different: the corruption, luxury, and social inequities of city life are stressed, while the prospect of abandoning it all and going back to a nomadic existence in the desert holds out spiritual advantages.[51] But this feeling seems to have been peculiar to ancient Israel (even there it was limited to certain eras) and is not representative of common sentiment in the ancient Near East, especially in the early period.

[T]he basic attitude of Mesopotamian civilization toward the city as a social phenomenon . . . is one of unconditional acceptance of the city as the one and only communal organization. There is nothing here of that resentment against the city which in certain passages of the Old Testament still echoes the nomadic past with nostalgia and which goes hand in hand with the rejection of that type of storage agriculture that forms the basis of a redistribution system. Neither are there in these cities any vestiges or even memories of a tribal organization such as have left their unmistakable imprint on Muslim cities.[52]

The hard-won accomplishments of civilization were not to be lightly despised.

The one exception to all this—and, therefore, the first example of pastoral attitudes to be discussed—is the remarkable passage describing the "education" of Enkidu in the Akkadian Epic of Gilgamesh. Enkidu is characterized in this work as a wild-man or savage (Tablet I iv 6); the same word is used to denote the primeval man created by the god Marduk in the *Enūma elish*, the Akkadian Epic of Creation:

I will establish a savage, "man" shall be his name.
Verily, savage-man I will create.
He shall be charged with the service of the gods that they might be at ease!
[Tablet VI, 6–8][53]

50. Oppenheim (1977), 111.
51. Albright (1935), 429–32.
52. Oppenheim (1977), 111.
53. Pritchard (1969), 68; for the similarities in vocabulary, see E. A. Speiser's notes *ad loc.*

It seems, then, that the account of Enkidu in his original wild state is meant to convey some sense of the advantages of the primitive:

[Sha]ggy with hair is his whole body,
    He is endowed with head hair like a woman.
The locks of his hair sprout like Nisaba (the goddess of grain).
He knows neither people nor land;
    Garbed is he like Sumuqan (the god of cattle).
With the gazelles he feeds on grass,
With the wild beasts he jostles at the watering-place,
With the teeming creatures his heart delights in water.

[I ii 36–41][54]

Enkidu's strength is immense; he is the mightiest creature in the land. He destroys the traps for wild animals set by hunters and prevents them from practicing their profession. In order to put an end to this nuisance, the hunters procure from Gilgamesh in Uruk a "pleasure-girl," who begins the process of integrating Enkidu into civilization, where he will join with Gilgamesh—first in rivalry, then in friendship—and eventually lose his life as a result of their exploits. The famous episode narrating Enkidu's encounter with the "pleasure-girl" reads as follows in the (late) Assyrian version:

For six days and seven nights Enkidu comes forth,
    Mating with the lass.
After he had had (his) fill of her charms,
He set his face toward his wild beasts.
On seeing him, Enkidu, the gazelles ran off,
The wild beasts of the steppe drew away from his body.
Startled was Enkidu, as his body became taut,
His knees were motionless—for his wild beasts had gone.
Enkidu had to slacken his pace—it was not as before;
But now he had [wi]sdom, [br]oader understanding.
Returning, he sits at the feet of the harlot.
He looks up at the face of the harlot,
His ears attentive, as the harlot speaks;
[The harlot] says to him, to Enkidu:
"Thou are [wi]se, Enkidu, art become like a god!
Why with the wild creatures dost thou roam over the steppe?
Come, let me lead thee [to] ramparted Uruk. . . ."

[I iv 21–36][55]

The Old Babylonian version of the epic, composed about 2000 B.C., tells the same story in a somewhat more laconic fashion:

Enkidu sits before the harlot.
The two of them make love together.

54. Pritchard (1969), 74.
55. Ibid., 75.

He forgot the s[tep]pe where he was born.
For six days and seven nights Enkidu came forth
Mating with the l[ass].
Then the harlot opened her mouth,
Saying to Enkidu:
"As I look at thee, Enkidu, thou art become like a god;
Wherefore with the wild creatures
Dost thou range over the steppe?
Up, I will lead thee
To broad-marted Uruk. . . ."

[II ii 4–15][56]

On their journey to Uruk Enkidu and his companion stop at a shepherd's cottage. It is here, at this kind of cultural halfway house, that Enkidu
makes his transition from the wilderness to human society—and it is in the
following description that the poem acquires its strongest pastoral overtones:

Holding on to his hand,
She leads him like a child
To the shepherd-hut,
The place of the sheepfold.
Round him the shepherds gathered

[II ii 31–35]

[lacuna]

The milk of wild creatures
He was wont to suck.
Food they placed before him;
He gagged, he gaped
And he stared.
Nothing does Enkidu know
Of eating food;
To drink strong drink
He has not been taught.
The harlot opened her mouth,
Saying to Enkidu:
"Eat the food, Enkidu,
As is life's due;
Drink the strong drink, as is the custom of the land."
Enkidu ate the food,
Until he was sated;
Of strong drink he drank
Seven goblets.
Carefree became his mood (and) cheerful,
His heart exulted

56. Ibid., 77.

And his face glowed.
He rubbed [the *shaggy growth*],
The hair of his body,
Anointed himself with oil,
Became human.

[II iii 1–25][57]

From this point forward, Enkidu becomes a champion of civilization. Whereas he had earlier destroyed the hunters' traps, implicitly defending the wilderness from human incursion and frustrating the arts of forestry, he now turns his formidable powers *against* the wilderness and places them instead at the service of civilization.

He took his weapon
To chase the lions,
That shepherds might rest at night.
He caught wolves,
He captured lions.
The chief cattlemen could lie down;
Enkidu is their watchman,
The bold man,
The unique hero!

[II iii 28–36][58]

Enkidu's conversion, however beneficial to the shepherds it may be, will eventually prove his own undoing, and on his deathbed he will momentarily regret his fateful encounter with the "pleasure-girl" (Tablet VII iii 5–32). In this way, through its careful balance of the refinements of civilized life against the mysterious power and energy of the wild, its deliberate ambivalence about the relative advantages of nature and culture, the Gilgamesh epic manages to achieve something of a pastoral effect. "One can easily detect in the praise of the joys of civilized living in Uruk and the idyllic descriptions of the shepherds and their way of life the expression of a relationship between city and country that is unique in Mesopotamia. In lieu of an emphasis on the customary contrasts that separate these ways of life, politically, socially, and in other respects, we find a sentimental interest in rusticity. The poet characterizes Enkidu as a "noble savage." Since early Old Babylonian versions of the epic show the same attitude . . . [the poet's] praise of Uruk and his praise of rustic activities are [possibly] reflections of the earliest Akkadian versions of the epic."[59]

Turning now to the relations between farmer and shepherd within the civilized communities, the historian confronts a situation at once more

57. Ibid.
58. Ibid.
59. Oppenheim (1977), 261; cf. Albright (1935), 423–24; Berg (1974), 15–17.

subtle and more complex. Farming and animal husbandry constituted the two basic sources of food and surplus wealth in the ancient Near East; as such, they were clearly interdependent. Yet the skills required by each of them were sharply differentiated. The pressures of specialization consequently gave rise to distinct modes of life and separate sets of economic ties to the centers of administration. Agriculture could flourish only where the land was irrigated by a sophisticated exploitation of groundwater, whereas animals could graze on more arid land, usually in regions far removed from areas under intensive cultivation. These conditions tended to place the shepherd, at least part of the time, on the border between civilization and the wild.[60] That is, of course, exactly where Enkidu found him in the Gilgamesh epic. It is no accident that Enkidu encounters herdsmen precisely at the intermediate stage of his own transition from the untamed potency of nature to the ordered, hierarchical power of urban culture. The herdsman is properly a *liminal* figure: he moves back and forth between two worlds, exposed to the menace of wild animals yet bound by his livelihood and by cultural conditioning to the settled communities. The "shepherd-hut" is an appropriate setting for Enkidu's socialization, his integration into human society, because it represents a kind of border-station on the frontier between nature and culture.[61]

James M. Redfield has argued that the Homeric epics reveal a similar understanding and valuation of the pastoral locale.

The sharpest demarcation in the Homeric landscape, second only to the distinction between land and sea, is the line between tillable lowland and hill or grazing land. On the alluvial plain there are fields, gardens, cities, and houses; the plain is the properly inhabited world of family life and political community. Around the plain runs the mountain wall, and those who climb this wall find themselves in a separate world: the *agrou ep' eschatiēn*, the land beyond the limit of agriculture. Here the herds live (except in the fallow season) with the herdsmen who care for them. The herdsmen do not live in proper houses but in *stathmoi*, lean-tos or sheds, and there are no families; herding is a task for young men (xvii. 20–21), before they reach an age to have a wife, an *oikos*, and a *klēros*—a family, a house, and a tract of agricultural land (xiv.64). The hill land is included in the description of the Shield in a kind of three-line footnote to the third ring (XVIII.587–589). This land beyond the limit of the

60. For information about the life of shepherds in the ancient Near East, see F. R. Kraus, *Staatliche Viehhaltung im altbabylonischen Lande Larsa,* Mededeelingen der Koninklijke Nederlandse Akademie van Wetenschappen, Afd. Letterkunde, Nieuwe Reeks, Deel 29 (Amsterdam, 1966); J. N. Postgate, "Some Old Babylonian Shepherds and Their Flocks," *Journal of Semitic Studies,* 20 (1975), 1–21; recently, M. A. Morrison, "Evidence for Herdsmen and Animal Husbandry in the Nuzi Documents," in *Studies on the Civilization and Culture of Nuzi and the Hurrians in Honor of E. R. Lacheman,* ed. M. A. Morrison and Owen (Winona Lake, Ind.: Eisenbrauns, 1981), 257–96; cf. L. Beck, "Herd Owners and Hired Shepherds: The Qashqa'i of Iran," *Ethnology,* 19 (1980), 327–51.

61. Cf. Berg (1974), 16.

sown is a no-man's land between nature and culture; men share it with the wild beasts who also live there: lions, wolves, jackals, wild boar, and deer. The *agrou ep' eschatiēn,* then, is a marginal environment . . . . a vertical frontier; it marks both the limit of the community and a no-man's-land between communities.[62]

The process by which a vertical frontier between communities acquires additional significance and comes to be associated with the horizontal frontier between gods and men may defy logical analysis, but it should nonetheless be familiar to students of the ancient world. To become inhuman is to move in two directions at the same time—toward the world of natural phenomena and toward the world of the gods. The farther removed one is from human culture, the nearer one approaches to animals, weather, fire, and the forces of nature; as Aristotle said, the man without a city is "either a beast or a god."[63] The physical isolation of the herdsman from village life seems to have suggested to the ancients a withdrawal from participation in human culture, and exposure to the vicissitudes of nature implied a correspondingly freer commerce with divinity. As one of Virgil's pastoral characters says, "habitarunt di quoque siluas/Dardaniusque Paris" (*Buc.* 2.60–61: "the gods have also dwelt in the woods—Dardanian Paris, too!"). It was while Paris was apart from his fellow Trojans, pasturing his flocks on Mount Ida, that the three goddesses appeared to him and asked him to judge their beauty; the lonely scene was evocatively described by Euripides (*Iph. Aul.* 573–86), who calls Paris a *boukolos* (574). The ancient literary record indicates that herdsmen were frequently molested by divinities in out-of-the-way places. In the *Theogony* (22–34), Hesiod informs us that he was accosted by the Muses while shepherding lambs below Mount Helicon (23: ἄρνας ποιμαίνονθ' Ἑλικῶνος ὕπο ζαθέοιο) and taught to sing truly about the future, the past, and the generation of the gods who are forever. A Homeric Hymn to Aphrodite eloquently relates how the goddess was overcome by desire for Anchises when he, like his compatriot Paris, was herding cattle on Mount Ida (5.54–55: ὃς τότ' ἐν ἀκροπόλοις ὄρεσιν πολυπιδάκου Ἴδης/βουκολέεσκεν βοῦς); Anchises had been left all alone at the sheds (*stathmoi*) by the other herdsmen and was wandering here and there playing loudly upon his cithara when the goddess approached and seduced him (5.76–80).[64]

Perhaps the most beautiful and intimate of all such encounters is described in the Old Testament (1 Sam. 16: 1–13). God has rejected Saul and sent his priest, Samuel, under the pretense of performing a sacrifice, to anoint a king from among the sons of Jesse in Bethlehem. As soon as

62. Redfield (1975), 189–91.
63. Ibid., 107–08.
64. Cf. Berg (1974), 15–22.

Samuel sees Jesse's sons, he thinks he knows which one of them God has selected (namely, Eliab). "But the Lord said to Samuel, 'Do not look on his appearance or on the height of his stature, because I have rejected him; for the Lord sees not as man sees; man looks on the outward appearance, but the Lord looks on the heart'" (16:7). Seven of Jesse's sons pass in review before Samuel, and God chooses none of them.

And Samuel said to Jesse, "Are all your sons here?" And he said, "There remains yet the youngest, but behold, he is keeping the sheep." And Samuel said to Jesse, "Send and fetch him; for we will not sit down till he comes here." And he sent, and brought him in. Now he was ruddy, and had beautiful eyes, and was handsome. And the Lord said, "Arise, anoint him; for this is he." [16:11–12][65]

Because God does not see as man sees—unlike men, He does not value a person's outward appearance—His judgment is not likely to coincide with that of most people (not even with that of Samuel, who from childhood has been His priest), and so He does not seek out Israel's future king in cities, where men find favor in other men's eyes. By neglecting the city entirely and lighting upon David in the isolation of the pasture, the working of God's grace accentuates the contrast between man's outward appearance and his inner state. To be sure, there is also a suggestion that removal from society carries with it a comparative innocence or moral rectitude and that the kingship, which has been a corrupt urban institution modeled on that of Israel's heathen neighbors, can be purified or spiritualized by drawing on more humble, rural stock than the house of Saul. But the very inwardness of God's vision and the privacy of his dealings with the individual human heart seem to require, as a kind of objective correlative, the physical and social isolation of the person under divine scrutiny. Moses, it will be recalled, heard the voice of God speak to him out of a burning bush only after he had inherited a flock from his father-in-law, Jethro, and had led it "to the west side of the wilderness,"[66] thence to Mount Horeb (Exod. 2:16–3:4).

Thanks to his liminal position and increased exposure to divinity, the ancient herdsman could perform the function of a mediator between the human community and the mysterious powers beyond it. Herdsmen therefore came to assume considerable prominence in the religious life (or at least in the religious literature) of early cultures.[67] We have to jettison our domesticated image of the shepherd—a legacy of the later artistic tradition which adapted this awesome figure for the drawing room and the delectation of polite society. The arduous duties of ancient herdsmen (see Columella 7.3.26) served both to estrange them from direct and frequent in-

---

65. May and Metzger (1977), 352–53.
66. Ibid., 69.
67. See Duchemin (1960), especially 57–84, 127–66.

volvement in village life and to preserve the possibilities for occasional contact and exchange between them and their more sedentary neighbors. This proved to be an ideal posture for mediation. The herdsmen of the Bronze Age were in a position vis-à-vis the settled townships which resembles, in its detachment, its ambiguity, its mixture of the familiar and the alien, the position of the holy man in late antiquity, whose links with both the mysterious spirit world and the organized local communities have been so well described and evaluated by Peter Brown. According to Brown, "the ascetics of Syria called themselves the tūraiē—the men of the mountains— and the ra'ie—the shepherds. . . . Many a holy man had lived this free and rootless life before. Symeon Stylites had guarded his brother's herds on the mountains around Şiş (near Nicopolis). . . . [The holy man] belonged to a world that was not so much antithetical to village life as marginal."[68] The task of bringing the local community into some sort of relation with otherwise unattainable sources of power and authority, whether human or divine, seems to have been shared alike by the early herdsmen and their late antique descendants, although the form and techniques of mediation were quite different.

The life of the holy man (and especially in Syria) is marked by so many histrionic feats of self-mortification that it is easy, at first sight, to miss the deep social significance of asceticism as a long drawn out, solemn ritual of dissociation—of becoming the total stranger. For the society around him, the holy man is the one man who can stand outside the ties of family, and of economic interest; whose attitude to food itself rejected all the ties of solidarity to kin and village that, in the peasant societies of the Near East, had always been expressed by the gesture of eating. He was thought of as a man who owed nothing to society . . . by [virtue of] going to live in the desert, in close identification with an animal kingdom that stood, in the imagination of contemporaries, for the opposite pole of all human society. Perched on his column, nearer to the demons of the upper air than to human beings, Symeon was objectivity personified.

Brown also recognizes certain aspects of religious continuity implicit in the function and behavior of the holy man. "The rise of the holy man as a bearer of objectivity in society is, of course, a final playing out of the long history of oracles and divination in the ancient world. The 'god-bearing' hermit usurped the position of the oracle and was known to have done so."[69] The association of oracular wisdom with a physical withdrawal or dissociation from society is a constant theme in Graeco-Roman religion; it is reflected, in a manner relevant to our concerns, by a remarkable passage of Tacitus' *Dialogus* which describes the process of poetic inspiration: "The mind retreats into unspoiled, gentle places and has what amounts to a sacred

68. Brown (1971), 83–84.
69. Ibid., 91–93.

dwelling. These places are the source of eloquence, its inmost shrines. In this guise and aspect did it first become accessible to mortals and flow into breasts pure and untouched by sin. This is how the oracles used to speak."[70] The removal of the herdsman from among his fellow citizens to the lonely desolation of distant pastures would have brought him closer to such an access of mysterious wisdom.

It was chiefly in the religious sphere, rather than in the social or political ones also discussed by Brown, that the ancient Near Eastern shepherd performed his function as an arbitrator. To be sure, such arbitration could be carried out by a variety of figures in ancient Near Eastern religion and not by any means were all (or even most) of them dissociated from their cultures by remote habitation or a unique mode of life. But the ambiguous position of marginal outsider seems to have lent itself extremely well to the techniques of mediation. Elijah, as he is described in the two books of Kings in the Old Testament, maintained precisely such a wavering relation to the settled communities, and it is perhaps no accident that he appeared in a vision to Symeon Stylites—as if to reinforce the implicit cultural and typological connections between them.[71] The prophet Amos is called a *noqed,* a lowly sort of shepherd, in an editorial superscription to the book of the Old Testament which bears his name and which articulates his pastoral-religious creed: "I am no prophet, nor a prophet's son; but I am a herdsman, and a dresser of sycamore trees, and the Lord took me from following the flock, and the Lord said to me, 'Go, prophesy to my people Israel'" (7:14–15).[72] The "religious aura" traditionally surrounding the figure of the herdsman and his prophetic colleagues also clings to Orpheus and, in historical times, to Hesiod; it can be traced back from the Daphnis of Greek lyric poetry and cult all the way to the Sumerian shepherd-god Dumuzi.[73] Indeed, a recent interpreter has emphasized Dumuzi's role as a "mediator between . . . nature and culture."[74]

Returning, then, to Sumer, we may conjecture that it was perhaps the mediating function of the shepherd in the ancient Near East that led to the transfer of the vocabulary of husbandry from the profession of the herdsman to that of the political leader. The earliest traditions, as recorded in the Sumerian King List, refer to the shepherd Dumuzi as the fifth of the antediluvian kings, with a reign of thirty-six thousand years. Dumuzi is later attested in the same document as king of Uruk (significantly, the city sacred

---

70. Quoted by Berg (1974), 4.
71. Cf. Brown (1971), 97.
72. May and Metzger (1977), 1115.
73. Cf. Duchemin (1960), 70–84; Berg (1974), 15–22.
74. Alster (1972), 14.

to Inanna), although now he is called a fisherman; his reign occurs between
those of the legendary heroes Lugalbanda—called a shepherd in this passage—and Gilgamesh, "whose father was a nomad (?)."[75] Whether the
Sumerians ascribed political leadership to the god Dumuzi in one or several
of his various aspects or whether Dumuzi was originally a historical figure
subsequently deified by tradition are matters of continuing controversy and
are best left to one side.[76] According to the currently accepted manipulation
of the data in the King List,[77] the first monarch after the Flood was Etana of
Kish, also characterized as a shepherd. He is "the first ruler of Sumer whose
deeds are recorded . . . [and he] may have come to the throne quite early in
the third millennium B.C.," according to Samuel Noah Kramer. That
would place Etana about a thousand years before the document which
mentions him and which goes on to say that he "made firm all the lands"
and "ascended to heaven." A Semitic poem in Akkadian from the early
second millennium (for which there is currently no known Sumerian ante-
cedent) tells the story of Etana. He was afflicted by childlessness and therefore resolved to obtain the "plant of birth" which grew in heaven; for this
purpose he enlisted the aid of an eagle. The legend is probably quite old and
was very popular, to judge by the number of recensions preserving it and
by the multitude of cylinder seals from the Old Akkadian period which
depict a mortal rising to heaven on the wings of an eagle.[78] The text breaks
off at a crucial point, leaving Etana's success in doubt; he may have prevailed in one version, but a funerary dirge for him has been discovered and
he is also mentioned as residing in the nether world on the seventh tablet of
the Gilgamesh epic (VII iv 49). That Etana, a shepherd, was the subject of
an elegy strengthens his typological resemblance to Dumuzi; in any case,
the ability of both figures to mediate between man and god lends a more
precise and significant meaning to their pastoral identity. Something of the
same interpretation regarding the liminal function of the shepherd might
conceivably be placed on that group among the earliest Sumerian cylinder
seals which depict scenes of shepherds defending their cattle against wild
beasts.[79]

Whether the common referent had to do with mediation or simply
with protection, the pastoral and political metaphors seem to have become
fused at an early date. Thus, the office of "shepherdship" is placed eighth

75. Kramer (1963a), 328–29 (translation of the Sumerian King List).
76. See Alster (1972), 9–15.
77. Hallo and Simpson (1971), 37–42.
78. Kramer (1963a), 43–44; Pritchard (1969), 114–18 and 517.
79. Kramer (1963a), 100.

(between "the exalted throne" and "kingship") in a list of one hundred elements of civilized life in a Sumerian poem entitled "Inanna and Enki: The Transfer of the Arts of Civilization from Eridu to Erech."[80] The shepherd's crook was part of the insignia of authority in Sumer no less than in Egypt, and the image of the ruler as shepherd was ubiquitous throughout the ancient Near East and Egypt (especially during the Middle Kingdom) long before Homer applied it to Agamemnon. The god Enlil, ruler of the Sumerian pantheon, is called a shepherd in the great "Hymn to Enlil, the All Beneficent" (line 84). In "Man and his God," which has been called a Sumerian variation on the Job motif, the sufferer complains:

> With me, the *valiant,* my righteous shepherd has become angry, has looked
>   upon me inimically,
> My herdsman has sought out evil forces against me who am not (his)
>   enemy. . . .   [33–34][81]

The context implies that the speaker intends "my king" by these periphrases. Other metaphors from the profession of animal husbandry besides the title of shepherd are extended to the political domain. For example, to enforce peace on people under one's authority is to make them lie down in the pastures. The two dimensions of such language are often combined, as in the subcategory of Sumerian hymns designated *sir-namsipad-inanna-ka,* "hymns of the shepherdship of (the goddess) Inanna." (In the Sumerian poem entitled "Enki and the World Order," Inanna is told, "You have taken charge of the crook, staff, and wand of shepherdship, Maid Inanna, what, what more shall we add to you?") The pastoral idiom refers, presumably, not only to Inanna's exalted authority but also to her union with the shepherd Dumuzi celebrated in the sacred marriage rite; it is not clear whether *namsipad* ("shepherdship") here alludes to Dumuzi's literal profession of shepherd, to his role of husband (and hence authority over Inanna), or to his royal power as god and, more specifically, as the ritual identity of the king during the marriage ceremony itself.[82]

The frequent—though less insistent (perhaps because less apt)—use of agricultural language to characterize the ruler indicates the equally important role played by the farmer in both the economic life and the consciousness of the Sumerians. The complementarity of shepherd and farmer, so obvious a feature of the ancient Near Eastern economy, is expressed in the literature by a constant pairing and balancing of the two figures. In the following passage from a sacred marriage text, for example, the ruler is

80. Ibid., 116.
81. Pritchard (1969), 574, 590.
82. Kramer (1963a), 51, 183, 207.

compared to both (although his office and its insignia are described in exclusively pastoral terms):

> Over all Sumer and Akkad give him the staff (and) the crook,
> May he exercise the shepherdship [*nam-sipad*] of the blackheads [i.e., the
>   Sumerians] (wherever) they dwell,
> May he make productive the fields like the farmer,
> May he multiply the sheepfolds like a trustworthy shepherd [*sipad-zi-gim*].
>
> [17–20][83]

The shift from a metaphorical to a literal use of the pastoral analogy within the space of two lines is remarkable; it seems to be occasioned by a strong sense that the farmer cannot be mentioned without the shepherd, even if this requires an abrupt change in the levels of language employed. Such parallelism in the treatment of shepherd and farmer is common in Sumerian literature. In "Enki and the World Order," for instance, a myth narrating the invention of the arts and institutions of civilized life, the complementary roles of farmer and shepherd are emphasized by coordinate and carefully balanced descriptions: Enki invents or blesses—in a sequential arrangement which may be compared, with interesting results, to the chronology provided by the archaeological record—the plow, yoke, ox, furrow, grain, vegetables, pickax, brickmold, field grasses, cattle, stalls, and sheepfolds; he places the farmer-god Enkimdu (not to be confused with the Akkadian character Enkidu), called here "the farmer of Enlil . . . the man of ditch and dike," in charge of the cultivated field, while the shepherd-god Dumuzi, "the husband of holy Inanna," takes command of the sheepfolds with their fat (or butter) and milk.[84] When these two figures reappear in another text, the complementarity of shepherd and farmer is the basis of rivalry between them. The conflict of values embodied in their struggle creates a familiar impression, and this poem, to which we now turn, is the second work discussed so far which can lay claim to a pastoral identity in the literary sense.

"In a country like Mesopotamia, in which the chief industries were sheep-herding and farming, it is only natural that these two modes of life should form favorite subjects of comparison and evaluation. Which is the better, the more important, the more useful? . . . The liveliest treatment of the theme . . . is given in a myth entitled 'The Wooing of Inanna.'"[85] The text is inscribed on three tablets from Nippur dating to the first half of the second millennium B.C. It is generally called "Dumuzi and Enkimdu: The

83. Kramer (1963b), 501–02; Pritchard (1969), 641.
84. Kramer (1963a), 173–74, 180–81.
85. Jacobsen (1949), 180.

Dispute between the Shepherd-God and the Farmer-God." When the text first becomes comprehensible, Inanna's brother, the sun-god Utu, is attempting to persuade her to marry Dumuzi; Frank Kermode singled out her reply as a possible early example of pastoral and compared it to the Twentieth Idyll of Theocritus.[86]

Her brother, the hero, the warrior, Utu,
Says [to] the pure Inanna:
"O my sister, let the shepherd marry thee,
O maid Inanna, why art thou unwilling?
His fat is good, his milk is good,
The shepherd, everything his hand touches is bright,
O Inanna, let the shepherd Dumuzi marry thee,
O thou who . . . , why art thou unwilling?
His good fat he will eat with thee,
O *protector of* the king, why art thou unwilling?"
"[*Me*] the shepherd shall not marry,
In his new [*garment*] he shall not *drape* me,
When I . . . he shall not . . . me,
Me, the maid, let the farmer marry,
The farmer who makes *plants* grow abundantly,
The farmer who makes grain grow abundantly. . . .   [10–25]

After a lacuna, Dumuzi makes a long speech in self-defense and self-justification, then drives his flock to the riverbank.

To him who is a shepherd, the farmer [*approached*],
The farmer Enkimdu [*approached*].
Dumuzi, the farmer, the king of dike and ditch . . . ,
In his plain, the shepherd in his [plain starts] a quarrel with him,
The [sh]epherd Dumuzi in his plain starts a quarrel with him.
"I against thee, O shepherd, against thee, O shepherd, I against thee
Why shall I strive?
Let thy sheep eat the grass of the riverbank,
In my *meadowland* let thy sheep walk about,
In the bright fields of Erech let them eat grain,
Let thy *kids* and *lambs* drink the water of my *Unun* canal."
          [69–79][87]

Although the identity of the victor for Inanna's hand remains a matter of dispute among scholars, Thorkild Jacobsen has rightly emphasized the reconciliatory character of the poem, which accords well with the many literary expressions of the essential complementarity of farmer and shepherd

86. Kermode (1952), 19–20, using Jacobsen's 1949 translation, which differs considerably from the one cited here.
87. Pritchard (1969), 41–42.

already noted. Relations between them may often have been strained, but Sumerian literature tends to pair them off and set them against the example of nomadic tribesmen. "[E]ven that antagonism between city-dwellers and those who live in the open countryside, which is characteristic of many urban civilizations, cannot be found in the cuneiform sources. Only nomadic invaders and the uncouth inhabitants of the Zagros mountains are sometimes despised as being devoid of the essential qualities of civilized people with regard to personal behavior, the care for the dead, and willingness to submit to organized government."[88]

From what has been said so far, it seems possible to detect in the literature of the ancient Near East two kinds of pastoral elements, or rather two classes of compositions which can be considered pastoral according to different conceptions of the term. Works belonging to the first category convey the outlook or view of life we have come to recognize as pastoral, in the modern, extended sense of that word. Works belonging to the second category prefigure some of the conventions and themes of the formal literary tradition we are accustomed to call by the name of pastoral. A remarkable feature of the ancient Near Eastern texts under discussion here is the clarity with which they observe, indeed illustrate this distinction: they often express pastoral *attitudes* quite independently of obeying pastoral *conventions* (although it is still not hard to see how the two could later be conjoined). Thus, nothing in the Gilgamesh epic marks it as a formal pastoral poem in the traditional sense, yet Enkidu is plainly a pastoral figure. By contrast, we would not be inclined to regard the "Dispute" between Dumuzi and Enkimdu as a pastoral, did it not appear to anticipate the motif of the scorned shepherd. The expression of pastoral attitudes in the ancient Near East does not require a traditionally pastoral locale or cast of characters as a vehicle, while the idealization of the shepherd and the literary exploitation of his liminal associations do not necessarily involve the articulation of pastoral attitudes. That such attitudes did in fact exist and could be expressed by means of figures other than the shepherd is evident from the Gilgamesh epic. Nonetheless, the significance attached to the herdsman by early cultures indicates that he was already being fashioned for the role he would

---

88. Oppenheim (1977), 111. This statement seems hard to square with one made earlier by Oppenheim (p. 82): "[The] contrast between city-dwellers and those in the open country cuts across the fabric of Mesopotamian society and represents an eternal source of conflict. . . . The tension, city against surrounding country, affected the history of the region but should not be regarded as a typically Mesopotamian phenomenon, since the entire ancient Near East had to face this problem in varying intensity and in several periods. . . ." Jacobsen (1970), 59, even speaks of "the bitter and deep antagonism between shepherd and farmer, which is ever present in ancient cultures."

subsequently play in the pastoral tradition, although the union of the pastoral outlook with its appropriate spokesman had to wait until the poetry of Theocritus, or perhaps even Virgil, for its consummation. What we find in the ancient Near East is on the one hand a widely diffused habit of mind or figure of thought, presumably shared by a much larger population than the limited number of writers and as yet unincorporated in any specific, formal literary devices, and on the other the crystallization of pastoral attitudes around certain characters whose artistic depiction is gradually becoming conventionalized. Let us turn now to a series of texts in which both of these tendencies make themselves felt in different degrees and in varying proportions.

A Sumerian hymn to Nidaba, goddess of grasses, grain, and reeds, pauses from its litany of ceremonial praise to sketch a pastoral scene combining all the traditional elements—leisure, music, and the therapeutic effect of art.

> Nidaba, where you are not heaped up
> people are not settled, cities not built,
> no palace is built, no king is raised to office,
> the gods' handwashings (before offerings) are not performed correctly
> Nidaba, where you are not near
> no cattle pen is built, no sheepfold constructed,
> and the shepherd soothes not the heart with his reed pipe.[89]

Another Sumerian poem contains a passage which "shows Sumerian pastoral life from its idyllic side," according to its translator, who went on to entitle this fragment "Bucolic." It was found inscribed on material from Nippur, dating to 1700 B.C. or earlier, and describes Geshtinanna, the sister of Dumuzi.

> His sister of the sweet-voiced lyre,
> Maid Geshtin-anna, sits in the fold,
> She milks the ewe and gives to the lamb,
> She milks the goat and gives to the kid,
> In her right hand she carries the churn,
> In her left the young woman has a lyre and a harp.[90]

The Sumerian sacred marriage texts produce something of a pastoral effect through their conflation of erotic and agricultural imagery. In one such text, Dumuzi is addressed: "Oh my lord who has come to the house— approach her, Approach her with a chant, a heart (moving) melody," and Inanna(?) appears to reply, "Oh wild bull, 'eye' of the land, I would *fulfill*

89. Jacobsen (1976), 10.
90. Jacobsen (1970), 215.

all its *needs,* Would make its lord carry out justice in the princely house, Would make its seed . . . justice in the palace" (60–61; 66–69). The poem concludes:

> Oh lady, your breast is your field,
> Inanna, your breast is your field,
> Your wide field which "pours out" plants,
> Your wide field which "pours out" grain,
> Water flowing from on high—(for) the lord—bread, bread from on high,
> [*Pour*] out for the "commanded" lord,
> I will drink it from you.
>
>   [70–79]

The union of erotic and agricultural imagery is even more striking in another sacred marriage text beginning "I gazed on all the people, called Dumuzi to the godship of the Land." The speaker, Inanna, at one point composes a song about her vulva, likening it to a horn, the "Boat of Heaven," the new crescent, fallow land, a field, and a hillock; after some fragmentary lines describing her sexual union with Dumuzi, the text goes on to convey their consequent prosperity:

> At the lap of the king, the high-standing cedar . . . ,
> The plants stood high by (his) side, the grain stood high by (his) side,
> The . . . garden flourished luxuriantly by his side.

The work continues with Inanna's request to the king to provide her with rich fresh milk, cheese, and cream, and breaks off after her repeated promises to preserve the prosperity of the palace.[91] Suggestive as these passages are, it would perhaps be best not to insist on their pastoral qualities.

Two other works celebrating the ritual marriage of Inanna and Dumuzi take on more intense pastoral coloring. In the first, Inanna blesses the stall and sheepfold with her presence.

> The faithful shepherd, he of the sweet chant,
> Will utter a resounding(?) chant for you,
> Lordly Queen, you who sweeten all things,
> Inanna, it will bring joy to your heart.
>
> Lordly Queen, when you enter the stall,
> Inanna, the stall rejoices with you,
> Hierodule, when you enter the sheepfold,
> The stall rejoices with you. . . .
> The holy sheepfold is filled with cream because of you,
> In the sheepfold there is rejoicing. . . .

91. Pritchard (1969), 642–44.

Here, the wished-for harmony is projected into a time in the future. The other poem, which recounts Dumuzi's meeting with his sister Geshtinanna in the countryside, begins with a nostalgic glance at the happiness of former times:

> Those were days of plenty, those were nights of abundance,
> Those were months of pleasure, those were years of rejoicing—
> In those days, the shepherd to make the heart rejoice,
> To go to the stall, to brighten its spirit,
> To light up the holy sheepfold like the sun,
> The shepherd Dumuzi took it into his holy heart.

After several idyllic descriptions of the sheepfold and its bounty, the remainder of the poem is devoted to Dumuzi's entertainment of his inexperienced sister, which seems to consist of showing her the incestuous practices of animals (perhaps with an immediate human lesson to be drawn from them).[92] Such delight in the innocent and free behavior of the countryside and in its lack of social and sexual inhibitions is, it has been noted, a prominent component of pastoral.

The Sumerians did not lack a myth of the Golden Age, as can be seen from this extract of a heroic poem entitled "Enmerkar and the Land of Aratta":

> Once upon a time, there was no snake, there was no scorpion,
> There was no hyena, there was no lion,
> There was no wild dog, no wolf,
> There was no fear, no terror,
> Man had no rival.

> Once upon a time, the lands Shubar and Hamazi,
> Many(?)-tongued Sumer, the great land of princeships' divine laws,
> Uri, the land having all that is appropriate,
> The land Martu, resting in security,
> The whole universe, the people in unison,
> To Enlil in one tongue gave praise.[93]

Another "golden age" account combines the notion of a lost paradise (the Sumerian Dilmun) with the description of a *locus amoenus*. "Enki and Ninhursag: A Paradise Myth" may exhibit what one scholar has called "the inane formalism of conventional literary texts" from the ancient Near East,[94] but it is not for that reason less significant:

---

92. Kramer (1969), 102–03.

93. S. N. Kramer, *From the Tablets of Sumer: Twenty-five Firsts in Man's Recorded History* (Indian Hills, Colo.: Falcon's Wing Press, 1956), 259.

94. Oppenheim (1977), 26.

[The *place*] is [pure] . . . , . . . [the land] Dilmun is pure;
[The land Dilmun] is [pu]re . . . , the [la]nd D[il]mun is pure;
The land Dilmun is pure, the land Dilmun is clean;
The land Dilmun is clean, the land Dilmun is most bright.
Who had lain by himself in Dilmun—
The place, after Enki had lain with his wife,
That place is clean, that place is most bright;
(Who had lain) by himself (in Dilmun)—
The place, (after) Enki (had lain) by Ninsikilla,
That place is clean, (that place is bright).
In Dilmun the raven utters no cries,
The *ittidu*-bird utters not the cry of the *ittidu*-bird,
The lion kills not,
The wolf snatches not the lamb,
Unknown is the kid-devouring *wild dog,*
Unknown is the grain-devouring . . . ,
[*Unknown*] is the . . . widow,
The bird on high . . . s not its . . . ,
The dove *droops* not the head,
The sick-eyed says not "I am sick-eyed,"
The sick-headed (says) not "I am sick-headed,"
Its old woman (says) not "I am an old woman,"
Its old man (says) not "I am an old man,"
Unbathed is the maid, no sparkling water is poured in the city,
Who crosses the river utters no . . . ,
The wailing priest walks not round about him,
The singer utters no *wail,*
By the side of the city he (utters) no *lament.*

[1–30][95]

It is worth noting that descriptions of *loci amoeni* occur sporadically throughout the literature of the ancient Near East. The *locus amoenus* also represents a
favorite topic of Egyptian poetry toward the end of the second millennium.[96]

One Sumerian literary genre in particular—one that does not seem to
have been very popular with subsequent inhabitants of Mesopotamia—
anticipates a prominent feature of the pastoral tradition: the disputation or
quarrel-poem (called *adaman-duga*). Aside from the pastoral contests in Theocritus and Virgil, so widely imitated by later poets, it will be recalled that
the content of "bucolic" was almost entirely restricted to the rhetorical
debate in literary theory during the Middle Ages. It is clear that the anteced-

95. Pritchard (1969), 38.

96. See the material contained in J. L. Foster, *Love Songs of the New Kingdom* (New York,
1974), especially 36–37 and 86–95; Foster comments: "[T]he final effect, however idyllic, is
not at all rural. It is more like pastoral, perhaps the first instances of the long pastoral tradition
in literature, with, instead of shepherds, milkmaids, and flocks, a panorama of fowlers, bird-
catchers' daughters, and hunting in the marsh" (xv–xvi).

ents of the *altercatio, Streitgedicht,* or *tenzone* are very old indeed. In addition to "Dumuzi and Enkimdu: The Dispute . . ." (already discussed), which may belong to this type, twelve other examples are known in Sumerian and three in Akkadian.[97] Not all concern pastoral subjects: four are set among the inmates of a Sumerian school and one, between two unnamed ladies, is written in the Emesal dialect reserved for women. Comparison with the classical and Hellenistic mime is inevitable but ought perhaps to be resisted for the moment. Of particular interest for this survey are "The Dispute between Cattle and Grain" and "The Dispute between Emesh and Enten." The former work relates the quarrel between Lahar, the cattle-goddess, and her sister Ashnan, the grain-goddess. The poem begins with a description of the primitive state before the creation of the two goddesses when neither husbandry nor agriculture existed and the children of An (the heaven-god) "knew not the eating of bread, Knew not the dressing of garments, Ate plants with their mouths like sheep, Drank water from the ditch." Then:

> At the pure word of Enki and Enlil,
> Lahar and Ashnan descend from the Duku,
> For Lahar they (Enlil and Enki) set up the sheepfold,
> Plants and herbs in abundance they present to her.

> For Ashnan they establish a house,
> Plough and yoke they present to her.
> Lahar standing in her sheepfold,
> A shepherdess increasing the bounty of the sheepfold is she;
> Ashnan standing among the crops,
> A maid kindly and bountiful is she,
> Lifting (her) head in trusting fashion from her field.[98]

At the feast held by the gods to celebrate these achievements, the two goddesses drink quantities of wine, quarrel with one another, and extol their own contributions while denigrating each other's. Ashnan is declared the victor.

"The Dispute between Emesh and Enten" concerns a quarrel between two divine brothers who represent summer and winter or, alternately, shepherd and farmer.[99] The former interpretation is more likely, as each brother is given a share of both pastoral and agricultural duties:

---

97. Oppenheim (1977), 275; Kramer (1963a), 217–23. Cf. Dundes, A., Leach, J. W., and Özkök, B. "The Strategy of Turkish Boys' Verbal Dueling Rhymes." *Journal of American Folklore,* 83 (1970), 325–49.

98. Kramer (1963a), 220–22; the final line is supplemented from Jacobsen (1970), 108. I have not been able to locate a full translation of this text.

99. The former identification is Kramer's (1963a), 218; the latter, Jacobsen's (1949), 180.

Enten made the ewe give birth to the lamb, the goat to give birth to the
    kid,
Cow and calf to multiply, fat and milk to increase,
In the plain he made rejoice the heart of the wild goat, sheep, and donkey,
The birds of heaven—in the wide earth he made them set up their nests,
The fish of the sea—in the canebrake he made them lay their eggs,
In the palm grove and vineyard he made honey and wine abound,
The trees, wherever planted, he caused to bear fruit,
The gardens he decked out in green, made their plants luxuriant,
Made grain increase in the furrows,
Like Ashnan, the kindly maid, he made it come forth sturdily.
Emesh brought into being trees and fields, made wide the stalls and
    sheepfolds,
In the farms he multiplied produce, bedecked the earth . . . ,
Caused the abundant harvest to be brought into the houses, the granaries to
    be heaped high,
Cities and habitations to be founded, houses to be built in the land,
Temples to rise mountain high.

As the two brothers are bringing offerings from this abundance to their
father, Enlil, they quarrel, and Emesh challenges his brother's claim to be
"farmer of the gods." Enlil decides in favor of Enten.[100]

    In each of these poems value seems to be placed on agriculture rather
than on husbandry; once again, the motif of the scorned shepherd appears.
Furthermore, the normative dualism of these works and the preference
evinced in the second for the prosperity of the country over the greatness of
the city help build pastoral contrasts. Even in one of the non-pastoral dis-
putes, however, an exchange of insults contains a topic of enduring significance for the tradition of the rustic quarrel. One schoolboy says to another:

You have a harp, but know no music,
You who are the "water boy" of (your) colleagues,
(Your) throat (?) can't sound a note,
You stutter (your) Sumerian, can't make a straight speech,
Can't sing a hymn, can't open (your) mouth,
And you are an accomplished fellow![101]

One immediately recalls the retort made by Comatas to Lacon in the Fifth
Idyll of Theocritus:

τὰν ποίαν σύριγγα; τὺ γὰρ ποκα, δῶλε Σιβύρτα,
ἐκτάσω σύριγγα; τί δ' οὐκέτι σὺν Κορύδωνι
ἀρκεῖ τοι καλάμας αὐλὸν ποππύσδεν ἔχοντι;

                                                        [5–7]

100. Kramer (1963a), 218–19.
    101. Ibid., 222–23. For an example of an Akkadian disputation in a rustic context, see the
"Quarrel between the Tamarisk and the Date Palm," in Pritchard (1969), 410–11, 592–93. See
also Hallo and Simpson (1971), 167; S. N. Kramer, "Sumerian Literature and the Bible," in
Studia Biblica et Orientalia, 3 (Oriens Antiquus) = *Analecta Biblica*, 12 (Rome, 1959), 195n.

What syrinx do you mean? Did *you* ever own a syrinx, you slave of Sibyrtas? Why are you no longer content to take a hollow piece of straw and toot it with Corydon?

The more famous example of such pastoral abuse occurs in Virgil's Third Eclogue:

> Cantando tu illum? aut umquam tibi fistula cera
> iuncta fuit? non tu in triuiis, indocte, solebas
> stridenti miserum stipula disperdere carmen?
>
> [25–27]

Did you say *you* beat *him* at singing? Did you ever have a wax-joined set of pipes? Didn't you, idiot, use to squander your wretched song at the crossings, playing on a whistling hollow stalk?

The interest in *Kleinleben* or "low life" conceivably displayed by these homely disputations skillfully recast into literary form may be compared to that found in the Egyptian laboring-songs and in other portrayals of "popular" expression during the Eighteenth Dynasty.[102] Callimachus seems to have drawn on these traditions for his fables concerning quarrels between plants in his *Iambi.*

One of the sacred marriage texts reads remarkably like a traditional *pastourelle:*

> Last night, as I, the queen, was shining bright,
> Last night, as I, the queen of heaven, was shining bright,
> As I was shining bright, as I was dancing about,
> As I was uttering a song at the brightening of the *oncoming* night,
> He met me, he met me,
> The Lord Kuli-Anna (i.e., Dumuzi) met me,
> The lord put his hand into my hand,
> Ushumgalanna embraced me.
>
> "*Come now,* wild bull, set me free, I must go home,
> Kuli-Enlil, set me free, I must go home,
> What shall I say to deceive my mother!
> What shall I say to deceive my mother Ningal!"
>
> [1–12][103]

The conversation proceeds predictably to the affair's consummation.

Most prominent, however, among Sumerian experiments in the pastoral form is the dirge or funeral elegy. The pastoral elegy represented only one kind of dirge; and the dirge itself was included in the more general category of lament, along with some narrative poems bewailing the destruction of Sumerian cities, a genre familiar to us from the (much later) book of Lamentations in the Old Testament. According to Jacobsen, the original purpose of the lament was not to sway the divine heart to pity—the

102. E.g., Pritchard (1969), 469–70.
103. Ibid., 639–40.

intent generally perceived in later versions; rather, "in the lament the vividness of recall and longing was an actual magical reconstitution, an attempt to draw back the lost god or temple by recreating in the mind the lost happy presence."[104] Such is the avowed design of much (though by no means all) pastoral elegy: compare the rival songs about Daphnis in Eclogue 5 and the corresponding failure of the singers to evoke "the lost happy presence" in Eclogue 9. Elegy enters a pastoral context in Sumerian literature when it concerns the death of the shepherd-god Dumuzi. The original identity of Dumuzi is much disputed,[105] but it is generally agreed that he was a divine figure associated in some way with the pastoral economy, that he died or was killed, and that he was the subject of ritual mourning which continued into historical times and of which traces still persist today.

A large number of ancient laments for Dumuzi have survived and it is well worth quoting from them. Some of them, including "The Most Bitter Cry" and a dirge spoken by Dumuzi's sister Geshtinanna (as if for a family member in a private context), lack an intensely pastoral color.[106] The same can be said of Geshtinanna's lament contained in a new text from Ur that belongs to the cycle of "Inanna's Descent."[107] The rest, however, exhibit striking pastoral features. Here is a selection from "The Wild Bull Who Has Lain Down," one of the best known among these documents:

> The wild bull who has lain down, lives no more,
>   the wild bull who has lain down,
>   lives no more,
> Dumuzi, the wild bull, who has lain down,
>   lives no more,
> . . . the chief shepherd, lives no more,
> the wild bull who has lain down, lives no more.
>
> O you wild bull, how fast you sleep!
>   How fast sleep ewe and lamb!
> O you wild bull, how fast you sleep!
>   How fast sleep goat and kid!
>
> . . . .
>
> On his couch you have made the jackals lie down,
> in my husband's fold you have made the raven dwell,
> his reed pipe—the wind will have to play it,
> my husband's songs—the north wind will have to sing them.[108]

104. Jacobsen (1976), 15.
105. See, most recently, W. Burkert, *Structure and History in Greek Mythology and Ritual,* Sather Classical Lectures, 47 (Berkeley, Calif., 1979), 99–122, especially 105–08.
106. For translations of these texts, see Jacobsen (1976), 49–52.
107. Kramer (1963b), 492–93, lines 38–46.
108. Jacobsen (1976), 53–54.

The musical legacy of the dying herdsman and the transfer of his talents to a new agency in nature are prominent topics in the First Idyll of Theocritus, who describes how Daphnis gave his syrinx to Pan (123–30), and they were taken up again by Virgil in the Second Eclogue:

> est mihi disparibus septem compacta cicutis
> fistula, Damoetas dono mihi quam dedit olim,
> et dixit moriens: "te nunc habet ista secundum."
>
> [36–38]

I have a set of pipes composed of seven unequal pieces of hemlock which Damoetas once gave me as a gift, and as he died said, "Now you're its second master."

Another interesting example of the pastoral lament comes from a poem entitled "My Heart Plays a Reed Pipe":

> My heart plays a reed pipe of dirges
>   for him in the desert,
> plays where the lad dwelt,
> plays where Dumuzi dwelt,
> in Aralli, on the Shepherd's Hill—
> my heart plays a reed pipe of dirges
>   for him in the desert—
> where the lad dwelt, he who is captive,
> where Dumuzi dwelt, he who is bound,
> where the ewe surrendered the lamb—
> my heart plays a reed pipe of dirges
>   for him in the desert—
> where the goat surrendered the kid.[109]

A lament for Dumuzi is also included in the Sumerian myth concerning the quarrel between Inanna and Bilulu:

> (My) lady gave birth to a song to her young husband, fashioned a song to
>   him,
> Holy Inanna gave birth to a song to Dumuzi, fashioned a song to him:
> "O you who lie at rest, shepherd who lie at rest, you stood guard over
>   them,
> Dumuzi, who lie at rest, you stood guard over them,
> Ama-ushumgal-anna, who lie at rest, you stood guard over them,
> Rising with the sun you stood guard over my sheep,
> Lying down by night (only), you stood guard over my sheep!
>
> [80–87][110]

The elegiac text which holds the greatest interest for students of the pastoral tradition is "Dumuzi's Dream," for in it the protagonist himself

---

109. Ibid., 54–55.
110. Jacobsen (1970), 64–67.

utters the lament and asks the natural world to mourn with him. The poem begins:

> His heart was filled with tears, he went out to the plain,
> The lad—his heart was filled with tears, he went out to the plain,
> Dumuzi—his heart was filled with tears, he went out to the plain.
> He carried a stick on his shoulder, and cried again and again:
> "Set up a lament, set up a lament, O Plain, set up a lament,
> O Plain, set up a lament, O Swamp, set up a cry!
> O *Crabs,* set up a lament *in* the river,
> O Frogs, set up a cry in the river!
>   My mother will call,
> My mother, my Duttur, will call,
> My mother will call for the five breads,
> My mother will call for the ten breads!
> If she does not know the day when I am dead,
> You, O Plain, can inform my mother who bore me,
> Like my little sister may you weep for me!"
>
> [1–14]

Dumuzi then lies down, sleeps, and has an ominous dream:

> "Rushes were torn out for me, but rushes kept growing for me,
> A single reed was shaking the head for me,
> A twin reed—one was being removed from me,
> Tall trees in the forest were uprooted by themselves for me,
> Water was poured on my pure coal for me,
> The cover of my pure churn was being removed from me,
> My pure drinking cup was torn down from the peg where it hung,
> My shepherd's stick disappeared from me,
> An *eagle* took a lamb in the house of the sheep,
> A falcon caught a sparrow in the reeds of the fence,
> My male goats were dragging their lapis-lazuli beard in the dust for me,
> My male sheep were scratching the earth with their thick legs for me,
> The churns were lying (on their side), no milk was poured,
> The drinking cups were lying (on their side), Dumuzi was dead, the fold
>   was made into a wind."
>
> [27–40][111]

In short, it is difficult to avoid seeing in the figure of Dumuzi a true "forebear" of Daphnis. One scholar has even suggested that the Greek herdsman's name is derived from that of his Sumerian ancestor.[112]

One might well inquire at this point how much relevance all this ancient Near Eastern material has for the study of pastoral poetry in general

---

111. Alster (1972), 52–57; the importance of this text for the history of pastoral origins was first noted by Berg (1974), 17.

112. Trencsényi-Waldapfel (1966), 29–30; cf. Berg (1974), 197, n. 28. See, generally, my forthcoming essay, "The Forebears of Daphnis."

or for Hellenistic literature in particular. Surely the superficial similarities of diction, *topoi,* themes, or plot structure do not argue (much less establish) a historical relation between the works compared, and the vast intervals of time separating Sumerian literature from the products of the Hellenistic period seem to prohibit decisively the workings of influence. What sort of relation, then, between man's earliest literary experiments and the sophisticated artifacts of Hellenistic Alexandria can be inferred from the preceding discussion?

Two points need to be made. First of all, the working definition of pastoral set forth at the end of part I represents (it was argued) a modern literary concept. Nonetheless, the concept is a powerful and suggestive one; it enables the contemporary critic to assemble, relate, and analyze jointly different literary works from a variety of periods, cultures, and genres— works whose affinities as well as differences would be overlooked so long as there was no common framework within which to compare them. The Greek bucolic poets have been prominent members in this ecumenical congregation of pastoralists; they are also, either incidentally or significantly (depending on the critic), the earliest such contributors to the canon according to established chronology. This circumstance has led ineluctably to the tendency to regard Theocritus as the inventor of pastoral poetry. It is indeed clear that Theocritus was an original talent whose name was connected with a distinct variety of poetic composition (as his ancient and modern critics alike have recognized). Both he and his scholarly contemporaries called his invention "bucolic." The content of that invention remains to be identified. The foregoing discussion has attempted to suggest that because all the components of pastoral poetry can be found long before Theocritus, the ground of his originality will always remain obscure so long as the equation of bucolic with pastoral is retained, because the pastoralism of Theocritus did not represent a sufficiently startling departure from what had gone before him. Not only was the invention of pastoral poetry not a conscious and, therefore, strictly speaking, *historical* achievement on the part of Theocritus (to deny this, I have argued, would in effect import a modern conceptual distinction into a literary and cultural context where it does not properly belong): even from a modern comparative or "synchronistic" perspective, what we mean by pastoral cannot be judged to have found its original expression in the poetry of Theocritus. For the constitutive elements of pastoral were older not only than Theocritus but also than the specific cultural tradition to which Theocritus belonged.

There is a second point to be made, perhaps a more speculative one. The definitive account of the diffusion of Sumerian literature throughout the ancient Near East and the dynamics of the complex cultural interaction among the early inhabitants of that region has yet to be written; it would occupy many volumes. But the crucial importance of the Sumerian achievement is becoming increasingly manifest. It stands behind not only the formation of the Old Testament, as has long been acknowledged, but also a good deal of Greek cult and literary expression. Kramer noted in 1963 that

the ideas and ideals of the Sumerians . . . permeated to a greater or lesser extent the thoughts and writings of all the peoples of the ancient Near East including Palestine. So too, did the Sumerian literary forms and themes—their plots, motifs, stylistic devices, and aesthetic techniques. And since, as is becoming ever more apparent, the interconnections between Ancient Mesopotamia, Palestine, and the Aegean world were manifold and far-reaching, it is not unlikely, *a priori,* that traces of Sumerian influence may be found even in the literatures of the ancient Greeks and Hebrews. . . . [I]n the second millennium B.C. Akkadian was the *lingua franca* of practically the entire literary world. Akkadian literary works must therefore have been quite familiar to men of letters, even in the Palestinian and Aegean world. But not a few of these Akkadian literary works went back to Sumerian prototypes, remodeled and transformed over the centuries.[113]

Whether the path of diffusion of Sumerian literature is traced back from the Greeks, via either the Phoenicians (Canaanites) or the Hittites to the Hurrians and thence to Kassite Babylonia,[114] or by some other route, the fact of such diffusion is not in doubt; there is already a sizable body of scholarship on this topic.[115] But this is not to assert the direct influence of Sumer on Greece— only to identify it as the ultimate point of origin for many cultural forces pervading the ancient Near East and providing it with a common currency of ideas and values. What is important to understand is that the chronological priority of Sumerian culture, as well as its numerous typological correspondences with subsequent cultures, establishes a privileged status for the information it imparts about the character of man's earliest spiritual expression. That this character underwent many changes, was displaced and replaced by subsequent cultural events, is beyond question, but such evolution took place, we now know, only very gradually. The process of cultural transformation, the specific forms which the borrowed material assumed in new contexts and under which it can still be recognized, the degree to which influence is discernible and the nature of the complex sources in which it can still, perhaps, be detected—all these issues are likely to remain controversial, even more for Greek literature than they have already proved in the case of Genesis, the Song of Songs, and many other portions of the Old Testament.

---

113. Kramer (1963b), 487.

114. Hallo and Simpson (1971), 154.

115. For references to this large corpus, see Oppenheim (1977), 354, n. 26; Kramer (1963b), 486, n. 2; Sandars (1972), 57; also Oppenheim (1977), 73, 379, n. 37; Kramer (1963b), 486–88; Damon (1961), ch. 1, especially 270–71. For a recent illustration, see W. L. Moran, "An Assyriological Gloss on the New Archilochus Fragment," *HSCP,* 82 (1978), 17–19.

But there can be no doubt that "Mesopotamian influence and ideas are so pervasive" that their content may legitimately "be considered to have been part of the general cultural environment"[116] of the ancient Near East and therefore to have shaped, in subtle and at times imperceptible ways, the development of early Western thought.

It is clear that the ancients did not lack an approximate concept of pastoral: what they lacked was an interest in using such concepts of pastoral as they had to group artistic works or to differentiate one kind of aesthetic response from another. A survey of pastoralism in pre-Theocritean literature suggests that no sophisticated, erudite, and widely informed Alexandrian *littérateur,* such as Callimachus (a prominent member of Theocritus' readership), could possibly have thought that the originality of bucolic poetry as it had been invented lay in its rustic or pastoral qualities. Pastoralism had been present in literature since time immemorial, as Egger pointed out long ago; it is inconceivable that Callimachus, a native of Cyrene in Libya, where local pastoral festivals were still taking place more than six hundred years later, as the bishop Synesius reports (in a document already cited by Egger),[117] could be ignorant of such long-lived traditions reflected both in peasant culture and in art. If Theocritus' reputation as an original artistic talent is to be upheld, it must rest on some other foundation than the claim of having invented pastoral poetry.

116. Jacobsen (1976), 152. Cf. Sandars (1972), 46: "It is less a case of prototypes and parentage than of similar atmosphere."

117. Egger (1862), 258n.; see Knaack (1897), col. 1010; Trencsényi-Waldapfel (1966), 3.

CHAPTER SEVEN

Bucolic and Pastoral in Theocritus

Yet even should it be conceded, as indeed it must, that Theocritus is the first
writer to employ a fully elaborated system of pastoral conventions to express the outlook or set of attitudes we regard as distinctively pastoral and
that this fusion, further consolidated by Virgil, would subsequently dominate an important part of European poetry, Theocritus' claim to originality
is still not free of difficulty. The originality of Theocritus takes on a different meaning when it is viewed from the vantage point of the previous
artistic tradition instead of with the steady gaze of historical hindsight. A
survey of pastoral literature before Theocritus demonstrates that the peculiar character of his own poetic achievement and the factors contributing to
his reputation for originality in the ancient world must continue to remain
obscure so long as we persist in identifying bucolic poetry with what is
understood today by pastoral. To be sure, Theocritus does develop the
pastoral setting of many Idylls with a power and immediacy as unprece-
dented in his forebears as it is unsurpassed by his followers.[118] William
Berg, although he admits that "Theocritus would hardly have known what
we meant" in calling his first experiments in country mime " 'the earliest of
his pastoral poems,' "[119] nonetheless furnishes a precise account of Theocritus' originality in pastoral terms. According to Berg, the pastoral
achievement of Theocritus does not consist in his depiction of a rustic
locale, but in the self-consciousness with which he exploits the countryside's metaphorical value. After noting the traditional use of natural

118. Cf. Parry (1957), 14; Hieatt (1972), 7–11. For a lively appreciation of Theocritus as a
pastoralist, see the 1846 essay of C.-A. Sainte-Beuve, "Théocrite," *Derniers Portraits littéraires*
(Paris, 1858), 3–43, especially 3–29.

119. Berg (1974), 8; see also 25: Theocritus "had never heard of 'pastoral poetry.' "

metaphors for artistic creativity in archaic and classical poetry, Berg declares:

When a Greek poet contemplates and characterizes his own work in a poem, one or more of these natural metaphors will often appear. The more self-conscious the poet becomes, the more he imagines himself . . . [engaged] in an imitation of natural processes. Around him flourish the works of nature, his first model: a landscape appears in the mind. Inevitably a type of poetry emerged which sustained the landscape and permitted the poet to dwell within it at greater length. . . . The conscious recognition of this landscape, however, had to await an era of self-conscious poetry, a literary atmosphere in which the poet, divorced from all civic function, was alone with his Muse, so to speak, and free to look within himself, to reflect on the nature of his art.[120]

Berg goes on to say, quite rightly, that this interior landscape was consciously discovered in the Hellenistic age and to credit Theocritus more than anyone else with its discovery.[121]

Despite these valid observations, a variety of factors combine to prohibit equating Theocritus' invention of bucolic poetry with the heightened description of pastoral scenes or the self-conscious discovery of a spiritual landscape, distinctive and characteristic features of his art as these things may be. First of all, such innovations may not be deemed to constitute a sufficiently radical departure from previous literary tradition; as Dover points out, "The fact that no one in antiquity regarded any poet earlier than Theokritos as having written bucolic poetry is a warning to us not to underrate the originality of Theokritos or to overrate the bucolic element in the poets" who preceded him.[122] Much more important, however, the association of bucolic poetry with either an elaborately developed pastoralism or a self-conscious exploitation of it creates a mass of contradictions between Theocritus' supposed programme and his observable practice which are impossible to reconcile so long as such an association continues to be made.

120. Ibid., 5.

121. Cf. Legrand (1898), 438–39: "Le poète des Idylles n'a pas appelé l'attention de ses contemporains sur la campagne et sur la vie champêtre; il n'a pas écrit le premier des pièces empreintes d'un bout à l'autre de l'esprit 'idyllique'; mais il connut mieux que son entourage les réalités rustiques, ou il en connut de plus intéressantes, et il les exposa dans des œuvres d'une forme nouvelle"; Rohde (1932), 81, and 90: "Es ist festzuhalten . . . dass es keine Bukolik vor Theokrit gibt, dass aber alle Elemente dieser Bukolik zum Greifen bereit lagen, als er auf den Plan trat"; cf. Knaack (1897), col. 1004; Stark (1963), 366–67. Rosenmeyer (1969), 31, is more unqualified in his judgment: "In the case of pastoral, the inquiry [into origins] has been confounded by a natural reluctance to accept the fact that there was no pastoral poetry prior to Theocritus"; even he, however, admits, "All of the elements which [Theocritus] combined to construct a new kind of poetry were available in earlier achievements, but scattered and suspended in other compounds" (41).

122. Dover (1971), lxi.

The Seventh Idyll of Theocritus is generally acknowledged by recent
interpreters to be a conscious showpiece of his art and a manifesto of his
poetic ideals as they are embodied in bucolic poetry. Between the opening
of the poem, with its promise of an inspirational visit to a rustic harvest
festival, and the closing lines, in which the promise is seen to have been
abundantly fulfilled, occurs the speaker's encounter with Lycidas, the quin-
tessential goatherd; the center of the work is occupied with their exchange
of songs, concluding with the symbolic consecration of the city poet by the
goatherd. The action, which is modeled on Hesiod's encounter with the
Muses at the beginning of the *Theogony* and on the meeting of Odysseus
and Eumaeus with the goatherd Melanthius in the seventeenth book of the
Odyssey, is charged with a special significance both for the poet's own
relation to the literary tradition in general and for the particular place he
defines for himself within it.[123] The poem's narrator, whom the goatherd
calls Simichidas, proposes the poetic contest thus:

> ἀλλ᾽ ἄγε δή, ξυνὰ γὰρ ὁδὸς ξυνὰ δὲ καὶ ἀώς,
> βουκολιασδώμεσθα.

[35–36]

But come—for ours is a common road and a common morning—let's bucolize!

Lycidas replies:

> ἀλλ᾽ ἄγε βουκολικᾶς ταχέως ἀρξώμεθ᾽ ἀοιδᾶς,
> Σιμιχίδα· κἠγὼ μέν—ὄρη, φίλος, εἴ τοι ἀρέσκει
> τοῦθ᾽ ὅτι πρᾶν ἐν ὄρει τὸ μελύδριον ἐξεπόνασα.

[49–51]

But come, let's begin our bucolic song right away, Simichidas. For my part, I—see,
friend, if you like this ditty which I just worked out in the mountains.

When Lycidas has finished, the narrator of the poem responds:

> Λυκίδα φίλε, πολλὰ μὲν ἄλλα
> Νύμφαι κἠμὲ δίδαξαν ἀν᾽ ὤρεα βουκολέοντα. . . .

[91–92]

Lycidas, my friend, the Nymphs taught me, too, many such things while I was
tending cattle [*boukoleonta*] on the mountains.

There can be little doubt that what has taken place is an exchange of bucolic
poems as Theocritus understands the word.

If our current understanding of the verb *boukoliasdesthai* is correct, the
speaker's exhortation to Lycidas in line 36 should mean something of the
order "let's make like cowherds," or, more specifically, "let's speak cow-
herd-talk." As the second passage quoted above clearly indicates, however,

---

123. Van Sickle (1976), 23–24, with a survey of recent scholarship.

Lycidas understands the word to refer to the making of "bucolic" song; and as neither of the two compositions entered in the contest bears the slightest relation to cowherds or to their talk, it is abundantly obvious that *boukoliasdesthai* signifies, at least in this context, the process of creating a bucolic poem—it is the *terminus technicus* for the poetic activity, just as *boukolika* is the name of the product. Lycidas goes on to assert that he composed his piece in the mountains (ἐν ὄρει) and the narrator replies that the Nymphs taught him, too, many noble things while he was plying the cowherd's trade on the mountains (ἀν' ὤρεα βουκολέοντα), with a glance at the *Theogony* (22–23):

αἵ νύ ποθ' Ἡσίοδον καλὴν ἐδίδαξαν ἀοιδήν,
ἄρνας ποιμαίνονθ' Ἑλικῶνος ὑπο ζαθέοιο.

. . . [the Muses] who once taught Hesiod fair song as he was shepherding lambs below holy Helicon.

Thus, the language used by the two interlocutors and the larger literary significance surrounding their encounter emphatically characterize their compositions as typical, exemplary, and preeminent specimens of bucolic poetry. The unwary reader of Theocritus, accustomed to the conventional association of bucolic poetry with a pastoral subject, expects a rustic scene of rich and sensuous description shot through with vivid, realistic detail— the sort of landscape at which our poet excels and which is actually exemplified at the conclusion of Idyll 7 itself.[124] But the two bucolic songs composed by Theocritus contain hardly a trace of these features which are met with in such abundance elsewhere in the Idylls.

Indeed, had not Theocritus specifically labeled the two poems "bucolic" and singled them out as showpieces of the "genre," no modern critic would be inclinded to regard them as exemplary bucolics (meaning "ancient pastorals"). The song of Lycidas is an amatory send-off poem for a traveler, a *propemptikon* with erotic overtones, addressed to one Ageanax. The poem's wit lies in the artful manner with which its emphasis is shifted from parting salutations to seductive overtures; the fervent wishes expressed by Lycidas are "as much for Ageanax's complaisance as for his safety."[125] At this point, the song veers off to anticipate a series of imagined

124. The surprising contrast between the opulent pastoral tones at the close of Idyll 7 and the absence of such qualities in its explicitly bucolic portions was noted, though differently interpreted, by Legrand (1898), 412; Cholmeley (1919), 24, flatly called Idyll 7 "pseudopastoral."

125. Gow (1952), II, 145. On the *propemptikon* form and its relevance to Lycidas' poem, see Cairns (1972), 7–16, 27–28, 163–64. Note Wilamowitz's warning against interpreting the poem of Lycidas within the conceptual framework furnished by this rhetorical form (cited by Kühn [1958], 48n.).

events, including a rustic celebration graced by pastoral musicians, and culminates in an impossible wish for the companionship of the legendary goatherd and singer Comatas. Despite the heightened pastoral tones introduced here, the erotic theme continues to predominate—as a glance at the two songs performed at the anticipated picnic indicates. The pastoral subject of the first (the heartbreak of Daphnis and the countryside's mourning for him) should not be allowed to obscure the fictive song's true purpose— namely, to harmonize with the feelings of nostalgia and bittersweet longing which Lycidas pictures himself as indulging on the occasion of Ageanax's eventual departure: Lycidas can thereby demonstrate (by implication) the genuineness of his passion for Ageanax in the present moment. The story of the Muses' rescue of Comatas, the subject of the second song, and Lycidas' expression of desire for his companionship are subtly designed to inflate those praiseworthy qualities of Comatas which are also shared by the speaker, Lycidas (himself a goatherd and a poet), and to provide examples of appropriate action for Ageanax to follow: save me as the Muses saved Comatas; long to share my company as I long to share his.[126]

It is noteworthy that Lycidas, though a goatherd, dissociates himself somewhat from his rustic company in these scenes: he envisions himself reclining comfortably by a fire, garlanded and drinking wine, while two shepherds pipe and Tityrus sings. The pastoral element is imported into his world, it seems, almost as if he were a city dweller; indeed, the only time he chooses to remind us of his rustic identity is at the end of his composition, when he is seeking to be compared implicitly with Comatas and is presenting his own longing as a model for Ageanax's projected desire:

ὥς τοι ἐγὼν ἐνόμευον ἀν' ὥρεα τὰς καλὰς αἶγας
φωνᾶς εἰσαΐων, τὺ δ' ὑπὸ δρυσὶν ἢ ὑπὸ πεύκαις
ἁδὺ μελισδόμενος κατεκέκλισο, θεῖε Κομᾶτα.

[87–89]

So might I have herded your fair goats on the mountains, hearkening to your voice, while you, under the oaks or under the pines reclined, sweetly warbling, divine Comatas.

Otherwise, all the pastoral color in the poem is provided exclusively by the rustic trio of performers called in to help Lycidas celebrate his imagined erotic victory. Their songs create a pretty backdrop to what is otherwise an urbane and witty love poem addressed to a boy with a stikingly antipastoral name.[127] It may be objected, of course, that Lycidas' tendency to quail

126. Kühn (1958), 50–52. For an opposing interpretation, see Lawall (1967), 89–91, 93–95.

127. Kühn (1958), 49–50; Lawall (1967), 88. Lawall's belief that Ageanax's name implies a specifically aristocratic origin and identity was decisively refuted by Giangrande in his review of Lawall (JHS, 88 [1968], 170).

before erotic difficulties and to escape instead into the realm of the imagination represents a classically pastoral alternative and is consistent, moreover, with Priapus' characterization of goatherds, in Idyll 1.85–91, as inept and backward in matters of love; besides, the very mention of Daphnis and Comatas seems to glance at the most pastoral of Theocritus' Idylls. But all this, true though it may be, cannot erase the impression made by Lycidas' flirtation with a non-pastoral persona for his poetic voice and by his treatment of a non-pastoral theme: infatuation with a foreign youth.

Simichidas' reply, which even Berg considers "more urbane than pastoral,"[128] opens with an expression of sympathy for the erotic plight of his friend Aratus (the addressee of Idyll 6), who is also in love with a boy. Hints of sarcasm and mockery are initially concealed. The speaker proceeds to invoke the aid of Pan, using elements of the hymn form to dwell on the more disreputable aspects of the god's cult, and the help of the Erotes as well; he then abruptly drops this pretense of identification with Aratus' feelings, pointing out that the boy is in any case past his prime and not worth sighing over, and begs not to be pressed into any more nightlong vigils on his doorstep. The cynical and humorous tone of Simichidas' poem contrasts with the sentimentality of Lycidas' appeal to Ageanax, producing a typically Theocritean effect: one need only recall Priapus' mocking speech to Daphnis in Idyll 1, Milon's robust and sarcastic advice to the lovesick Bucaeus in Idyll 10, the exchanges between the largely ironic Battus and the sentimental Corydon in Idyll 4, or the conversation between Aeschinas and Thyonichus in Idyll 14 in order to appreciate the pattern. Thus, although Simichidas ostensibly takes no notice of Lycidas' song and offers an independent composition, his poem has the effect of a personal rejoinder.[129]

If the song of Simichidas can be said to have a setting, the sensitivity to social disgrace which it exploits and the mention of nocturnal serenades seem to place it in the city rather than in the country. It combines hymnic, epistolary, and komastic poetic forms[130] with that of the *paraclausithyron* (a serenade of sorts), and while Theocritus can adapt each of these four types to a rustic context on occasion (Idylls 22, 11, and 3), Simichidas' modified *kōmos* or *paraclausithyron* introduces a note of sophisticated urbanity no less than does Lycidas' modified *propemptikon*. Neither poem elaborates natural scenes, recasts mythological narratives into a new and arresting form, or

---

128. Berg (1974), 23; cf. Coleman (1969), 115–16: "Moreover, the songs which Lycidas and Simichidas sing in their competition, though full of pastoral colour, have more in common with the erotic themes of other genres."

129. Kühn (1958), 52–61; Ott (1969), especially 142–59, 212–13; F. Cairns, "Theocritus Idyll 10," *Hermes*, 98 (1970), 38–44, who discusses Theocritus' fondness for portraying the clash between an *amator* and an *irrisor amoris*.

130. Cf. Cairns (1972), 201–04.

incorporates folkloric poetic structures—unlike the one work which scholars have customarily taken to be typical of Theocritean bucolic poetry: the Daphnis-song of Thyrsis in Idyll 1. Not that pastoral elements are utterly absent from Simichidas' song: he begins by saying that he loves Myrto as much as the goats love the spingtime (96–97). The invocation of Pan, the description of Arcadian cult practices, and the threatened curse of miserable pasturage may also be thought to contribute a certain pastoral coloring. Pan's identity as patron deity of pederasts (cf. Call., fr. 689 Pfeiffer) is perhaps more relevant in the context, however, and in any case the learned exposition of local customs was a favorite theme of urban, Alexandrian poetry (Arcadia may be included for its primitive obscurity rather than for its rustic charm).[131] In short, the poem of Simichidas is urban in setting, didactic in intent, and ironically humorous in tone: it is not pastoral.

The songs of Lycidas and Simichidas, taken together, illustrate and exemplify bucolic poetry as Theocritus understood it. They demand comparison with many other aspects of his work and with much of Alexandrian poetry in general. Their artistic excellence has been increasingly appreciated in the last twenty-five years. Nevertheless, they raise serious problems for the interpretation of Theocritus which have yet to be properly confronted. In particular, an analysis of the two songs in their context seems utterly to prohibit the equation of bucolic poetry in the sense intended by Theocritus with pastoral poetry as it is currently understood by literary critics. When the rest of Theocritus' oeuvre is examined with this problem in mind, a surprising number of additional factors appear which weaken even further the conventional identification of Greek bucolic with pastoral poetry.

It has already been pointed out that the contrasting attitudes contained in the songs of Lycidas and Simichidas in Idyll 7 recall a similar conflict of values expressed in the conversation between Milon and Bucaeus in Idyll 10. In Idyll 10 as in Idyll 7 the encounter culminates in an exchange of songs which are separate and distinct but opposed to one another and mutually referential. The significance and pervasiveness of this normative dialectic in Theocritus' work have been discussed by Josef-Hans Kühn, who argues that Theocritus, by representing two important and characteristic features of his poetry under the guise of two concrete figures, set out to reveal the manifold resources of his own artistry.[132] That it is impossible to decide without a context whether Kühn's remarks refer to Idyll 7 or to Idyll 10

131. Kühn (1958), 53–54, 56. Cf. G. Jachmann, "L'Arcadia come paesaggio bucolico," *Maia,* 5 (1952), 161–74; E. Panofsky, "*Et in Arcadia Ego:* Poussin and the Elegiac Tradition," *Meaning in the Visual Arts* (New York, 1955), 295–320, especially 297–301; L. Alfonsi, "Dalla Sicilia all'Arcadia," *Aevum,* 36 (1962), 234–39; further references to the scholarship on this topic are cited by Schmidt (1964), cols. 965–66.

132. Kühn (1958), 61.

demonstrates the extent of the similarities between the two poems. And yet, whereas Idyll 7 is generally held to be one of the most representative and influential of Theocritus' pastoral efforts, Idyll 10 is related only marginally to the pastoral mode. Its protagonists are reapers, agricultural day laborers, and one of them identifies himself with a poetic tradition of fieldworkers' songs which he traces to the legendary hero Lityerses.[133] Now Gilbert Highet maintains, as we have seen, that "ploughmen and field workers are not introduced" into pastoral, "because their life is too laborious and sordid." Rosenmeyer has emphasized that "*otium* is a keyword in the discussion of the pastoral" and has devoted a lengthy discussion to the importance of leisure and tranquillity in pastoral literature.[134] The identification of pastoral with bucolic imports a theoretical distinction between Idylls 7 and 10 into the Theocritean corpus where it is alien to the spirit of the two poems and violates the more pertinent similarities of structure and theme connecting them.

Pastoral criticism has, on occasion, made allowances for agricultural subjects, however, and it may be prudent not to insist on the inadmissible qualities of Idyll 10. There are other unities and correspondences within the Theocritean corpus with a more urgent claim on our attention. The Eleventh Idyll of Theocritus demands comparison with its companion piece, Idyll 13. Both are poetic epistles addressed to Nicias, whose name occurs in the same position of the same line of each poem—at the beginning of the second verse (a logical place for the dedication, which, if it occurred earlier, would risk becoming part of the title). Both Idylls deal with mythological subjects drawn from heroic legend—with the Cyclops and with Hylas, respectively—and both exploit the comic possibilities latent in these subjects.[135] Idyll 11 has eighty-one lines, Idyll 13 seventy-five. But whereas the former is almost classically pastoral, the latter is not pastoral at all: it describes an incident during the voyage of the Argonauts—the drowning (or nympholepsy) of Hylas, the beloved of Heracles, and the mighty hero's desperate, unsuccessful search for the boy.

In the case of Idylls 11 and 13, then, it is clear that the distinction between pastoral and non-pastoral is foreign to the common thrust of the

---

133. On this tradition, see Trencsényi-Waldapfel (1966), 22–25; Gow (1952), II, 204, *ad* 10.41, who notes a few pages earlier that "*Id.* 10 differs from the other bucolic Idylls in that its setting is agricultural, not pastoral" (193).

134. Rosenmeyer (1969), 67; more generally, 65–97.

135. The humorous incongruities in Idyll 11 need little commentary; on Idyll 13, see Mastronarde (1968); Effe (1978), 60–64. For a more general discussion of Theocritus' impertinent treatment of mythological material, see Legrand (1898), 184–95; Horstmann (1976), 57–113; Effe (1978), 48–77. But see Poggioli (1975), 4, on the inherent antagonism between the heroic epic and pastoral.

poems and obscures their similarities of form, theme, and technique. The further possibility that *both* Idylls 11 and 13 may have belonged to the bucolic corpus of Theocritus creates additional difficulties for those who wish to equate bucolic with pastoral. Although Idyll 11 is nowhere explicitly characterized as a bucolic poem, it shares many features (such as its rustic locale, use of Doricisms, preoccupation with the importance of song, and ironic treatment of unsophisticated speech) with the indisputably bucolic Idylls. It has the same subject as Idyll 6—the courtship of Galatea by Polyphemus; both Idylls 6 and 11, moreover, begin as poetic epistles addressed, respectively, to Aratus and Nicias. Virgil's extensive imitations of Idyll 11 in his own *Bucolics* also provide a clue to its "generic" identity. Similarly, Idyll 13, despite its lack of pastoral qualifications, is expressly included among Theocritus' bucolic compositions by a scholiast commenting on Apollonius Rhodius *Argonautica* 1.1236: Θεόκριτος ἐν τοῖς Βουκολικοῖς ἐν τῷ ῞Υλα ἐπιγραφομένῳ. Virgil, for what it is worth, inserts the Hylas story into the song of Silenus in Eclogue 6.43–44. The vexed question concerning the dialect of Idyll 13 will be discussed in its place (part III, chapter 8); for the moment, it is sufficient to point out that since by late antiquity the bucolic "genre" had become associated with the Doric dialect, the repeated assertions in the textual tradition—from the Antinoe papyrus on through the manuscripts—that Idyll 13 is composed in Doric, in spite of some evidence to the contrary, may reflect a long-standing and ancient notion about its bucolic identity. Such a classification of Idyll 13, if accepted, would prohibit the synonymous usage of bucolic and pastoral.

A similar comparison might be made between Idylls 1 and 2. In this case there is no question of dialectal deviation. Both poems are composed in similar versions of Doric, and both—unique in this respect among all the Idylls—make use of a recurrent refrain or intercalary verse which breaks up the narrative into "stanzas" of varying length and represents a highly anomalous ("lyric") element in continuous hexameter poetry. Furthermore, the plethora of Homeric forms and the metrical irregularities in both poems place them within the same stylistic subgroup according to established Theocritean stylometry.[136] Both poems investigate the pathology of love and share numerous elements of feeling, expression, and technique.[137] The First Idyll is 152 lines long; the Second is fourteen verses longer. But whereas the First Idyll, set in the countryside, relates a conversation between two herdsmen and introduces into world literature the pastoral hero *par excellence*—

---

136. Di Benedetto (1956), 48–60; cf. Fabiano (1971), 535.

137. On the various points of resemblance between the two poems, see Lawall (1967), 14–33; Segal (1975), 123; Van Sickle (1976), 24–25.

Daphnis the dying neatherd, the prime subject of rustic song and genius of the Sicilian landscape—the Second Idyll takes place entirely within the humble (not to say squalid) dwelling of a lower-middle-class teenager on the outskirts of a large city. Once again, the distinction between pastoral and non-pastoral serves only to create artificial divisions between poems which otherwise would naturally complement each other.

Pastoral or not, Idylls 1 and 2 share a strong claim to be considered bucolic. The song of Thyrsis in Idyll 1 is emphatically designated bucolic by each of its numerous refrains; its singer is said to be an adept at bucolic poetry (20:καὶ τᾶς βουκολικᾶς ἐπὶ τὸ πλέον ἵκεο μοίσας). The exchange of compliments at the poem's opening is widely imitated by later bucolic aspirants and its first line is cited by Terentianus Maurus (2123–30) as an example of the so-called bucolic diaeresis. Hermogenes also refers to the poem as an instance of bucolic (περὶ ἰδεῶν 2.306, p. 323.19–22 Rabe). The Second Idyll belongs on stylometric grounds, and perhaps on the evidence of the manuscript tradition as well, to that group of Theocritus' poems which includes Idylls 1 and 7—the most self-consciously bucolic works in the Theocritean corpus. The anti-pastoral locale of Idyll 2 should not raise a serious objection to including the poem among the bucolic Idylls and it certainly did not prevent Virgil from using Idyll 2 as the model for the second half of his Eighth Eclogue. To be sure, Virgil's reworking of the Second Idyll places the speaker in a rustic setting and culminates in the countryside's victory over the lure of the city; the beloved's name is also changed, significantly, from Delphis to Daphnis.[138] This is quite in keeping with Virgil's own aesthetic objectives throughout the Eclogues. However, if Virgil did not consider Idyll 2 bucolic, why did he go to the trouble of incorporating such an irrelevant and (from the pastoral point of view) almost unassimilable work into his own *liber bucolicon?* And why did he balance his imitation of it so carefully against an imitation of Idyll 1 in the first half of the Eighth Eclogue? The very difficulty of adapting Theocritus' poem to suit his purposes might point to some external or formal constraint shaping Virgil's choice.

Once again, the Antinoe papyrus and all the manuscripts that preserve a titulus for the Second Idyll label it a "Doric" composition. But the manuscript tradition contains clearer indications of its "generic" identity. Several manuscripts preserve a wretched little poem bidding farewell to Theocritus which concludes the bucolic portion of their holdings. The anonymous epigrammatist, like Artemidorus of Tarsus (whose famous couplet served him as a model), "casts himself not merely as a fellow poet but as the

138. Coleman (1977), 253–55.

herdsman of the tradition, expressing the critic's role in a metaphor drawn
from the matter."[139] The Byzantine scholar's use of this figure, along with
his specific verbal reminiscences of Artemidorus, tell a good deal about the
sources of his inspiration.

Σιμιχίδα Θεόκριτε, σοφῶν ὄϊων ποιμάντορ
καὶ τοκάδων αἰγῶν αἰπόλε μηκάδων,
τὰς Ἑλικωνίτιδες βοτάναι θρέψαν καλλίστως·
οὐ περὶ μάνδραν ἔδυν τεήν, ἀλλὰ σποράδας
ἐξ ὀρέων συνέλεξα καὶ ἐς μίαν ἤγαγον μάνδραν
βουκολικὰς Μοίσας, αἱ γέννημα σέθεν.
οὐ πλειόνων δ᾽ ἐπέτυχον, ἐπεί γε μόλις καὶ τῶνδε.

Simichidas Theocritus, shepherd of wise sheep and goatherd of prolific, bleating
goats, which the pastures of Helicon nourished splendidly: I did not slink about your
fold—rather, I collected the Bucolic Muses, your offspring, from the mountains
where they had scattered, and led them into one fold. I happened on no more than
these (and even these with difficulty!).

In the Vatican manuscripts UEA these lines are followed by the notation
Τέλος τῶν Θεοκρίτου Βουκολικῶν ("conclusion of Theocritus' Bucolics"); in U and E, the poem and notation occur at the end of Idyll 18 and
separate it from the *Syrinx,* one of the ancient bucolic glyphs or *Technopaegnia;* in A, they divide the Theocritean material from non-Theocritean portions of the manuscript. In the Laurentian manuscript G the poem and
notation follow Idyll 14 and separate it from the *Alae* ("Wings") of Simias.
The Laurentian manuscript P, however, retains the poem after the end of
Idyll 14 but omits the concluding notation, for in P, Idyll 14 is not followed
by any of the *Technopaegnia,* whether attributed to Theocritus (as the *Syrinx*
usually is) or to other poets, but by Idyll 2, the *Lament for Bion,* and Idyll 16,
in that order. Clearly the notation Τέλος τῶν Θεοκρίτου Βουκολικῶν was
inappropriate in P, where the scribe was about to continue copying Idyll 2
and perhaps as many as two more genuinely bucolic works by Theocritus
after Idyll 14.[140] The little valedictory poem, however, had become attached by convention to the end of that Idyll and remained there. One
might object that the language of the Byzantine scholiast's poem to Theocritus, with its pastoral imagery, Doric intonation, and explicit claim of
terminating the bucolic corpus, excludes Idyll 2 from the bucolic composi-

---

139. Van Sickle (1976), 27.

140. P. 333 Wendel; viii–x, for the order of the poems in the mss. Generally, references to
the manuscripts and to the order of the poems in them are based on Gow (1952), I, xxxvii–
xlvii, but in the case of P and a few other mss. the divisions of Gallavotti, which Gow uses,
depend on the character of the preserved text and so cut across the order of the poems in the
mss. (Gow, xxxiv n.). That the omission of the concluding notation in P was due to simple
error or to negligence cannot, of course, be ruled out. Note that the *Lament for Bion* is ascribed
to Theocritus in CDS and Tr, though not in P.

tions of Theocritus more decisively than the mitigating evidence of the omitted notation argues for its inclusion. It should be recalled, however, that the scholiast's verses occur in the manuscripts at the end of Idylls 14 and 18, which are in any case the *least* pastoral of Theocritus' works (the former relates a highly colloquial exchange between two mercenaries, the latter is an epithalamium for Helen and Menelaus). Therefore, the poem cannot be construed to mark the end of what is conventionally understood as the bucolic corpus; furthermore, it is clear that the poem's usual function, that of separating the Idylls from other material, is suspended in P (the manuscript under discussion). Given, then, that the position of dedicatory poem cannot in any event be presumed to divide the pastoral Idylls of Theocritus from his nonpastoral (and hence "non-bucolic") corpus, it is the omission of the concluding notation in P before Idyll 2 which may be deemed significant and which perhaps identifies Idyll 2 as a bucolic poem.

The possible bucolic identity of Idylls 10, 13, and 2, as well as the connection which Theocritus establishes between them and Idylls 7, 11, 6, and 1, agrees with the evidence afforded by an examination of the songs in the Seventh Idyll in warning us not to treat the bucolic poetry of Theocritus as a primitive version of pastoral. The lack of congruence between the ancient usage of *bucolic* and the modern meaning of *pastoral* was first pointed out by B. A. van Groningen, who noted that the early fifth-century compendium of Stobaeus preserves a number of poems in Doric hexameters, ascribed to the Greek bucolic poets Moschus and Bion under the title of *Bucolics*, which make no mention of herdsmen or flocks and hardly any reference to the countryside.[141] Although the first fragment of Moschus (in Gow's edition) develops a typically pastoral contrast between the hazards of life at sea and the easeful tranquillity of the countryside, the remaining two fragments preserved by Stobaeus ἐκ τῶν Μόσχου τοῦ Σικελιώτου Βουκολικῶν ("from the Bucolics of Moschus the Sicilian") are devoted entirely to erotic subjects. To be sure, the frustrated chain of lovers in fragment 2 includes Pan, Echo, a Satyr, and an otherwise unknown Lyde, but their names are the only hint of a pastoral setting, if one is actually implied. The third fragment, reproduced below, is a mythological piece with an erotic point about the union of Alpheus and Arethusa. That Alpheus was a river in Arcadia, the home of Pan, does not seem relevant; as already noted, Arcadia is not a pastoral landscape in the Greek tradition, and Moschus had not read Milton. Except for the connection of Arethusa with Syracuse in Sicily, the supposed birthplace of Theocritus and for that reason

---

141. van Groningen (1958), 296–300; cf. Knaack (1897), col. 1009: "Moschos und Bion zeigen in ihrem Nachlass keinen wirklich bukolischen Charakter mehr, es sind nur erotisch-sentimentale Tändeleien und Spielereien."

the putative origin of bucolic poetry, Arethusa can have had no conceivable
pastoral associations (although it may have had bucolic ones: see Idyll 1.117;
Lament for Bion, 77) until Virgil used it in the Tenth Eclogue to symbolize
the unadulterate tradition of bucolic inspiration.

> Ἀλφειὸς μετὰ Πῖσαν ἐπὴν κατὰ πόντον ὁδεύῃ,
> ἔρχεται εἰς Ἀρέθοισαν ἄγων κοτινηφόρον ὕδωρ,
> ἔδνα φέρων καλὰ φύλλα καὶ ἄνθεα καὶ κόνιν ἱράν,
> καὶ βαθὺς ἐμβαίνει τοῖς κύμασι τὰν δὲ θάλασσαν
> νέρθεν ὑποτροχάει, κοὐ μίγνυται ὕδασιν ὕδωρ,
> ἁ δ' οὐκ οἶδε θάλασσα διερχομένω ποταμοῖο.
> κῶρος δεινοθέτας κακομάχανος αἰνὰ διδάσκων
> καὶ ποταμὸν διὰ φίλτρον Ἔρως ἐδίδαξε κολυμβῆν.

> When Alpheius, from Pisa departing, journeyeth under the sea,
> He brings Arethusa the waters that nurture the olive-tree,
> Bears bridal-gifts, fair leaves and flowers of the sacred soil.
> Deep under the billows he plunges: far under the sea like oil
> He races, for never mingle his streams with the water's flow:
> Of the river that rusheth through her nothing the sea doth know.
> That knavish Boy, that teacher of naughtiness, mischief-contriver,
> Love, by his spells made even a river a deep-sea-diver!
>
> [trans. A. S. Way]

The subject of the story is erotic—Love can teach even rivers new tricks—
and whatever pastoral flavor may be judged to accompany it is plainly
subordinated.

The fragments of Bion selected by Stobaeus ἐκ τῶν Βίωνος βουκολικῶν (from the bucolics of Bion) are even more conclusive on this score. They
include verses on love and poetry (fr. 3):

> Μοίσας Ἔρως καλέοι, Μοῖσαι τὸν Ἔρωτα φέροιεν.
> μολπὰν ταὶ Μοῖσαί μοι ἀεὶ ποθέοντι διδοῖεν,
> τὰν γλυκερὰν μολπάν, τᾶς φάρμακον ἄδιον οὐδέν.

> Let Eros summon the Muses, the Muses bring Eros.
> The Muses ever grant my constant desire a song,
> a sweet song, than which there is no pleasanter medicine.

The allusion in the last line to the Eleventh Idyll of Theocritus does not alter
the fact of the lack of pastoral elements in the poem. Somewhat the same
theme occurs in fragment 1, which recounts Apollo's search for an antidote
to his sorrow at the death of Hyacinth, and in fragment 9, an elaboration of
the interdependence of love and poetic inspiration (Lycidas, the name of the
beloved in line 10, is the only suggestion of a pastoral context). Fragment 13
tells the story of a young bird-catcher who tried to bag Eros and is given
some sage advice by an old plowman. Fragment 2, which may report a

conversation between two rustics, is nevertheless exclusively taken up with a discussion about the respective merits of the seasons. It is noteworthy that in fragment 10, the cowherd commissioned by Aphrodite to instruct Eros how to sing restricts his bucolic themes to aetiological topics and stories about the discovery of various musical instruments.[142]

ἐγὼ δ᾽ ὅσα βουκολίασδον . . .
ὡς εὗρεν πλαγίαυλον ὁ Πάν, ὡς αὐλὸν Ἀθάνα,
ὡς χέλυν Ἑρμάων, κίθαριν ὡς ἁδὺς Ἀπόλλων. . . .

But no matter how much I bucolized about how Pan
discovered the flute, Athena the pipe,
Hermes the lyre, sweet Apollo the cithara. . . .

The fragments of Moschus and Bion are similar in spirit to a Doric hexameter poem of unknown authorship which was ascribed to Theocritus in a fifteenth-century manuscript and usually inserted in bucolic collections after the Ἔρως Δραπέτης of Moschus (poem 1). Although no authority identifies it as bucolic, its resemblance to other bucolic fragments is so striking (not to mention its unswerving observance of the so-called bucolic diaeresis) that its presence in the Theocritean corpus becomes difficult to explain only if the identification of bucolic with pastoral is rigorously upheld:

τὸν κλέπταν ποτ᾽ Ἔρωτα κακὰ κέντασε μέλισσα
κηρίον ἐκ σίμβλων συλεύμενον, ἄκρα δὲ χειρῶν
δάκτυλα πάνθ᾽ ὑπένυξεν. ὁ δ᾽ ἄλγεε καὶ χέρ᾽ ἐφύση
καὶ τὰν γᾶν ἐπάταξε καὶ ἅλατο, τᾷ δ᾽ Ἀφροδίτᾳ
δεῖξεν τὰν ὀδύναν, καὶ μέμφετο ὅττι γε τυτθόν
θηρίον ἐντὶ μέλισσα καὶ ἁλίκα τραύματα ποιεῖ.
χἁ μάτηρ γελάσασα· "τὺ δ᾽ οὐκ ἴσος ἐσσὶ μελίσσαις,
ὃς τυτθὸς μὲν ἔεις τὰ δὲ τραύματα ἁλίκα ποιεῖς;"

[Idyll 19]

A cruel bee once stung the thievish Love-god as he was stealing honey from the hives, and pricked all his finger-tips. And he was hurt, and blew upon his hand, and stamped and danced. And to Aphrodite he showed the wound, and made complaint that so small a creature as a bee should deal so cruel a wound. And his mother answered laughing, "Art not thou like the bees, that art so small yet dealest wounds so cruel?" [trans. Gow]

A similar argument might be made for Idyll 21, which, though it could be viewed as part of the (later and largely derivative) tradition of the piscatory eclogue, seems very much out of place in a pastoral anthology; yet it shares many characteristics with the bucolic poems examined thus far.

142. But see van Groningen (1958), 297, for a warning that these stories may conceal pastoral motifs.

A survey of the works ascribed to Theocritus, Moschus, and Bion which can be identified as bucolic on the basis of internal or external evidence has demonstrated that the modern tendency to equate bucolic with pastoral is not only historically inaccurate but also fails to account for the nature of the very poems it is designed to elucidate. The general argument can be substantiated by examining the entry under Theocritus in the Byzantine *Suda,* the relevant portion of which reads: "He wrote the so-called Bucolic hexameter poems in the Doric dialect. Some also ascribe to him the following works: *Proetides, Elpides* [Expectations], *Hymns, Heroines, Dirges* [*epikēdeia*], *Lyrics* [*melē*], *Elegies and Iambs, Epigrams.*" Although the testimony of the *Suda* must be used with care, the traditional Theocritean bibliography preserved in this passage may aid in the task of distinguishing the bucolic from the non-bucolic works of Theocritus.[143]

About the *Proetides* nothing is known. It may have been an epyllion about the punishment of the daughters of Proetus. The story is alluded to by Silenus in the course of his song in Virgil's Sixth Eclogue (line 48) and it is possible that the poem of Theocritus in question, if it existed, was numbered among his bucolic compositions, not identified as a separate work. But the evidence afforded by Virgil is in this case hardly consequential, and in the absence of further information it is impossible to pursue the matter beyond the point of speculation.

Idyll 21 concludes with a moral about the foolishness of being deluded by dreams and false hopes. As such, it might qualify as part of the (otherwise lost) *Elpides.* However, Idyll 21 has come down to us with its own title (though it is attested in only one branch of the Laurentian manuscript tradition) and does not appear to be an excerpt; nor is it likely that this short poem, similar in formal, thematic, and stylistic respects—not the least of which are meter and dialect—to Idylls 4, 10, 14, and 1.39–44, should have been singled out and classified as a separate work. If some longer poem of Theocritus is intended by this entry, it is unknown (and may never have existed).

The opening line of Idyll 22 identifies it as a hymn to the Dioscuri. To be sure, the poem contains stichomythy, dramatic monologues, and other features traditionally foreign to the hymn form, but Theocritus' fondness for contaminating poetic conventions, in itself a common characteristic of Alexandrian poetry in his day, may well be judged to overrule formal objections to its inclusion in the category of hymns. Nor do the many Doric readings of the manuscripts diminish the good reasons for classifying Idyll 22 among the putative *Hymns* of Theocritus rather than among his bucolic poems. Idylls 24 and 26 have also been advanced as candidates for inclusion

---

143. See the discussions of Cholmeley (1919), 52–53, and Gow (1952), I, xxiv–xxv, on which the following paragraphs are based.

among the *Hymns;* only the latter contains hymnic elements—such as the closure beginning Χαῖροι μὲν Διόνυσος ("farewell, Dionysus" [33]). It is composed in Doric,[144] moreover, and makes a very strange, short hymn, but—in the light of Callimachus' example—matters of dialect and convention need not be considered insuperable obstacles to identifying all these poems as hymns. Finally, the encomia to Hieron and Ptolemy, Idylls 16 and 17 (more plausibly the latter, with its grandiloquent opening and epic diction), might be enrolled among the *Hymns,* if necessary, along with Idyll 18, the Doric epithalamium for Helen and Menelaus.

The only Idyll conceivably appropriate for inclusion among the Theocritean *Heroines* is Idyll 26 again, which retells the story of the *Bacchae* in condensed form. It seems too self-contained to be part of a series or longer poem and, if subjective impressions are worth anything, its emphasis does not suit it to be numbered among mythological tales of heroic women. In any case, Idyll 26 cannot very well be reckoned *both* a hymn and a heroine poem. Gow has suggested that the *Europa* and *Megara* of Moschus (nos. 2 and 4) might be enrolled in this category. The latter is certainly attributed to Theocritus in some manuscripts (in C and Tr, for example), the former more rarely so (only in the 1516 editions of P. Giunta and Z. Callierges), but if the tradition reported by the scholiast is correct in asserting that Moschus was called Theocritus, the ascription of these poems to Theocritus' authorship is perfectly credible.[145] The other poems of Theocritus which treat feminine subjects, Idylls 2 and 15, could hardly be supposed to deal with heroines.

Bion's *Lament for Adonis* is ascribed to Theocritus by C and by the Iuntine and Calliergian editions; the disputed *Lament for Bion,* usually claimed by Moschus, is attributed to Theocritus by CDS and Tr. That there were other, similar pastoral elegies in circulation at one time is demonstrated by the survival of the poem Εἰς Νεκρὸν Ἄδωνιν in bucolic manuscripts. It is possible that the bibliographical tradition preserved by the *Suda* included these in the title *Dirges.* It is worth pointing out, however, that because all these works—except the Εἰς Νεκρόν Ἄδωνιν and the *Europa* and *Megara* of Moschus—are largely similar to the bucolic Idylls in meter, dialect, and subject, they cannot positively be excluded from the bucolic corpus itself. A number of funerary epigrams have come down to us under the name of Theocritus (7, 9, 11, 15, 16, 20, 23, conceivably 6 and 19, and the dubious 25);

144. But see Di Benedetto (1956), 48n.

145. Σ Prol. A.a.: κατὰ γοῦν τινας Μόσχος καλούμενος Θεόκριτος ὠνομάσθη (p. 1.13–14 Wendel). Whether we are meant to understand that Moschus assumed this name as a gesture of deference to the reputation of his master or was assigned it through the confused admiration of his readers remains uncertain. For the manuscript ascriptions see Gow (1952), I, xxxv–xlvii.

it cannot be determined beyond doubt that the *Dirges* mentioned in the *Suda* do not refer to them.

Unless we take *epikēdeia* as the modifier of *melē* and treat the two words as a single entry, the bibliographical tradition cited in the *Suda* furnishes one category for which surviving works of Theocritus can unquestionably be found. Idylls 28, 29, 30, and 31 are composed in lyric meters and in a version of the Aeolic dialect. The Antinoë papyrus and a few manuscripts take note of these poems' Aeolic identity. There is no reason to doubt that the four poems represented part of Theocritus' efforts in the melic genre.[146]

Little needs to be said about the remaining titles. No trace has survived of the *Elegies and Iambs*,[147] if indeed they ever existed. Twenty-six epigrams ascribed by one source or another to Theocritus are extant and some are undoubtedly genuine.

To sum up: the value of the bibliographical tradition transmitted by the *Suda* is highly questionable. It apparently attributed to Theocritus several works of alien authorship, such as the pastoral *Laments* or perhaps other works by the later Greek bucolic poets, and it lists two or more titles (*Proetides, Iambs,* probably *Elpides* and *Heroines* as well) which cannot be accounted for by the slightest preserved scrap of Theocritean poetry. Furthermore, it passes over in silence some of the genuine, presumably non-bucolic works of Theocritus which have survived: unless the *Berenice* (a fragment in Epic hexameters is preserved by Athenaeus, 284a) is to be classed among the *Hymns* or *Heroines,* it represents an aspect of Theocritus' poetic endeavor otherwise unattested—and the same might be said, though with considerably more diffidence, about the works of Theocritus alluded to by Eustathius and the *Etymologicum magnum*.[148] As Gow remarks, "Such a list firmly presented as describing Theocritus' range would command little confidence; and this is not so presented, for the entry in Suidas asserts only that 'some ascribe' such works to Theocritus. We cannot be certain that the enigmatic ascriptions were wrong, but the absence of citations in antiquity, and the negative evidence of the papyri, discourage the belief that they were right."[149]

Nevertheless, the critical reader will be struck by the number of poems in the Theocritean collection left unaccounted for by the bibliographical tradition—so long as a work's admission to the bucolic corpus depends on

146. West (1967).

147. Idyll 8 contains a passage in elegiac distichs; this led Cholmeley (1919), 52, to class it among the hypothetical elegies of Theocritus. Idyll 8 identifies itself quite unambiguously as bucolic, however, although its elegiac segment may have led the originator of the bibliographical tradition preserved in the *Suda* to invent a separate category for it. On the problem of classification, see Schmidt (1972), 38, 282.

148. The value of these allusions is in doubt; see Gow (1952), II, 520.

149. Ibid., I, xxv.

its pastoral qualities.[150] More than half of the collection, eighteen Idylls in all, lack such qualities almost entirely: Idylls 2, 12, 13, 14, 15, 16, 17, 18, 19, 21, 23, 24, 25, 26, 28, 29, 30, and 31. Of these, Idylls 2, 12, 13, 14, 15, 19, 23 (along with Idylls 16, 21, and 24 in all probability) cannot be attributed to whatever works, now lost, might have been associated with Theocritus' name in antiquity according to the evidence of the *Suda*. Moreover, these Idylls include some of Theocritus' genuine and most distinctive master-pieces (Idylls 2, 13, 14, 15, 16, and 24). This fact has been taken, by Gow and others, to impugn even further the value of the bibliographical tradition preserved in the *Suda*. But one should recall that the *Suda* ascribes to The-ocritus only "the so-called Bucolic hexameters in Doric dialect" with any confidence. And another scholion points out that Theocritus' reputation rested on his bucolic compositions: περὶ δὲ τὴν τῶν βουκολικῶν ποίησιν εὐφυὴς γενόμενος πολλῆς δόξης ἐπέτυχε.[151] It is likely that more of The-ocritus' bucolic poetry would have survived than his efforts in other forms. Although the testimony of the *Suda,* then, is not so authoritative as to compel us to include all the unaccounted Idylls in the bucolic corpus, it does suggest the strong possibility that more of Theocritus' surviving poems figured in it than the current equation of bucolic and pastoral allows us to recognize.

A case has been made already for the possible bucolic identity of Idylls 2 and 13. The Twenty-fourth Idyll shares with the Thirteenth an interest in Heracles and is labeled "Doric" by the Antinoë papyrus (which, though inconsistent, preserves more Doric forms in the doubtful text of this poem than does the manuscript tradition). It is perhaps no coincidence, then, that Virgil imitated Idyll 24 in his own *Bucolics.* The speaker of Alphesiboeus' song in Eclogue 8 instructs her maidservant:

fer cineres, Amarylli, foras riuoque fluenti
transque caput iace, nec respexeris.

[101–02]

Take out the ashes, Amaryllis, and throw them behind you into a running stream, and don't look back.

This injunction recalls Tiresias' advice to Alcmena in Idyll 24:

ἦρι δὲ συλλέξασα κόνιν πυρὸς ἀμφιπόλων τις
ῥιψάτω, εὖ μάλα πᾶσαν ὑπὲρ ποταμοῖο φέρουσα
ῥωγάδας ἐς πέτρας, ὑπερούριον, ἂψ δὲ νεέσθω
ἄστρεπτος.

[93–96]

150. According to Muecke (1975), 171, "Of the twenty-two or so authentic *Idylls* only eight can be counted as bucolic."
151. Σ Prol. A.a. (p. 1.11–13 Wendel).

In the early morning let one of your handmaids collect the ash from the fire and, when she has brought all of it across the river to the broken rocks, well beyond our boundaries, cast it away, and then come back without turning to look behind her.

Although Virgil's version is more condensed, according to the needs of his narrower compass, it remains faithful to the Theocritean original. A passage from the non-pastoral Idyll 18 (lines 29–31) might even have provided a model for Virgil in two different Eclogues (5.32–34, 7.65–68).[152] Did Virgil, then, consider Idylls 24 and 18 bucolic?

In the light of the many correspondences between the pastoral and non-pastoral Idylls, some recent scholarly efforts to distinguish the bucolic poems of Theocritus within the larger collection of his work according to the presence or absence of pastoral elements must be considered to have been misplaced. Although Charles Segal, for example, commenting on parallels between Idyll 1 and "the non-bucolic Second *Idyll*," calls attention to "the continuity within the totality of Theocritus' *oeuvre*," he finds it necessary to insist on the peculiar "coherence" among the bucolic landscapes. But the qualities which in his view set apart the bucolic landscapes are often arbitrary (cypresses are *akrokomoi*, "high-leaved," in Idyll 22.41 but not in the "bucolic" poems), vague ("complete fusion of surface and latent meaning"), or derived from post-Theocritean definitions of pastoral (wild forests cannot be part of an authentic bucolic landscape).[153] Similarly, Robert Coleman persists in conflating bucolic with pastoral even while acknowledging that "the boundaries of the [pastoral] genre remain indeterminate" in Hellenistic poetry and admitting, "Although there can be little doubt that Theocritus invented the pastoral genre, it is not at all clear that he regarded the pastoral poems as distinct from the rest of his idylls in anything but their rural setting."[154] Coleman does not appear to grasp how devastating is his admission, which he goes on to amplify in considerable detail, for the conventional understanding of ancient bucolic poetry. The ultimate paradox created by pastoralist criticism of bucolic poetry is provided by Gilbert Lawall, who, arguing that the first seven Idylls of the Vatican manuscripts (nos. 1–7 in the normal modern arrangement) form a separate poetry book, is obliged to include the intractably non-pastoral (but possibly bucolic) Second Idyll among the "Coan Pastorals" of that collection and to plead for its pastoral identity.[155]

The many continuities within the Theocritean corpus spanning the pastoral and non-pastoral Idylls represent only one of the current interpreta-

152. See Gow (1952), I, lx, n. 4.
153. Segal (1975), 123, 131–32, 115.
154. Coleman (1975), 140.
155. Lawall (1967), 14–33, cf. Grant (1965), 64–65.

tive problems which any new and rigorous historical definition of bucolic
poetry must attempt to solve. The lack of an appropriate designation for
those poems which are without pastoral characteristics yet share other features with the pastoral Idylls also suggests the kind of vacuum which such a
definition, in order to be successful, must fill. There is no reason to insist
that all, or even most, of the Idylls—or those unaccounted for by the
bibliographical tradition in the *Suda*—be assimilated to a single formulation
of bucolic poetry.[156] It is legitimate to presume, however, that the distinctive mark of a successful definition will be the ease and naturalness with
which it is able to encompass the great variety of material contained in
many of the Idylls and help make sense of (or, at least, not violate) the many
similarities of form and content connecting otherwise dissimilar poems in
the Theocritean corpus.

---

156. Cf. Hermog. περὶ ἰδεῶν 2.306: καὶ τὰ πολλὰ τῶν βουκολικῶν, ἵνα μὴ τὰ πάντα
λέγω, τοιαῦτά ἐστι (p. 323.21–22 Rabe).

PART III

The Thematic Structure of Bucolic Poetry

CHAPTER EIGHT

Rules of Evidence

In order to arrive at an accurate historical assessment of Theocritus and the nature of his poetic achievement, it will be necessary first of all to jettison any conventional assumptions that still remain about what can and cannot qualify as "bucolic," since the meaning of the term has yet to be understood.[1] As B. A. van Groningen argued in 1958, there is but a single valid method for recovering the ancient meaning of *bucolic:* to study the texts which the ancients actually called by that name. "It is pointless," van Groningen wrote, "to settle on a definition in advance and then apply it to the texts in such a way as to accept some [as authentic specimens] and reject others. Our task is to conform to the rules, or rather to the customs, of the ancients."[2] Had van Groningen adhered unswervingly to the methodological principles enunciated at the outset of his study, he would have largely obviated the need for the present continuation of it. But unfortunately, after surveying all the works or fragments labeled "bucolic" by ancient authorities and extracting from them some rough and ready criteria which might have been used to distinguish the genuinely bucolic poems within the Theocritean corpus, van Groningen decided to exclude from his investigation (though not without some misgivings) Idylls 2, 12–18, 22–24, and 26, as well as all the epigrams except nos. 2–6, on the fatal grounds that these poems do not possess the requisite minimum of pastoral, or even rustic, elements.[3] The following paragraphs will renew van Groningen's experiment, in a sense, by complying more fully with his prohibition against

1. Cf. Effe (1978), 49.
2. van Groningen (1958), 293–94.
3. Ibid., 300–01.

selecting textual evidence according to some prior supposition and by attempting to refine his methodology.

The case of Idyll 13 (identified as bucolic only in a scholion on Apollonius, as we have seen) should alert us to the possibility that other works of Theocritus might have qualified as bucolic in antiquity without being so named in the surviving testimonia. Indeed, the very paucity of such explicit testimonia must weaken the credibility of any hypothesis about the meaning of *bucolic* based too rigidly on them alone. As it was argued in the preceding chapter, the lack of appropriate designations in the ancient bibliographical tradition for many of the non-pastoral Idylls, together with Virgil's imitation of Idylls 2, 24, and (conceivably) 18 in his own *Bucolics,* suggests that more of Theocritus' poetry was actually deemed bucolic than the few outright assertions of ancient authorities about the status of individual poems might lead us to believe. Nonetheless, although the *Bucolics* of Theocritus have the only secure claim on his authorship in the *Suda* and are closely associated with his name in other ancient sources, it would be wrong to suppose that everything Theocritus wrote was considered bucolic in antiquity.[4] Athenaeus cites a passage of more than five lines from a poem by Theocritus which bore the title of *Berenice* (7.284a: ἡ ἐπιγραφομένη Βερενίκη) and is otherwise unknown. Furthermore, if *bucolic* was correctly construed in my introduction to be a technical designation for a kind of poetry rather than a merely descriptive term, it is unlikely to have been applied indiscriminately to the lyrics, epigrams, and hexameter poems of Theocritus, inasmuch as these categories were strictly differentiated according to the highly formalistic system of literary classification current in the Hellenistic and Roman periods.

Bucolic poetry, then, cannot be presumed to have originated within more than one of the three generic classes represented among the surviving compositions of Theocritus. Only the hexameter poems contain explicit declarations of bucolic identity.[5] The epigrams ascribed to Theocritus, some of which are doubtless authentic, are distinguished from the hexameter corpus by their meters, by their magnitude (or lack of it), and by their obvious relation to an independent, clearly recognizable poetic tradition.

---

4. Gallavotti's belief (truly a counsel of despair) that *bucolic* signified to Artemidorus of Tarsus and his generation any poem by a bucolic poet can be refuted by a survey of the evidence bearing on the formal classification of bucolic poetry in antiquity (see part IV, chapter 10). Gallavotti's opinion is discussed in a general commentary on the problem by Van Sickle (1976), 31–33.

5. Although the Second Epigram of Theocritus pictures Daphnis καλᾷ σύριγγι μελισδ-ων/βουκολικοὺς ὕμνους ("warbling bucolic hymns on his pretty syrinx"), it in no way claims to be a bucolic poem itself—and the reference to "hymns" may even suggest hexameter poetry.

They constitute a separate generic group within the Theocritean collection. A similar case can be made for Idylls 28–31, composed in lyric meters and in a version of the Aeolic dialect, which therefore deviate from the metrical and linguistic norms exhibited by the self-proclaimed bucolic Idylls. Moreover, the meters and dialect of Idylls 28–31 identify them as belonging to the melic genre of poetry, and to an archaizing conception of it at that. The relative dialectal uniformity displayed by this group[6] as well as the thematic cohesiveness of the last three argues for their separate and unique status— and for their isolation from the remainder of the Idylls.[7] Hence the ancient division of Theocritus' poetry into Bucolics, Lyrics, Epigrams, and sundry other categories.

If dialect constitutes a second criterion (in addition to meter) which can be used to segregate the melic poems from other works of Theocritus, might it not also serve to distinguish the bucolic compositions within the larger collection of the hexameter Idylls? Scholars have long recognized the significance of dialect as the most important of the stylistic devices available to ancient Greek writers for generic labeling (in prose as well as in verse).[8] Theocritus' elaborate attention to matters of dialect has evoked comment from students of his art from antiquity to the present day; recent research has shown him to be conscious and deliberate, if not always easy to interpret at this remove in time.[9] Nevertheless, a close study of Theocritus' linguistic practice demonstrates that his use of dialect is not sufficiently unambiguous to permit making divisions among the hexameter Idylls on the basis of it alone. Because this conclusion contradicts an important and venerable tendency in Theocritean criticism, it is worth reviewing the interpretative tradition which associates bucolic poetry with a specific dialect.

As it happens, all the Idylls of Theocritus explicitly characterized by their speakers as bucolic are composed in versions of the Doric dialect. Such

6. Fabiano (1971), 533n.

7. West (1967); on the correspondences between Idyll 28 and the epigram form, see the views of Wilamowitz (cited by Stark [1963], 371) and Rossi (1971a), 85.

8. That matters of dialectal variation in Greek poetry must be referred to the stylistic considerations involved in generic labeling—rather than, say, to the local origin of the poet—was established systematically for the first time in 1852 by H. L. Ahrens, "Ueber die Mischung der Dialekte in der griechischen Lyrik," *Kleine Schriften*, I (Hanover, 1891), 181: "Der Grund liegt . . . in dem Umstande, . . . dass mit den Klängen bestimmter Dialekte sich die Eindrücke ihrer eigentümlichen Dichtungsweisen für jedes hellenische Ohr untrennbar verbanden und selbst durch ein leises Anschlagen der Saiten eines jedes Dialektes sympathetisch erweckt werden konnten" (cited by Rossi [1971a], 87, n. 2).

9. Di Benedetto (1956), 49, points out several examples of Theocritus' conscious manipulation of details of dialect and glossography in Idylls 12.13–14 (but see now Gallavotti [1978]), 15.87–93 and 18.48; cf. also 2.156. The major study of Theocritus' language is C. Gallavotti, *Lingua, tecnica e poesia negli idilli di Teocrito* (Rome, 1952); for a good general introduction to the linguistic variety of the Idylls, see Dover (1971), xxvii–xlv.

explicit declarations occur in Idyll 1, where the unnamed goatherd compliments Thyrsis on his accomplished mastery of bucolic song (20: τᾶς βουκολικᾶς ἐπὶ τὸ πλέον ἵκεο μοίσας), and Thyrsis' ode identifies itself as a *boukolika aoida* in each one of its famous refrains. In Idyll 5 Lacon calls the proposed singing match bucolic in his invitation to Comatas (44: ἀλλὰ γὰρ ἔρφ', ὧδ' ἔρπε, καὶ ὕστατα βουκολιαξῇ); after some further wrangling, Lacon repeats the invitation in similar terms at line 60 (αὐτόθε μοι ποτερισδε καὶ αὐτόθε βουκολιάσδευ) and explains the contest to Morson as follows: ἄμμες γὰρ ἐρίσδομες, ὅστις ἀρείων/βουκολιαστάς ἐστι ("we contend over who is the better bucoliast" [67–68]). The usage of Idyll 7 established that *boukoliasdesthai* is the technical term for the activity of creating bucolic poetry (only in later antiquity, when such words as *boukoliasmos* and *boukolismos* first appear, is it construed to mean "hold a rustic competition" or "hold a song contest among herdsmen");[10] the use of that verb in Idyll 7 marks the exchange of poems between Lycidas and Simichidas as bucolic— if not the entire Idyll as well. The same verb is featured at the opening of the Ninth Idyll (1: Βουκολιάζεο, Δάφνι) and is repeated at line 5 (ἐμὶν δὲ τὺ βουκολιάζευ), while the poem's close is signaled by an invocation of the Bucolic Muses (28: Βουκολικαὶ Μοῖσαι, μάλα χαίρετε).[11] This list is not exhaustive; there are many other mentions of *boukoloi* and *boutai* which can perhaps be understood programmatically, and it might be perverse to overlook the beginning of Idyll 8:

Δάφνιδι τῷ χαρίεντι συνάντετο βουκολέοντι
μῆλα νέμων, ὡς φαντί, κατ' ὤρεα μακρὰ Μενάλκας.

[1–2]

Menalcas, so they say, while pasturing his flocks in the high mountains, met the charming Daphnis tending cattle [*boukoleonti*].

especially since these lines appear to glance at Simichidas' boast to Lycidas in Idyll 7.91–93:

πολλὰ μὲν ἄλλα
Νύμφαι κἠμὲ δίδαξαν ἀν' ὤρεα βουκολέοντα
ἐσθλά. . . .

The Nymphs taught me, too, many other noble things while I was tending cattle [or wandering][12] on the mountains. . . .

---

10. Cf. Dover (1971), lv. That such an understanding of *boukoliasdesthai* does not date to an earlier period is demonstrated by the passage from Idyll 8.31–32, quoted below, in which the poet feels compelled to specify that the songs are not only bucolic but also amoebean.

11. The inclusion of Idylls 8 and 9 in this survey does not imply any opinion about their authorship or their trustworthiness as exemplars of bucolic poetry. For an imaginative discussion of the closure of Idyll 9 and its conceivably "generic" implications, see Van Sickle (1976), 26–27, 32.

12. On the deliberate ambiguities surrounding the meaning of *boukoleonta* in this passage, see Giangrande (1968), 509–11.

The programmatic message in the opening lines of Idyll 8 becomes explicit when the narrator of the poem introduces the singing contest between Daphnis and Menalcas:

εἶτα δ' ἀμοιβαίαν ὑπελάμβανε Δάφνις ἀοιδάν
βουκολικάν· οὕτω δὲ Μενάλκας ἄρξατο πρᾶτος.

[31–32]

Then Daphnis took up the alternating [amoibaian] bucolic song, and Menalcas was the first to begin.

All these passages, and many other more subtle ones no doubt, served to identify portions or totalities of Idylls 1, 5, 7, 8, and 9 as bucolic—or, in the case of the spurious poems, were intended by their authors to do so. In style and subject, these bucolic works closely resemble Idylls 3, 4, 6, 10, and 11. To an inexperienced or negligent eye, moreover, Idylls 1 and 3–11 appear to be composed alike in the Doric dialect. It seems reasonable to conclude that Theocritus used the Doric dialect as a stylistic device to distinguish his bucolic compositions from the rest of his poetry; such a conclusion has indeed been widely made by modern scholars. The inference appears to be corroborated by the observation that all ten of the foregoing Idylls are imitated by Virgil and can be assimilated to post-Virgilian notions of pastoral poetry.[13]

Let us dispose of the most obvious fallacies first. Virgil, as we have seen, also imitated the non-pastoral Idylls 2 and 24. Furthermore, the "Doric corpus" of Theocritus, however loosely defined, is not in any case coextensive with the canonical bucolic (that is, pastoral) corpus: it includes not only Idylls 1 and 3–11, but also Idylls 2, 14, 15, 18–21, 23, 27, and probably 26.[14] More important, the traditional inventory of bucolic poems postulates a greater degree of linguistic uniformity among them than actually exists.

As Doric is no strictly local dialect, the Doric element alone is already so differentiated that it makes up an unlimited reserve of expression: from common-Doric forms, which may be occasionally endowed with the dignity of choral-lyric tradition, to strictly local and provincial Doric forms. In the idylls where the Doric element prevails phonetic surprises follow one another without any apparent rule; furthermore the plight of the manuscripts is such as to make it impossible for editors to restore the original dialectal form.[15]

If certain stylometric divisions can be made among those poems of Theocritus in which "the Doric element prevails," the results of modern re-

---

13. Cf. Servius' famous remark: "sane sciendum, VII. eclogas esse meras rusticas, quas Theocritus X. habet" (p. 3.20–21 Thilo)—"Virgil wrote only seven pure and uncontaminated pastorals, whereas Theocritus wrote ten."

14. I refer to Gow (1952), I, lxxii, for the conventional list of Theocritus' Doric Idylls. Di Benedetto (1956), 48n., has questioned the authenticity of the Doric forms in Idyll 26.

15. Fabiano (1971), 529, citing numerous examples; see also Dover (1971), xxxviii–xlii.

search into the matter, far from upholding the traditional canon, utterly prohibit the distinction between the pastoral and non-pastoral Idylls or between Idylls 1 and 3–11 and the other so-called Doric poems. Rather, the analysis of Vincenzo Di Benedetto divides the Doric Idylls into two subgroups according to the quantity of guaranteed Homeric forms contained in them, and his division clearly cuts across thematic boundaries (as they have been traditionally understood, at any rate). Ranking the Idylls in order of the increasing frequency of Homeric forms, Di Benedetto lists them as follows: 11, 15, 10, 18, 5, 14, 3, 1, 4, 2, 6, 7. He observes that Idylls 11, 15, 10, 18, 14, and 5 lack both the quantity and the variety of Homeric forms exhibited by the other so-called Doric poems. Di Benedetto's metrical analysis substantially confirms his linguistic subdivision of the Doric Idylls; arranged according to their increasing conformity to Callimachean norms of prosody, they fall into the order: 11, 15, 18, 10, 14, 5, 3, 2, 7, 1, 6, 4.[16] Di Benedetto's results agree with the conclusion of Gianfranco Fabiano, who asserts:

Although the varying convention of dialect shifts from an artificial Doric absolutely devoid of uniformity in the Bucolic Idylls, where the Doric coloring varies strongly in degrees according to the character of each idyll, and in the Urban Mimes (including also *Idylls* 18 and 26) . . . to a learned attempt to reproduce Sappho's and Alcaeus' Aeolic in *Idylls* 28, 29, 30 and 31, Theocritus' language, no matter what the dialect, is almost always made dynamic in a series of oppositions between Homerisms and rough Doric forms, high artificiality and colloquialisms, realism in some details and refusal of a consistent realistic poetics, personal tone and literary stimuli.[17]

The language of Theocritus is consistent in its inconsistency throughout the Idylls; it serves to unify, rather than to distinguish, pastoral and urban, bucolic and epic, and Doric and non-Doric works.

An interesting by-product of Di Benedetto's analysis is the observation that whereas linguistic and metrical developments seem to correspond in the majority of so-called Doric poems, they are sharply at odds in the case of Idylls 8 and 9. The style of Idylls 8 and 9 represents an amalgam of different elements which the authors of these poems considered typical of Theocritus but which they combined through free variation of his usual practice (witness the introduction of a passage in elegiac distichs into Idyll

16. Di Benedetto (1956), 55–58.
17. Fabiano (1971), 533; cf. the remarks of J. A. Hartung, more than a century ago: "Theocritus has not chosen a popular dialect, his language is the Homeric which prevails in the epic and lyric poetry of Greece, only with a somewhat stronger admixture of Dorisms than is found in Pindar; this Doric colouring varies in degree according to the character of each idyll" (quoted by Cholmeley [1919], 36). Kroll (1924), 204, remarks on the contamination of dialects in Theocritus but persists in regarding the use of Doric as proper to bucolic poetry.

8.33–60, for example).[18] This suggests that the critical reinterpretation of bucolic poetry had already begun in the generations immediately following Theocritus. Van Sickle, who has done more than anyone else to establish and investigate the post-Theocritean evolution of bucolic concepts, points to the Eighth Idyll as the start of the process of literary and critical revaluation, a process continuing with the composition of Idyll 9 and with the later bucolic collection and systematization of Artemidorus of Tarsus (whose famous prefatory epigram recalls the language of the closure of the Ninth Idyll). Although no major reorientation seems to have taken place before Virgil, the evolution of bucolic concepts proceeded thereafter at an accelerated pace. "From the actual texts . . . ctitics abstract conceptions of genre according to the tastes, interests, received and new ideas—intellectual currency of their own time. Abstracted, then, and cast in simple and intelligible form, they begin a tralatitious life in ambivalent, quasi independent relation to their texts of origin. . . . [T]he conception of bucolic genre, too, has a history, developing in distinct stages, progressively incorporating the ideas of contemporary criticism and in the process gradually cutting itself off from the texts where it began."[19] The history of this process (as it is reflected in the scholiastic tradition) still remains to be traced, but the methodological ramifications of positing a changing or developing concept of bucolic poetry in the ancient world after Theocritus are momentous. The meaning of *bucolic,* as it appears in the scholia and in other ancient sources, can no longer be considered stable or unequivocal. What we confront in the conspectus of ancient opinions is not a consistent, reliable, and authoritative tradition based on a correct (and now, unfortunately, lost) understanding of Theocritean poetics, but rather a gradual accretion of speculation and hypothesis (especially after Virgil's influential popularization of bucolic poetry) designed to explain something that was already mystifying to ancient scholars.[20] The widespread confusion in antiquity about the nature of bucolic poetry becomes all the more understandable if Theocritus, as it has been conjectured, did not in fact collect, arrange, and publish his own works.[21] Classical scholars are naturally reluctant to surrender the few sources of information available from the ancient world that bear on bucolic poetry. But although much of the ancient testimony must now be consid-

18. Di Benedetto (1956), 58–59; cf. Rossi (1971b); Van Sickle, "The Structure of [Theocr.] VIII," *Museum Criticum,* 8/9 (1973–74), 200–01; *contra,* H. White, "On the Structure of Theocritus' Idyll VIII," *MPhL,* 4 (1981), 181–90.

19. Van Sickle (1976), 18; cf. 25–28, 31–34.

20. Cf. Van Sickle (1975), 49; Schmidt (1972), 16–17, argues for the contrary view, "that no evolution of the pastoral genre itself actually occurred in antiquity." Schmidt, however, regards Virgil as the norm of ancient bucolic poetry.

21. Gow (1952), I, lix–lxii, discusses the evidence.

ered suspect, the new interpretation holds out the possibility of distinguishing those scholiastic comments which are pure expressions of contemporary critical tastes and attitudes from those belonging to a dissident—and so, perhaps, more ancient and authentic—tradition.

The evolving conception of bucolic poetry in the ancient world can be illustrated by a survey of the differing constructions placed upon Theocritus' linguistic practice by his successors and commentators. The earliest post-Theocritean evidence indicates that the multitude of Doric forms in the Idylls was initially mistaken for a consequence of the poet's native origin. Such, at least, appears to have been the view of whoever wrote the *Lament for Bion,* for the epithets "Dorian" and "Doric" are liberally used (lines 1, 12, 18, 96, 122)—interchangeably, it appears, with "Sicilian" and "Syracusan"—as synonyms for *bucolic.* Particularly striking is the following passage:

> ὅττι Βίων τέθνακεν ὁ βουκόλος, ὅττι σὺν αὐτῷ
> καὶ τὸ μέλος τέθνακε καὶ ὤλετο Δωρὶς ἀοιδά.
>
> [11–12]

Bion the cowherd has died; with him poetry has died as well, and Doric song has perished.

The epithet "Doric" serves to localize the source of bucolic poetry; it is as much an ethnic as a linguistic term. Nevertheless, it is likely that the diction and imagery of the *Lament,* to say nothing of its own language, had the effect of associating bucolic poetry with the Doric dialect.

In later antiquity, when bucolic poetry came to be seen as the distinctive expression of rustic folk culture[22] or, more important, as a direct

---

22. This notion is implicit in the various scholiastic accounts of the invention of bucolic poetry by herdsmen (as Dover [1971], lix–lx, points out), as well as in the view of Athenaeus (14.619ab), that the genre called *boukoliasmos* is essentially a type of folk song belonging to cowherds (cf. Diomedes, p. 17.10–13 Wendel: "quamquam est et alia opinio, circum pagos et oppida solitos fuisse pastores composito cantu precari pecorum ac frugum hominumque proventum, atque inde in hunc diem manere nomen et ritum bucolicorum"). Donatus (p. 18.10–18 Wendel), followed by Iunius Philargyrius (p. 20.6–11 Wendel), says that some suppose bucolic poetry sacred to various gods of husbandry—from Apollo Nomius to Pan—because they are "id genus numinum principi, quibus placet rusticum carmen" (cf. Servius, p. 21.1–4 Wendel: "alii non Dianae, sed Apollini Nomio consecratum carmen hoc volunt, . . . alii rusticis numinibus a pastoribus dicatum hoc asserunt carmen, ut Pani, Faunis, Nymphis ac Satyris"). And according to Diomedes (p. 16.14–15 Wendel), "bucolica dicuntur poemata secundum carmen pastorale composita" (cf. Isidore of Seville, p. 21.28–30 Wendel: "Bucolicum, id est pastorale carmen, plerique Syracusis primum compositum a pastoribus opinantur"). The doctrine that bucolic poetry derives from folk culture was widely espoused in the nineteenth century and is asserted as fact by Christ (1890), 445–46.

representation of rustic life itself,[23] a new interpretation was placed on Theocritus' use of Doric forms. The commentators of late antiquity combined their "simple mimetic conception" of bucolic poetry, as Van Sickle terms it, with a decreased sensitivity to nuances of linguistic variation to produce the dogma, still current in the nineteenth century,[24] that the bucolic poems of Theocritus possess a uniform, characteristic dialect, a unique blend of Doric which approximates most perfectly of all the available Greek dialects the actual habits and manner of speech of Sicilian (or Coan) herdsmen.[25] The most accessible, though not the most complete, articulation of this doctrine is provided by the commentary on Virgil's *Bucolics* attributed to Probus (pp. 326–27 Hagen):

Bucolica Theocritus facilius videtur fecisse, quoniam Graecis sermo sic videtur divisus, ut Doris dialectos, qua ille scripsit, rustica habeatur. Opportunum fuit ergo ei, qui pastores inferebat, ea lingua disputasse. Vergilio tanto factum opus maius, quanto una lingua loquens sensus rusticos aptare elaboravit sine reprehensione sermonis.

Theocritus, it appears, composed Bucolics more easily than Virgil: for speech is differentiated (stylistically) among the Greeks in such a way that the Doric dialect, in which he wrote, is considered rustic. It was convenient for Theocritus, inasmuch as he was bringing herdsmen onto the scene, to have discoursed in that language. Virgil's achievement is superior to the degree that, while speaking an undivided language, he managed to accommodate rustic sentiments without committing any faults of style.

Byzantine scholarship took a somewhat more sophisticated approach— if the so-called *Anecdoton Estense,* a lengthy and discursive prolegomenon contained in a fifteenth-century manuscript, is a typical specimen. This treatise, which has been ascribed to the authorship of Joannes Tzetzes in the

---

23. Servius: "qualitas autem haec est, scilicet humilis character. . . . in bucolicis humilem pro qualitate negotiorum et personarum: nam personae hic rusticae sunt, simplicitate gaudentes, a quibus nihil altum debet requiri. . . . unde nihil in his urbanum, nihil declamatorium invenitur; sed ex re rustica sunt omnia negotia, comparationes et si qua sunt alia" (pp. 1.16–2.5, 4.11–13 Thilo). Ps.-Probus: "Sunt quaedam propria, heroico carmine sublimia, sed in bucolico humilia, quae apte divisisse Vergilius notatus est. . . . In hoc etiam carmine quosdam versus posuit, qui possint heroico carmini aptari . . . et quoniam intellegebat, sublimius se dixisse, novissimum versum attenuavit, quo rustico sensu carmen aptius fecit" (p. 327.5–23 Hagen). Σ Prol. D (p. 5.2–5 Wendel): εἰς ὅσον δ᾽ οἷόν τέ ἐστι, τὰ τῶν ἀγροίκων ἤθη ἐκμάσσεται αὕτη ἡ ποίησις, τερπνῶς πάνυ τοὺς τῇ ἀγροικίᾳ σκυθρωποὺς κατὰ τὸν βίον χαρακτηρίζουσα (= *Anec. Est.* 3.6 [p. 11.19–20 Wendel]). *Anec. Est.* 3. 6 (p. 11.30–33 Wendel): ἐννοίαις τε γὰρ (τοῦ βουκολικοῦ ποιήματος) ἀνάγκη χρῆσθαι προσηκούσαις ἀγροίκοις. . . . ἄλλως γὰρ ἀσύμφωνος αὐτὸς ἑαυτῷ ἔσται ὁ λόγος. Σ *ad* Hermog. περὶ ἰδεῶν, 2.375: οὕτω δὲ λέγεται (ἡ τομὴ βουκολικὴ) διὰ τὸ ταύτῃ χρήσασθαι τοὺς τὰ βουκολικὰ ποιήσαντας ποιήματα, βουκόλους μιμούμενοι, ὡς ὁ Θεόκριτος (cited by Legrand [1898], 423n.). For a critique of these ancient theories, see Schmidt (1972), 23–25.

24. E. g., Christ (1890), 451; cf. Di Benedetto (1956), 49; Fabiano (1971), 521n.

25. See Σ Prol. F. (pp. 5–6 Wendel); Schmidt (1972), 27–28.

twelfth century,[26] attempts to account for Theocritus' dialect without succumbing either to the simpleminded view that Theocritus wrote in Doric
merely because he was a Dorian or to the mimetic conception of bucolic
poetry; although it succeeds momentarily in rebutting each of these two
critical tendencies, it reverts to them in time of need. More ominously, the
author of the *Anecdoton Estense* shares with ps.-Probus and with the other
commentators of late antiquity the habit of regarding Theocritus' dialect as
a stable, uniform, and undifferentiated system. The essay devoted to dialect
begins auspiciously enough: ὅτι Δωρίδι διαλέκτῳ χρῆται οὐ μόνον, διότι
Συρακούσιος ἦν, οἳ Δωριεῖς ἦσαν, οὐδ' ὅτι διὰ ταύτης μᾶλλον μιμεῖται
τὰς τῶν ἀγροίκων φωνάς—χρῆται γὰρ αὕτη τῷ ᾱ καὶ τῷ ω̄-μέγα τὰ
πολλά, ἃ δὴ παχεῖαν ἀπεργάζεται τὴν φωνὴν ἅτε προφερόμενα τοῦ στό-
ματος ὅτι μάλιστα ἠνεῳγμένου, τοιαύτη δὲ καὶ ἡ τῶν ἀγροίκων φωνή
(these two explanations, then, were the ones currently accepted by Byzantine scholars when the treatise was composed)—, ἀλλ' ὅτι ἢ ἂν ἄλλῃ παρὰ
ταύτην καὶ τὴν Αἰολίδα ἐχρήσατο, ἢ λέξεσιν ὑψηλαῖς ἂν ἐχρήσατο ταῖς
ἐννοίαις οὐ προσηκούσαις, ὅπερ τῶν ἀτόπων ἐστίν, ἢ πάντῃ
ἀφελέστατον ἂν ἐπεποιήκει τὸν λόγον καὶ ἀγροῖκον αὐτόχρημα (p.
12.4–13 Wendel). In other words, Theocritus did not write in Doric merely
because he happened to be Syracusan, as ps.-Probus had implied, or because
the Doric dialect approximated the sound of rustic speech, but because if he
had employed any other dialect (with the exception of Aeolic), he would
either have been forced to use a high-flown diction and thereby to violate
the decorum called for by realistic treatment of a lowly subject or he would
have risked going to the other extreme and making his language entirely
simple and vulgar. The *Anecdoton* takes no cognizance whatever of the
variation in Theocritus' diction—of the frequent epicisms or the intermin-
gling of so-called *lexeis hypsēlai* with colloquialisms. The influence of the
mimetic conception of bucolic poetry continues to be felt.

The Doric dialect, our anonymous critic goes on to say, has the advantage of preserving a fresh and untrite diction while harmonizing gracefully
with the humble design of bucolic poetry: ἡ δὲ Δωρὶς διάλεκτος τῷ μὴ
κατημαξευμένας ἔχειν τὰς λέξεις ὁμοῦ τε μιμεῖται εἰς ἄκρον ⟨ἀγροίκων
ὁμιλίας⟩ ἐννοίαις χρωμένη χθαμαλαῖς καὶ ἡδονὴν οὐκ ὀλίγην καὶ τέρψιν
ἀγροικίας ὁμοῦ καὶ ποιητικῆς ἐμμελείας μεστὴν παρέχει τοῖς ἀκροαταῖς
(p. 12.14–18 Wendel). This statement anticipates more nearly than anything
else to be found in the scholia the recent view that Theocritus' language
represents an attempt to *donner un sens plus pur aux mots de la tribu*—to avoid
the process of linguistic leveling associated with the spread of *koinē* Greek in

26. P. xxii Wendel.

the third century B.C. and to tap potential sources of fresh tonality and color available in various dialects and in everyday speech.[27] But just as the author of the *Anecdoton,* in claiming that the Doric dialect imitates rustic intercourse, seems to have retreated from his original statement that Theocritus did not choose it merely because it sounds like rustic speech, so he now abandons his other position and explains that Theocritus preferred Doric to Aeolic because of his native origin: χρῆται δ' ἔσθ' ὅτε καὶ Αἰολίδι, σπανίως γε μὴν διὰ τὸ Δωριέα εἶναι, οὐκ Αἰολέα. καὶ Ἰάδι χρῆται, καὶ ταύτη σπανίως, ἐπειδὰν ἀνεγεῖραι βούληται τὸν νοῦν τῶν ἀκροατῶν (p. 12.18–20 Wendel). The writer ignores the traditional role of dialectal variation in generic labeling, and so does not comment on the concentration of Theocritus' Aeolic forms in the lyric poems; he is obliged instead to invent a number of specious motives for it as well as for the Ionic and occasional Aeolic forms dispersed throughout the Idylls. He then goes on to differentiate between two kinds of Doric and to assert that Theocritus uses the more delicate and humble variety (p. 12.21–25 Wendel). The most explicit articulation of the view that Theocritus wrote in Doric in order to represent rustic speech occurs at the beginning of the *Anecdoton*'s chapter on bucolic poetry: Ὅτι τῶν τὰ βουκολικὰ συγγραψάντων ἴδιον τὸ Δωρίδι χρῆσθαι διαλέκτῳ, τὸ μιμεῖσθαι εἰς ἄκρον ἀγροίκων ὁμιλίας καὶ νομέων χαριέντως αὐτὰς ἐκφράζων (p. 7.8–10 Wendel). The similarities between this statement and the opinion of ps.-Probus already quoted suggests that much of the *Anecdoton* derives from a tradition considerably anterior to Tzetzes. In any case, the association of bucolic poetry with the Doric dialect, however the logic of that connection was explained, eventually became canonical, as the entry for Theocritus in the *Suda* testifies: οὗτος ἔγραψε τὰ καλούμενα Βουκολικὰ ἔπη Δωρίδι διαλέκτῳ ("he wrote the so-called Bucolic hexameter poems in the Doric dialect"). The flatness of this assertion conceals the gradual accretion of scholarly conjecture and speculation underlying it.

That the mimetic conception of bucolic poetry cannot furnish an adequate account of Theocritus' language has been evident since Legrand published his masterly study in 1898. In a chapter of exemplary clarity[28] Legrand, while conceding that Doric had served Epicharmus and Sophron as the vehicle for the realistic portrayal of common people long before Theocritus, maintains that during the period when the three principal Greek dialects were widely spoken, no one in particular was singled out as representative of rustic speech; he also notes that Herodas, a younger contemporary of Theocritus, though himself a Dorian writing for and about Dorians

27. Fabiano (1971), 530–31.
28. Legrand (1898), 234–48.

and doing so in a highly realistic vein, used the Ionic dialect because it was associated with the iambic metrical form in which he had elected to compose. Legrand goes on to observe that Theocritus' Doric resembles the language of Epicharmus, Sophron, Alcman, Pindar, Stesichorus, and choral lyric less than it does the dialect of Callimachus' Doric Hymns, a mixed dialect actually spoken nowhere in the third century and so hardly a replica of popular speech. Aware that even in the so-called Doric Idylls Theocritus is not consistent or uniform in the matter of dialect, that he contaminates his language with "dissident" forms drawn neither from Doric nor from *koinē*, and that the number of manuscript variants complicates the entire issue, Legrand concludes that "the majority of dissident forms are epicisms connected by an ancient tradition with the use of the hexameter. . . . Neither the selection of unchanging dialectal features, nor the varying admixture of Doric elements, nor the distribution of dissident forms was inspired more than minimally by a concern for local color or by a desire to align form and substance." Following up Legrand's arguments, Di Benedetto objects, further, that the "Probian" (that is, mimetic) theory of Theocritean linguistic behavior fails to explain why Idyll 18, an epithalamium, is written in Doric; why the performer in Idyll 15 sings in Doric; and why Theocritus himself uses Doric to introduce the erotic vicissitudes of the Cyclops in Idyll 11. Di Benedetto points out that Theocritus' Doric does not reflect one specific strain of spoken dialect but comprehends different forms not attested contemporaneously in any of the Doric provinces.[29] In short, the tradition affirming the mimetic qualities of Theocritus' language can no longer compel conviction.

But there are other reasons of a more general literary nature for rejecting the mimetic interpretation of Theocritus' use of dialect, and they enable us to grasp how closely the traditional view is in fact related to a specific critical prejudice on the part of ancient commentators (and on the part of modern scholars who share it). "The dialectizing tendency of Hellenistic poets is not intended merely to enroll individual poems in a particular, dialectally-coded literary genre or to elevate poetry above everyday speech, but to exploit the greater possibilities of vocalic variation for the purpose of distancing us from an accustomed sound-pattern and to strive through a new use of sound for a heightened musicality of the verse."[30] As Fabiano remarks, "The adaptation of the language to the theme is not always necessarily a realistic one . . . : it may be a far more eccentric adaptation, occasional or allusive. . . . Theocritus never follows Aristophanes' procedure in

29. Di Benedetto (1956), 50; similar observations are made by Gow (1952), I, lxxii–lxxiii.

30. Stark (1963), 374; cf. Fritzsche-Hiller (1881), 18–21.

reproducing dialects, not even in the Urban Mimes; on the contrary his artistic language always holds fast to its artfulness, so that stylistic variation inside the same idyll does not depend on breaks in the convention of the dialect but on differences of vocabulary, theme and feelings. . . . "[31] The failure of the ancient critics and their more recent epigones to recognize the autonomy of Theocritus' poetic language was what led them to formulate a variety of explanatory theories postulating a mimetic relation between the dialect and subject of the Idylls. The association of the bucolic Idylls, whichever they may be, with the use of Doric forms is, at best, a myth, like the simple mimetic conception of bucolic poetry itself.[32] It is a myth which achieves a certain clarity at the expense of ignoring both the very real linguistic fluctuation in those Idylls explicitly labeled bucolic and the overall uniformity of Theocritus' somewhat idiosyncratic linguistic practice as a whole. The myth cannot account for the thematic diversity among the poems in which "the Doric element prevails" nor can it help in the classification of the Idylls which are not predominantly Doric but are infused, in varying gradations and for no easily discernible reason, with Doric forms (many of them contested in the manuscripts). There is, therefore, no positive linguistic criterion available to the modern scholar, despite the contrary claims of the interpretative tradition, for distinguishing the bucolic from the non-bucolic poems of Theocritus within the larger body of the hexameter Idylls.

Thus, we return to the problem of identifying the bucolic poems more clearly aware of a difference not only in the relative utility of metrical and linguistic evidence but also in the methodologies appropriate to the task of interpreting each kind of evidence. The meter of a poem, after all, cannot easily suffer corruption or editorial emendation unnoticed, especially when the meter in question is as regular and familiar as the dactylic hexameter; moreover, the ancients learned from their experiments with metathesis how metrical rearrangement affects the aesthetic impact of a poem.[33] Since meter is not liable to editorial alteration and since, moreover, we know that meter constituted the basis of the generic classification of poetry in the intellectual community to which Theocritus belonged when he was composing the Idylls, we can confidently separate the hexameter poems from the Idylls in lyric meters and from the epigrams without fear of succumbing to prejudice or of importing into the ancient literary context a modern preconception alien to it. Linguistic evidence, however, can hardly inspire the same feeling

31. Fabiano (1971), 522–23.
32. See Van Sickle (1976), 18, on generic conceptions as "myths."
33. See N. A. Greenberg, "Metathesis as an Instrument in the Criticism of Poetry," *TAPA*, 89 (1958), 262–70.

of certainty. Because variations in the dialect of a poem are often metrically interchangeable, and because the elucidation of a poem's dialect can involve implicit judgments about that poem's generic status, the evidence of our transmitted texts may reflect the editorial interpretation of an author's intentions rather than the original state of the composition. At any point in the transmission of a text, an editor can feel justified in altering a previous editor's readings in the belief that they derive from a false interpretation of a work's generic identity—or, at least, from one at odds with the later editor's own view of the matter. To be sure, whenever the text of a poem exhibits consistent and recognizable linguistic behavior, there is little chance of such corruption taking place on a large scale and almost none at all of its passing unperceived (so long as the text is transmitted in several families of manuscripts). In the case of certain poems of Theocritus, however, a great deal of linguistic tampering has taken place and continues to take place.[34] A few illustrations from the recent textual history of the Idylls are sufficient to establish this point.

In general, modern editors of Theocritus are quick to "restore" Epic and Ionic forms to the texts of disputed poems and slow to "introduce" Doric ones. Gow and Beckby follow Ahrens and Wilamowitz in "purifying" Idylls 12, 22, and 25 of all Doric forms. Idyll 12 is indeed called Ionic in all its preserved tituli and in a scholion attached to it in eight manuscripts;[35] Idyll 22 identifies itself as a hymn in its first line, and Idyll 25 has the form of a fragmentary epic narrative. As such, these poems may naturally be assumed to have been composed in Ionic, not in Doric. And in fact a certain amount of Doricizing corruption has occurred in the process of their transmission. Nonetheless, it is far from evident that the linguistic elements of each poem were ever as internally consistent or homogeneous as the systematic editorial policy of alteration seems to imply.[36] Even in Idyll 12 a certain mixture of dialects may conceivably be authentic—if the play of language in the poem turns (as commentators have traditionally assumed) on the erudite distinction between the Thessalian term ἀίτης and the Laconian εἰσπνηλος, words hardly current in "the common (koinē) Ionic dialect" so insistently attributed to this poem by the scholia.[37]

---

34. See, generally, Dover (1971), xxxi–xxxvii.

35. P. 249 Wendel.

36. See the apparatus of Gallavotti (1955), who reports the dialectal variants more fully than does Gow (1952); what appear to be obvious examples of Doricizing corruption can be found at 12.25 and 12.31. Giangrande (1970a), 76–77, however, maintains that Ionicizing corruption is far more frequent in Hellenistic epic texts and should be more widely suspected. See also Fabiano (1971), 533, n. 39.

37. Di Benedetto (1956), 49; but see Gallavotti (1978). Giangrande (1971), 98, n. 13, argues that most of the Doric forms in Idyll 12 are authentic; see, generally, Giangrande (1970b) for supporting arguments.

When we come to those poems of Theocritus in which different dialects are more promiscuously blended, the literary judgments implicit in modern editorial decisions appear in correspondingly sharper relief. As Gow remarks, these poems confront an editor with "the problem . . . [of] how to choose where the mss are divided between Doric and non-Doric forms. An editor has no means of solving it and can have no confidence that his choices, even if they reproduce what was presented by the archetype of the mss, will be true to the poet's original text." The editor's literary judgments will therefore play a role in the process of selecting among variant dialectal forms. Gow goes on to say that he "followed Wilamowitz rather than introduce Doric forms at the invitation of the papyrus" into Idyll 24, although the papyrus labels the poem "Doric" and contains (however inconsistently) more Doric lections than does the manuscript on which the traditional text is based.[38] How extensively Gow's decision was influenced by an appreciation of the presumptive epical qualities of Idyll 24 can only be conjectured; in the case of Idyll 13, however, his literary prejudice is a matter of record. Like Idyll 24, Idyll 13 bears the heading Δωρίδι ("in Doric") in the Antinoe papyrus codex (dated c. 500), which, though sloppy, is our fullest source for the vulgate text of Theocritus in the ancient world. Titular notations attached to Idyll 13 in six manuscripts and scholia contained in another three are in unanimous agreement with the papyrus on this point.[39] Yet the text of Idyll 13, as it is transmitted by these same manuscripts, displays a multitude of well-attested Epic and Ionic forms and reveals traces of Ionicizing corruption (in 13.20, for example, η has twice been substituted for α in the genitive singular of a feminine noun). Hence, the editor of Idyll 13 is obliged not only to choose between variant dialectal readings but also to weigh the authority of the tituli and scholia against the linguistic evidence of the transmitted text. In his approach to the textual difficulties of Idyll 22, Gow had given credence to the tituli and scholia: while admitting that the three manuscript headings which label Idyll 22 "Ionic" are hardly more authoritative than the chorus of titular notations calling Idyll 13 "Doric"—especially since one annotator, Tr, who vouches for the Ionic dialect of Idyll 22, actually mistakes the Epic diction of Idyll 25 for Doric—Gow nonetheless proceeded to remove all Doric variants from Idyll 22 and, relying on the precedent set by previous modern editors and on the testimony of the scholion on Idyll 12, to change to Ionic even unanimously attested Doric readings supported by the papyrus. But when faced with a similar challenge in the case of Idyll 13, Gow reversed his practice; for at an earlier point Gow had claimed that "*Id.* 13 is not bucolic"

38. Gow (1952), I, lxxvii. See, generally, K. Latte, "Zur Textkritik Theokrits," *Gött-Nach* (1949), 225–32 (cited by Fabiano [1971], 529n.).
39. P. 257 Wendel.

(indeed, it is not pastoral) and had deduced from the Apollonian scholiast's inclusion of Idyll 13 among the *Bucolics* of Theocritus that the term *bucolic* was applied to "poems other than the bucolic Idylls"[40] (indeed, it was not restricted to the pastoral works of Theocritus, as we have seen); in conformity no doubt with this literary judgment about the non-bucolic status of Idyll 13, Gow allowed its well-attested Epic and Ionic forms to remain unmolested, even though the tituli and scholia—the very sources whose authority he had invoked to warrant purifying the text of Idyll 22—are now unanimous in their endorsement of the Doric dialect in Idyll 13. Whereas the consensus of the notations in the papyrus and the manuscripts, then, is not sufficient to persuade Gow to restore Doric readings to the texts of Idylls 24 and 13, the relatively untrustworthy tituli attesting the Ionic dialect of Idyll 22 provide adequate justification for expunging all Doric lections from its text.[41] It is hardly necessary to point out the role played in these editorial decisions by considerations of "genre," more specifically by the tendency to equate bucolic with pastoral poetry and, accordingly, to view Theocritus' language as a mimetic system: predictably, Gow follows ps.-Probus in considering the use of Doric "something of a mannerism or conscious rusticity" in Theocritus' day, and therefore as more appropriate to the composition of pastorals than to the creation of supposed hymns, such as Idyll 22, or miniature epics, such as Idylls 13 and 24.[42]

The foregoing paragraphs have not been intended to imply that the specific editorial decisions discussed in them are wrong, but merely to suggest that recent editors of Theocritus, in their approach to linguistic matters, have at times behaved inconsistently in interpreting textual evidence, because they have been guided by their own critical assessments of a poem's "generic" status—and, more important, that their behavior illustrates a tendency which may be plausibly ascribed to earlier editors in the textual history of the Idylls.[43] After all, it is by no means obvious that the strange mixture of dialects in certain works of Theocritus does not accu-

40. Gow (1952), I, lxi, n. 2.

41. On the tendency of ancient editors and modern scholars to "trivialize" the complex dialect of Hellenistic epic texts by reducing their linguistic richness to a standard brand of Ionic, see Giangrande (1970a), 76–77; (1970b), 266–68; (1971), 98, n. 13; "A Passage of Apollonius," *CQ,* n.s. 21 (1971), 146–48, especially 147, n. 4.

42. Gow (1952), I, lxxiii. Di Benedetto (1956), 48n., notes that Gallavotti, despite the opposing views of Wilamowitz and Legrand, included Idylls 13 and 24 among the Doric poems of Theocritus. Cholmeley (1919), 419, was even more cautious.

43. A fascinating example is discussed by J. Moore-Blunt, "A Theocritus Fragment: *P. Oxy.* 2945 Theocritus Id. XIV, 30–50," *MPhL,* 5 (1981), 68–71: "the 'mistakes' in the text are consistent: they are not mere mechanical errors but are deliberate 'corrections' inserted by the scribe or scribes responsible for the papyrus. Their aim was to produce a consistently Doric text, and this is reflected both in the morphology and in the accentuation" (68–69).

rately express the poet's artistic objectives, for a similar linguistic jumble can be found in the verses of Theocritus' approximate contemporary, Isyllus of Epidaurus, which are preserved on stone and therefore have not suffered from editorial interference in transmission (although the oddities of diction in Isyllus are perhaps more easily explained).[44] In fact the practice of contaminating dialects seems to have been part of a deliberate poetic programme in some literary circles in Hellenistic Alexandria; Callimachus discusses the issue explicitly in his Thirteenth Iambus, although the mutilated state of the papyrus prevents us from grasping the ultimate thrust of his remarks or the view advocated therein:

> ἀλλ' εἴ τι θυμὸν ἢ 'πὶ γαστέρα πγεγϙ.[
> εἶτ' οὖν ἐπ. . . ἀρχαῖον εἴτ' ἀπαι . [,
> τοῦτ' ἐμπ[έ]πλεκται καὶ λαλευσ[. . .] . [
> Ἰαστὶ καὶ Δωριστὶ καὶ τὸ σύμμεικ[τον.
> τ[ε]ῦ μέχρι τολμᾶς; οἱ φίλοι σε δήσ[ουσι,
> κ[ἢ]ν νοῦν ἔχωσιν, ἐγχέουσι τὴν[κρᾶσιν
> ὡς ὑγιείης οὐδὲ τὤνυχι ψαύεις

[fr. 203.15–21 Pfeiffer]

But if something (appeals) to the heart or the stomach, . . . this has been interwoven and they(?) speak . . . Ionic and Doric and a mixture of both. How far dare you go? Your friends will bind you, and, if they have sense, will pour out (a libation to Sanity), as you don't touch sanity even with your finger-tips. . . . [trans. C. A. Trypanis]

The real disadvantage of scholarly intervention, however necessary, into the dialect of Theocritus as it has been transmitted to us is that we are thereby deprived of the possibility of using linguistic evidence in making literary judgments about individual poems. As Legrand sensibly remarks, "It is undoubtedly legitimate, when one is obliged to choose one [dialectal] form among several, to take literary considerations into account; but then, once the text has been established, one must obviously refrain from examining it to discover what principle the poet has followed, lest one discover nothing more than what one has just put there oneself."[45] Legrand's warning has a broader application. Because all the evidence bearing on the dialect of a particular poem, from readings of the transmitted text to editorial superscriptions in the manuscripts and the testimony of the scholia, derives indifferently from post-Theocritean interpretative traditions, it may never be possible to decide which, if any, of these sources best reflects the poet's original composition in a specific instance: to judge the value of the marginalia by the readings of the manuscripts (or vice versa), except in obvious

---

44. Gow (1952), I, lxxvii; cf. Giangrande (1970b).
45. Legrand (1898), 241.

cases, is simply to pit one interpretation of the text against another and to engage in an exercise in circular reasoning.

An awareness of such liability to critical deconstruction should inform new attempts at classification of the hexameter Idylls. The possibility must be faced that all the so-called hard evidence we possess from antiquity that bears on this question—the dialect of an individual poem, the order and grouping of the Idylls in the papyri and manuscripts, editorial remarks, and the interpretations offered by the scholia and commentaries—has been affected in varying degrees by certain critical assumptions about the nature of bucolic poetry which are either known to be false, such as the mimetic conception, or which we do not share, or whose very existence is entirely unsuspected. The proper methodology is exemplified by Van Sickle in a detail of his argument. Van Sickle, after using Di Benedetto's stylometry to uphold the inclusion of Idyll 2 among the bucolic poems of Theocritus, concludes:

> The second idyll . . . [is] closely linked by stylistic features, theme, and language to the bucolic poems, yet usually segregated from them by critics who expect rustic drama in this group rather than a portrayal of urban characters in an urban scene. The critics invoke the simple conception of bucolic as a mimetic genre even here where it now appears that the generic idea would separate in theory what Theocritus in poetic practice joined. . . . [W]e have already seen enough of Theocritus to warn that mime (and realistic imitation) do not begin to exhaust his own generic ideas. . . . If the simple mimetic conception of the genre developed . . . by gradually losing touch with important elements in Theocritean poetics, then its authority can no longer be invoked to separate the second idyll from its stylistic fellows.[46]

In a note, Van Sickle considers the implications, which run contrary to his own view, of the order of Idyll 2 in the arrangement of Theocritus' poems in the papyri; he decides, correctly, that because the grouping of the Idylls in the textual tradition may reflect nothing more than the conceptions of bucolic poetry which prevailed among the scholars of late antiquity and which are now known to be mistaken, such evidence cannot be seriously weighted. Indeed, the exclusion of Idyll 2 from the canonical bucolic corpus (Idylls 1 and 3–11) in the order of the poems in the Antinoe papyrus (written about the same time that the commentary of ps.-Probus was composed) only testifies to the influence on editors, no less than on commentators of the period, of the mimetic conception of bucolic poetry.[47]

---

46. Van Sickle (1976), 24–25, noting the insufficiency of Lawall's arguments from similarities of theme "to change such a long and firmly entrenched belief" about the essential differences between Idyll 2 and the canonical bucolic Idylls.

47. Van Sickle (1976), 39, n. 22. For the probable order of the poems in the Antinoe papyrus, see Gow (1952), I, xlix–l, who comments (lxix) on their essentially haphazard or arbitrary arrangement both in the papyri and in the archetype of the manuscripts; Hunt and Johnson (1930), 3, express a similar opinion.

Despite the difficulty of interpreting it properly, however, the ancient evidence can still be forced to yield a certain amount of information. As noted earlier, a greater understanding of the evolution of critical tastes and attitudes in the ancient world makes it possible to distinguish dissenting views (such as the Apollonian scholiast's inclusion of Idyll 13 among the *Bucolics* of Theocritus) from those of the majority and to understand the purpose behind what seem to us to be obvious and self-evident errors. One may inquire, for example, why the Antinoe papyrus prefixes the notation Δωρίδι ("in Doric") to two poems so linguistically diverse as Idylls 2 and 24. One cannot rule out carelessness or indifference, of course, especially in the case of such a hastily written codex and such an ignorant annotator. But as one examines the titular notations in the papyrus as a whole, a certain pattern begins to emerge. Except for the title of Idyll 30, which the papyrus lists as Παιδι]κα Αιολ[ικα, the only titular notation of dialect in the codex is the single word Δωρίδι. This word is added to the tituli of Idylls 2, 13, 14, 15, 18, 24, and 26 despite the considerable linguistic diversity they display; the canonical bucolic Idylls, however, for all their abundance of Doric forms, lack such annotations.[48] It has been shown that in late antiquity, when the papyrus in question was written, bucolic poetry was associated with a rural subject and with the Doric dialect. Perhaps, then, the annotator of the Antinoe papyrus felt the need to comment on the language of the non-pastoral "Doric" Idylls, almost as if to authenticate and to safeguard their linguistic features. But the Antinoe papyrus is not a scholarly edition—far from it: whatever intent may lie behind its annotations must therefore be ascribed to some earlier editor in the history of our text. A plausible hypothesis presents itself: The notation Δωρίδι in the Antinoe papyrus represents an echo of the genuine tradition—which can be glimpsed in the practice of Virgil and in the scholion on Apollonius 1.1236 but is otherwise lost—that included Idylls 2, 13, 14, 15, 18, 24, and 26 among the bucolic poems of Theocritus. An editor of the Idylls, influenced by this tradition, sought to express his understanding of the identity of the non-pastoral bucolic Idylls by labeling them "Doric," which in his view signified a distinguishing characteristic of bucolic poetry (the language of the *Lament for Bion* helps explain how the association of bucolic poetry with supposedly Doric features might have begun before the mimetic conception had firmly established itself). Such a label was not necessary for the Idylls explicitly identified in their texts as bucolic or for those closely associated with them, but was required for those poems which might otherwise slip away and become separated from the corpus (as indeed they have). The annotations of this editor, later reduced in significance by the passage of

---

48. Unless the conjecture of Hunt and Johnson (1930), 63, is accepted.

time to purely linguistic comments, were copied by the editor of the Antinoe papyrus, even though he did not happen to share the critical attitudes
responsible for producing them or consider Idyll 2 bucolic. This hypothesis
is supported by the stylometric and thematic criteria linking Idyll 2 and, to a
lesser extent, Idyll 13 to Theocritus' bucolic corpus; interpretation of the
other poems is more problematic. At all events, the point is not to prove the
imagined editor's motives correct but to elucidate quite simply what they
were, if possible, or are likely to have been, so that they may be weighed in
the balance with the rest of the evidence for the bucolic identity of Theocritus' poems. In this case the hypothesis, if accepted, would confirm the
methodological procedure followed here of attempting to abstract a historical definition of bucolic poetry from Theocritus' hexameter Idylls as a
whole.

CHAPTER NINE

Three Scenes on an Ivy-Cup

The ambiguous nature of the so-called hard evidence from antiquity forces on the modern literary historian the still more hazardous task of formulating a definition of bucolic poetry from internal evidence and with no firmer basis than sound interpretation of the relevant texts. Despite the uncertainties inherent in such a procedure, a measure of encouragement can be derived from what we know about the self-consciousness of Theocritus and his contemporaries. "[P]oetic practice in Alexandria is itself designed to show the literary interests of the writer. Alexandrian poetry, made by poets conscious of their craft and its traditions, acts as a form of criticism, offering judgments implicit but intelligible to careful readers. Thus even without critical writing from Theocritus, we should be able to reconstruct his literary ideas."[49] The present attempt at reconstruction begins with an examination of the importance of the ivy-cup in Idyll 1 for Theocritean poetics and in particular for the thematic structure of bucolic poetry.[50]

---

49. Van Sickle (1976), 19; cf. Stark (1963), 383: "Theokrit hatte selbst ja . . . nicht theoretisiert, sondern durch seine Kunstwerke unmittelbar dargestellt, wie er sich das Verhältnis zwischen Inhalt und formaler Gestaltung bei den gewählten Themen dachte."

50. Most of the extensive literature surrounding the ivy-cup in Idyll 1 is concerned with its shape and decoration or with the possible connections between Theocritus' description of it and such artifacts of Alexandrian or Hellenistic workmanship as are known or can be reconstructed. The most important studies of the cup itself, aside from those to be found in the major commentaries on Theocritus, are: O. Ribbeck, "Theokriteische Studien," *RhM*, 17 (1862), 543–77, especially 549–51; R. Gädechens, *Der Becher des Ziegenhirten bei Theokrit*, Programm zum 100. Jahrestag des Todes Winckelmanns (Jena, 1868); K. Zacher, "Der Becher des Ziegenhirten bei Theokritos (1, 27ff.)," *NJbb*, 129 (1884), 285–88; S. Rossi, "Ricostruzione di un 'κισσύβιον,'" *Rivista di storia antica*, 4 (1899), 104–17; A. S. F. Gow, "The Cup in the First Idyll of Theocritus," *JHS*, 33 (1913), 207–22; Mastrelli (1948); Dale (1952); Gallavotti (1966); G. Giangrande, "Theocritus 1.32," *Liverpool Classical Monthly*, 1 (1976), 17–18; and W.

Recent critics have called attention to the symmetry and balance which characterize the relation of the dramatic frame of Idyll 1—the conversation between Thyrsis and an unnamed goatherd—to the Daphnis-song which it encloses. Although the ode of Thyrsis is in a sense the showpiece of the poem, it is also set against the long description of the ivy-cup which occupies a large part of the dramatic frame. According to Salvatore Nicosia, "The *ecphrasis* constitutes a counterweight, a pendant to the lengthy song of Thyrsis, and so it makes the structure of the First Idyll conform to that of the other pastoral Idylls which are always divided among the speakers into individual parts."[51] Taking this line of reasoning a step further, Ulrich Ott has strikingly reemphasized the traditional observation that the form of Idyll 1 is that of Theocritus' other poems featuring pastoral competitions—but with one of the contestants missing! All the other customary elements are present in their normal order: encounter of two herdsmen, discussion of their musical/poetic abilities, reciprocal invitations to perform, description of an appropriate setting or locale, discussion of the victor's prize, performance, response of the audience or narrator, award of the prize, and return to the business of herding. But in the First Idyll, an actual exchange of song is prevented (conveniently enough for Theocritus' purpose) by a disparity in the talents of the two herdsmen—one sings, the other plays the syrinx—and by the prohibition against piping at noontime laid upon the goatherd by rustic convention.[52] As Ott concludes, "The First Idyll does not, to be sure, contain a contest, but it does possess the balanced, bi-partite structure featured in Theocritus' pastoral competitions."[53] The result is a sense of unmitigated triumph for Thyrsis and his song. Since Thyrsis' distinction, as enunciated by the goatherd, is to have achieved mastery in the field of bucolic poetry with an ode about Daphnis which, incidentally, proclaims its bucolic identity in each of its refrains, what emerges from his uncontested victory in Idyll 1 is the easy preeminence of bucolic "genre" itself. Everything in the poem conspires to glorify this new achievement: instead of a

---

G. Arnott, "The Theocritus Cup in Liverpool," *QUCC*, 29 (1978), 129–34. Studies of a more general nature which bear, either directly or indirectly, on the cup and its relation to Hellenistic art include: H. Brunn, "Die griechischen Bukoliker und die bildende Kunst," *Sitzungsb. beyer. Akad. Wiss.*, Philos.-philolog. Klasse, 2 (1879), 1–21; Friedländer (1912); Perotta (1923); Webster (1964), especially 160–61; Nicosia (1968); Ott (1969); and N. Himmelmann-Wildschütz, "Lo bucolico en el arte antiguo," *Habis*, 5 (1974), 141–52.

51. Nicosia (1968), 36; the same observation had been made by Couat (1882), 416, and Gallavotti (1966), 421, among others.

52. On the distinction between piping and singing in Theocritus, with its hierarchical implications, see Serrao (1971), 21–28.

53. Ott (1969), 85, 132. Ott's observation was anticipated in varying degrees by Legrand (1898), 407; Friedländer (1912), 13; and by Deubner (1921), 369, citing his two predecessors.

competition between two herdsmen or (in this case) a rivalry between cup and song, there is only a harmonious agreement among all the parts of the poem, united in the central task of unfolding and revealing the poet's literary discovery. But the structure of Idyll 1, with its symmetrical balance of song and dramatic frame, divides the leading roles in this chorus of praise between the ode about Daphnis (the perfect example of bucolic poetry) and the goatherd's description of the ivy-cup (the figure and emblem of the new "genre"). Whether the relation of cup to song is interpreted as one of parallelism, expansion, or contrast,[54] there can be no doubt that Theocritus intended each artifact to be set against the other as complementary illustrations of the bucolic "genre."

Theocritus elaborates the connection between cup and song in several ways. On the most literal level, the cup is offered in exchange for the song, a gift conditional upon satisfactory performance: αἰ δέ κ᾽ ἀείσῃς/ὥς ὅκα . . . ᾇσας ἐρίσδων, / αἶγά τέ τοι δωσῶ διδυματόκον ἐς τρὶς ἀμέλξαι . . . καὶ βαθὺ κισσύβιον (23–27: "if you sing as once . . . you sang in competition, I will give you to milk three times a goat that has borne twins . . . and a deep *kissybion* or ivy-cup"). According to rustic notions of value, then, the song is equivalent to the cup in worth (plus three draughts of goat's milk to round it off). When his condition is seen to be abundantly fulfilled, the goatherd makes over the cup to Thyrsis readily, though not without a just appreciation of its value: ἠνίδε τοι τὸ δέπας· θᾶσαι, φίλος, ὡς καλὸν ὄσδει (149: "Behold! here is the cup. See, friend, how fair it smells"). Second, both cup and song are rustic artifacts. The cup was acquired from a ferryman of Calydna (probably an island off Cos) for the price of a goat and a large cheese of white milk (57–58); a goat, appropriately named *Kissaetha,* is milked into it at the end of Idyll 1 (143–44, 151). We are told that the cup has been freshly chiseled and sealed with beeswax (27–28), so we know it is a wooden vessel; the humble material out of which it is made accords with its origin and circulation in a world of simple people, for whom it is an αἰπολικὸν θάημα (56), something a goatherd can marvel at.[55] The song of Thyrsis derives from an equally humble context: it was composed by a shepherd and was entered in a competition against one Chromis from Libya, whose name and native origin suggest alike a pastoral milieu.[56] Finally,

54. Cf. Ott (1969), 133, 135; Lawall (1967), 30–31. Their disagreement is largely a difference of emphasis.

55. For the elucidation of the text and its meaning, see Gow (1952), II, 13, *ad loc.* For a different view of the cup as alien, imported, "an intruder on this scene" of rusticity, see Lawall (1967), 27; G. B. Miles, "Characterization and the Ideal of Innocence in Theocritus' Idylls," *Ramus,* 6 (1977), 139–64, especially 146–49.

56. On the name of Chromis, see Gow (1952), II, 6, *ad loc.;* in Virgil's Sixth Eclogue Chromis is the name of a shepherd-lad (or faun?) who binds the sleeping Silenus.

both cup and song are "sweet" or "pleasant." The cup is κεκλυσμένον ἁδέι κηρῷ (27): the wax with which it is sealed comes from a honeycomb and smells sweet (cf. line 149, quoted above). Similarly, Thyrsis boasts of his "sweet" voice at the beginning and at the conclusion of his song: Θύρσιδος ἁδέα φωνά (65); καὶ ἐς ὕστερον ἅδιον ᾀσῶ (145). The goatherd concurs:

> πλῆρές τοι μέλιτος τὸ καλὸν στόμα, Θύρσι, γένοιτο,
> πλῆρες δὲ σχαδόνων, καὶ ἀπ᾽ Αἰγίλω ἰσχάδα τρώγοις
> ἁδεῖαν, τέττιγος ἐπεὶ τύγα φέρτερον ᾄδεις.

[146–48]

May your fair mouth be filled with honey, Thyrsis; may it be filled with the honeycomb; and may you munch the sweet dried figs of Aegilus, since you sing better than a cicada.

It has been argued that "sweetness" constitutes a generic attribute of bucolic poetry, in which pleasure is detached from considerations of utility.[57] At all events, cup and song share many properties.

More important, both the cup and the song are in their different ways virtuoso performances, the work of skilled professionals. That is to say, not only are they both masterpieces of craftsmanship, *tours de force,* but they evoke alike responses of enthusiastic yet detached appreciation. Thyrsis concludes his tragic, sentimental account of the sorrows of Daphnis by demanding his appointed reward and making the professional singer's farewell salute to the Muses; the goatherd's reaction to the tale is one of unqualified aesthetic pleasure.[58] Similarly, the scenes on the cup arouse only wonder at the skill of its carving. The sense of personal remoteness and uninvolvement, *dégagement,* which characterizes the spectator's response to a professional performance was well understood by the Greeks; it is a prominent topic in Homer, who seems to dwell on the aesthetic effect of a performance especially in instances when it creates dissonance. The re-

---

57. Schmidt (1972), 27–32; Van Sickle (1975), 54–56; idem (1976), 26. Cf. Koster (1970), 81; Segal (1974b), 6, 14–16; Walker (1980), 131.

58. Cf. Rosenmeyer (1969), 121: "the song is, at its termination, characterized as a performance. The joy that the listeners derive from it is more substantial than any mourning in which they might be encouraged to share. . . . The pleasure that the herdsmen-listeners take in the musical offerings brought by their friends is a portion of the pleasure which the pastoral bower holds as its birthright. Against this background, the grief of a lament is dulled, as is the bravado of the dying hero and the veneration paid to his deified spirit. The simplicity of the pleasance endorses the freedom and the genuine aspirations of the herdsmen; the relaxing beauty of the *otium* mutes the poignancy of the challenge." Rosenmeyer is discussing here not the song of Thyrsis but the songs of Mopsus and Menalcas in Virgil's Fifth Eclogue. The programmatic importance of aesthetic distance in Theocritus is emphasized by Effe (1978), 50–53. I am indebted to Professor Phillip W. Damon, of the University of California at Berkeley, for the analogy between cup and song in terms of "performance."

sponse of Alcinous to Odysseus' tale of woe is instructive. Odysseus had begun:

> σοὶ δ' ἐμὰ κήδεα θυμὸς ἐπετράπετο στονόεντα
> εἴρεσθ', ὄφρ' ἔτι μᾶλλον ὀδυρόμενος στεναχίζω.

[*Od.* 9. 12–13]

But your heart is resolved that I tell you my grievous troubles, so that I may mourn and grieve all the more.

Alcinous refers to Odysseus' adventures in the same terms, but the wandering hero's travails are the Phaeacian king's delight.

> σοὶ δ' ἔπι μὲν μορφὴ ἐπέων, ἔνι δὲ φρένες ἐσθλαί,
> μῦθον δ' ὡς ὅτ' ἀοιδὸς ἐπισταμένως κατέλεξας,
> πάντων Ἀργείων σέο τ' αὐτοῦ κήδεα λυγρά. . . .
> καί κεν ἐς ἠῶ δῖαν ἀνασχοίμην, ὅτε μοι σὺ
> τλαίης ἐν μεγάρῳ τὰ σὰ κήδεα μυθήσασθαι.

[11.367–69, 375–76]

You have the gift of arranging words, but your wits are noble, and you recounted skillfully, as a bard would, the story of all the Argives' baneful troubles and your own. . . . I could hold out even till the bright dawn, if only you would endure to tell the story, here in the palace, of your troubles.

The repetition of κήδεα ("troubles"; see also 9.15), the unusual enjambement of 11.375–76, and the pointed application of τλαίης ("endure") to Odysseus lend vigor and wit to the entire exchange. Alcinous had in any case announced his aesthetic views and philosophy of poetic pleasure earlier when he had inquired of Odysseus (whose identity was still unknown) what cause there might be for weeping at Demodocus' tales of the Trojan War.

> εἰπὲ δ' ὅ τι κλαίεις καὶ ὀδύρεαι ἔνδοθι θυμῷ
> Ἀργείων Δαναῶν ἰδὲ Ἰλίου οἶτον ἀκούων.
> τὸν δὲ θεοὶ μὲν τεῦξαν, ἐπεκλώσαντο δ' ὄλεθρον
> ἀνθρώποις, ἵνα ᾖσι καὶ ἐσσομένοισιν ἀοιδή.

[8.577–80]

Say why you lament and mourn in your heart, hearing the doom of the Greeks and of Ilium. That was the gods' devising—they ordained destruction for the peoples, so that future generations might have the possession of song.

In both instances Odysseus is affected by the matter of the story, personally implicated as he is in its events, whereas Alcinous is moved only by the manner of its recitation and derives nothing but enjoyment from the experience. The unmixed pleasure attendant on hearing a tale which, told in other circumstances, might produce only pain, is a characteristic feature of the aesthetic response to a certain type of literary expression currently called "romance." The passages just quoted from the *Odyssey* illustrate this response admirably. The wanderings of Odysseus, representing the first romantic comedy in Western art, have been a source of unqualified delight to all but the wanderer himself; similarly, it is a distinctive mark of the world of the *Odyssey*—and of Phaeacia in particular—that what still passes for high seriousness in the *Iliad* should be assimilated to romantic comedy in the epic sequel.[59] "Naive romance, being closer to the wish-fulfilment dream, tends to absorb emotion and communicate it internally to the reader. Romance, therefore, is characterized by the acceptance of pity and fear, which in ordinary life relate to pain, as forms of pleasure."[60] The song of Thyrsis is characterized as romantic fiction not only by the kind of aesthetic response which it evokes but also by its selection and treatment of themes.

> The hero of romance moves in a world in which the ordinary laws of nature are slightly suspended. . . . In romance the suspension of natural law and the individualizing of the hero's exploits reduce nature largely to the animal and vegetable world. . . . The hero's death or isolation thus has the effect of a spirit passing out of nature, and evokes a mood best described as elegiac. The elegiac presents a heroism unspoiled by irony. . . . The mode of romantic comedy corresponding to the elegiac is best described as idyllic, and its chief vehicle is the pastoral.[61]

The special and almost indefinable charm of Thyrsis' song, like that of the *Odyssey,* has to do with its blend of what Frye calls "romantic comedy" and "romantic tragedy." Into an idyllic world that cannot be taken seriously Theocritus somehow infuses a note of tragic grandeur and creates a heroism unspoiled by the irony which colors our perception of the interlocutors in the surrounding rustic frame. "Daphnis, indeed, lives in a world where it is possible to be a hero. But this world is no longer quite the poet's own—or the audience's. . . . By a subtle device, it is the very magical unreality of the poetic landscape in the First Idyll that prevails upon us to accept Daphnis' words as straightforward heroic speech, and to take pleasure in them as spontaneous dramatic utterance; for this unreality wins us to itself. The unreality, be it noted, is not that of the exotic and far-away; rather, it is the unreality of happy simplicity. . . . Pastoral might be described as a cover in an age of irony."[62] Precisely the same qualities are

---

59. Cf. C. P. Segal, "The Phaeacians and the Symbolism of Odysseus' Return," *Arion*, 1, no. 4 (1962), 17–64, especially 27–28; on the relation of the two poems, see Redfield (1973); G. Nagy, *The Best of the Achaeans* (Baltimore, 1979), 15–65; on aesthetic distance in Homer generally, see J. Griffin, "The Divine Audience and the Religion of the *Iliad*," *CQ*, n.s. 28 (1978), 1–22. I view the *Odyssey* as a comedy insofar as it represents a story in which there is a reversal of fortune from bad to good and a general predominance of *ēthos* over *pathos:* see part IV, chapter 11.

60. Frye (1957), 37. Because Frye is discussing the peculiar deflection of strong feeling characteristic of romance, there is no question here of "aesthetic distance," which for Frye "is almost a tautology: wherever there is aesthetic apprehension there is emotional and intellectual detachment" (66; cf. Aristotle *Poet.* 1448b8–19; *Rhet.* 1371b4–11).

61. Frye (1957), 33–43; on romance generally, 186–206.

62. Parry (1957), 11–14; cf. Spofford (1969).

shared by the scenes on the ivy-cup. Framed above and below by the winding tendrils of helichryse and vine with grape clusters, the scenes of erotic frustration, struggle, and suspense, which by themselves might create a certain discomfort or (conversely) provoke amused contempt, are isolated and detached from our immediate apprehension by the device of their being carved on a "simple" rustic artifact. Once again an aura of magical unreality is created, only in this case by the convention of *ecphrasis* and by stress on the ornamental artificiality of the floral border in which the scenes are arranged, a series of glimpses into a world of disarming simplicity, yet one sufficiently familiar for us to be able to enter. We are thus presented with a series of romantic moments. Like the Daphnis-song, "what matters about these echoes of the world beyond the pleasance is that they are stilled, frozen into sculptured beauty, hemmed in by the ivy frame that winds around the lip of the cup."[63] Through the double framing of the decorative border and the larger context of the *ecphrasis* as a whole, the scenes on the cup can gain a kind of direct access to our feelings.

Before returning to examine these scenes more closely, we must ascertain that the cup itself, no less than the song, can figure as an emblem for bucolic poetry. First it should be pointed out that the ivy-cup (although its design and decorative patterns can be paralleled in other artifacts actually surviving from the Hellenistic period or otherwise known to us) is essentially a literary article.[64] This much can be gauged from the discussion devoted to the word *kissybion* ("ivy-cup") by Athenaeus (11.476–77) in the course of his alphabetical survey of drinking vessels. The most famous pre-Theocritean literary usage of *kissybion* occurs in the *Odyssey* when Odysseus introduces the Cyclops to the use of wine and persuades him to drink (from one of his own bowls, no doubt):

καὶ τότ᾽ ἐγὼ Κύκλωπα προσηύδων ἄγχι παραστάς,
κισσύβιον μετὰ χερσὶν ἔχων μέλανος οἴνοιο

[9.345–46]

And then I stood close by the Cyclops and addressed him, holding in my hands a *kissybion* of dark wine.

This passage indicated to later scholars that the vessel in question was a capacious one, appropriate for imbibing large quantities; as Athenaeus,

---

63. Rosenmeyer (1969), 91; on the literary tradition of the pastoral cup, 305–06, n. 54. According to Lawall (1967), 27, the decorative frame "marks the boundary between the world of Thyrsis and the goatherd with its action and conversation on the one hand and the timeless, unchanging world of the cup scenes on the other."

64. Ott (1969), 94–95. I derive my information about the ancient sources of the word *kissybion* from Dale (1952), but in surveying the literary antecedents of Theocritus I follow, for the most part, the reasoning of Nicosia (1968), 19–22; similar arguments were advanced earlier by Mastrelli (1948).

commenting on the equation made by Dionysius of Samos between *kymbion* and *kissybion*, remarks, οὐκ ἔστι δὲ μικρὸν τὸ διδόμενον αὐτῷ (τῷ Κύκλωπι) κισσύβιον παρ' Ὁμήρῳ· οὐ γὰρ ἂν τρὶς πιὼν μέγιστος ὢν τὸ σῶμα ταχέως ἂν ὑπὸ τῆς μέθης κατηνέχθη (481e; cf. 477de); earlier in the same discussion Ulpian had speculated, at greater length and in almost identical language, on this very matter: οὔκ ἐστι μικρὸν τὸ παρ' Ὁμήρῳ διδόμενον τῷ Κύκλωπι ὑπ' Ὀδυσσέως κισσύβιον. οὐ γὰρ ἂν τρὶς πιὼν οὕτως κατηνέχθη ὑπὸ μέθης τηλικοῦτος ὤν. ἦν οὖν καὶ τότε μεγάλα ποτήρια, εἰ μὴ αἰτιάσεταί τις τὴν δύναμιν τοῦ οἴνου, ἣν αὐτὸς Ὅμηρος ἐξηγήσατο, ἢ τὸ ἄηθες τῆς πόσεως τοῦ Κύκλωπος, ἐπεὶ τὰ πολλὰ ἐγαλακτοπότει (11.461d: "The *kissybion* given to the Cyclops by Odysseus in Homer is no small vessel. For a creature of such size would not have been so overcome with drunkenness after only three draughts. They must have had great drinking vessels even in those days, unless one is to impute the wine's effect to its potency, which Homer himself explains, or to the Cyclops' being unaccustomed to liquor, since he was mostly used to drinking milk"). Similarly, a scholiast commenting on Theocritus' qualification of the *kissybion* as ἀμφῶες (1.28: "two-handled"), points out: διὰ τούτου δὲ τὸ μέγεθος παριστᾷ ("by this he establishes its magnitude").[65] More important, Homer associated *kissybia* with rustic and uncouth contexts. Although the scene in the Cyclops' cave had perhaps the greatest effect in creating this association for later writers, there are two other passages in the *Odyssey* which mention *kissybia* in connection with the simple life of primitive folk. Both involve the hospitality of Odysseus' swineherd, Eumaeus. In the first, Eumaeus uses a *kissybion* as a mixing bowl in preparing wine for Odysseus and Telemachus:

> ἐν δ' ἄρα κισσυβίῳ κίρνη μελιηδέα οἶνον·
> αὐτὸς δ' ἀντίον ἷζεν Ὀδυσσῆος θείοιο.
>
> [16.52–53]

And then he mixed the honey-sweet wine in a *kissybion*, and himself sat down opposite godlike Odysseus.

The lines seem to recall an earlier scene in which Eumaeus entertains the disguised Odysseus:

> ἐν δ' ἄρα κισσυβίῳ κίρνη μελιηδέα οἶνον,
> αὐτὸς δ' ἀντίον ἷζεν, ἐποτρύνων δὲ προσηύδα.
>
> [14.78–79]

And then he mixed the honey-sweet wine in a *kissybion*, and himself sat down opposite, and addressed him encouragingly.

65. P. 39 Wendel; for the alternate tradition that *kissybia* had only one handle, see the opinion of Philemon, mentioned by Athenaeus (477a), and the pictorial evidence cited by Dale (1952), 130.

After the meal, Eumaeus fills his own wine-cup—obviously not a *kissybion* (Eumaeus, after all, is not a Cyclops)—and gives it to his guest.

καί οἱ πλησάμενος δῶκε σκύφος, ᾧ περ ἔπινεν,
οἴνου ἐνίπλειον.

[14.112–13]

And then he filled the very cup from which he drank and gave it to him brimful of wine.

This, the only use of *scyphus* in Homer, was interpreted in a treatise "On Nestor's Cup" by Asclepiades of Myrlea, one of the earliest and most authoritative commentators on Theocritus,[66] to distinguish the sort of people who drink from a *kissybion,* such as Polyphemus, or a *scyphus,* such as Eumaeus, from city dwellers (Ath. 477bc; cf. 498f.). Asclepiades' example illustrates the attention paid by ancient students of Theocritus—and no doubt by Theocritus himself—to the literary contexts surrounding the term *kissybion* in the earlier poetic tradition.[67] In the *Odyssey,* then, a *kissybion* seems to be a large bowl, used by rustics, probably made of wood—in short, a humble implement belonging to a primitive economy.

Later Greek writers, conscious as they are of the language of these episodes in Homer, seem embarrassed by the "outlandish" word *kissybion* and avoid it, substituting a variety of periphrases. Its association with the world of humble people may also explain why the word is not attested in fifth-century tragedy.[68] But such an association commended the word to Hellenistic poets, and when *kissybion* reappears after a lapse of many centuries in the *Aetia* of Callimachus, its original meaning, whatever it was, has been lost—or at least has been subordinated to other semantic considerations. Like many other technical words for items of household equipment in Homer which survived in epic or elegiac diction but remained quite foreign to common Attic usage, the term *kissybion* continued to exert a certain lexical pressure on the minds and vocabularies of poets, while ceasing to correspond to any specific, concrete object.[69] Hence, Callimachus is not interested in the physical shape, size, or function of the cup—Athenaeus (477cd) taxes him with this neglect—but rather is eager to exploit its connotations of humility and unpretentiousness. Speaking of the man with whom he shared a couch at a feast given by his Athenian friend Pollis, Callimachus says:

66. On Asclepiades, see Gow (1952), I, lxxxii; Pfeiffer (1968), 272–73.

67. The drunken Cyclops attracted the attention of Theocritus in another passage (7.151–53).

68. Dale (1952), 131. Cf. Epicharmus *Cyclops,* fr. 83 Kaibel; Euripides *Cyclops* 388–91; *Alcestis* 756–57; *Andromeda,* fr. 146N² (according to Athenaeus 476f–477a, Neoptolemus of Parium recognized these words as a periphrasis for *kissybion*); Timotheus, *Cyclops* (Ath. 465c).

69. Nicosia (1968), 21–22.

ἦν δὲ γενέθλην
Ἴκιος, ᾧ ξυνὴν εἶχον ἐγὼ κλισίην
οὐκ ἐπιτάξ, ἀλλ᾽ αἶνος Ὁμηρικός, αἰὲν ὁμοῖον
ὡς θεός, οὐ ψευδής, ἐς τὸν ὁμοῖον ἄγει.
καὶ γὰρ ὁ Θρηϊκίην μὲν ἀπέστυγε χανδὸν ἄμυστιν
οἰνοποτεῖν, ὀλίγῳ δ᾽ ἥδετο κισσυβίῳ

[fr. 178.7–12 Pfeiffer]

He was an Ician by birth, and I shared a couch with him—not by design, but the saying of Homer is not false that God ever brings like to like [Od. 17.218]. For he too hated the greedy Thracian draught of wine, and liked a small cup [kissybion]. [trans. Trypanis]

If Callimachus implies, contrary to the traditional interpretation, that kissybion refers to a small vessel, it is because he is attempting to focus attention entirely on one set of its literary associations, namely, those that can be made to accord with the value terms of his poetic ideology. In stating his preference for moderate drink, Callimachus uses language that recalls the familiar polaritites of his polemical literary manifestos. The kissybion figures not only smallness of quantity but fineness of quality: the burden of signification is borne by the word itself, with its ancient lineage (Homeric descent), its obscurity and arcane preciosity, along with connotations of rusticity and even frivolity. Like the ὀλίγη λιβάς ("small trickle of water") transported by bees from the holy fountain, which Callimachus contrasts with the filth of the great Assyrian river in his Hymn to Apollo (108–12), the ὀλίγον κισσύβιον ("small kissybion") is opposed to the vulgar superfluity of the Thracian draught and so becomes part of the vocabulary for expressing Callimachean norms of good taste. Its literary origin in the Odyssey, and in what came to be viewed as the most comic and anti-heroic episodes of the poem, makes the word kissybion congenial to Callimachus, accustomed as he was to appeal for literary precedent to the earliest examples of "fineness" (leptotēs) in the epic genre itself: the catalogues and ecphrases in the Iliad, the scenes of humble folk and comedy of manners in the Odyssey, the learned and didactic poetry of Hesiod. The importance of these signals of generic ancestry is attested by the scholiast on Theocritus 1.27, who ascribes the relevant verse of the Aetia passage to Hesiod[70] (Callimachus is correctly cited by Athenaeus, 477c).

Similarly, Theocritus' use of kissybion in Idyll 1 serves to indicate the ultimate source of his inspiration as well as the nature and dimensions of his poetic ideals. Like Callimachus, he intends his choice of diction to glance at Homer, particularly at the Odyssey (which corresponds so closely to many of the Idylls in theme and technique), because he is engaged in precisely the

70. P. 38 Wendel.

same kind of poetic self-definition and is appealing to analogous standards of good taste. Nonetheless, although Theocritus cites the same literary precedents as Callimachus and does so for an equally programmatic purpose, he puts the identical Homeric material to a different use, developing it in such a way as to bring out a set of aesthetic values distinct from the antithetical terms of Callimachean poetics. Specifically, Theocritus expands upon the humble and comic associations acquired by the ivy-cup in Homer, associations subsequently exploited by later writers. In his *Cyclops,* for example, Euripides—who seems to have believed that *kissybion* meant a vessel made of ivy-wood—has Odysseus relate his encounter with Polyphemus as follows:

κρατῆρα δ' ἐξέπλησεν ὡς δεκάμφορον,
μόσχους ἀμέλξας, λευκὸν εἰσχέας γάλα.
σκύφος τε κισσοῦ παρέθετ' εἰς εὖρος τριῶν
πήχεων, βάθος δὲ τεσσάρων ἐφαίνετο.

[388–91]

He filled up a mixing bowl that held about ten amphorae by milking his heifers and pouring their white milk into it, and he set out a *scyphus* of ivy, three cubits wide and four deep.

Note that the article in question can be employed as a milk-cup here no less than in the First Idyll. The rustic associations of the ivy-bowl stand out even more clearly in the passage quoted by Athenaeus from the *Andromeda* of Euripides, where the same etymology of the word *kissybion* is assumed:

πᾶς δὲ ποιμένων ἔρρει λεώς,
ὁ μὲν γάλακτος κίσσινον φέρων σκύφος
πόνων ἀναψυκτῆρ', ὁ δ' ἀμπέλων γάνος. . . .

[477a = fr. 146N²]

All the shepherd folk came running out, one man carrying an ivy-wood *scyphus* of milk that gives refreshment from labors, another the gladdening fruit of the vine. . . .

Once again, the rustic qualities of the vessel are highlighted by its use as a milk container, for milk is the countryman's beverage *par excellence.* In Lucian's comic dialogue between Zeus and Ganymede the uncouth and rather stupid peasant lad, mistaking his function in heaven, tells Zeus uncomprehendingly, οἶδα γὰρ ὡς χρὴ ἐγχέαι τὸ γάλα καὶ ἀναδοῦναι τὸ κισσύβιον—"I know how one ought to pour out milk and pass the *kissybion*" (*D.D.* 4.211; a scholiast on Theocritus 1.27 glosses *kissybion* as γαλακτοδόχον ἀγγεῖον, a vessel for holding milk, among other things).[71] Eu-

---

71. Ibid., 39; the word κισσοῦβι may mean a "milking-pail" in parts of modern Greece, according to Fritzsche-Hiller (1881), 43, *ad* Idyll 1.27–28; Dale (1952), 130.

ripides turns these associations of the ivy-cup to good effect in the *Alcestis,* where he describes Heracles, whom he treats in a comic fashion, ποτῆρα δ' ἐν χείρεσσι κίσσινον λαβών (756: "taking in his hands the ivy-wood drinking-vessel"), and getting drunk with the uncultivated abandon of a Cyclops. Given that ivy-vessels seem to have acquired these boorish connotations, if only because of their size, it is little wonder that Asclepiades of Myrlea, in his *Nestoris,* made this judgment concerning them: σκύφει καὶ κισσυβίῳ τῶν μὲν ἐν ἄστει καὶ μετρίων οὐδεὶς ἐχρῆτο, συβῶται δὲ καὶ νομεῖς καὶ οἱ ἐν ἀγρῷ. Πολύφημος μὲν τῷ κισσυβίῳ, θατέρῳ δὲ Εὔμαιος (Ath. 11.477bc: "No inhabitant of a city, even of modest means, ever used a *scyphus* or *kissybion,* but only swineherds, herdsmen, and country folk. Polyphemus used a *kissybion,* Eumaeus the other"). Whether Asclepiades had Theocritus in mind when he wrote these words cannot be ascertained, but it is likely that when he read the First Idyll, he attributed Theocritus' use of *kissybion* to the propriety of introducing an ivy-vessel into a rustic milieu.[72] At all events, the connotations surrounding the word *kissybion* throughout its career in pre-Theocritean literature would seem to suit it to the immediate context of Idyll 1 (and if the term can also function as a figure of "fineness," or *leptotēs,* in the *Aetia,* perhaps it is because Callimachus inherited from the programmatic First Idyll something of a ready-made literary symbol).

But Theocritus departs from the traditional poetic treatment of *kissybia* in several respects. First of all, he makes it clear that he has a different understanding of the word's etymology:

> καὶ βαθὺ κισσύβιον κεκλυσμένον ἁδέι κηρῷ,
> ἀμφῶες, νεοτευχές, ἔτι γλυφάνοιο ποτόσδον.
> τῶ ποτὶ μὲν χείλη μαρύεται ὑψόθι κισσός,
> κισσὸς ἑλιχρύσῳ κεκονιμένος. . . .

[27–30]

. . . and a deep *kissybion* sealed with sweet beeswax, two-handled, newly fashioned, still smelling of the chisel. Along its lips, above, winds ivy—ivy dusted with helichryse. . . .

Theocritus emphasizes his original derivation of *kissybion* by his repetition of the key word, *kissos* ("ivy"). The ivy-vessel is so named not because it is made of ivy-wood (which in any case is highly unfeasible) but because it is decorated with a pattern featuring an ivy-motif, an idea which Theocritus may have borrowed from similar conjectures about Polyphemus' cup in the

---

72. Other ancient scholars, such as Neoptolemus of Parium, Eumolpus, and Athenaeus, associated *kissybia* with rustic contexts because they understood the word to mean a vessel made of ivy-wood, and only peasants drink from wooden cups (Ath. 477ad; Σ *ad* Theoc. 1.27acde [pp. 38–39 Wendel]). For the later history of *kissybion,* see Mastrelli (1948), 104n.

Homeric scholia.[73] Second, Theocritus' innovative etymology calls attention to his other original supplement to the tradition—the carving of the bowl. Earlier commentators, including Brunn, Wilamowitz, and Gow, interested as they were in the actual design of the cup and in the disposition of its separate figural elements, remarked only that Theocritus seems to have transferred to a new medium, somewhat mischievously, the sort of decoration attested (or surviving) only on embossed metal vessels; this view has been confirmed and supplemented by new studies of Hellenistic ceramics with relief decoration.[74] All of these scholars unfortunately failed to grasp the essential point of Theocritus' innovation: nowhere in the foregoing literary tradition is an ivy-vessel described as decorated in any way.[75] It is the elaborate carving embellishing the surface of the goatherd's simple wooden bowl which sets this *kissybion* apart from earlier accounts of the type and which allows it to serve as an emblem for Theocritus' distinctive contribution to Greek literature. The most obvious contrast to emerge from the goatherd's description—and one requiring the least knowledge of previous literary sources to appreciate—is that between the common, worthless material out of which the cup is made, as well as the humble environment in which it circulates, and the precious beauty of its exquisite carving. The contrast between the vessel's crude substance and the refined technique which characterizes its workmanship expresses a more general incongruity typical of Alexandrian literature, or of that part of it which aspires to Callimachean standards of elegance and good taste: the contrast between the prosaic subject or humble theme of a poem and the elaborately artistic means with which it is treated. The most notorious example of such an aesthetic is the work of Aratus, whose choice of an intractable subject (astronomy) was designed to highlight the refinement, skill, and ingenuity of his craftsmanlike versification and diction (for which he was duly and enthusiastically praised by Callimachus).[76]

But the carvings on the goatherd's ivy-cup are meant to do more than merely demonstrate by how much Theocritus' manner exceeds his matter. A comparison of Theocritus with his imitators, who reduce the refined delights of rusticity to a pure mannerism, points up the difference. In *Daphnis and Chloe* Longus also brings in an ornamented ivy-cup: the seducer Dorcon attempts to win Chloe's complaisance with such gifts as a *kissybion*

73. Dale (1952), 131–32. Nicosia (1968), 17–19, argues that Theocritus' etymology is in fact correct—it was echoed, at any rate, by Pollux; Mastrelli (1948), 104–05n.

74. Nicosia (1968), 26, 29–36; Ott (1969), 93–99, 137n.

75. Cf. Nicosia (1968), 21. To be sure, this point has not gone unnoticed but it has been insufficiently appreciated.

76. Clausen (1964), 183–84.

diachryson ("decorated with gold" [1.15.3]). Here, as everywhere throughout his romance, Longus prettifies the life of the countryside by adorning its humble artifacts with sophisticated embellishments—belts of straw and ivy buds with coral clasps and amber studs. The carving on Theocritus' ivy-cup, however, has a more complex function and is involved with the same issues of literary genealogy that were implicit in the passage quoted from Callimachus' *Aetia*.

In devoting such elaborate attention to the *kissybion*, Theocritus is rescuing from obscurity a precious detail from the Homeric epic and expanding upon it for its own sake. This loving attention to humble but significant matters of vocabulary and narrative detail is indeed typical of Theocritus' own poetry, but it also exemplifies his attitude toward Homer. Unlike the tragic poets of the fifth century, Theocritus and his Alexandrian colleagues are interested less in reinterpreting the grand themes, plots, or myths of Homer than they are in elaborating aspects of his art that had been pushed into the background or passed over by the literary tradition. The close scholarly study of the Homeric epics undertaken by Alexandrian critics and poets promoted a kind of democracy of detail among the parts of the Homeric epics, casting an even illumination over all the fine points of the ancient texts and bringing to the fore minutiae of language and narrative description which had previously been unable to compete for attention amid the great battle scenes and dramatic set pieces. Like the light falling on a coarse household cloth in a Rembrandt canvas, the poetic practice of Theocritus and his Alexandrian fellow workers sought to "salvage," to use Ortega y Gasset's term, the insignificant objects in the (literary) world around them, objects once thrust aside in favor of larger concerns but now deemed worthy of consideration in their own right.[77] The importance of appreciating the value of little things is emphasized by Lycidas in Idyll 7, when he confronts the distracted Simichidas with the latter's neglect of this world's minute beauties, in what are perhaps the most moving lines in Theocritus:

> ὡς τοι ποσὶ νισσομένοιο
> πᾶσα λίθος πταίοισα ποτ' ἀρβυλίδεσσιν ἀείδει.
>
> [25–26]

See how, at every step you take, the very pebbles spin singing from your boots.

The pebble's song contrasts with the mountainous works which ignorant poets, not knowing what to make of a diminished thing, heap up as high as the peak of Mount Oromedon (45–48). But, as Yeats reminds us,

---

77. J. Ortega y Gasset, *Meditaciones del Quijote, Meditaciones por José Ortega y Gasset*, I (Madrid, 1914), 15. For a different view of the matter, see Deubner (1921), 370.

Though the great song return no more
There's keen delight in what we have:
The rattle of pebbles on the shore
Under the receding wave.

Theocritus, however, does not share Yeats's self-lacerating irony: he celebrates not the moribund rattle of contemporary voices but the song readily
yielded up on all sides by nature's pedestrian musicians.

Theocritus himself articulates the literary analogue to such attentiveness to humble detail when he illustrates the power of art—his own art in
particular—in Idyll 16 by citing these examples:

οὐδ' 'Οδυσεὺς ἑκατόν τε καὶ εἴκατι μῆνας ἀλαθείς
πάντας ἐπ' ἀνθρώπους, 'Αίδαν τ' εἰς ἔσχατον ἐλθών
ζωός, καὶ σπήλυγγα φυγὼν ὀλοοῖο Κύκλωπος,
δηναιὸν κλέος ἔσχεν, ἐσιγάθη δ' ἂν ὑφορβός
Εὔμαιος καὶ βουσὶ Φιλοίτιος ἀμφ' ἀγελαίαις
ἔργον ἔχων αὐτός τε περίσπλαγχνος Λαέρτης,
εἰ μή σφεας ὤνασαν 'Ιάονος ἀνδρὸς ἀοιδαί.

[51–57]

Never had Odysseus won lasting fame, who wandered six score months through all
the world, and came alive to farthest Hades, and escaped from the cave of the baleful
Cyclops; never would the swineherd Eumaeus have been named, nor Philoetius,
busied with the cattle of the herd, nor the great-hearted Laertes himself, had not the
minstrelsy of an Ionian bard profited them. [trans. Gow]

To say that the Homeric heroes would have remained obscure without their
poet is a commonplace, but Theocritus, by interspersing among his allusions to them the names of Homer's more humble characters, implies more
than that: without Homer, Odysseus would be as obscure as Philoetius—
or, conversely, Homer's artistic power can be seen in the equally enduring
fame of the heroic wanderer and the lowly swineherd. Long before Horace,
then, Theocritus proclaimed the power of the poet to confer immortality on
any subject of his own choosing, however insignificant it might be; if
Homer could achieve lasting renown for Eumaeus, Theocritus can do the
same for Hieron.[78] Theocritus' elaboration of Homer's *kissybion,* a rare epic
word and forgotten article of rustic household equipment which the literary
tradition had consigned to obscurity or to the comic irrelevance of peasant
scenes, proclaims the character of his poetry and helps to define the place he
intends to occupy within the epic legacy of the great archaic poets. Unlike
them, he will not be ambitious or seek to treat long, large-scale dramas of
the human condition; he prefers to get his material from the most unpreten-

78. I wish to thank Professor F. T. Griffiths of Amherst College for suggesting this
interpretation.

tious parts of their narratives, from homely details, unheroic moments, humble or humorous circumstances, and forgotten episodes. Yet these will be treated with a fullness, exquisite refinement, and delicate irony sufficiently expressive to make them worthy offshoots, in their way, of the venerable tradition from which they derive. Theocritus' subjects, then, represent an amplification of topics touched on but not developed by earlier epic poets, an attempt to read between Homer's lines. F. T. Griffiths has interpreted the long speech of Lynceus in Idyll 22 in a similar fashion. "The great palace by itself is no longer a fit subject for a poetry of wit and λεπτότης, nor is heroic battle. Now it is the faces in the crowd that come alive. In an earlier age, Lynceus would be one of those anonymous souls who enhance some greater man's *aristeia,* falling to the dust after five or six pathetic lines about his father or wife. . . . Theocritus' preferred perspective on the great world of heroic myth, as of the Alexandrian elite, is that of the outsiders whose revealing incomprehension has become a precious commodity in a sophisticated age."[79] Theocritus finds such outsiders, characteristically, in the background of the Homeric epics—the rustic populace on Ithaca, the unidentified voices among the soldiery commenting on the action of the *Iliad,* the silent spectators at the heroic courts. Theocritus transfers them to a new medium in which they can command the audience's attention and express in fresh language their new and independent existence.

The goatherd's exposition of the decoration on the ivy-cup in Idyll 1 relates the subjects of Theocritus' poetry to the epic tradition in an even more suggestive way than the use of *kissybion* and the play of its literary associations had done. The long *ecphrasis* devoted to describing the physical appearance of a product of human craftsmanship, though it can certainly be paralleled in the work of Theocritus' contemporaries (or in poetry inspired by them) and even elsewhere in Theocritus himself (cf. Idyll 15.109–31), demands comparison with the two famous examples of *ecphrasis* in early epic: Homer's Shield of Achilles in *Iliad* 18 and the Shield of Heracles in a poem of that title ascribed to Hesiod by contemporaries of Theocritus (such as Apollonius of Rhodes).[80] Such a comparison, which Ott, among others, has undertaken with considerable thoroughness, establishes that the goatherd's description of the ivy-bowl is indeed closely modeled on the two archaic *ecphrases* in overall design as well as in more minute matters of diction, theme, and narrative technique.[81] But the fact of Theocritus' imitation of his

---

79. Griffiths (1976), 360.
80. Cf. Fritzsche-Hiller (1881), 46, *ad* Idyll 1.46; Friedländer (1912), 13–14. On Apollonius' theory about the authorship of the *Scutum,* see Pfeiffer (1968), 144.
81. Ott (1969), 100–05.

epic predecessors, important though it may be, is less significant than his use of their figurative method of exposition to articulate the thematic structure of his own literary innovation. For, as Lessing remarked about Homer's *ecphrasis,* the Shield of Achilles represents an "Inbegriff von allem, was in der Welt vorgeht."[82] Scholars have often remarked that one function of Achilles' Shield in the *Iliad* is to set forth in concentrated and static form the subjects of Homer's poetic world.[83] Thus, the technique of *ecphrasis* itself, besides linking bucolic poetry with the epic tradition, provides Theocritus with a means of announcing the thematic range of his hexameter poetry. "Just as Homer's Shield must be viewed as a picture of the world of his epic, so the *ecphrasis* in the First Idyll provides a picture of the life and feelings of little people, portrayed in situations that are not earthshaking, but whose aesthetic appeal represents a central discovery of Alexandrian poetry; they also constitute the chosen theme of Theocritus' poetic oeuvre."[84]

When the details of the scenes on the ivy-cup are examined, it becomes clear that Theocritus, through allusions to his forebears in the epic tradition, is calling attention to the continuities of theme and technique connecting his work with earlier epic; at the same time, by emphasizing the carefully calculated divergences of his *ecphrasis* from the example of his models, Theocritus also manages to define the distinctive qualities of his own individual contribution to the literary tradition he is refashioning.[85] This is most noticeable in the first of the scenes on the ivy-cup. The passage of the *Iliad* imitated by Theocritus had concerned a quarrel between two citizens of the City at Peace over the blood-price of a murdered man:

ἔνθα δὲ νεῖκος
ὠρώρει, δύο δ' ἄνδρες ἐνείκεον εἵνεκα ποινῆς
ἀνδρὸς ἀποφθιμένου. . . . οἱ δὲ γέροντες . . .
τοῖσιν ἔπειτ' ἤϊσσον, ἀμοιβηδὶς δὲ δίκαζον.

[18.497–506[

And there a quarrel arose over the blood-price of a dead man. . . . But the elders . . . then came forward with their scepters, and gave judgment by turns.

---

82. Quoted by Schadewaldt (1965), 352.

83. Ibid., 368–70: "So zeigt der Schild Homers im Kleinen, was in die Welt seines Epos im Grossen ist. Er zeigt als Zustand in ruhendem Bilde, was im vorwärtsdrängenden Gang der epischen Handlung mächtig bewegtes Geschehen ist. . . . [Man könnte manches darüber sagen,] wie die innere Ordnung, die in der Schildbeschreibung lebt, auch die Welt- und Lebensordnung der Ilias im ganzen ist"; C. H. Whitman, *Homer and the Heroic Tradition* (Cambridge, Mass., 1958), 205: "At the moment when the hero, self-doomed, is about to plunge into the final fatalities of the action, the poet universalizes that action by giving him a shield which is a summary picture of the world."

84. Ott (1969), 109.

85. Cf. Van Sickle (1975), 56.

Theocritus' version presents a sharp contrast:

> πὰρ δέ οἱ ἄνδρες
> καλὸν ἐθειράζοντες ἀμοιβαδὶς ἄλλοθεν ἄλλος
> νεικείουσ' ἐπέεσσι.

[33–35]

And next to her, two men with beautiful long hair quarrel with words, by turns, from each side of her.

Homer's language has been transferred by the Alexandrian poet to a scene of erotic contest for which there is no precedent in the early *ecphrases*. The point of this juxtaposition is to highlight Theocritus' major innovation in his treatment of epic themes: his substitution of an erotic for a heroic subject and his removal of agonistic strife from the battlefield to the everyday world of amorous and poetic competition.[86] Note that νεικείουσ' ἐπέεσσι ("quarrel with words") can refer to rivalry in hexameter verses as well as in simple speech and so anticipates the contests of poetic skill which figure in so many of the hexameter Idylls. The use of ἀμοιβαδίς ("by turns") confirms this impression and looks forward to the convention of "amoeboean song" which was destined to become a hallmark of the bucolic poetry of Theocritus and his imitators.[87] Whereas Homer's description is spare and lacking in extraneous detail, Theocritus adds καλὸν ἐθειράζοντες ("with beautiful long hair"), an observation immaterial to the story told by the figures but highly relevant to its erotic tonality. The treatment of erotic struggle on the cup is also consonant with Theocritus' general practice of taking a distant perspective of amused detachment on such matters, even when his own feelings are ostensibly involved. Finally, just as the lovers on the cup "struggle wearily and to no purpose" (38: ἐτώσια μοχθίζοντι) for the attentions of the woman, so in the Idylls of Theocritus all heterosexual love—and most homosexual love as well—is doomed to frustration (with the exception of Simichidas' convenient arrangement with Myrto in Idyll 7, mentioned only by way of contrast with Aratus' troubles, and the couple in the spurious Idyll 27).[88] One might even say that love in Theocritus has to be frustrated in order for erotic themes to be a fitting substitute for heroic ones: Theocritus' distinctive emphasis in his treatment of love may be conditioned by the character of the heroic tradition to which he is reacting—the agony of battle can be replaced only by the agony of desire. Thus, the first

---

86. Cf. Ott (1969), 105; Friedländer (1912), 14.

87. Cf. Idyll 8.31–32 (quoted above); Virgil *Buc.* 3.59: "alternis dicetis; amant alterna Camenae"; 7.20: "hos Corydon, illos referebat in ordine Thyrsis."

88. Cf. Lawall (1967), 28; L. Séchan, "Les Magiciennes et l'amour chez Théocrite," *Annales de la faculté des lettres et sciences humaines d'Aix,* Série classique, 29 (1965), 67–100.

scene on the cup is able to represent two major themes of Theocritean poetry: erotic frustration and verbal competition with alternating speech.

The second scene on the ivy-cup is based on a passage from the pseudo-Hesiodic *Scutum* (or *Shield of Heracles*).

δοιὼ δ' ἀναφυσιόωντες
ἀργύρεοι δελφῖνες ἐθοινῶντ' ἔλλοπας ἰχθῦς.
τῶν δ' ὕπο χάλκειοι τρέον ἰχθύες· αὐτὰρ ἐπ' ἀκταῖς
ἧστο ἀνὴρ ἁλιεὺς δεδοκημένος· εἶχε δὲ χερσὶν
ἰχθύσιν ἀμφίβληστρον ἀπορρίψοντι ἐοικώς.

[211–15]

Two spouting silver dolphins were feasting on scaly fishes. And before them bronze fishes fled in terror. But on the coast a fisherman sat watching; he held in his hands a casting-net for fish and seemed about to hurl it.

The relevant passage from the First Idyll is:

τοῖς δὲ μέτα γριπεύς τε γέρων πέτρα τε τέτυκται
λεπράς, ἐφ' ᾷ σπεύδων μέγα δίκτυον ἐς βόλον ἕλκει
ὁ πρέσβυς, κάμνοντι τὸ καρτερὸν ἀνδρὶ ἐοικώς.
φαίης κεν γυίων νιν ὅσον σθένος ἐλλοπιεύειν. . . .

[39–42]

Beside them are fashioned an old fisherman and a rough rock. On it the ancient is eagerly hauling a great net for a throw; he seems like a man straining mightily. You would say he is fishing with all the strength in his limbs.

The lines from the *Scutum* retain a certain heroic flavor and recall Homer's simile for the scattering of the Trojans before Achilles (*Il.* 21.22–24): ὡς δ' ὑπὸ δελφῖνος μεγακήτεος ἰχθύες ἄλλοι/φεύγοντες πιμπλᾶσι μυχοὺς λιμένος εὐόρμου,/δειδιότες. . . .("as in flight before a voracious dolphin the other fishes fill the hollows of the shore in their fear. . ."). Only a muted echo of Homeric battle[89] can be heard in the Theocritean passage, however, where the struggle is confined within the homely conditions of the old fisherman's world. Whereas in the *Scutum* the human figure had been a peripheral observer of the action, in Theocritus' version he occupies the center of the narrative focus. Much emphasis is placed on the old man's efforts to haul in his net—and on the verisimilitude with which it is portrayed—as well as on the contrast between his age (γέρων, πρέσβυς) and his youthful strength (44: τὸ δὲ σθένος ἄξιον ἄβας). The naturalism of Theocritus' portrait is typical of certain trends in Hellenistic art, which fre-

89. Patroclus hooks Thestor with a spear-thrust through the cheek and pulls him out of his chariot, ὡς ὅτε τις φὼς/πέτρῃ ἔπι προβλῆτι καθήμενος ἱερὸν ἰχθὺν/ἐκ πόντοιο θύραζε λίνῳ καὶ ἤνοπι χαλκῷ [ἕλκει]. . . . (16. 406–08: "as when a man sitting on a jutting rock [hauls] a fish out from the sea by means of a flaxen cord and gleaming bronze [hook]").

quently shows an interest in depicting the human body in postures of physical strain as well as in conveying a realistic picture of the lowest social classes—a general concern with *ēthos* in preference to *pathos*.[90] But, more important, the old fisherman is emblematic of a theme that pervades the poetry of Theocritus: the vicissitudes of "little people" amid their humble circumstances (*Kleinleben*). The lovelorn teenager of Idyll 2, the mercenaries of Idyll 14, or the Syracusan housewives of Idyll 15, sketched with a wealth of telling and veristic detail, would have aroused in Theocritus and his colleagues a social response hardly differentiated from that evoked by the countrymen of the pastoral Idylls; both groups are sufficiently distant from the poet's own social environment to facilitate a sense of aesthetic detachment, yet neither is excessively exotic: they share alike that aura of simplicity which contributes to the faint unreality surrounding their lives (when viewed from a sophisticated vantage). "The literary practice of the partial idealization and partial realization of an occupational or regional class that has thematic reference to the author's own more complicated one" reveals in Theocritus' hands "the capacity of an organic device employable for gaining perspective on any social group or cultural myth that one might wish."[91] The herdsmen of Theocritus should not be isolated, then, from his other low-life figures, for both fulfill essentially the same artistic and thematic function.

For the third scene on the cup Theocritus combined two passages from archaic epic. The first is part of a tableau on the shield of Achilles:

ἐν δὲ τίθει σταφυλῇσι μέγα βρίθουσαν ἀλωὴν
καλὴν χρυσείην· μέλανες δ᾽ ἀνὰ βότρυες ἦσαν. . . .

[18.561–62]

And he added a beautiful vineyard in gold, greatly laden with grape clusters, and on them were dark grapes. . . .

The second is drawn from the pseudo-Hesiodic *Scutum*:

παρὰ δέ σφισιν ὄρχος
χρύσεος ἦν . . . .
βριθόμενος σταφυλῇσι· μελάνθησάν γε μὲν αἵδε.

[296–300]

and next to them was a row of vines in gold, . . . laden with grape clusters, which were darkening.

The Theocritean version is the longest of the three; only the relevant portion follows.

90. Cf. Webster (1964), 168–71; Auerbach (1953), 30.
91. Hieatt (1972), 26.

περκναῖσι σταφυλαῖσι καλὸν βέβριθεν ἀλωά,
τὰν ὀλίγος τις κῶρος ἐφ᾽ αἱμασιαῖσι φυλάσσει
ἥμενος· ἀμφὶ δέ νιν δύ᾽ ἀλώπεκες, ἁ μὲν ἀν᾽ ὄρχως
φοιτῇ. . . .

[46–49]

With reddening grape clusters a vineyard has been beautifully laden; a small lad, sitting on a wall of stones, guards it, and on either side are two foxes, one going up and down the rows of vines. . . .

The older poets describe aspects of the vintage, whereas Theocritus has chosen to portray a boy outwitted by foxes. The contrast between a panorama of a typical laboring scene, with its broad general outlines depicting a multitude of activities, and the concentration on a single humorous incident is programmatic for Theocritus' art. The poet expresses his delight in the trivial but amusing situation, in a miniature scene that can be conveyed with delicacy and wit. Once again we find a good-natured, almost irresponsible detachment: the cup's decorator is not concerned with either the value of the grapes or the boy's dereliction of his duty, only with the piquancy of the scene and the possibility of communicating the boy's rapt self-absorption. This sense of unencumbered delight is characteristic of much of Theocritus' poetry; his herdsmen savor the enjoyment of leisure no less than the boy on the ivy-cup.[92] Also, Theocritus' language brings out the cuteness of the miniature scene by emphasizing its diminuitive scale: he begins with τυτθὸν δ᾽ ὅσσον (45: "a tiny way off"), then goes on to call the boy an ὀλίγος τις κῶρος (47: "a small lad"), and a παιδίον (50: "little child"). In this Theocritus exemplifies the taste of his age for what T. B. L. Webster calls "child art."[93] But there is another aspect to the scene. The playful child came to be a fitting figure for the Alexandrian poet dedicated to upholding standards of artistic modesty and avoiding the grand themes of "serious" literature. The most famous instance is Callimachus' self-characterization in the *Aetia* prologue (fr. 1.5–6 Pfeiffer): ἔπος δ᾽ ἐπὶ τυτθὸν ἑλ[ίσσω/παῖς ἅτε, τῶν δ᾽ ἐτέων ἡ δεκὰς οὐκ ὀλίγη ("I roll my poem a tiny distance, like a child, though my years are numbered in many decades"). The import of Theocritus' miniature was not lost on Virgil, who portrays himself at the end of his *Bucolics* engaged in an occupation resembling that of the boy on the ivy-cup—similarly combining πόνος and παίγνιον, *meditari* and *ludere*, work and play—and almost as irresponsibly absorbed (10.71). In the later Greek bucolic poets such cuteness became a mannerism that grew to dominate the treatment of other themes.

92. Ott (1969), 106.
93. Webster (1964), 158, 161–62; cf. Giangrande (1968), 496n.; Rosenmeyer (1969), 55–59.

One last comparison will conclude this discussion of Theocritus' use of epic models and of their programmatic value in helping to define the thematic structure of his poetry. It indicates clearly that the ivy-cup is not only an emblem for the range of subjects in the Idylls in general but for the thematic structure of bucolic poetry in particular. The final portion of the pseudo-Hesiodic *ecphrasis* begins:

θαῦμα ἰδεῖν καὶ Ζηνὶ βαρυκτύπῳ, οὗ διὰ βουλὰς
Ἥφαιστος ποίησε σάκος μέγα τε στιβαρόν τε. . . .

[318–19]

It was a marvel to behold even for deep-thundering Zeus, by whose will Hephaestus made the great and sturdy shield. . . .

When this passage is incorporated in line 56 of the First Idyll, it undergoes a typically Theocritean transformation:

αἰπολικὸν θάημα· τέρας κέ τυ θυμὸν ἀτύξαι.

It is something a goatherd can marvel at; it's a sight that will amaze your heart.

The shield of Heracles, so marvelous in its decoration, is a source of wonderment to Zeus the Thunderer who commissioned it and is not unused to wonders; the ivy-cup is an awesome apparition to the lowly goatherd and his ilk. Theocritus' choice of rustic in this passage is significant, for it marks the completeness of his inversion of the traditional figure: a goatherd is the lowliest of herdsmen in the same measure as Zeus is king and father of the gods. But the phrase αἰπολικὸν θάημα is also important as an explicit acknowledgment that the cup, no less than the song of Thyrsis, is an example of bucolic *chef-d'oeuvre* and hence an emblem for the new brand of poetry. To maintain this is not to blur the conventional distinction between the various grades of herdsmen. Indeed, the traditional hierarchy is not only preserved but is even emphasized in the First Idyll. An orderly progression in the use of the terms *boukolikos* (20), *poimenikos* (23), and *aipolikos* (56) can be found in the goatherd's speech; the same ranking of the pastoral professions according to their decreasing prestige occurs in a single line of the Daphnis-song, as if to mirror in concentrated form the hierarchy suggested by the goatherd: ἦνθον τοὶ βοῦται, τοὶ ποιμένες, ᾡπόλοι ἦνθον (80: "came the cowherds, the shepherds, the goatherds came"). Similarly, the poet reminds us of Daphnis' status as a *boukolos* with a peculiar insistence (lines 92, 105, 113, 116, 120–21) and underscores his point by means of a startling contrast in line 86: βούτας μὲν ἐλέγευ, νῦν δ᾽ αἰπόλῳ ἀνδρὶ ἔοικας ("you were called a cowherd, but now you are like a goatherd"). The various grades of herdsmen are hardly interchangeable.[94] Nonetheless,

94. Cf. van Groningen (1958), 313–17; Rossi (1971b), 6; Van Sickle (1978), 172n.; but see Schmidt (1969).

there are grounds for arguing that the term *aepolic* can be understood to include the cup within the general range of Theocritean bucolic poetry.

Aepolic in its literary sense is a coinage of Theocritus no less than *bucolic,* although both possess linguistic precedents. A scholiast[95] explains the preference for *bucolic* over *aepolic* as a generic term in the following manner: τὰ δὲ βουκολικὰ ἔχει ⟨κατὰ⟩ διαφορὰν τὴν τῶν ποιημάτων ἐπιγραφήν· καὶ γὰρ αἰπολικά ἐστι καὶ ποιμενικὰ καὶ μικτά. τὴν μέντοι ἀπὸ τῶν βοῶν εἴληφεν ἐπιγραφὴν ⟨ὡς⟩ κρατιστεύοντος τοῦ ζῴου· διὸ καὶ βουκολικὰ λέγονται πάντα ("Bucolic poetry differs from its title in that it is aepolic [of goatherds], poemenic [of shepherds], and mixed. Nevertheless, it took its title from cattle because they are the mightiest animals. Therefore, all this poetry is called bucolic.") Whatever one may think of the cogency of this explanation, it at least confirms that *bucolic* is the broad generic term and therefore comprehends poetry involving other kinds of rustic figures (indeed, it includes poetry lacking rustic subjects entirely), a conclusion which could have been drawn from a cursory examination of the poems explicitly designated bucolic by Theocritus. The importance of the ancient pastoral hierarchy may have to do with differentiating levels of dignity and seriousness within the bucolic world. For example, van Groningen observed that whereas the conversation between a goatherd and a shepherd in Idyll 5 is vulgar and unpleasant, that between two cowherds in Idyll 6 is polite and amicable; moreover, the cowherd's sexual proclivities (he is never homosexual) set him apart from the shepherd and, especially, from the goatherd.[96] It is all the more remarkable, then, that Theocritus, in selecting spokesmen for his literary programme, should favor goatherds. The best example is Lycidas in Idyll 7:

> ἐσθλὸν σὺν Μοίσαισι Κυδωνικὸν εὕρομες ἄνδρα,
> οὔνομα μὲν Λυκίδαν, ἧς δ' αἰπόλος, οὐδέ κέ τίς νιν
> ἠγνοίησεν ἰδὼν ἐπεὶ αἰπόλῳ ἔξοχ' ἐῴκει.

[12–14]

By the grace of the Muses we came upon a noble man of Cydonia, Lycidas by name; he was a goatherd, nor could anyone who saw him mistake him, since he looked conspicuously like a goatherd.

The emphasis in these lines is noteworthy, as is the collocation of Lycidas' profession with heroic terms of praise (such as *esthlos*). The solution to this paradox becomes apparent when we recall the inverse snobbery of Alexandrian *littérateurs,* who tended to disparage the nobility, grandeur, and importance of their work in proportion as they prided themselves on its delicacy, refinement, and sophistication. This inversion of values can be

95. Σ Prol. C. a. (pp. 3–4 Wendel); for a full conspectus of sources, see Schmidt (1969), 194–95.
96. van Groningen (1958), 314; cf. Gow (1952), II, 20, *ad* 1.86.

seen in Theocritus' stress on the simplicity and unpretentiousness of his poetry; far from contradicting his boasts about its high artistic quality, such self-deprecation constitutes a sign of adherence to the highest Alexandrian aesthetic ideals.[97] Something of the same tactics can be seen in Callimachus' epigram (22 Pfeiffer; 36 Page) in which the poet's modesty consists in calling himself and his colleagues shepherds while reserving the honorific epithet of goatherd for Astacides, the object of his praise:

> Ἀστακίδην τὸν Κρῆτα τὸν αἰπόλον ἥρπασε Νύμφη
> ἐξ ὄρεος, καὶ νῦν ἱερὸς Ἀστακίδης.
> οὐκέτι Δικταίῃσιν ὑπὸ δρυσίν, οὐκέτι Δάφνιν,
> ποιμένες, Ἀστακίδην δ᾽ αἰὲν ἀεισόμεθα.

Astacides, the Cretan, the goat-herd, a nymph carried off from the hill, and now Astacides is made holy. No more beneath the oaks of Dicte, no more of Daphnis shall we shepherds sing, but always of Astacides. [trans. A. W. Mair]

The conclusion of van Groningen: "Among poets, the 'goatherd' will signify he who exhibits 'bucolic' characteristics clearly and vigorously. Most of all in his poetry: he will treat, above all, the trivial pleasures, futile sufferings, petty conflicts, and vulgar passions of even the littlest people. His realism will be down-to-earth, even crude at times. To be sure, this excess of 'bucolicism' does not at all exclude a sincere sympathy for these little people, much less an artistic value of the highest order: Hellenistic literature unquestioningly admits the combination of an impeccable form with a vulgar, or even scabrous, subject."[98] It is not necessary to agree completely with van Groningen's characterization of bucolic poetry in order to accept his view that the word *aepolic,* because of its lowly associations, represents an intensified or strengthened form of the more general term *bucolic.* That *aepolic* can therefore signify by synecdoche what is meant by *bucolic* was already pointed out by the ancient scholiast on Idyll 1.56 (the very passage under discussion), who commented: διὰ τῶν αἰπόλων δηλοῖ καὶ τοὺς ποιμένας καὶ τοὺς βουκόλους ("by goatherds he indicates both shepherds and cowherds").[99] But a comparison with the passage from the pseudo-Hesiodic *Scutum* makes Theocritus' choice of vocabulary clearer. The cup is a source of wonder to people who are lowly in proportion as Zeus is great—not cowherds, then, but goatherds. The selection of the social rank *within* the bucolic frame of reference is dictated by a desire to invert as fully as possible the phraseology of the epic model.[100] There is accordingly no impediment to interpreting the words *aipolikon thaēma* in line 56 as an

---

97. Cf. Servius *ad* Virg. *Buc.* 10.77.
98. van Groningen (1958), 316.
99. P. 52. Wendel.
100. Ott (1969), 109–10.

explicit signal of the connection between the ivy-cup and the newly invented "genre" of bucolic poetry.

At this point it may be worth rehearsing the arguments in favor of
viewing the goatherd's ivy-cup in the First Idyll of Theocritus as a figure for
the themes of bucolic poetry. First of all, the cup balances the song, which is
explicitly identified as bucolic, in the structure of the poem; both share the
task of unveiling, illustrating, and expounding Theocritus' literary discovery. Cup and song are connected by the exchange of one for the other. Both
are rustic artifacts; both are sweet as honey; both are virtuoso performances
which arouse the keen but detached pleasures associated with purely aesthetic appreciation and with the response to what is now called romance.
Furthermore, although the scenes on the cup depict familiar, not to say
archetypal, aspects of human experience,[101] they have been wondrously
refashioned by the artisan and, when juxtaposed to one another, form a new
synthesis; similarly, the Daphnis-song incorporates traditional material
from Sicilian legend and cult practice, possibly borrowing its subject from
the lyric poem by Stesichorus as well as from other previous works, and
casts it into the novel form of a rustic ballad complete with the refrain so
characteristic of folk poetry. Second, the language Theocritus employs to
describe the cup enables it to function as a literary symbol. He refers to the
cup by the rare, Homeric word *kissybion* and plays on the various associations surrounding that word in the earlier poetic tradition. The literary
derivation of *kissybion* also empowers Theocritus to use the ivy-cup programmatically to define his relationship to the early epic poets and the place
which he claims to occupy within the epic tradition, while the ecphrastic
convention provides a traditional means of articulating figuratively the thematic content of his art. Theocritus does not fail to exploit this convention.
By carefully manipulating his epic models he reveals, through a delicately
contrived interplay of similarities and differences between his scenes and
those of his forerunners (in matters of tone, diction, narrative technique,
and in the subject represented), the thematic structure of his own poetry.

Finally, as the comparison with pseudo-Hesiod makes plain, Theocritus explicitly labels the cup a bucolic artifact. This is not to say that the
substitution of *aipolikos* for *boukolikos* is emptied of literal meaning on the
one hand (the cup belongs to a goatherd) or of figurative literary value on
the other (*aepolic* signifies "intensely bucolic"), merely that the words
aipolikon thaēma ("something a goatherd can marvel at") serve to incorporate the cup within the range of bucolic material. Like bucolic poetry, the
cup is brand-new: it is freshly carved, redolent of the chisel, and has never

101. Lawall (1967), 28–31.

been used before now, but preserved inviolate: οὐδέ τί πω ποτὶ χεῖλος ἐμὸν θίγεν ἀλλ᾽ ἔτι κεῖται/ἄχραντον (59–60: "nor has it yet touched my lip at all; rather, it lies still undefiled"). If Idyll 1 stands first, without exception, in all the collections of Theocritus' poetry that have come down to us whether in manuscript or on papyrus, it is most likely because the poem was regarded in the ancient world as programmatic—as the best introduction to the realm of Theocritus' literary imagination and the best critical prolegomenon to an understanding of his art.[102] Just as Thyrsis indicates his authorship of the Daphnis-song at the outset, by signing his name[103] at the top of the page (as Virgil would say, *Buc.* 6.12), in line 65 (Θύρσις ὅδ᾽ ὡξ Αἴτνας καὶ Θύρσιδος ἀδέα φωνά—"I am Thyrsis from Aetna and Thyrsis' voice is sweet"), so Theocritus places his personal emblem on his work in the form of the poetic manifesto implicit in the collocation of the ivy-cup and Daphnis-song. (The latter will be discussed in part 4, chapter 11.) Where Thyrsis is naive and concrete, Theocritus is highly sophisticated. As Berg concludes, "This cup is obviously meant as the poet's *sphragis,* the signature upon his work: it forecasts, for the first poem of the collection, Theocritus' poetic programme. . . . [As for the scenes on the cup,] these static vignettes, these *eidyllia,* are the stuff of Theocritean poetry. The reader hovers peacefully in the herdsman's dream world, admiring and even enjoying a panorama of human struggle framed forever in ivy and acanthus. The cup, which foreshadows the nature of the Idylls, is represented as a fair exchange for Thyrsis' 'Lament for Daphnis.' The goatherd is willing to stake all of Theocritus' themes for the theme *par excellence,* that of a herdsman-musician sacrificed on love's altar."[104]

Now it remains only to substantiate Berg's claim that the scenes on the ivy-cup not only typify Theocritus' art but actually represent the themes of bucolic poetry itself. It will be recalled from part 2, chapter 7 that by using the modern concept of pastoral to account for the thematic structure of bucolic poetry, it was possible to identify only thirteen of the twenty-seven

102. Σ *ad* Idyll 1, arg. b (p. 23.5–11 Wendel); *Anec. Est.* 3.5 (p. 11.4–10 Wendel); Van Sickle (1976), 41, n. 58.

103. This frequent observation has been restated most recently by A. Rist, trans., *The Poems of Theocritus* (Chapel Hill, 1978), 24: "Thyrsis' song . . . opens with a verse 'signature,' an establishment of copyright."

104. Berg (1974), 13–14; a similar interpretation of the ivy-cup was articulated by A. Rostagni, *Poeti alessandrini* (Turin, 1916), 97–98: see Mastrelli (1948), 103–04. The same view has recently been restated by Walker (1980), 36–37: "Just as the earlier exchanges between the goatherd and the shepherd distinguished Theocritus' sophisticated verse from its rustic counterpart, so this passage presents a symbolic image of the nature of Theocritus' new poetic genre. . . . The cup is the symbol of Theocritus' pastoral *ars poetica,* his poetic credo." Observe that the scenes on the cup are not all pastoral, however.

hexameter Idylls in the Theocritean collection, leaving some of the most successful and distinctive of Theocritus' poems (Idylls 2, 13, 14, 15, 16, and 24) without a plausible generic designation. That the cup *can* serve as a device for representing figuratively the themes of bucolic poetry has been established by a discussion of the ecphrastic convention and by an examination of the programmatic way in which Theocritus alters and refashions his epic models. That the cup *does* in fact represent the themes of bucolic poetry can be decided only on the basis of the ease and naturalness with which the scenes on the cup can be made to account for the diversity of subject matter in the Idylls. This diversity has forced on critics a certain vagueness in their formulations of bucolic thematics. Thus, Van Sickle, the only scholar to attempt a radical redefinition of the "genre," has written that bucolic "might be defined not as narrowly mimetic but as encompassing a calculated range of rural-urban themes and poetic forms in a kind of generic mingling, interplay."[105] Perhaps the scenes on the ivy-cup can provide an account of Theocritus' thematic range which is at once more precise, more comprehensive, and better grounded historically than the *ad hoc* critical formulations hitherto advanced.

We have seen that the first scene on the cup, the picture of contention and erotic frustration, is emblematic of Theocritus' treatment of love in the Idylls. We have also seen that Theocritus adapts his Homeric model so as to highlight his own emphasis on the themes of love and competition. The following Idylls are chiefly concerned with an erotic subject: 2, 3, 6, 7, 10, 11, 12, 13, 14, 20, 23, and 27; the erotic theme also figures importantly in Idylls 1, 4, 5, 8, 15, 18, and 19. This accounts for a total of nineteen out of twenty-seven Idylls. The theme of erotic or poetic rivalry is also present in Idylls 5, 6, 7, 8, 9, 10, 22, and, to a lesser extent, in Idylls 1, 4, 12, and 14. The two motifs combined account for twenty-one Idylls in all: Theocritus may quite legitimately have considered the first scene on the ivy-cup representative of his individual contribution to the themes of hexameter poetry. The second scene, portraying the old fisherman, is a figure for Theocritus' interest in *ēthos* and, particularly, in the world of little people—drawn from the most insignificant sectors of society and sketched with veristic detail. This aspect of Theocritus' art is represented by Idylls 1–11, 14, 15, 20, 21, 24, and 27—seventeen poems in all. Finally, the third scene on the cup, the boy outwitted by foxes, reflects the comic, ironic, or playful strain in Theocritus' poetry and in his choice of subjects. The playful boy, rapturously intent on his weaving, stands in opposition to the fisherman toiling

---

105. Van Sickle (1976), 25.

with his net—a figure of *ponos* (artistic labor, exertion);[106] they belong not only to different ages of man but to different conceptions of the poet's task. Humorous or pointed miniature scenes can be found in Idylls 2–15, 19, 20, 22, 24, 25, and 27—twenty poems in all.

It is therefore possible, by formulating the themes of bucolic poetry according to the hints provided by the poet himself rather than by attempting to impose on his text thematic notions derived from modern critical presuppositions, to account for twenty-four of the twenty-seven hexameter poems of Theocritus: Idylls 1–15, 18–25, and 27. Of the excluded poems, Idyll 26 suffers perhaps from insufficient appreciation hitherto of its irony; the same might be said for Idylls 18, 22, and 25.[107] Idylls 16 and 17, it has been recently suggested,[108] constitute two parts of a composite argument whose purpose is to undermine, through an ironic juxtaposition of disparate elements, the conventional *topoi* of the encomium form. It is interesting to note, further, that the poems with the weakest link to the bucolic corpus, as it has been newly defined, are also those most easily comprehended by one of the other categories mentioned in the bibliographical tradition preserved in the *Suda*. The result of this analysis, then, is not a grab bag of motifs one or several of which can be found in any poem by Theocritus, but rather a selection of those subjects which furnish the material essential to the creation of a particular kind of poetry.

The foregoing interpretation of the significance of the ivy-cup in Idyll 1 makes possible a consistent and plausible description of bucolic thematics. It certainly shows that a coherent set of defining criteria for the subject matter of bucolic poetry can be more easily reconstructed by examining the imagery and poetic technique of Idyll 1 than by invoking modern notions of pastoral. What remains puzzling is the exact relation of the various themes identified here to one another and to some more fundamental conception of bucolic poetry as a whole. We have seen that Theocritus' "criteria for similarity and difference—his conception of the parameters of a poetic group—was more complex, versatile than the critics' simple mimetic scheme."[109] But it remains to discover what those criteria for similarity and difference were, how they could accommodate the diverse themes selected

---

106. On πόνος, see Schmidt (1972), 33–34.

107. Cf. Effe (1978), 64–76; on Idyll 22, Horstmann (1976), 72–79.

108. By S. Scofield, in a paper delivered to the American Philological Association at New Orleans in December 1980. See also F. T. Griffiths, *Theocritus at Court,* Mnemosyne supp. 55 (1979).

109. Van Sickle (1976), 24.

by Theocritus. What do the subjects of bucolic poetry have in common, what permits them to exist side by side in the Idylls without incongruities or dissonance? According to what principles did Theocritus choose and combine them? These are the questions for which an answer will be sought in the final part of this inquiry.

PART IV

The Formal Structure of Bucolic Poetry

CHAPTER TEN

Meter and Genre

Fieri certe potuit ut ingeniosus poeta, quum novum poesis genus induceret, formam quoque novam ejusmodi, quæ nihil commune haberet cum pastorum cantu, inveniret atque excoleret.[1]

What was this "new form" that Theocritus pioneered together with the "new genre" of bucolic poetry he had invented? To ask such a question is equivalent to inquiring into the generic definition of bucolic poetry itself, inasmuch as the ancient determinants of genre were largely formal: according to L. E. Rossi they included, in addition to thematics (or content), structure, or the disposition of the parts and the dimensions; language, or the dialect and stylistic level; and meter—as well as music and dance, whenever present. These elements, in varying combinations and proportions, imparted to individual works of ancient literature that distinctive profile, *quella particolare fisionomia,* that led both the poets and scholars of antiquity, and leads us as well, to assign them to one or another of the principal generic categories.[2] Of the ancient determinants of genre enumerated by Rossi, the last (music and dance) can be ignored in the case of Theocritus, since the Idylls are primarily intended to be read from the written page rather than publicly recited, sung, accompanied by movement, or other-

1. Strähler, *De cæsuris versus Homerici,* diss. Breslau (1889), 46 (cited by Legrand [1898], 423n.): "It could well be that Theocritus, a gifted poet, in bringing forth a new kind of poetry also discovered and refined a new form that had nothing in common with the song of herdsmen."
2. Rossi (1971a), 71.

wise performed:[3] the musical element which might, for poetry of an earlier period, have contributed to our understanding of an individual work's generic identity is here lacking. Language, moreover, does not provide an adequate or reliable tool for generic classification of the Idylls: the dialect employed by Theocritus is not a stable or consistent system, nor do its variations correspond discernibly with variations in theme (except in the case of the Aeolic poems), while the poet's diction—far from adhering to a single stylistic level—exhibits extreme fluctuation.[4] The thematic component of bucolic poetry, with its diversity of possible subjects, does not immediately betray an underlying common interest, and Rossi cautions us against deriving generic determinants solely from our reading of the poems rather than from the critical formulations of the ancients.[5] The "dimensions and disposition of the parts" as well as the meter remain to be studied. They constitute not only what might be called in modern terminology the formal structure of bucolic poetry but also represent the most important criteria for generic classification according to Hellenistic literary and critical practice.

Theocritus was of course intimately acquainted with the principles of contemporary criticism. The close connection between poetry and scholarship in Hellenistic Alexandria, where the great practitioners of either discipline were often the same individuals, has been emphasized by Rudolf Pfeiffer, whose authoritative account should be quoted at some length.

The new generation of about 300 B.C. living under a new monarchy realized that the great old poetical forms also belonged to ages gone forever. . . . Poetry had to be rescued from the dangerous situation in which it lay, and the writing of poetry had to become a particularly serious work of discipline and wide knowledge, τέχνη and σοφίη. The new writers had to look back to the old masters, especially of Ionic poetry, not to imitate them—this was regarded as impossible or at least as undesirable—but in order to be trained by them in their own new poetical technique. Their incomparably precious heritage had to be saved and studied. This was felt to be, first of all, a necessity for the rebirth and future life of poetry, and secondly an obligation to the achievements of past ages which had given birth to the masterpieces of Hellenic literature. . . . Thus a novel conception of poetry, held by the poets themselves, led the way to the revival of poetry as well as to a new treatment of the ancient poetical texts and then of all the other literary monuments. . . . For the new poetical technique could not be successfully practised without the constant help of

---

3. Legrand (1898), 413–32, who observes that the circumstantial allusions to musical performance in the Idylls of Theocritus and in the Hymns of Callimachus are "allusions dont l'à-propos est purement fictif" (p. 429); see also T. G. Rosenmeyer, "Elegiac and Elegos," *CSCA*, 1 (1968), 219: "In the pastoral lyric, the characters claim to be singing lines which are in fact not sung but recited. This should remind us that it will not do to confuse the poetic reality with the circumstances of production." Cf. Giangrande (1971), 99.

4. Fabiano (1971), especially 534n.

5. Rossi (1971a), 71.

the old masters. Glossaries, invaluable in the first place for the choice of words, helped also to give an understanding of the great poetry of the past.[6]

The first representative of this new age was Philetas of Cos, revered by Theocritus (see 7.39–41) and by Callimachus as well,[7] who articulated the aesthetic ideal, if not the name, of *leptotēs* or "fineness" in poetry (see fr. 10 Powell), whose compilation of glosses immediately became famous throughout the Greek world, and whom Strabo called "both poet and critic" (14.657 : ποιητὴς ἅμα καὶ κριτικός), a combination of words never before applied to any one individual. According to the later tradition, Philetas was appointed to undertake the education of Ptolemy II Philadelphus (308–246), the second ruler of Hellenistic Egypt, and he numbered among his pupils the poets Theocritus and Hermesianax as well as the scholar Zenodotus; the latter initiated the systematic study and recension of the Homeric epics and eventually succeeded his teacher in the office of royal tutor.[8] About the time that Zenodotus was engaged in editing the text of Homer, Callimachus undertook to devise a system for arranging all the works currently being assembled in the libraries of the Alexandrian Museum, a task which resulted in "a critical inventory of Greek literature" called the *Pinakes* or "Tables of all those who were eminent in any kind of παιδεία [intellectual or artistic culture] and their writings in 120 books" (as Hesychius and the *Suda* describe it).[9] The most productive period of Theocritus' artistic career, then, appears to have coincided with the first, and perhaps the greatest, burst of creative energy in Alexandrian scholarship, and it would be astonishing if a poet who demonstrates in so many other ways his vigorous and self-conscious participation in the contemporary literary movement were unaffected by the critical theories both directing and emerging from the work of his colleagues. Two closely related but distinguishable critical notions which took shape during this period—and which found their clearest and most definitive expression in the canonical lists of the foremost authors drawn up for each of the literary genres by Aristophanes of Byzantium at the end of the third century—are especially pertinent to an understanding of Theocritus' theoretical formation and principles of poetic practice: they are the metrical criterion for generic classification and the doctrine of the separateness and fixity of the literary genres.

It will be convenient to examine each of these critical principles independently in order to chart their eventual convergence in Alexandria. The Hellenistic emphasis on meter as the most important of literary differentiae

6. Pfeiffer (1968), 87–90.
7. If Pfeiffer (1968), 89, has correctly reconstructed *Aetia*, fr. 1.9–12.
8. Couat (1882), 69; Pfeiffer (1968), 88–92.
9. Pfeiffer (1968), 126–28.

was not merely a symptom of excessive formalism on the part of certain
critics, as it appears today, but on the contrary an attempt to isolate a stable
criterion which might serve to distinguish the various types of poetry according to their social function and the cultural factors responsible for producing them. In archaic Greece, different kinds of poetry were closely
bound to the contexts in which they were performed; the specific occasion
determined the choice of music, theme, and diction, and furnished an appropriate name for the type of poetry as well.[10] But the nature of these
divers occasions had ceased to be understood, while in the case of melic
poetry the unity of music and language had broken down in the fourth
century; the metrical form, however, remained. Alexandrian critics were
justified in their approach insofar as metrical variations accurately reflect the
varying circumstances of performance or conditions of public expression.[11]
Different metrical featurees do seem in fact to have accompanied the very
broadest divisions of Greek poetry (separating epic and melic poetry, for
example), and these were the very divisions on which Callimachus' arrangement of Greek literature was based.

As for the finer distinctions between metrical units, this subject would
appear to have been left, from the end of the sixth century B.C. at least, to
the province of musicians.[12] It was probably in the fifth century that a
terminology was developed to define the most important metrical units,[13]
and the first person to treat meter as an aspect of language rather than of
music was Hippias the sophist, thus preparing the way for Aristotle's sepa-
ration of diction and meter from rhythm.[14] In the seventh book of the
Laws, Plato categorizes poets by the meters in which they compose: λέγω
μὴν ὅτι ποιηταί τε ἡμῖν εἰσίν τινες ἐπῶν ἑξαμέτρων πάμπολλοι καὶ τρι-
μέτρων καὶ πάντων τῶν λεγομένων μέτρων . . . (810e: "Now mark my
words. We have a great number of poets, in hexameter verse, in iambic
trimeter, in a word in all the recognized meters . . .").[15] The principle of
generic classification according to meter was evidently formulated suffi-

---

10. Harvey (1955); West (1974), 1–39; Calame (1974), 117–21.

11. Cf. Pfeiffer (1968), 181–82; Maas (1962), 52–53, however, argues that the meter of
archaic Greek poetry was originally "neutral in respect of ethos," that is, unrelated to thematic
or social contexts, and only gradually came to be conditioned by the developing poetic
tradition.

12. Pfeiffer (1968), 53.

13. West (1974), 6–7, 22–25, 38; see Plato's references to Damon, *Rep.* 400bc.

14. Pfeiffer (1968), 53, 76.

15. All English quotations from the *Laws* are from A. E. Taylor's translation in *The
Collected Dialogues of Plato,* ed. E. Hamilton and H. Cairns, Bollingen Series, 71 (Princeton,
1961), 1226–1513.

ciently well by the fourth century to elicit Aristotle's famous rebuttal in the opening paragraphs of the *Poetics* (1447b13–20):

οἱ ἄνθρωποί γε συνάπτοντες τῷ μέτρῳ τὸ ποιεῖν ἐλεγειοποιοὺς τοὺς δὲ ἐποποιοὺς ὀνομάζουσιν, οὐχ ὡς κατὰ τὴν μίμησιν ποιητὰς ἀλλὰ κοινῇ κατὰ τὸ μέτρον προσαγορεύοντες· καὶ γὰρ ἂν ἰατρικὸν ἢ φυσικόν τι διὰ τῶν μέτρων ἐκφέρωσιν, οὕτω καλεῖν εἰώθασιν· οὐδὲν δὲ κοινόν ἐστιν Ὁμήρῳ καὶ Ἐμπεδοκλεῖ πλὴν τὸ μέτρον, διὸ τὸν μὲν ποιητὴν δίκαιον καλεῖν, τὸν δὲ φυσιολόγον μᾶλλον ἢ ποιητήν.

People do link up poetic composition with verse and speak of "elegiac poets," "epic poets," not treating them as poets by virtue of their imitation, but employing the term as a common appellation going along with the use of verse. And in fact the name is also applied to anyone who treats a medical or scientific topic in verses, yet Homer and Empedocles actually have nothing in common except their verse; hence the proper term for the one is "poet," for the other, "science writer" rather than "poet."[16]

To be sure, Aristotle's specific complaint in this passage is directed against those who would make meter the sole criterion for distinguishing poetry from other sorts of literature—as Gorgias, in his encomium on Helen (9D–K), and Gorgias' pupil Isocrates, in his eulogy of Evagoras (10–11) or in his *Antidosis* (45–47), had done[17]—but Aristotle's remarks reflect the existence of an older tradition, otherwise unknown to us, which tended to classify the different kinds of poetry according to meter (1447b15 : κατὰ τὸ μέτρον). Aristotle did not object to using meter in making generic divisions within poetry and he distinguished tragedy from epic by metrical criteria as well as by manner of representation, length of composition, and number of constituent parts (1149b11–17; cf. 1459b17). Moreover, although Aristotle's vocabulary is precise and consistent throughout the *Poetics,* his usage betrays the influence of the tradition against which he protested. For example: *epos,* which Aristotle employs only to designate a certain kind of poetry, is also the name of a meter (cf. Plato, *Phaedrus* 241d; *Laws* 682a), whereas the term used by Aristotle to refer to the dactylic hexameter is *to hērōikon* (1459b32–1460a5), a word derived from the conventional subject matter of poetry in that meter. Elsewhere, Aristotle refers to the epic as *hē en hexametrois mimētikē* (1449b21). Such a close association of metrical and generic names in Aristotle, though it does not produce any confusion in the *Poetics,* was to encourage the tendency to identify genre with meter, a tendency

16. All citations from the *Poetics* are based on R. Kassel's text, reprinted in D. W. Lucas, ed., *Aristotle: Poetics* (Oxford, 1968), and all translations are by G. F. Else, trans., *Aristotle: Poetics* (Ann Arbor, 1967).

17. Koster (1970), 22–24, 80–81, 83.

whose results are illustrated by the usage of *metrum* in later Latin.[18] Furthermore, Aristotle stresses that different meters each have individual characters: iambic is the most speakable of meters (hence most fit for dialogue in tragedy) because it is closest to the natural rhythm of conversation (1449a22–27); metrical variations are also held to determine variations in diction (1459a8–13). Aristotle's most ambitious characterization of the innate qualities of the various meters occurs in the following passage (1459b34–1460a1): τὸ γὰρ ἡρωικὸν στασιμώτατον καὶ ὀγκωδέστατον τῶν μέτρων ἐστίν (διὸ καὶ γλώττας καὶ μεταφορὰς δέχεται μάλιστα . . .), τὸ δὲ ἰαμβεῖον καὶ τετράμετρον κινητικὰ καὶ τὸ μὲν ὀρχηστικὸν τὸ δὲ πρακτικόν ("For the hexameter is the slowest moving and weightiest of all verses—that is why it is the most receptive to foreign words and metaphors. . . . The iambic trimeter and trochaic tetrameter, on the other hand, are verses suited to movement, the one to moral action, the other to dancing"; cf. *Rhet.* 1408b32). In the light of these attitudes, it is evident that the Alexandrian systems of generic classification represent not the imposition of rigid formalistic criteria on a wealth of diversified literary expression so much as an attempt to arrange in an orderly and coherent way the different types of Greek literature according to the norms that had traditionally defined them.

The literary taxonomy of Callimachus must have been worked out mainly in the process of compiling his *Pinakes,* for the immense scope of the task would have called for clear organizational principles, and the project must have been motivated, at least to some extent, by the need for a satisfactory system of classification to be used in the Museum library. The results of this enormous labor have now vanished except for a few pitiful fragments and references, but the little knowledge we have can be supplemented by surviving information about the revisions or additions to Callimachus' work by Aristophanes of Byzantium.[19] Callimachus divided the entire body of Greek literature into classes, ten of which have been identified, with varying degrees of certainty, by Pfeiffer, who notes that "there were probably many more and a number of subdivisions." Most of Pfeiffer's identifications bear on Callimachus' classification of prose; what is known of his poetic subdivisions suggests that he was quite willing to part with metrical criteria when there was a clear advantage to be gained, such as the likelihood of duplicating the categories in use by the poets themselves or by their contemporaries. For example, Callimachus classed the epinician odes of Pindar separately from the rest of his triadic poetry and subdivided

18. Behrens (1940), 15–16, especially n. 40; Steinmetz (1964), 462.
19. Pfeiffer (1968), 183–84, argues persuasively for a continuity from Callimachus to Aristophanes in the methods of arranging and classifying literature at Alexandria.

them according to the location of the games at which the contests were held. The victory songs of Simonides were apparently arranged by the type of competition entered; the dithyrambs of Bacchylides were also separated from his paeans. The poems of Sappho, however, may have been ordered by meter or alphabetically by the *incipit* of each work.[20] In any case, all the broader divisions of poetry made by Callimachus were consistent with metrical differentiae: there are references to epic, lyric, tragic, and comic classes; the lists of canonical authors drawn up by Aristophanes, no doubt in connection with his revision of the *Pinakes,* were arranged by metrical categories as well and included iambic, lyric, elegiac, tragic, comic, and epic poets.[21]

More important for an understanding of Theocritus' practice and aesthetic objectives is the cultural tradition which emphasized the peculiar genius and function of each of the poetic genres and contrasted the proper qualities belonging to each with those belonging to the others. The doctrine of the fixity and separateness of the poetic genres is closely related to the practice of classifying poetry according to metrical criteria (because every important kind of meter is also unique and distinct from every other); in fact, the doctrine of fixity is probably older than the metrical schemes of generic classification, which represent in all likelihood merely a taxonomic corollary to it. An early expression of the feeling that all works composed in a single genre belong somehow to an indivisible body may be seen in the original practice of ascribing all epic narratives to one "Homer."[22] Whatever the nature of the unwritten laws defining the boundaries of the poetic genres in the archaic period, the first explicit articulation of the principle of generic fixity occurs in Plato's *Ion* (534bc)

ἅτε οὖν οὐ τέχνῃ ποιοῦντες καὶ πολλὰ λέγοντες καὶ καλὰ περὶ τῶν πραγμάτ-ων . . . ἀλλὰ θείᾳ μοίρᾳ, τοῦτο μόνον οἷός τε ἕκαστος (ὁ ποιητὴς) ποιεῖν καλῶς ἐφ' ὃ ἡ Μοῦσα αὐτὸν ὥρμησεν, ὁ μὲν διθυράμβους, ὁ δὲ ἐγκώμια, ὁ δὲ ὑπορ-χήματα, ὁ δ' ἔπη, ὁ δ' ἰάμβους· τὰ δ' ἄλλα φαῦλος αὐτῶν ἕκαστός ἐστιν

Therefore, since their making is not by art, when they utter many things and fine about the deeds of men . . . but is by lot divine—therefore each [poet] is able to do well only that to which the Muse has impelled him—one to make dithyrambs, another panegyric odes, another choral songs, another epic poems, another iambs. In all the rest, each one of them is poor. . . . [trans. Lane Cooper]

Since a poet does not produce his works by his own craft but through the

20. Pfeiffer (1968), 128–30, argues for an alphabetical arrangement of Sappho's works; cf. Harvey (1955), 159, and Calame (1974), 121, who postulate a metrical scheme of classification.
21. Pfeiffer (1968), 128, 204–07; generally, Steinmetz (1964), 462.
22. Pfeiffer (1968), 43–44.

intervention of the Muse, the creative talent is a gift of the gods and, like each of their gifts to man, is specific and circumscribed. Socrates spoke of artistic ability as a θεῖα μοῖρα, something bestowed on a poet as a divine portion or allotment, a strictly bounded capacity to which nothing can be added; its limitations are made palpable in human terms by the incommensurable divisions between the various genres.[23] Plato's observation in the *Republic* (395a) that the same poet cannot compose successfully both tragedies and comedies, although of all the genres these two are the most similar to one another, seems to be a confirmation or illustration of this view. Plato reemphasizes the separate and proper function of each genre in his discussion of the "laws of music" (νόμοι περὶ τὴν μουσικήν) in the third book of the *Laws:* (700ab)

διῃρημένη γὰρ δὴ τότε ἦν ἡμῖν ἡ μουσικὴ κατὰ εἴδη τε ἑαυτῆς ἄττα καὶ σχήματα, καί τι ἦν εἶδος ᾠδῆς εὐχαὶ πρὸς θεούς, ὄνομα δὲ ὕμνοι ἐπεκαλοῦντο· καὶ τούτῳ δὴ τὸ ἐναντίον ἦν ᾠδῆς ἕτερον εἶδος—θρήνους δέ τις ἂν αὐτοὺς μάλιστα ἐκάλεσεν—καὶ παίωνες ἕτερον, καὶ ἄλλο, Διονύσου γένεσις οἶμαι, διθύραμβος λεγόμενος. . . .

Our music was then divided into several kinds and patterns. One kind of song, which went by the name of a *hymn,* consisted of prayers to the gods; there was a second and contrasting kind which might well have been called a *lament; paeans* were a third kind, and there was a fourth, the *dithyramb,* as it was called, dealing, if I am not mistaken, with the birth of Dionysus. . . .

Each of these genres was absolutely fixed and determined (700bc): τούτων δὴ διατεταγμένων καὶ ἄλλων τινῶν, οὐκ ἐξῆν ἄλλο εἰς ἄλλο καταχρῆσθαι μέλους εἶδος ("Now these and other types were definitely fixed, and it was not permissible to misuse one kind of melody for another"). Plato goes on to contrast the good old days of aesthetic orderliness with the chaos that ensued when poets began to mingle genres (700d):

μετὰ δὲ ταῦτα, προϊόντος τοῦ χρόνου, ἄρχοντες μὲν τῆς ἀμούσου παρανομίας ποιηταὶ ἐγίγνοντο φύσει μὲν ποιητικοί, ἀγνώμονες δὲ περὶ τὸ δίκαιον τῆς Μούσης καὶ τὸ νόμιμον, βακχεύοντες καὶ μᾶλλον τοῦ δέοντος κατεχόμενοι ὑφ' ἡδονῆς, κεραννύντες δὲ θρήνους τε ὕμνοις καὶ παίωνας διθυράμβοις, καὶ αὐλῳδίας δὴ ταῖς κιθαρῳδίαις μιμούμενοι. . . .

Afterward, in course of time, an unmusical license set in with the appearance of poets who were men of native genius, but ignorant of what is right and legitimate in the realm of the Muses. Possessed by a frantic and unhallowed lust for pleasure, they contaminated laments with hymns and paeans with dithyrambs, actually imitated the strains of the flute on the harp. . . .

23. See Trimpi (1973), 8–9, for a discussion of the *non omnia possumus omnes* theme in ancient literary critical theory.

The practice of *catachresis* or mingling of genres evidently began long before the Hellenistic period, when it became the hallmark of the new poetry.

Aristotle also protested against the contamination of meters, a practice for which he cited the *Centaur* of Chaeremon as an example (1447b20–23, 1460a2; cf. Ath. 608c). In Aristotle's view, the distinctive qualities of the individual genres should not be seen as determined by such a purely formal criterion as meter; rather, each genre as constituted should possess a meter appropriate to its own nature.[24] Aristotle's position on the issue of generic fixity can be gauged from his remarks about the proper role of different meters. Speaking of the poetry of invective, he says (1448b30–34): ἐν οἷς κατὰ τὸ ἁρμόττον καὶ τὸ ἰαμβεῖον ἦλθε μέτρον—διὸ καὶ ἰαμβεῖον καλεῖται νῦν, ὅτι ἐν τῷ μέτρῳ τούτῳ ἰάμβιζον ἀλλήλους. καὶ ἐγένοντο τῶν παλαιῶν οἱ μὲν ἡρωικῶν οἱ δὲ ἰάμβων ποιηταί ("In them [the invectives], in accordance with what is suitable and fitting, iambic verse also put in its appearance; indeed that is why it is called 'iambic' now, because it is the verse in which they used to 'iambize,' that is, lampoon, each other. And so some of the early poets became composers of epic, the others of iambic, verses"). Similar reasoning can be found in Aristotle's discussion of the shift from the trochaic tetrameter to the iambic trimeter for use in the dialogue portions of tragedy. The trochaic is connected with dance and was appropriate to tragedy before spoken parts were introduced; λέξεως δὲ γενομένης αὐτὴ ἡ φύσις τὸ οἰκεῖον μέτρον εὗρε (1449a23–24: "but when speech came along the very nature of the case turned up the appropriate verse"). Aristotle's comments on the appropriateness of the dactylic hexameter to epic poetry are in line with this point of view and are even more emphatic (1459b31–1460a5):

τὸ δὲ μέτρον τὸ ἡρωικὸν ἀπὸ τῆς πείρας ἥρμοκεν. εἰ γάρ τις ἐν ἄλλῳ τινὶ μέτρῳ διηγηματικὴν μίμησιν ποιοῖτο ἢ ἐν πολλοῖς, ἀπρεπὲς ἂν φαίνοιτο. . . . διὸ οὐδεὶς μακρὰν σύστασιν ἐν ἄλλῳ πεποίηκεν ἢ τῷ ἡρῴῳ, ἀλλ᾽ ὥσπερ εἴπομεν αὐτὴ ἡ φύσις διδάσκει τὸ ἁρμόττον αὐτῇ αἱρεῖσθαι.

As for the epic verse, it has found its way to the mark by a process of trial. If someone should compose a narrative imitation in any other verse form, or in several, it would strike one as incongruous. . . . Hence nobody has composed a long poem in any other verse than the hexameter; instead, in the way we have indicated the very nature of the genre teaches one to choose the verse that fits it.

We have already seen that a poet's choice of diction should vary with the meter (1459a8–13), not indeed because meter is the most basic aesthetic component but rather because the rule of propriety creates such an intimate

24. Cf. Koster (1970), 52n.

association between meter and genre that the former can become a kind of shorthand for the latter. Aristotle's observations illustrate the natural connection between the metrical principle of generic classification and the doctrine of fixity which underlies it.

The combination of the two notions, though it can be found only in the writings of Roman authorities, is so widely accepted by them that it has been taken to be a fundamental principle of Alexandrian criticism.[25] According to Cicero, for example, "poematis enim tragici comici epici melici etiam ac dithyrambici . . . suum cuiusque est, diversum a reliquis. . . . suus est cuique certus sonus et quaedam intellegentibus nota vox" (*De opt. gen. orat.* 1.1: "Of the tragic, comic, epic, lyric, and dithyrambic poem . . . there belongs to each a proper quality that is different from the rest. . . . Each has its own fixed style and a certain tone familiar to persons of discernment"). Speaking elsewhere of the parts of an oration, Cicero sought to discover the distinguishing characteristics and standard type of each (*Orat.* 23.75: "ut cuiusque generis nota quaeratur et formula"). Horace also lent weight to the notion that each branch of literature requires what is uniquely appropriate to it (*AP* 72, 86–87, 92).[26] The doctrine was well summed up by Quintilian: "sua cuique proposito [*or* proposita] lex, suus cuique decor est" (*Inst.* 10.2.22: "to each subject its proper law, to each its proper quality"). But there are sufficient indications in contemporary sources to establish that the rules for differentiating the various genres from one another were already in full force when Theocritus was composing the Idylls. Most important in this regard is a passage from the Thirteenth Iambus of Callimachus in which the poet, protesting the charges of πολυ-είδεια leveled against him by his critics (according to the *Diegesis*), apparently voices resentment at the notion that a writer should be confined to composing in one genre rather than in another, and in a few rather than in many. Callimachus' remark demonstrates the strength and pervasiveness of the doctrine of fixity and its combination with the principle of metrical classification, for the language Callimachus uses makes it plain that each genre was identified with a specific meter:

τίς εἶπεν αυτ [. . . .]λε . . ϱ . [. . . .].
σὺ πεντάμετϱα συντίθει, σὺ δ' η[ϱῶο]ν,
σὺ δὲ τϱαγῳδε[ῖν] ἐκ θεῶν ἐκληϱώσῳ;
δοκέω μὲν οὐδείς, ἀλλὰ καὶ το.δ. .κεψαι

[fr. 203.30–33 Pfeiffer]

. . . who said "Do you compose pentameters and you epics; the gods have allotted that you write tragedies"? Nobody, I believe, but. . . . [trans. Trypanis]

25. Steinmetz, 461–62, 465.
26. Cf. Hack (1916), especially 21–22.

It might be reasonable to conclude that the way to discover the form, and hence the generic concept, underlying the bucolic poetry of Theocritus would be to examine his use of the dactylic hexameter for what it can tell us about the relation between bucolic and the other kinds of poetry traditionally composed in that meter.

But, as one commentator on the *Iambi* of Callimachus has noted, it was already something of an anachronism to protest against the laws of generic fixity when Callimachus was writing, for not only he but a number of other Hellenistic poets had long since abandoned the practice of composing in one genre;[27] what is more, the Alexandrians seem to have taken up and refined the technique, which earlier had been tried only intermittently and without complete success (if the judgments of Plato and Aristotle on this point can be trusted), of mixing different generic elements together *within* the same poem. The Alexandrian practice of generic contamination has come in for increased attention from classical scholars in this century and is now thought to constitute one of the distinguishing features of Hellenistic and Roman poetry. Wilhelm Kroll is often credited with being the first to form a just appreciation of the significance of this phenomenon and with coining the phrase *die Kreuzung der Gattungen* to describe it, but in fact the concept—at least as it applies to the study of Theocritus, if not in its broader implications—had been fully articulated by Couat and Legrand.[28] Legrand also anticipated Kroll in linking the practice of generic contamination to the bookish quality, *le caractère livresque,* of Alexandrian poetry.[29] At all events, the Hellenistic tendency to mix and combine generic elements further complicates the task of defining bucolic poetry by detracting from the taxonomic significance of its formal structure. For in the context of a widespread "crossing of literary breeds" in Alexandrian poetry, Callimachus' complaint against the traditional rules of generic composition seems less an act of defiance directed at currently prevailing literary norms than a programmatic utterance designed to proclaim the independence of the new poetry in general and of the *Iambi* in particular from the very principles of contemporary criticism actually being laid down and employed by Call-

27. C. M. Dawson, "The Iambi of Callimachus: A Hellenistic Poet's Experimental Laboratory," *YCS,* 11 (1950), 130.

28. Kroll (1924), especially 203n.; but see Couat (1882), 395, 258 (on Callimachus); Legrand (1898), 413–36, especially 418, 431, 434; Deubner (1921), 361–68.

29. Legrand (1898), especially 430–31; Kroll's views on the connection between generic contamination and the rise of the book as a literary medium were first set forth in an article, "Hellenistisch-römische Gedichtbücher," *NJbb. klass. Altert.,* 37 (1916), 93–106, especially 94–95, 101 (where the phrase *die Kreuzung der Gattungen* also occurs). On the importance of the book for the character of Hellenistic poetry, see Kroll (1924), 202; Pfeiffer (1968), 102–03; Giangrande (1971), 98, n. 11; idem (1970a), 47.

imachus and his colleagues in their scholarly activity of classifying Greek literature.

The relation between the Alexandrian critical doctrines of generic fixity and metrical determination on the one hand and the Alexandrian poetic practice of generic contamination on the other has been investigated by Rossi, who speaks of an inversion, a *normatività a rovescio:* the scholarly principles of literary classification devised in this period are meant to apply *positively* and *descriptively* to the literature of the past, but over the literature of the present day they exercise an influence at once *prescriptive* and *negative*. It is almost as if the Alexandrians undertook to analyze and define the rules of the classic genres in order to be able to violate them all the more vigorously.[30] The chief exponent and theorist of this *nuova normatività,* according to Rossi, is the author of the Thirteenth Iambus. The scope of the new literary fashion can be illustrated by such oddities as two epinician odes in elegiac distichs and a Doric hymn in the same meter, by Callimachus; a philosophical work by Cercidas of Megalopolis in lyric meters, Doric dialect, and in the style of the new dithyramb; a hymn to Pan in trimeters by Castorion of Soli; a hymn to Demeter composed entirely in stichic choriambic hexameters by Philicius of Corcyra; and Boiscus' invention of the iambic octameter.[31] What strikes the historian about these literary experiments is "their intellectualism, their virtually absolute arbitrariness."[32] If Theocritus' choice of poetic forms should prove to be equally arbitrary, it will be impossible to extract an understanding of the "generic" identity of bucolic poetry from its formal structure. The very notion of genre may be deemed inappropriate and alien to the aesthetic intent of the poems.

This may in fact appear at first to be the case. Kroll treats Theocritus' pastoral dialogues as a mixture of elements derived from "bucolic" (the term is left undefined) and from mime; he also comments on the different rhetorical structures contained in the Idylls, such as the *propemptikon* of Lycidas and the *paraenesis* of Simichidas in Idyll 7.[33] The dependence of Idylls 2 and 15 on Sophron's Γυναικεῖοι ("Women's Mimes"), the use of stichomythy in Idylls 22 and 27, the combination of bucolic themes with the epyllion, the mixture of dialects, and the presence of a range of meters (from the dactylic hexameter in most of the Idylls to the elegiac distichs in Idyll 8 and in many of the Epigrams, to the lyric meters of Idylls 28–31 and the *Syrinx*) are all adduced as further evidence.[34] More subtle is Theocritus'

30. Rossi (1971a), 83.
31. Ibid., 83–84; 93, n. 76; Pfeiffer (1968), 157; Legrand (1898), 435.
32. Rossi (1971a), 84.
33. Similarly, Giangrande (1971), 96–98, identifies Idyll 12 as an ἐπιβατήριον.
34. Kroll (1924), 203–06; cf. Rossi (1972) and (1971a), 84–85; Deubner (1921), 375–76.

contamination of narrative poetry in recitative meter with lyric elements: refrains, symmetrical (if not quite strophic) divisions, and various folkloric forms originally lyrical in structure (such as the fieldworkers' song in Idyll 10 or the lullaby in Idyll 24.7–9).[35] This evidence leads Fabiano to conclude that

a procedure falling within the Hellenistic ideal of ποικιλία . . . is the blending of traditional genres inside the same poem; in this procedure, technically correspond-ing to the use of various dialects in their work, to the combination of dialects in the language of the same poem, to the mixture of elements of learned origin with others of popular derivation, Hellenistic poets are really constraining the genres [instead of being constrained by them] as earlier poets had never done before. In this respect almost every Theocritean idyll is a mosaic: the intrusion of alien elements is more noticeable in the Epyllia, particularly in the *Hymn to the Dioskouroi,* but it can be found in the Urban Mimes too . . . and is even the rule in the Bucolic Idylls, where an obvious stylistic distinction depends not only on the character of each poem but also on the color of various parts of the same poem, which can consist of narrative, dialogue and sung sections at the same time.[36]

Fabiano goes on to speculate about the problem of how to define The-ocritus' style, if indeed such a task can even be attempted, in the light of the Hellenistic ideal of stylistic variation. His discussion is extremely relevant to the undertaking here, which is to uncover the original identity of bucolic poetry in the context of the Alexandrian technique of generic contamina-tion. "At this point one must ask oneself whether it will be possible from the critical point of view to propose a unitary interpretation of such a differentiated system of expression and composition, that is to say, whether it will be legitimate to speak of only one style in an author whose most conspicuous peculiarity is his mastery of all styles and genres in order to allow himself the refined pleasure of mingling them together. To such a question traditional stylistic analysis would give a negative answer and would limit itself to registering the differences of tone or, at most, to remarking mechanically the variation of style as it coincides approximately with the variation of genre." Fabiano pursues instead something of a struc-turalist approach and is able to arrive at a unitary conception of Theocritus' style:

What seems chiefly to characterize Theocritus' poetic language is the instability of the system at every level, from the least phonetic unity, which always enjoys a considerable autonomy inside the changeable convention of the dialect, to the struc-ture of the *Idylls* as complex syntheses of different literary genres. In Theocritus' poetry it is usual to meet with extravagant elements which apparently derive from other fields and clash with the fundamental character of the poem where they

35. Rossi (1971a), 85–86; cf. Dover (1971), xlviii–l.
36. Fabiano (1971), 526–27.

appear . . . : the impact of these elements on the others is so typical of Theocritus' poetry that it is to be envisaged as one of the features which most distinguish his style. . . . I am inclined to think that variation of the level of style, which appears not only in the pastoral but in almost every idyll, is one of the main aspects of poetic unification.[37]

Fabiano's conclusion is somewhat paradoxical. Theocritus' style is characterized by an avoidance of clear stylistic indicators, or rather by a superabundant and incongruous mixture of them. His style can be identified by a complete absence of discrete stylistic levels, an absence achieved by inclusive and inconsistent treatment of style-specific terms. Theocritus' poetry lacks a traditional style; it can only be said to possess an anti-style—or, better, a meta-style.

It is tempting to adopt a similar strategy to define the generic concept underlying bucolic poetry. Bucolic, accordingly, would be a kind of hybrid, a meta-genre, composed of elements drawn from all the traditional genres alike and combined in varying proportions into an exotic assemblage. The boundaries of the "genre" would be determined by none of the usual criteria, such as a specific meter, but would be distinguished by their fluidity, by their ability to accommodate many different formal structures. Actually, this line of reasoning makes a certain amount of sense, and the definition of bucolic poetry proposed here will take account of it insofar as bucolic poetry will be viewed as a conscious reflection on and deliberate reversal of certain traditional determinants of a venerable genre. Bucolic poetry is indeed constituted in such a fashion as to play on conventional methods of literary definition. Nonetheless, it is quite plain that the meta-generic interpretation of bucolic poetry, in and of itself, is inadequate. First of all, it is not sufficiently informative and cannot account for the specific elements contributing to the thematic range of bucolic poetry, nor does it explain Theocritus' choice of the dactylic hexameter as the metrical pattern for the vast majority of the Idylls. Second, the tendency to combine various generic elements is not unique to Theocritus' poetry and it is therefore difficult to see how the technique of generic mingling alone could distinguish the Idylls, as a whole or individually, from other contemporary productions which exhibit similar features. In fact, Ludwig Deubner logically proposed, on the basis of similar reasoning, to group Idylls 2 and 15 together with the Second, Fifth, and Sixth Hymns of Callimachus in virtually the same genre of *sakrale Solomimen,* by which he meant hymnic material cast into the form of mimetic dramatizations of religious ritual featuring a monologue by a speaker who appears to be an active and vocal

37. Ibid., 527–29, 536.

participant in the ceremony.[38] But we know that the bucolic Idylls of
Theocritus represented in antiquity a separate and recognizable subdivision
of his poetry with a distinctive literary profile of their own. The meta-
generic conception of bucolic poetry not only risks dispersing individual
Idylls among sundry other hypothetical categories (by analogy with the
practice of other Alexandrian poets), but in the context of contemporary
literary experiments it also fails to reveal what it was that led ancient readers
to assign a number of Theocritus' poems to a specific literary class. Third,
the meta-generic conception ignores certain aspects of consistency and continuity throughout the Idylls which may be pertinent to an understanding of
the formal structure of bucolic poetry. It is these aspects of Theocritus'
work that we must now consider.

Despite a complete—and, in the light of later discoveries, one might
almost say exaggerated—awareness of generic contamination in the Idylls,
Legrand also noticed a common feature present throughout most of Theocritus' poetry: "no one, to my knowledge, either before Theocritus or
among his contemporaries, practiced generic mingling with such freedom
as he did—*narrating* songs, for example, or interspersing his narrative with
dramatic dialogue. . . . Of these irregularities . . . there is one at all events
on which it is fitting to insist: the predilection of the author of the Idylls for
the dactylic hexameter."[39] To Legrand, of course, Theocritus' adherence to
the epic meter regardless of changes in the subject of his poems represented
simply another anomaly, hardly unparalleled in Alexandrian poetry, in the
use of metrics. But since the practice of Theocritus appears to be consistent
in this one regard, it may be legitimate to inquire whether a coherent
identity can be constructed for a sizable number of poems within the group
of hexameter Idylls, an identity whose coherence is not vitiated by the
combination of divers generic elements within those poems. Kroll's objection that Theocritus mixes his meters is thereby avoided: with the exception
of the spurious Eighth Idyll, no combination of different meters exists
within the same poem in the Theocritean corpus; the poems composed in
meters other than the hexameter belong to the collection of epigrams or to
the Aeolic group, which, as we have seen, constitute separate subdivisions.
To be sure, the influence of the mime form on many of the hexameter Idylls
is unmistakable, but it has been vastly exaggerated by critics who have
appealed to it as a solution to the problem of identifying the generic determinants of bucolic poetry.

It cannot be demonstrated that Idylls 14 and 15, for example, are actu-

38. Deubner (1921), 376.
39. Legrand (1898), 434.

ally "mimes in hexameter"[40] or that contemporaries of Theocritus would have confounded them with mimes. First of all, the traditional mime form did not include meter; mimes by convention were composed entirely in prose (although recent fragments show Sophron's prose to have been highly rhythmical), as Aristotle attests by associating the mimes of Sophron and Xenarchus with Socratic dialogues in the same "nameless" category (1447b10–11). When Herodas undertook to adapt the mime to a literary treatment in his *mimiamboi*, he achieved this objective by reviving (however imperfectly) the Eastern Ionic dialect and choliambic meter of Hipponax, and both the subject and style of his poems—unlike the subject and style of the hexameter Idylls—are invariably those of the mime form as we know it.[41] Moreover, the traditional setting of mime ("everyday life in the humbler levels of society"),[42] which certain Idylls do share, is not itself tied to any particular genre or form in the Hellenistic period, but on the contrary is used to color in varying degrees the treatment of many different themes in both literature and the arts.[43] Such an interest in the life of "little people" can be found in both the *Hecale* of Callimachus and the *Heracliscus* (Idyll 24) of Theocritus, each of which is devoted, ostensibly, to a heroic subject yet lays its scene in a humble domestic setting, and neither of which is ever confused with mime by ancient or modern commentators. Critics have fastened onto the formal similarities linking the urban and rustic dialogues of Theocritus with mime, but it is not clear that issues involving the *mode of imitation* in poetry which are raised by the presence of the dialogue form would have played as decisive a role in generic differentiation for the Alexandrians as they had for Plato and Aristotle or would again for the late antique followers of Plato and Aristotle. Just as Herodas took over many of the features of the mime form in the process of creating his own original poetic synthesis, so Theocritus borrowed a dramatic form from the mime in creating his urban and rustic dialogues, poems whose setting closely resembles that of many other works by Theocritus and his contemporaries which happen not to possess a dialogue form. Clearly, the question is one of the relative importance of different sets of formal criteria in differentiating genres. Because the evidence indicates that metrical considerations far outweighed mimetic ones in the Hellenistic period—even if some poets honored conventional metrical norms of genre more in the breach than in the observance—it is likely that the differences between the Idylls of Theocritus and the Mimes of Sophron or Herodas were more striking to the Hellenistic

40. Kroll (1924), 204.
41. Cunningham (1971), 3–17.
42. Ibid., 10.
43. Cf. Webster (1964), 168–71.

reader than were the similarities. Just as epic language and narrative techniques are widely employed in poetry of the archaic and classical periods without causing any real generic confusion, so in literature of the Hellenistic age, through a characteristic inversion of styles, features common to the mime form are introduced to add variety, freshness, humor, or irony to many different kinds of poetry. While it cannot and need not be denied, then, that Theocritus derives certain formal and thematic elements from mime (the dialogue form and the social setting, respectively), it is by no means probable that he regarded the presence or absence of such elements as differentiating the hexameter Idylls generically from one another; rather, his consistent use of the dactylic hexameter suggests that he wished to create an underlying unity among them despite their diversity.[44] All the remaining objections to the formal coherence of the hexameter Idylls made by adherents to the *Kreuzung der Gattungen* theory similarly depend on matters of stylistic, as opposed to generic, variation.

But it may be objected that Theocritus' metrical practice itself is hardly consistent enough to use as a basis for a unitary conception of bucolic poetry. Minor variations in meter, of course, can be ascribed to the technique of stylistic fluctuation already discussed. The phenomenon of the so-called bucolic diaeresis is more problematic, for it has been regarded in and of itself as an important formal component of bucolic poetry. According to one view, the bucolic diaeresis is the most prominent of the various devices by which Theocritus adapted the meter of the Homeric epics to an antiheroic subject. A naive version of this thematic interpretation of the bucolic diaeresis is exemplified by a scholiast on Hermogenes who, appealing to the mimetic conception of bucolic genre current in his own day, seems to regard the bucolic diaeresis as imitative of the verse form actually employed by cowherds: οὕτω δὲ λέγεται (ἡ τομὴ βουκολικὴ) διὰ τὸ ταύτῃ χρήσασθαι τοὺς τὰ βουκολικὰ ποιήσαντας ποιήματα, βουκόλους μιμούμενοι, ὡς ὁ Θεόκριτος ("the bucolic caesura is so called because it is used by the composers of bucolic poems, such as Theocritus, in imitating cowherds").[45] But the opinion expressed here was exceptional in antiquity: most of the ancient authorities who mention the bucolic diaeresis do so with reference to Homer or to other (non-bucolic) epic poets, and they account for its name by alluding to its frequency in the work of Theocritus rather

44. Cf. Todorov (1976/77), 160: "The fact that a work 'disobeys' its genre does not make the latter nonexistent; it is tempting to say that quite the contrary is true. . . . because transgression, in order to exist as such, requires a law that will, of course, be transgressed. One could go further: the norm becomes visible—lives—only by its transgressions."

45. Cited by Legrand (1898), 423n. Perhaps the phrase "imitating cowherds (*boukoloi*)" is merely intended as a gloss on *bucolic,* however.

than by ascribing to the phenomenon itself some kind of inherently bucolic or rustic quality.[46] The thematic interpretation was resurrected in the modern age in the form of a theory—fortunately now discarded—which connected the end of Theocritus' hexameter with the fragmentary dactylic rhythms of folk poetry.[47] It still survives in the notion that the stately verse of Homer was made more humble, and therefore more suitable to the requirements of its subject, by Theocritus' use of the bucolic diaeresis—a formulation that has become axiomatic in recent Theocritean criticism.[48] But the high incidence of bucolic diaeresis in the Homeric hexameter (62 percent in the *Iliad*, 59 percent in the *Odyssey*) and in its Alexandrian imitations (58 percent in Aratus, 62 percent in Apollonius, and 67 percent in Callimachus), though it falls short of Theocritus' practice in Idylls 1–7 and 9–11 (76 percent),[49] argues against any theory which would make this metrical feature alone into a distinguishing characteristic of bucolic poetry: would a difference of at most 15 percent change the nature of the verse so radically or impart to it such a distinctive identity as to impress its singularity upon the reader and provide an immediate signal of a shift in genre? After all, Sophocles and Euripides make frequent use of the bucolic diaeresis when composing monodies in hexameters—perhaps to break up the line

46. Legrand (1898), 423; O'Neill (1942), 166. Juba, a second-century A.D. writer, simply points out the high incidence of bucolic diaeresis in both Homer and Theocritus, according to a fragment cited by Bassett (1919), 351. It is noteworthy that Marius Victorinus, one of the few ancient grammarians who account for the name of the so-called bucolic diaeresis by noting its frequency in Theocritus, describes Theocritus' metrical practice in such exaggerated terms that it is clear he has never read the Idylls; see Bassett (1919), 354n., who also quotes (358) the relevant passage of Marius Victorinus: "quam legem per omne opus sui carminis Theocritus Syracusanus exceptis tribus aut quattuor ferme versibus . . . custodit" ("which law Theocritus observes throughout the entire body of his poetry, except in about three or four verses").

47. Fritzsche-Hiller (1881), 13–14; Christ (1890), 446; Legrand (1898), 422–24. A more sophisticated version of this theory can be found in Bassett (1920), who derives the bucolic tetrapody from the Priapean (which does occur in folk poetry, specifically in the fragments cited by the scholiasts in their account of the ritual origin of bucolic poetry, and which was called "bucolic" by Byzantine metricians).

48. Rosenmeyer (1969), 92–97, for example, discussing Theocritus' various techniques of *Tonmalerei*, seems to view Theocritus' segmented verse structure as a metrical corollary to the "disjunctive" or "disconnective" nature of his syntax, with its concentration on the simplicity of each *Ding an sich* (45–54). Berg (1974), 10, similarly speaks of Theocritus' "'rustication'" of heroic verse through the use of repeated sounds, refrains, and the bucolic diaeresis, all intended to break up the continuity of the otherwise uninterrupted hexameters. It is, of course, quite possible to accept this description of Theocritus' technique without subscribing to the view that the formal device of word end following the eighth position in the hexameter reflects the distinctive subject matter or harmonizes with the humble design of bucolic poetry.

49. These figures derive from Kunst (1889), 854, and from a compilation made by Van Sickle (1978), 108n. (and independently checked by me), of the statistical data supplied by O'Neill (1942), 138–50 (tables 1–3, 6, 8, 10, 11, 14, 16–18, 23, 24, and 28).

and give it more "strophic" or lyrical quality;[50] one might also compare the oracular speech of Neoptolemus in Sophocles' *Philoctetes* 839–42, which contains diaeresis after the fourth foot in each line. These passages, presumably, are not freighted with rustic or humble associations. Second, as Legrand demonstrated, there is no difference in the frequency of bucolic diaeresis between the purportedly sung and spoken portions of Idylls 1, 3, 5, 7, and 10; even in the "sung" portions of the pastoral Idylls Theocritus does not accentuate the bucolic diaeresis (by means of anaphora and other devices) in relation to other conventional caesurae. "One thing at least is certain: in the poems combining 'speech' and 'song' neither meter nor technique conveys more than very imperfectly the difference between the purported types of utterance."[51] The issue is far more complex than has been suggested here, however; I have therefore included a detailed technical consideration of the matter in an appendix.

To sum up: at the time Theocritus was composing the Idylls, the principle of classifying poetic genres according to meter and the doctrine of the fixity and separateness of the poetic genres had been long and powerfully established. Although the laws regulating generic composition were often deliberately contravened by the very poets who had, in commenting on the practice of their predecessors, helped to formulate those laws, the technique of "crossing literary breeds" does not seem to have affected the formal coherence of bucolic poetry—its consistent use of the dactylic hexameter. Finer sorts of metrical distinctions, such as the presence or absence of the bucolic diaeresis, cannot be shown to have had significance for the "generic" identity of individual Idylls—as Rosenmeyer says, "these are subtleties of texture."[52] No obstacle remains, then, to following the procedure enunciated at the outset. The most reasonable way to discover the form, and hence the "generic" concept, underlying the bucolic poetry of Theocritus is to regard his use of the dactylic hexameter as programmatic and to investigate the relation between bucolic poetry and other kinds of poetry traditionally composed in that meter. For of all Theocritus' innovations, his metrical practice had the longest influence. "The gross fact re-

50. Legrand (1898), 424; cf. Stark (1963), 377.

51. Legrand (1898), 422–25. Legrand's argument is designed to prove that the Idylls are meant to be read, not sung, but individual points of his discussion also tell against the thematic interpretation of the bucolic diaeresis; similar arguments had been made by Kunst (1889), 854. Theocritus' metrical practice does vary somewhat throughout the hexameter Idylls, and the bucolic diaeresis is indeed more frequent in Idylls 1–7 (and in the *Lament for Bion*) than in the rest of Theocritus' hexameter poetry. Daniel Heinsius first pointed this out in 1604 (O'Neill [1942], 166); more recent discussions of these issues can be found in Kunst (1889); Bassett (1920); O'Neill (1942), 108; Maas (1962), 93–96; Dover (1971), xxii–xxvii; Van Sickle (1978), 107n.; and in my appendix.

52. Rosenmeyer (1969), 14.

mains that pastoral lyric was at first composed in the same verse form as epic, and remained faithful to the pattern for over 1700 years."[53]

Already in the fourth century B.C. Theophrastus had designated as *epos* the fixed and determinate genre of poetry distinguished by its use of the dactylic hexameter.[54] Theophrastus' two treatises *peri poiētikēs* are not extant, but Diomedes quotes his definition of tragedy, and it has been argued that the following anonymous definition of *epos* in Diomedes derives from the same Greek source as the definition of tragedy (I, 483 Keil): "Epos dicitur Graece carmine hexametro divinarum rerum et heroicarum humanarumque comprehensio; quod a Graecis ita definitum est, ἔπος ἐστὶν περιοχὴ θείων τε καὶ ἡρωικῶν καὶ ἀνθρωπίνων πραγμάτων" ("*Epos* is the Greek word for hexameter poetry encompassing divine, heroic, and human deeds"). The term *epos* no longer refers to the poet's words or to the metrical lines of his poetry in isolation but has become instead the name of a genre. Here for the first time is *epos* used in place of the more customary ἐποποιΐα or ἐπῶν ποίησις as a proper literary critical term. Its semantic transformation from "word" [ἔπος] to "poet's words" [ἔπεα], to "what is composed in a poet's words" [ἐποποιΐα] to a generic label [ἔπος] is now complete.[55] Unless the Greek text presented by Diomedes is a reflection of the latter's critical vocabulary, it would seem that the generic name of the class to which bucolic poetry belonged had been established even before the time of Theocritus. In Theocritus' own day, Callimachus could compare the didactic hexameter poem of Aratus with its generic ancestor in the same terms:

> Ἡσιόδου τό τ' ἄεισμα καὶ ὁ τρόπος· οὐ τὸν ἀοιδόν
> ἔσχατον, ἀλλ' ὀκνέω μὴ τὸ μελιχρότατον
> τῶν ἐπέων ὁ Σολεὺς ἀπεμάξατο· χαίρετε λεπταί
> ῥήσιες, Ἀρήτου σύμβολον ἀγρυπνίης
>
> [27 Pfeiffer; 56 Page]

Hesiod's is both the theme and the manner [*or* the (didactic) character and the style], although I must admit that the poet of Soli did not copy that bard to the end but took for his pattern only the sweetest part of his [hexameter] verses. Hail refined discourses, token of Aratus' wakefulness.[56]

---

53. Rosenmeyer (1969), 14, who neglects to follow up the implications of this gross fact. The argument contained in the following paragraphs was first sketched out by Van Sickle (1975); cf. also Schmidt (1972), 38, 282–83.

54. On the early history of *epos*, see A. L. Ford, "Early Greek Terms for Poetry: *Aoidē, Epos, Poiēsis*," diss. Yale (1982).

55. Koster (1970), 85–87, 91.

56. My translation of this variously interpreted epigram has been guided by the commentary of Gow-Page; Wilamowitz's reading in line 1 (ἀοιδῶν), if correct, would make matters of epic genealogy central to the epigram. For an alternate reading of the last line, see G. Lohse, "ΣΥΝΤΟΝΟΣ ΑΓΡΥΠΝΙΗ," *Hermes*, 95 (1967), 379–81.

To be sure, Callimachus is using *epos* here not in its technical literary sense (that is, as a generic category) but in its more general meaning of hexameter verse or poetic word; nonetheless, its role in the epigram is to reinforce the generic connections between Hesiod and Aratus as similar practitioners of (didactic) epic poetry. By choosing to compose in hexameters, Theocritus also was assimilating bucolic poetry to the genre of *epos*.

The word *epos* continues to be used in Roman literature as the name of a genre. It is from this period that most of our information about the ancient classification of bucolic poetry derives. The Alexandrians had brought about the complete fusion of the principles of metrical classification and generic fixity, with the result that versification came to be considered the essential determinant of genre. Horace accordingly regarded Virgil's bucolic poetry as a variety of *epos;* because his famous judgment, *molle atque facetum,* is so often lifted out of context, Horace's words are usually construed as neuter singulars with an adverbial function, but a glance at the entire passage[57] indicates that the two adjectives are attributes of the noun *epos:*

> arguta meretrice potes Dauoque Chremata
> eludente senem comis garrire libellos
> unus uiuorum, Fundani, Pollio regum
> facta canit pede ter percusso; forte epos acer
> ut nemo Varius ducit, molle atque facetum
> Vergilio adnuerunt gaudentes rure Camenae:
> hoc erat experto frustra Varrone Atacino
> atque quibusdam aliis melius quod scribere possem
> inuentore minor. . . .
>
> [*Serm.* 1.10.40–48]

You alone among living writers, Fundanius, can rattle off little books elegantly portraying old man Chremes tricked by Davus and a clever prostitute [books in the style of the New Comedy]; Pollio sings the deeds of kings, three beats to a verse [in the dialogue meter of tragedy]; fierce Varius spins out the heroic *epos* better than anyone, while the Camenae who delight in the countryside have granted Virgil a tender and polished *epos* [bucolic *epos*]; it was this sort of *epos* [satire] that I could write better than Varro of Atax, who, along with several others, tried his hand at it in vain, though I am inferior to its originator. . . .

The *fortis/mollis* polarity occurs again[58] in the epigram by Domitius Marsus on the death of Tibullus, which contrasts the heroic epic of Virgil with the love poetry of Tibullus by attaching value terms not only to their subjects but also to the meter in which each poet composed:

---

57. Fraenkel (1957), 130; Van Sickle (1975), 50–51.

58. Fraenkel (1957), 130–31n. C. N. Jackson, "Molle atque Facetum," *HSCP,* 25 (1914), 117–37, argues that Horace's terminology, unlike that of Domitius Marsus, refers to the contrast between the plain style and the grand style.

> Te quoque Vergilio comitem non aequa, Tibulle,
> mors iuuenem campos misit ad Elysios,
> ne foret, aut elegis molles qui fleret amores
> aut caneret forti regia bella pede.

To keep Virgil company an unjust death sent you, too, Tibullus, in your youth to the Elysian fields, lest anyone be left to lament tender love affairs in elegiac distichs or to sing the battles of kings in heroic verse.

The *fortis pes* of the last line is clearly the dactylic hexameter of epic poetry, a meter treated as vigorous in comparison with elegy and its voluptuous themes. In the Horatian passage, the dichotomy between *fortis* and *mollis* is applied to a difference of theme and stylistic level within *epos* itself and recalls the Alexandrian distinction, about which more will be said later, between "great *epos*" and "slight *epos*." Virgil's *Bucolics* belong to the latter category.[59]

Other examples of Roman schemes for classifying *epos* are more obscure. Hardly any reference is ever made to the important proem to the second book of Manilius' *Astronomica* which reviews all the previous masters of the poetic tradition that Manilius claims to carry forward—the tradition of didactic *epos*. Manilius begins by mentioning the poet of the *Iliad* and the *Odyssey* (1–11), then goes on to praise Hesiod for both the *Theogony* and the *Works and Days* (11–24). Next, he speaks of certain unnamed astronomical poets who described the myths associated with each constellation (25–38). He then introduces Theocritus, but both his assessment of bucolic subject matter and the language he uses to describe it betray, as so much else in Manilius, the influence of Virgil:

> quin etiam ritus pastorum et Pana sonantem
> in calamos Sicula memorat tellure creatus,
> nec siluis siluestre canit perque horrida motus
> rura serit dulcis Musamque inducit in arua.

[39–42]

The son of the Sicilian land tells the ways of shepherds and Pan playing upon his reeds, and he sings to the woods in no uncouth fashion, and through the rough countryside he sows sweet excitation, bringing the Muse into the fields.

The identification of Theocritus in this passage is confirmed, as Housman notes, by its similarity to Terentianus Maurus' later periphrasis for him (2127): "Siculae telluris alumnus" ("the nursling of the Sicilian land"). Manilius continues with a reference to Nicander and concludes his survey with the observation that all the subjects of didactic *epos* are used up (49: "omne genus rerum doctae cecinere sorores") except for astronomy, a field

---

59. Cf. Ovid *Tristia* 2. 537–38: "Phyllidis hic idem teneraeque Amaryllidis ignes / bucolicis iuuenis luserat ante modis."

in which he can aspire to originality. The verses devoted to Theocritus contain two textual problems (*ritus pastorum* in line 39 and *arua* in line 42 are emendations), but whatever solutions are adopted, it is clear that Manilius, despite an understanding of Theocritean thematics filtered by his reading of Virgil, agrees with Horace in classing bucolic poets together with other practitioners of *epos,* in this case with Homer, Hesiod, and Nicander, among others.[60]

Horace and Manilius are joined by Quintilian, whose inclusion of bucolic poetry in the category of *epos* is well known. Quintilian has decided to set forth the "kinds of reading matter especially appropriate to those proposing to become orators" (10.1.45: *genera ipsa lectionum quae praecipue conuenire intendentibus ut oratores fiant*), and indeed he organizes his discussion according to literary classes. Beginning his survey with the greatest poet, Quintilian first discusses Homer; then he goes on to mention the other *epici* whom Homer surpasses: Hesiod, Antimachus, and Panyasis. At this point, before mentioning any Hellenistic poets, Quintilian pauses to explain that Apollonius (along with the others) was not included in the Alexandrian canon because Aristarchus and Aristophanes, the two critics who devised it, omitted their contemporaries from consideration (10.1.54). Thereupon follows the contrasting treatment of Aratus and Theocritus already discussed in the introduction. Quintilian remarks that he does not intend to give an exhaustive account, and so will not specify his reasons for omitting Peisander, Nicander, and Euphorion, "whose 'songs composed in Chalcidic verse' Virgil would surely never have mentioned in his own *Bucolics* had he not admired him" (10.1.56: *quem nisi probasset Vergilius, idem numquam certe conditorum Chalcidico versu carminum fecisset in Bucolicis* [cf. *Buc.* 10.50–51] *mentionem*). When Quintilian turns to the Roman epic poets, he confines himself to discussing Virgil's *Aeneid* and neglects the non-heroic works in hexameter.

Theocritus is also classed with Apollonius in the treatise *On the Sublime* ascribed to Longinus. The question to be resolved at the outset of chapter 33 is whether "grandeur attended by some faults of execution" (μέγεθος ἐν ἐνίοις διημαρτημένον) is better than "a modest degree of success, though wholly sound and free from fault" (τὸ σύμμετρον μὲν ἐν τοῖς κατορθώμασιν ὑγιὲς δὲ πάντα καὶ ἀδιάπτωτον), an issue pertaining very closely to the notion of the sublime. The alternatives are illustrated in the field of epic by Homer on the one hand and by Apollonius and Theocritus on the other (33.4): ἐπείτοιγε καὶ ἄπτωτος ὁ Ἀπολλών⟨ιος ἐν τοῖς⟩ Ἀργοναύταις ποιητής, κἂν τοῖς βουκολικοῖς πλὴν ὀλίγων τῶν ἔξωθεν ὁ

---

60. Cf. Koster (1970), 135–37; G. P. Goold, ed., *Manilius,* Loeb Classical Library (Cambridge, Mass., 1977), adopts the reading *aulas* in line 42.

Θεόκριτος ἐπιτυχέστατος· ἆρ' οὖν "Ομηρος ἂν μᾶλλον ἢ 'Απολλώνιος ἐθέλοις γενέσθαι; ("Apollonius makes no mistakes in the *Argonautica;* Theocritus is very felicitous in the *Bucolics,* apart from a few passages not connected with the theme; but would you rather be Homer or Apollonius?" [text and translation by D. A. Russell]). The writer is thinking in terms of genres, as he makes clear by going on to discuss examples from the lyric and tragic categories (33.5: ἐν μέλεσι . . . ἐν τραγῳδίᾳ). Theocritus figures along with Apollonius as a potential rival to Homer in the epic genre; his *Bucolics* are parallel to the *Argonautica*—both are titles or at least designations of unified poetic works. The title of Theocritus' poetic collection is similarly attested by Tzetzes in a heterodox account of the Hellenistic Pleiad contained in his "Life of Lycophron," where Theocritus appears in the company of Aratus, Nicander, and Apollonius (*TrGF,* CAT A5b.1–4, p. 55 Snell):

Θεόκριτος ὁ τὰ βουκολικὰ γράψας,
Άρατος ὁ τὰ Φαινόμενα γράψας καὶ ἕτερα,
Νίκανδρος,
Αἰαντίδης ἢ 'Απολλώνιος ὁ τὰ 'Αργοναυτικά. . . .

The poetry of Theocritus is also referred to as τὰ καλούμενα Βουκολικὰ ἔπη ("the so-called Bucolic *epos*") in the *Suda,* which thereby seems to imply that only the hexameter poems of Theocritus can qualify as bucolic. Finally, several sections of the "tabula Montefalconii," a tenth-century catalogue of outstanding writers of antiquity, list Theocritus as having composed διὰ στίχων, meaning in hexameter lines, a designation likewise applied to Homer, Hesiod, Apollonius, Aratus, Nicander, Oppian, Callimachus, and Dionysius the Periegete.[61] On the basis of the evidence supplied by Horace, Manilius, Quintilian, ps.-Longinus, the *Suda,* and the author of the "tabula Montefalconii," then, it can be determined that the bucolic poems of Theocritus belonged in antiquity to the genre of *epos* and that our poet is likely to have regarded his own compositions as a kind of "epic" poetry. (For the sake of convenience, I shall use *epic* as the adjectival form of *epos, heroic epic* to designate the modern concept of epic poetry).

---

61. O. Kroehnert, *Canonesne poetarum scriptorum artificium per antiquitatem fuerunt?,* diss. Königsberg (1897), 7, 10; cf. 20–21.

CHAPTER ELEVEN

The Bucolic Epos

The poem of the mind in the act of finding
What will suffice. It has not always had
To find: the scene was set; it repeated what
Was in the script.
                Then the theatre was changed
To something else. Its past was a souvenir.

It has to be living, to learn the speech of the place.
It has to face the men of the time and to meet
The women of the time. It has to think about war
And it has to find what will suffice. It has
To construct a new stage.

—Wallace Stevens,
"Of Modern Poetry"

How did Theocritus define his place within the epic tradition? He evidently managed in some as yet mysterious way to impart to his poetry a lasting and recognizable identity, rendering it distinctive without obliterating its relation to the genre of *epos*. This genre has at times been treated as rather colorless, as a formal critical concept lacking in thematic definition and based entirely on metrical factors.[62] While such an understanding of *epos* may have recommended itself upon occasion to ancient classifiers of literature, it is hardly adequate to explain the motivation of a poet, whose decision to compose in a specific meter necessarily carries with it a variety of

62. Steinmetz (1964), 460.

complex artistic considerations. If Horace can contrast Virgil with Varius, or ps.-Longinus compare Theocritus with Homer, we may legitimately suspect the existence of some underlying set of correspondences between these poets, correspondences more profound or substantive than those evoked merely by their different means of exploiting the medium of the dactylic hexameter.[63] What subterranean connection linked Theocritus' bucolic poetry to the heroic epic? Can any thematic correspondences be found to complement the formal ones? The issue was well formulated by Van Sickle: "It remains to be seen if anything in Theocritus and Virgil beyond their choice of meter shows consciousness of a generic relation to epic."[64] It is to this topic that the remainder of this chapter is devoted.

One passage in Theocritus betraying consciousness of a generic relation to epic has already been discussed, and it will be convenient to return to it before taking up others: the *ecphrasis* in Idyll 1. The convention of *ecphrasis*, as it was known to the Alexandrians, originated in epic poetry—in the eighteenth book of the *Iliad* and the pseudo-Hesiodic *Scutum,* both of which Theocritus imitates. The goatherd's description of the ivy-cup accords very well with the programmatic character of the First Idyll in that the tradition of *ecphrasis* in general and the minute verbal allusions to Homer and ps.-Hesiod in particular create a pattern of contrasts between old and new, between heroic and bucolic *epos*[65] which emphasizes, within the context of individual differences, the generic connection between the two already established by the meter. The very word *kissybion,* employed by Homer though fallen out of use during the intervening years, serves to remind the reader by its exotic (or perhaps specifically archaic) color that Theocritus' ultimate inspiration is the study of traditional epic; as Callimachus had recommended at the end of his *Hymn to Apollo* with the bee analogy, Theocritus draws his literary savor "from the original pure source, not from its polluted derivatives."[66] In particular, Theocritus appeals (as the associations of the word *kissybion* show) to the most comic and anti-heroic parts of the Homeric epics, to their descriptions of homely details, unpretentious settings, and humble or humorous incidents. As I suggested in an earlier chapter, Theocritus' subjects represent an amplification of topics touched on but not developed by previous epic poets. But the relation between traditional and bucolic *epos* implied by Theocritus' *ecphrasis* can be

---

63. Cf. Koster (1970), 143.

64. Van Sickle (1975), 51.

65. Fritzsche-Hiller (1881), 46, *ad* Idyll 1.46: "[dass Theokrit] bei dieser Schilderung, welche zu jenen Schildbeschreibungen des alten Epos ein bukolisches Gegenstück bilden sollte. . . ." Cf. Friedländer (1912), 13; Stark (1963), 378.

66. Pfeiffer (1968), 126.

characterized more precisely by examining a specific technique for creating opposing contrasts, a technique of major importance for the bucolic poet's recasting of traditional epic material.

This is the technique of inversion.[67] A heroic theme is inverted when it is detached from the heroic world and set instead amid the prosaic activities and humble personages of daily life—a life constituted and defined by its very distance from the aristocratic realm of kings, mortal struggle, and undying glory to which heroic themes had, at one time, properly belonged. Hence, the object so lavishly described by the goatherd in the First Idyll is not a piece of heroic armor but a rustic drinking cup or milking bowl, a token of homely simplicity. In place of the divine shield wrought by Hephaestus and decorated with gold and silver, a common wooden vessel (albeit exquisite in its decoration) is what elicits from the bucolic poet a mighty effort of figurative exposition. "In describing [the ivy-cup], Theocritus alludes obliquely to famous descriptions of artifacts in earlier epic . . . inviting comparison between slight and greater art. He thus defines implicitly the character and limits of his own work in relation to traditional epic."[68] Theocritus repeatedly uses the technique of inversion to incorporate in the Idylls subjects belonging to heroic literature, thereby reminding the reader that his poems represent in actuality a more modest, but nonetheless authentic, kind of *epos*. The consequent pattern of deliberately contrived thematic contrasts between great and slight in scale provides a framework for echoes of traditional language and helps to endow the lowly subjects of Theocritus' poetry with something of an almost magically enhanced dimension.[69]

The most prominent beneficiary of such enhancement is Daphnis. Although the ode of Thyrsis in Idyll 1 can be interpreted as an amalgam of the three bucolic themes represented on the ivy-cup, the significance of his song is not exhausted by them. To be sure, the myth of Daphnis is a tale of erotic love; it is set among the lowly inhabitants of the Sicilian countryside who fill the background of the scene, accompanied by their animals both wild

67. On the Hellenistic technique of *Umkehrung* or *renversement* and its relation to the *arte allusiva* of Theocritus, see Giangrande (1968), especially 494–501, 523–25, 529–31; also, 494, n. 9 (bibliography); when Giangrande speaks of "*Umkehrung* de motifs altiers, solennels, heroïques appliqués, par contraste allusif obtenu au moyen de réminiscences homériques, à un personnage humble" (530), he defines exactly what I mean by inversion. But Giangrande's notion of *Umkehrung* has both a broader application than the term employed here (in that it also includes the subversion of heroic subjects through a reduction in scale or dignity) and a narrower one (in that its operation is restricted for the most part to verbal or lexical, as opposed to thematic, reversals). See, further, Giangrande (1970a), 46–47, for references to his copious work on this topic.

68. Van Sickle (1975), 56.

69. Cf. Auerbach (1953), 31.

and domestic; it is told with a pointed naiveté most notable in the abusive encounter between Daphnis and Aphrodite. No one could accuse Daphnis of being a heroic figure in any traditional sense: he is too distant from us, and a full account of his deeds—whatever they may have been and however they may have led him to his current difficulties—is suppressed. But Daphnis is not merely a lovelorn cowherd served up for our ironical or sentimental delectation. He is a mysterious figure who seems to preside over the countryside as its tutelary deity, and his death is an occasion for universal mourning in the natural world (even Aphrodite is not unaffected). For Daphnis is nature's musician—his last act is to summon Pan from Arcadia to receive his syrinx—and he represents the power of art as a harmonizing catalyst in nature, the source of an accord among plants, animals, men, and gods.[70] Daphnis had long been the focus of certain religious and poetic traditions, and so Theocritus, in endowing the figure of Daphnis with mythic proportions, could draw on the stories surrounding him in Sicilian cult and on the ode of Stesichorus devoted to the tale.[71]

For this reason, Daphnis in Idyll 1 is fit to inherit from earlier figures in epic and drama something of a heroic grandeur and amplitude. His challenge to Aphrodite is couched in language that evokes both explicitly and by the nuances of its phrasing the battlefield of the *Iliad:*[72]

αὖτις ὅπως στασῇ Διομήδεος ἆσσον ἰοῖσα,
καὶ λέγε "τὸν βούταν νικῶ Δάφνιν, ἀλλὰ μάχευ μοι".

[112–13]

Why don't you approach Diomedes again and stand near him and say, "I vanquish Daphnis the cowherd: come, fight with me"?

The relation of Thyrsis' song to the grand literary tradition has not gone unnoticed. Some scholars have viewed Daphnis as standing in the shadow of such classical heroic prototypes as Hippolytus (because of his defiance of Aphrodite) and Prometheus (because he defends human values against the tyranny of the gods). Daphnis has been variously compared to Achilles, Ajax in the underworld, Aeschylus' Cassandra, Sophocles' Antigone and Electra, Euripides' Pentheus, and Virgil's Orpheus.[73] None of these analo-

---

70. Cf. C. P. Segal, *Landscape in Ovid's Metamorphoses: A Study in the Transformations of a Literary Symbol,* Hermes Einzelschr., 23 (Wiesbaden, 1969), 75.

71. On Daphnis, see Reitzenstein (1893), 243–63; Legrand (1898), 146–48; A. Rostagni, "Autonomia e svolgimento della letteratura greca di Sicilia," ΚΩΚΑΛΟΣ, 3 (1957), 3–17; R. M. Ogilvie, "The Song of Thyrsis," *JHS,* 82 (1962), 106–10; E. A. Schmidt, "Die Leiden des verliebten Daphnis," *Hermes,* 96 (1968/69), 539–52; F. J. Williams, "Theocritus, *Idyll* i 81–91," *JHS,* 89 (1969), 121–23.

72. Segal (1974b), 16–17.

73. G. Łanowski, "La Passion de Daphnis," *Eos,* 42 (1947), 175–94; Parry (1957), especially 11–14; W. Berg, "Daphnis and Prometheus," *TAPA,* 96 (1965), 11–23; Lawall (1967), especially 19–22; Segal (1974b).

gies can be pressed very far, but together they indicate a widely shared feeling on the part of his readers that Theocritus is "seeking to connect his art with the prior traditions of Greek tragic and heroic poetry. . . . In one sense Theocritus' Daphnis is descended from the mythical heroes who assert the independence of their emotional or spiritual life over against the busy, happy natural rhythms surrounding them. . . ."[74] Theocritus, in other words, has transferred thematic elements from the Greek heroic tradition to his treatment of a Sicilian cowherd. His inversion of these epic themes enables him to endow his quaint and distant subject with a certain depth and power "at a time when writers felt it impossible to deal with strong emotion directly and when literary works with reference to immediate experience were, for that reason, slight."[75] Yet, by the same token, Theocritus can capitalize on the comic incongruities arising from his juxtaposition of heroic and rustic motifs. Without attempting to give even the most cursory reading of the First Idyll, then, one can cite its technique as a prime example of Theocritean epic inversion.

The Second Idyll provides a less problematic example. The scene owes much to comedy and to mime, as scholars have often remarked. Simaetha's violent exchanges with her witless and frightened slave are part of the convention of abuse common in comedy,[76] and the scholia claim that Theocritus has incorporated portions of a mime of Sophron in this Idyll. The scholiasts also cite parallels from Menander which they seem to consider apposite.[77] Additional sources of humor are provided by Simaetha's naive exposition of events for which the reader can devise a more satisfactory interpretation than she, and by the contrasts between the simple, passionate girl and her cynical but suave seducer. Simaetha's extravagant exhibition of the full range of desperate emotions represents something of a lyric set piece (which in part betrays the influence of Sappho),[78] and the poem as a whole can be viewed as an example of the Hellenistic interest in details of erotic pathology. But all this notwithstanding, the very intensity of Simaetha's passion recalls the violent emotions of abandoned heroines and sorceresses from the high literary tradition, and in case we are disinclined to see her in the context of her heroic forebears, Simaetha makes the connection explicit:

χαῖρ', Ἑκάτα δασπλῆτι, καὶ ἐς τέλος ἄμμιν ὀπάδει,
φάρμακα ταῦτ' ἔρδοισα χερείονα μήτε τι Κίρκας
μήτε τι Μηδείας μήτε ξανθᾶς Περιμήδας.

[14–16]

74. Segal (1974b), 18–19.
75. Parry (1957), 14.
76. Dover (1971), 103, *ad* 19f.
77. Wendel (1914), 269–72, 276, 284.
78. Pretagostini (1977).

Hail, grim Hecate, and to the end attend me, and make these drugs of mine as potent as those of Circe or Medea or golden-haired Perimede. [trans. Gow][79]

Such epic parallels produce a comic effect on the reader, who is amused to hear a suburban teenager cite mythological precedent for her erotic entanglements. The incongruous introduction of Homeric diction and imagery produces a similar impression:

> ἀλλ᾽ ἦνθέ μοι ἅ τε Φιλίστας
> μάτηρ τᾶς ἁμᾶς αὐλητρίδος ἅ τε Μελιξοῦς
> σάμερον, ἀνίκα πέρ τε ποτ᾽ ὠρανὸν ἔτραχον ἵπποι
> Ἀῶ τὰν ῥοδόεσσαν ἀπ᾽ ὠκεανοῖο φέροισαι,
> κεῖπέ μοι ἄλλα τε πολλὰ καὶ ὡς ἄρα Δέλφις ἔραται.

[145–49]

But the mother of Philista, our flute-girl, and of Melixo came to me this morning, just when the horses of rosy Dawn were bearing her swiftly up the sky from the ocean, and told me a good many things, including that Delphis is in love.

The function of this juxtaposition—which is not essentially different from Eliot's "brings the sailor home from sea, The typist home at teatime," except perhaps for its greater impertinence—is to demonstrate the inappropriateness of traditional language to the task of conveying homely reality in verse. In addition to this disjunctive effect, however, the intrusion of heroic myth and language into Simaetha's world serves to remind us of the continuities: Medea in actuality may not have been a very different sort of person—or perhaps Simaetha is the closest thing to Circe that a modern inhabitant of Alexandria is likely to run across. The technique of inversion, of surrounding humble or vulgar occurrences with heroic reminiscences, allows Theocritus to prolong the life of the epic genre by transposing its language, its traditional subject matter, and its characters and situations into a contemporary social environment and into a modern form of poetic expression.

The poetic effect produced by these means is analogous to that obtained in more recent times by Edwin Arlington Robinson in his mock-heroic depiction of an old drunkard, Eben Flood, in "Mr. Flood's Party":

> Then, as a mother lays her sleeping child
> Down tenderly, fearing it may awake,
> He set the jug down slowly at his feet
> With trembling care, knowing that most things break;
> And only when assured that on firm earth
> It stood, as the uncertain lives of men
> Assuredly did not, he paced away,
> And with his hand extended paused again. . . .

[25–32]

79. On Perimede, see Gow (1952), II, 39 ad 15f.

An unobtrusive emotional accuracy and comic verve enable the poet simultaneously to convey Eben's extravagant concern for the jug's safety, his affection for the liquor it contains, a concomitant awareness that neither jug nor liquor is secure so long as they are in his hands, and a drunkenly exaggerated sense of the deceptiveness and contingency of earthly things. But the very elements that contribute to the humor of the portrait—the incongruous, grossly inapposite epic simile, the comic disproportion between content and style (that is, between Eben's mental processes and the artful language used to communicate them)—also create an ironic distance between the subject and the reader which allows the weighty themes of mutability and loss, and human dignity in the face of them, to be treated lightly, hence all the more compellingly. It is not for nothing that Eben Flood was likened in the preceding stanza to Roland at Roncesvalles.

Just as Daphnis and Simaetha, in their different ways, cast long shadows in the light of their grandiose literary prototypes, so the herdsmen of the pastoral Idylls can claim to stand at the end of a once lofty poetic tradition. The goatherd of Idyll 3, attempting to win the favors of the reluctant Amaryllis, cites for her edification five examples of virtuous or comely rustics from the legendary past who were rewarded with the love of beautiful women or goddesses. The first allusion, conforming to a version of the story known from Hesiod's *Catalogue of Women* (frs. 72–76 M-W) and from Philetas (fr. 18 Powell), concerns Hippomenes, who, though an old-fashioned hero and not a shepherd (according to the previous tradition, at least), is portrayed by the goatherd in Idyll 3 as winning the hand of Atalanta by means of a rustic gift of apples—no mention is made of their being golden—a gift paralleled by the goatherd's own offering of apples to Amaryllis (lines 10–11). Similarly, the goatherd's promise of a nannygoat and two kids (34–36) recalls another pastoral service performed by a hero,[80] who is named in the second allusion: Bias won Pero by recapturing the herd of cattle on Mount Othrys which had belonged to Pero's grandmother and which he acquired through the services of his brother, the seer Melampus; the story in its general outlines is known from the *Odyssey* (11.287–97). Next, the goatherd mentions Adonis and Endymion; the former is described "pasturing his flocks in the mountains" (46: ἐν ὤρεσι μῆλα νομεύων) and the latter was a herdsman in at least one account, a particularly congenial one to bucolic poets, as a reference in Idyll 20.37–39 attests. Endymion was later assimilated to the type of the herdsman who encounters a goddess in the wilderness: he appears, together with Iasion (who figures in the last of the goatherd's allusions), in a list of herdsmen and rustics beloved of goddesses in Nonnus (48.665–80). Iasion was in one

80. Walker (1980), 45–46.

version of the story a farmer, perhaps the first to sow seed, who was destroyed by Zeus after lying with Demeter in a thrice-sown field; the legend descends from the *Odyssey* (5.125–28) and from Hesiod's *Theogony* (969–71).[81] The unnamed goatherd of the Third Idyll is thus acutely conscious of his mythical forerunners and wishes to invoke the precedent of their success in advancing his hopeless suit. The disparity between the results of their efforts and his own heightens the comedy of his appeal. But however incongruous the mythological material may be in the rustic context of Idyll 3, it is certainly appropriate to the metrical form of the poem, as the epic sources (cited above) for other versions of the story illustrate, and Theocritus thereby recalls that other rustics have been fit subjects of *epos* in the past, even if his own character is but a poor relation to them.

Preeminent among these earlier rustics, of course, are the retainers of Odysseus immortalized by Homer. It is in the context of their gatherings, as well as in the scenes in the Cyclops' cave, that the *kissybion,* whose humble associations were later exploited in Idyll 1, is originally mentioned. Theocritus alludes to their fame as an index of the power of art in Idyll 16.51–57 by implying that the heroes, Odysseus and Laertes, and the laborers, Eumaeus and Philoetius, would alike have been obscure without Homer but that all are equally immortal because of his poetry. The *Odyssey* in particular abounds with humble figures who play a significant role in the action of the story and who inaugurate the epic lineage of Theocritus' countrymen. Comatas the goatherd in Idyll 5 is exceedingly mindful of his counterpart in the *Odyssey,* and he uses the Homeric analogy with wit and precision in order to make good his threat at the end of the poem:

οὗτος ὁ λευκίτας ὁ κορυπτίλος, εἴ τιν' ὀχευσεῖς
τᾶν αἰγῶν, φλασσῶ τυ, πρὶν ἢ ἐμὲ καλλιερῆσαι
ταῖς Νύμφαις τὰν ἀμνόν. ὁ δ' αὖ πάλιν. ἀλλὰ γενοίμαν,
αἰ μή τυ φλάσσαιμι, Μελάνθιος ἀντὶ Κομάτα

[147–50]

You there, the white, butting billy, if you mount one of the nannies before I've sacrificed the lamb to the Nymphs, I'll take my knife to you. There he goes again! If I don't take my knife to you, may I be Melanthius instead of Comatas.

Since Melanthius, Odysseus' disloyal goatherd, was castrated at the end of the twenty-second book of the *Odyssey,* the point of Comatas' speech, as Gow observes, is αὐτὸς φλασθείην: ("I'll be castrated myself [if I don't]"). In this way Odysseus' lordly revenge continues to resonate in the background of Comatas' threat.

Melanthius and the Odyssean setting figure importantly in the most

81. For information about the sources of these myths, see Gow (1952), II, 73–75; C. Segal, "Adonis and Aphrodite: Theocritus, *Idyll* III, 48," *AC,* 38 (1969), 82–88.

significant of Theocritus' refashioned epic scenes—Simichidas' encounter with the goatherd Lycidas in the Seventh Idyll.[82] To be sure, allusions can be found to several Homeric passages. The mention of the tomb (*sama*) of Brasilas (10–11: κοὔπω τὰν μεσάταν ὁδὸν ἄνυμες, οὐδὲ τὸ σᾶμα / ἁμῖν τὸ Βρασίλα κατεφαίνετο) has been viewed[83] as a reminiscence of Priam's journey to the tent of Achilles, similarly interrupted near a grave marker (*sēma*: οἱ δ' ἐπεὶ οὖν μέγα σῆμα παρὲξ Ἴλοιο ἔλασσαν, / στῆσαν ἄρ' ἡμιόνους τε καὶ ἵππους, ὄφρα πίοιεν, / ἐν ποταμῷ [Il.24.349–51], although it can also be taken as an instance of Theocritus' attention to details of local topography.[84] Similarly, Athena's appearance to Odysseus in the form of a shepherd-boy has been likened to the epiphany of Lycidas, although there are virtually no verbal resemblances between the two passages;[85] still, if one is to mention all examples of possible epic inversion in Idyll 7, one should not omit to suggest that Theocritus may have reversed Homer's description of the well-scrubbed Athena (13.223–24: παναπάλῳ, οἷοί τε ἀνάκτων παῖδες ἔασι, / δίπτυχον ἀμφ' ὤμοισιν ἔχουσ' εὐεργέα λώπην) in his sketch of the smelly goatherd (15–18: ἐκ μὲν γὰρ λασίοιο δασύτριχος εἶχε τράγοιο / κνακὸν δέρμ' ὤμοισι νέας ταμίσοιο ποτόσδον, / ἀμφὶ δέ οἱ στήθεσσι γέρων ἐσφίγγετο πέπλος / ζωστῆρι πλακερῷ). The construction of the scene on Cos also conforms somewhat to a formulaic pattern of the type used in Homer to describe a meeting between two or more individuals. But by far the most important Homeric precedent for the encounter between Simichidas and Lycidas is the meeting of Eumaeus and the goatherd Melanthius in the seventeenth book of the *Odyssey,* which results in the first pastoral competition in Greek literature— the exchange of insults between the two herdsmen.[86] It is worth comparing the two scenes in some detail.

82. Ott (1972), 143, sees in Theocritus' use of his epic model "das Bestreben, vorgegebene literarische Formen auf neue, unerwartete, ja spielerisch gelegentlich auf entgegengesetzte Bedingungen zu stellen und mit literarischen Vorbildern in einer Weise zu konkurrieren, die zwischen *imitatio* und Anspielung steht." Ott also sees the same artistic objectives behind the goatherd's *ecphrasis* in Idyll 1. Ott's formulation of Theocritus' technique of epic inversion differs from my own only in its lesser insistence on polarities, on the poet's deliberate reversal of great and slight in theme, style, and diction. For a helpful corrective to certain aspects of Ott's interpretation, see G. Giangrande, "Irony in Theocritus: Methods of Literary Interpretation," *MPhL,* 3 (1978), 143–46, and Williams (1978).

83. By Ott (1972), 144–45, among others.

84. Arnott (1979); G. Zanker, "Simichidas' Walk and the Locality of Bourina in Theocritus, *Id.* 7," *CQ,* n.s. 30 (1980), 373–77.

85. M. Puelma, "Die Dichterbegegnung in Theokrits 'Thalysien,'" *MH,* 17 (1960), 144–64, especially 148n.; Ott (1972), 144–45; Williams (1978); but cf. Giangrande (1968), 529–30.

86. Ott (1972) 144–48, whose discussion provides the basis for the following analysis— *pace* Williams (1978).

Simichidas and his companions are bound for the country, leaving the city behind them (2: εἴρπομες ἐκ πόλιος), whereas Odysseus and Eumaeus have set out from the countryside for the capital of Ithaca (182: τοὶ δ' ἐξ ἀγροῖο πόλινδε; 201: ὁ δ' ἐς πόλιν ἦγεν ἄνακτα). Lycidas is carrying an olive staff (19, 43: κορύνα), which he promises and eventually gives to Simichidas at the conclusion of their exchange (now called a λαγωβόλον [128]); before they start out, the swineherd gives Odysseus a stick to lean on (199: Εὔμαιος δ' ἄρα οἱ σκῆπτρον θυμαρὲς ἔδωκε; cf. 236: ῥόπαλον). Then follows the encounter itself.

ἀλλ' ὅτε δὴ στείχοντες ὁδὸν κάτα παιπαλόεσσαν
ἄστεος ἐγγὺς ἔσαν καὶ ἐπὶ κρήνην ἀφίκοντο
τυκτὴν καλλίροον, ὅθεν ὑδρεύοντο πολῖται,
τὴν ποίησ' Ἴθακος καὶ Νήριτος ἠδὲ Πολύκτωρ·
ἀμφὶ δ' ἄρ' αἰγείρων ὑδατοτρεφέων ἦν ἄλσος,
πάντοσε κυκλοτερές. κατὰ δὲ ψυχρὸν ῥέεν ὕδωρ
ὑψόθεν ἐκ πέτρης· βωμὸς δ' ἐφύπερθε τέτυκτο
νυμφάων, ὅθι πάντες ἐπιρρέζεσκον ὁδῖται·
ἔνθα σφέας ἐκίχανεν υἱὸς Δολίοιο Μελανθεὺς
αἶγας ἄγων, αἳ πᾶσι μετέπρεπον αἰπολίοισι,
δεῖπνον μνηστήρεσσι· δύω δ' ἅμ' ἕποντο νομῆες.

[204–14]

But when, as they were walking down the rugged road, they got close to the town and arrived at a man-made, sweet-flowing spring where the townspeople used to draw water—Ithakus made it, and Neritus and Polyktor; and about it, encircling it in every direction, was a grove of black poplars fed on water, and the cold water flowed down from above out of a rock; above that an altar of the Nymphs was fashioned where all travelers used to offer sacrifices—there Melanthius, the son of Dolius, fell in with them as he was driving she-goats, the choicest among all the goatflocks, to be a meal for the suitors, and two herdsmen followed along with him.

A few points are especially noteworthy. The spring on Ithaca is described in terms applied by Theocritus to the spring of Burina on Cos (both manmade and both termed a *krēnē*):

ταὶ δὲ παρ' αὐτάν
αἴγειροι πτελέαι τε ἐύσκιον ἄλσος ὕφαινον
χλωροῖσιν πετάλοισι κατηρεφέες κομόωσαι.

[7–9]

. . . and beside it black poplars and elms formed a shady grove with their arching, interwoven branches and luxuriant green foliage.

Theocritus was in any case thoroughly familiar with the Homeric passage, for he had adapted *Od.* 17.209–10, the lines immediately following the verse on which his description of Burina is modeled, in the First Idyll: τὸ καταχές / τὴν' ἀπὸ τᾶς πέτρας καταλείβεται ὑψόθεν ὕδωρ (1.7–8: "from the rock tumbles down the sounding water from above").[87] Both meetings are said to have taken place at a certain point along the journey, and Lycidas is first mentioned as "some traveler" (11: τιν' ὁδίταν), perhaps a reminiscence of Homer's travelers (211: ὁδῖται) in the same position of the verse. The emphasis of line 213, with its attention to the quality of the goats driven by Melanthius, may be reflected in Theocritus' famous characterization of Lycidas as a goatherd (13–14: αἰπόλος . . . αἰπόλῳ). Lycidas greets Simichidas with laughter and mockery, whereas Melanthius had assailed the two wayfarers with "quarrelsome and unseemly" words (215–16); and while the travelers in both the *Odyssey* and the *Thalysia* are suspected of intending to cadge free meals, Odysseus is called a "killjoy" or "scavenger of feasts" (220: δαιτῶν ἀπολυμαντῆρα), Simichidas merely asked, "Is it to a feast that you hasten uninvited?" (24: ἢ μετὰ δαῖτ' ἄκλητος ἐπείγεαι). Quite aside, then, from the passages of Hesiod's *Theogony*, on which the meeting of Lycidas and Simichidas is also modeled, the encounter of Odysseus and Eumaeus with Melanthius provides an epic precedent for Theocritus' scene. The tension in the Homeric narrative, with its careful character-drawing, its anticipation and artful postponement of Odysseus' revenge, is diffused in Theocritus' richly evocative version, with its new set of challenges and rivalries. Theocritus was no doubt much taken with the rustic comedy in the Homeric herdsmen's abusive exchange, but the Odyssean passage is less significant to his poetics for its claim to be an early instance of a pastoral competition than for its exemplification of the slight style in epic poetry. Although Theocritus avoids the grand themes of the Return and the dramatic tension accompanying its portrayal, the Seventh Idyll can be seen in part as an expansion of the anti-heroic material in the Homeric epic.[88] The allusions to the *Odyssey* thus provide a source of thematic continuity within the genre of *epos* which help to define the literary genealogy of bucolic poetry. Theocritus' reduction of Hesiod's awesome encounter with the Muses to a summer afternoon's diversion (anticipated in some respects by Archilochus)[89] is another example of epic inversion and can be thought of as functioning in a similar manner, although the significance of Hesiod for Theocritus has, to be sure, other dimensions as well.

87. These lines from the First Idyll were also inspired by Hesiod, *Theogony*, 785–87: ὕδωρ/ψυχρόν, ὅτ' ἐκ πέτρης καταλείβεται ἠλιβάτοιο/ὑψηλῆς. The resemblance between the Homeric and Hesiodic passages raises a separate question.

88. Ott. (1972), 149: "In entsprechender Weise verkörpern die 'Thalysien' die Gegenmöglichkeit gegen das zeitgenössische mythologische Epos: die Anknüpfung an die homerische Einzelszene in der epischen Kleinform mit nicht-mythischem Stoff."

89. See the helpful discussion of A. Kambylis, "Zur 'Dichterweihe' des Archilochos," *Hermes*, 91 (1963), 129–50, who does not, however, consider Idyll 7 to be part of the same tradition.

As we have seen, the anti-heroic material in Homer is particularly important to Theocritus because it furnishes him with an authoritative poetic precedent *within* the genre in which he elected to compose; it represents a traditional means of accomplishing his innovative purpose—to remake the genre of *epos* into a suitable vehicle for "modern" (Alexandrian) aesthetic ideals and themes. In this sense, Theocritus' inversion of epic subjects can be related to the composite nature of the comparisons in Homer's similes, for Homer is notoriously fond of juxtaposing the homely activities of humble people to the glorious struggle of the heroes. A few examples may be quoted by way of reminder; the first is the most famous.

ὡς δ' ὅτε τίς τ' ἐλέφαντα γυνὴ φοίνικι μιήνῃ
Μῃονὶς ἠὲ Κάειρα, παρήϊον ἔμμεναι ἵππων·
κεῖται δ' ἐν θαλάμῳ, πολέες τέ μιν ἠρήσαντο
ἱππῆες φορέειν· βασιλῆϊ δὲ κεῖται ἄγαλμα,
ἀμφότερον κόσμος θ' ἵππῳ ἐλατῆρί τε κῦδος·
τοῖοί τοι, Μενέλαε, μιάνθην αἵματι μηροὶ
εὐφυέες κνῆμαί τε ἰδὲ σφυρὰ κάλ' ὑπένερθε.

[4.141–47]

As when some Maionian woman or Karian stains ivory with crimson, to make it a cheek-piece for horses; it lies away in an inner room, and many a rider longs to have it, but it is laid up to be a king's treasure, to be both the beauty of the horse and the pride of the horseman: so, Menelaus, your shapely thighs were stained with blood, and your legs also and the fair ankles beneath them. [trans. Lattimore, adapted]

Without attempting to describe the total effect of this complex image, it is sufficient to point out that the main topic of comparison—the arresting visual contrast created by the sudden gush of blood over the fair skin of Menelaus—is a vivid sensuous image the appreciation of which is enhanced by analogy with an object that can serve, unlike the wounded flesh of the warrior in the midst of battle, as a focus of unqualified aesthetic pleasure. We can enjoy without restraint the beauty of the crimson-stained ivory cheek-piece for the very reason that it belongs to a world apart from the desperate contest in which Menelaus is engaged, to the quiet solitude of the princely chamber or to the workaday world of the skilled artisan. The poet invites us to transfer our mental image of the artifact with its contrasting colors to a clearer visualization of the onlooker's experience of Menelaus' spectacular injury. This is one of several respects in which the audience's capacity for evaluating and interpreting the heroic battlefield can be enlarged by means of an analogy with a world outside it.

The poet avails himself of a similar tactic to convey the pathetic death of one Simoesius. Here, the audience's attention is diverted from the battlefield to the humble activity of a craftsman:

ὁ δ' ἐν κονίῃσι χαμαὶ πέσεν αἴγειρος ὥς,
ἥ ῥά τ' ἐν εἰαμενῇ ἕλεος μεγάλοιο πεφύκει
λείη, ἀτάρ τέ οἱ ὄζοι ἐπ' ἀκροτάτῃ πεφύασι·
τὴν μέν θ' ἁρματοπηγὸς ἀνὴρ αἴθωνι σιδήρῳ
ἐξέταμ', ὄφρα ἴτυν κάμψῃ περικαλλέϊ δίφρῳ·
ἥ μέν τ' ἀζομένη κεῖται ποταμοῖο παρ' ὄχθας.

[4.482–87]

He dropped then to the ground in the dust, like some black poplar, which in the land low-lying about a great marsh grows smooth trimmed yet with branches growing at the uttermost treetop: one whom a man, a maker of chariots, fells with the shining iron, to bend it into a wheel for a fine-wrought chariot, and the tree lies hardening by the banks of a river. [trans. Lattimore]

Beauty and utility are more securely conjoined, and gradations of quality more sharply defined in the wheelwright's labor than in the ambiguous testing ground of mortal natures. The craftsman's discrminating choice of a fine material helps to communicate the strength, the abundant youthful vigor of Simoesius, and his peaceful and constructive task contrasts with the murderous ardor of Ajax, Simoesius' killer. At the same time the basic point of comparison—the underlying similarity of function shared by a spear, an instrument of war, with an ax (or some other tool for cutting)— produces a terrifying effect: both Ajax and the wheelwright manifest a businesslike indifference to the individual qualities of their victims, beyond exploiting their victims' common vulnerability to sharp metal implements, and so Homer's simile wrenches the audience's attention away from the fate of Simoesius to the clinical, ruthless objectivity which the craftsman shares with the professional warrior. Once again, our understanding of heroic struggle gains clarity and complexity from a comparison with the lowly activities of little people who do not participate in it.

In the two foregoing examples, Homer chooses a craft associated with the production of luxury articles—an ornamental piece of armor or a chariot—as a point of reference for his comparison; the effect is to suggest the conspicuous nobility of the aristocratic contestants on the battlefield at Troy and the expensive waste of precious lives occasioned by the fatalities. A different kind of Homeric comparison may provide a better illustration of the way Theocritus' technique of epic inversion is related to the combination of great and slight subjects in epic analogies.

ἦμος δὲ δρυτόμος περ ἀνὴρ ὡπλίσσατο δεῖπνον
οὔρεος ἐν βήσσῃσιν, ἐπεί τ' ἐκορέσσατο χεῖρας
τάμνων δένδρεα μάκρα, ἄδος τέ μιν ἵκετο θυμόν,
σίτου τε γλυκεροῖο περὶ φρένας ἵμερος αἱρεῖ,
τῆμος σφῇ ἀρετῇ Δαναοὶ ῥήξαντο φάλαγγας. . . . .

[11.86–90]

But at that time when the woodcutter makes ready his supper in the wooded glens of the mountains, when his arms and hands have grown weary from cutting down the tall trees, and his heart has had enough of it, and longing for food and for sweet wine takes hold of his senses; at that time the Danaans by their manhood broke the battalions. . . . [trans. Lattimore]

This is still a far cry from Rupert Brooke, but the contrast between the unencumbered independence, the humble tasks and pleasures of the lowly civilian long removed from war's clamor on the one hand and the martial valor of those whom duty will allow little respite on the other is designed to enhance the heroic glory and increase the brilliance surrounding the main characters. The woodcutter is engaged in a worthy but not wholly serious activity: the daily pattern of his life is marked by small concerns—weariness of labor, desire for refreshment—and by pedestrian chores. Just as Homer uses the woodcutter's simplicity and unpretentiousness as a foil to the mortal struggles of the Danaan host, so Theocritus, reversing the procedure, uses Homeric allusions to set off the unpretentiousness and charming triviality of his characters. In this sense, his technique of epic inversion can be viewed as an adaptation of the composite Homeric perspective to an antiheroic subject.[90] The memory of lofty themes hovers about the edges of Theocritus' poetry, as in Idyll 4, in which two herdsmen disparagingly discuss a colleague's departure to compete in the games at Olympia, or in Idyll 15, in which religious ceremonies at the royal palace are refracted through the dialogue of two participating housewives. Theocritus thereby reminds his readers of the heroic background of his chosen subjects, at once emphasizing his own lack of high seriousness and grandiose poetic ambition while carefully maintaining a thematic continuity with traditional versions of Greek *epos*.

So far, the device of epic inversion ascribed to Theocritus has been discussed as it relates to the construction of his plots, the setting of his narratives, or the personality of his characters. But the burden of maintaining generic links with heroic *epos* while exploiting the consequent incongruous resonances for their programmatic effect is borne by Theocritus' language itself. Indeed, signification in the poetry of Theocritus generally, as in much Alexandrian poetry, is achieved largely by minute linguistic means, as Giuseppe Giangrande stresses: the poet's learned manipulation of lexical nuances has a far greater share in determining his meaning in this period than do matters of mood, setting, or symbolism.[91] A complete

---

90. For an example of a modern poem that exhibits the same technique, see R. Hass, "Heroic Simile," *Praise* (New York, 1979), 2–3.

91. Giangrande's thesis is forcefully argued in his review of Lawall (*JHS*, 88 [1968], 170–73) and in an article on Theocritean irony (1971), especially 101–13; supporting evidence

study of epic words and phrases and their poetic role in Theocritus would easily occupy a separate volume; a few examples of epic inversion as it is created through details of language must suffice. Whereas the phrase ἔχον πόνον ("toiled") occurs in *Iliad* 15.416 in connection with the struggles of Hector and Ajax over the Achaean ships, it can be found in the same metrical position in Theocritus 7.139 referring to the chirping of cicadas. More startling, perhaps, is Theocritus' application to Amphitryon's slaves in Idyll 24.50 of the adjective ταλασίφρων ("with enduring spirit"), which in Homer is a constant epithet of Odysseus.[92] In the same poem Theocritus uses δινέω in connection with Alcmena, who is rocking her children to sleep in her husband's shield (instead of in a cradle): the word is traditionally associated with the revolving motion given to a shield by a warrior defending himself from a hail of missiles on the battlefield.[93] In Idyll 2, Simaetha's appropriation, for the purpose of characterizing her lover, Delphis, of the words used by Apollonius to describe Hylas in the *Argonautica*[94] may provide another example of Theocritus' general method of treating homely low-life scenes as if they were inverted heroic ones. This tendency, which makes itself felt in varying degrees throughout the Idylls, suggests that bucolic poetry should not be viewed simply as a series of realistic miniatures or genre scenes but as a recasting of the high traditions of Greek literature into an anti-heroic context where they can recover something of their original freshness and can accord with the tastes of the Alexandrian age. Theocritus thereby rescues the genre of *epos* from obsolescence.

The process of refashioning can be carried on by more than one means, and Theocritus' lexical practice reveals another method, which can be thought of as the exact opposite of the technique of inversion. In Idyll 13.19 the poet saddles Heracles with the epithet ταλαεργός ("enduring labor"), which is used only of mules in Homer and Hesiod.[95] In this passage, then, Theocritus reverses the procedure, whereby a Homeric epithet for Odysseus had been transferred to slaves, and instead qualifies a hero with a demeaning epithet. The technique of scaling down heroic subjects to fit the

---

has been marshaled in a series of scholarly studies by Giangrande (1967); (1968); (1970a), especially 46–47, for references to his previous work on the subject; (1973a); (1973b); and, generally, "The Utilization of Homeric Variants by Apollonius Rhodius: A Methodological Canon of Research," *QUCC* 15 (1973), 73–81. Among the examples of a lexical approach to understanding the poetry of Theocritus are: G. Perotta, "Studi di poesia ellenistica," *SIFC*, n.s. 4 (1925), 5–68; 85–280, especially 202–16, 234–49; Fabiano (1971); R. W. Garson, "An Aspect of Theocritean Humor," *CP*, 68 (1973), 296–97.

92. Fabiano (1971), 535.
93. Giangrande (1973b).
94. Webster (1964), 90.
95. Fabiano (1971), 535.

social environment of the Hellenistic reader, of portraying them according to the mimetic norm reserved for the veristic depiction of daily life, is also typical of Theocritus; without wishing to force the terminology into too stiff a pattern, one may speak properly of epic *subversion* in these cases. Just as heroic resonances are evoked to dignify or, alternately, to mock the pretensions of Theocritus' homely subjects, so disreputable or comic associations are employed to undermine the heroic figures treated by the poet. Although both techniques are paralleled in the work of Theocritus' contemporaries, they are particularly well adapted to the task of strengthening the connection between bucolic poetry and traditional *epos*. Theocritus' programme of reducing heroes and mythological figures to normal human proportions is announced at the beginning of Idyll 16:

Αἰεὶ τοῦτο Διὸς κούραις μέλει, αἰὲν ἀοιδοῖς,
ὑμνεῖν ἀθανάτους, ὑμνεῖν ἀγαθῶν κλέα ἀνδρῶν.
Μοῖσαι μὲν θεαὶ ἐντί, θεοὺς θεαὶ ἀείδοντι·
ἄμμες δὲ βροτοὶ οἵδε, βροτοὺς βροτοὶ ἀείδωμεν.

[1–4]

Always are Zeus' daughters, always are bards impelled to hymn the immortals, to hymn the glorious deeds of great men. Now Muses are goddesses—goddesses sing of gods—but we are mortals, and, being mortals, let us sing of mortals.

The traditional division of lofty poetic subjects into gods, heroes, and men—the division so memorably set forth by Pindar (though hardly unique to him) at the outset of the Second Olympian Ode: Ἀναξιφόρμιγγες ὕμνοι, τίνα θεόν, τίν' ἥρωα, τίνα δ' ἄνδρα κελαδήσομεν; ("what god, what hero, what man shall our songs resoundingly celebrate?")—is here reduced by Theocritus to the distinction between human and divine subjects. Heroes are left out, or rather are included among mortals (by being referred to as ἀγαθοὶ ἄνδρες: "great *men*"). Furthermore, the poet cheerfully surrenders divine themes to the province of the Muses.[96] Theocritus will occupy himself exclusively with mortal subjects, and whichever mythological or heroic figures are introduced into his poetry will be treated according to the same techniques of representation that are used to convey the poet's customary humble themes. Theocritus' portrayal of heroic subjects is indeed true to his principle. Once again, a good deal of work has already been done on Theocritus' subversion of epic themes,[97] and so I shall merely allude to the chief examples of this technique.

96. Koster (1970), 114–17.
97. Legrand (1898), 184–95; Perotta (1923); Horstmann (1976), 57–113; Effe (1978), including a thorough discussion of the scholarly tradition. Effe considers (mistakenly, in my opinion) Theocritus' use of ironic distance the single most important distinguishing characteristic, and hence the generic differentia, of his poetry (50–53).

The most famous of Theocritean subversions is the portrayal of the Cyclops in love. Theocritus, of course, was not the first to convert the Homeric episode to a comic purpose: the dithyramb of Philoxenus (*PMG* 815–24, pp. 423–28), also given over to an account of the Cyclops' erotic misadventures, had apparently enjoyed considerable popularity; moreover, Cratinus' comedy, *Odyssēs,* and Euripides' satyr play, *Cyclops,* may be viewed as evidence for the extent to which Greek audiences at an early date relished a debunking version of Odysseus' escapade. In Idyll 11 Theocritus seems to have exploited the element of grotesque pathos in Polyphemus' address to his ram in the *Odyssey* as well as the irony with which Homer treats the monster's self-pitying sentimentality.[98]

κριὲ πέπον, τί μοι ὧδε διὰ σπέος ἔσσυο μήλων
ὕστατος; οὔ τι πάρος γε λελειμμένος ἔρχεαι οἰῶν,
ἀλλὰ πολὺ πρῶτος νέμεαι τέρεν' ἄνθεα ποίης,
μακρὰ βιβάς, πρῶτος δὲ ῥοὰς ποταμῶν ἀφικάνεις,
πρῶτος δὲ σταθμόνδε λιλαίεαι ἀπονέεσθαι
ἑσπέριος· νῦν αὖτε πανύστατος. ἦ σὺ ἄνακτος
ὀφθαλμὸν ποθέεις, τὸν ἀνὴρ κακὸς ἐξαλάωσε
σὺν λυγροῖς ἑτάροισι, δαμασσάμενος φρένα οἴνῳ,
Οὖτις, ὃν οὔ πώ φημι πεφυγμένον ἔμμεν ὄλεθρον.

[9.447–55]

My dear old ram, why are you thus leaving the cave last of the sheep? Never before were you left behind by the flock, but long-striding, far ahead of the rest would pasture on the tender bloom of the grass and arrive first at running rivers, and you would be eager always to lead the way first back to the sheepfold at evening. Now you are last of all. Perhaps you are grieving for your master's eye, which a bad man with his wicked companions put out, after he had overcome my senses with wine, this Nobody, who I think has not yet got clear of destruction. [trans. Lattimore, adapted]

Since Odysseus, unbeknownst to the Cyclops, is at that very moment hiding underneath the ram, the monster's sentimental reflections are woefully misplaced: the ram is leaving the cave last because Odysseus has reserved it for his personal mode of conveyance—not because it is mourning for its master's eye, as he hopefully suggests—and Odysseus will indeed escape destruction at the hands of the Cyclops even as Polyphemus is solemnly and vehemently prophesying the contrary. The plight of Theocritus' enamored Cyclops does not differ essentially from the situation of Homer's creature: both are hapless, genuinely miserable, but irredeemably monstrous ogres destined for ill fortune. Theocritus anticipates Polyphemus' fate twice. The first allusion is made rather casually.

98. Berg (1974), 8–9.

καιόμενος δ' ὑπὸ τεῦς καὶ τὰν ψυχὰν ἀνεχοίμαν
καὶ τὸν ἕν' ὀφθαλμόν, τῶ μοι γλυκερώτερον οὐδέν.

[52–53]

Since you have set me on fire, you may consume my soul and my one eye, too, than
which I have no sweeter possession.

The irony of the second allusion is more heavy-handed and may not produce a uniformly happy effect on modern readers of the poem.

αἴ κά τις σὺν ναὶ πλέων ξένος ὧδ' ἀφίκηται,
ὡς εἰδῶ τί ποχ' ἁδὺ κατοικεῖν τὸν βυθὸν ὔμμιν.

[61–62]

. . . if but some stranger sail hither in his ship, that I may know what pleasure it is to
you [and yours] to dwell in the depths. [trans. Gow]

The most sinister detail occurs in line 51: ἐντὶ δρυὸς ξύλα μοι καὶ ὑπὸ
σποδῷ ἀκάματον πῦρ ("I have logs of oak and beneath the ash a weariless
fire");[99] in Homer's version Odysseus described in similar language his
preparation of the stake with which he put out the monster's eye: ὑπὸ
σποδοῦ ἤλασα πολλῆς ("I drove it beneath much ash"). By substituting an
erotic for a physical calamity, Theocritus has deprived Polyphemus of his
last doubtful claim to heroic dignity and has elaborated instead on the comic
possibilities already latent in the Homeric portrait of his grotesque self-pity.

Another hero who had been a similar target of ridicule long before the
time of Theocritus is Heracles. He appears in Theocritus' second erotic
epistle to Nicias, Idyll 13, where in the role of frustrated lover he replaces
the figure of the Cyclops, who had furnished the didactic example from
mythology in Idyll 11. Theocritus begins by emphasizing that he will view
Heracles in his mortal aspect; the reduction of the heroic to the human as
well as the neglect of divine themes, which Theocritus had announced at the
start of Idyll 16, becomes explicit in the case of Heracles from the opening
of Idyll 13:

Οὐχ ἁμῖν τὸν Ἔρωτα μόνοις ἔτεχ', ὡς ἐδοκεῦμες,
Νικία, ᾦτινι τοῦτο θεῶν ποκα τέκνον ἔγεντο·
οὐχ ἁμῖν τὰ καλὰ πράτοις καλὰ φαίνεται ἦμεν,
οἳ θνατοὶ πελόμεσθα τὸ δ' αὔριον οὐκ ἐσορῶμες·
ἀλλὰ καὶ Ἀμφιτρύωνος ὁ χαλκεοκάρδιος υἱός,
ὃς τὸν λῖν ὑπέμεινε τὸν ἄγριον, ἤρατο παιδός. . . .

[1–6]

Not for us alone, Nicias, as once we thought, was Love begotten by whosoever of
the gods begat him, nor does fair seem fair first to us, who are mortal and see not the
morrow. Even Amphitryon's iron-hearted son—he who withstood the savage
lion—loved a lad. . . . [trans. Gow]

99. For the text and its relation to the Homeric model, see Dover (1971), 177, *ad* 11.51.

Heracles represents, on the one hand, the mythical hero who ultimately obtained immortality and whose superiority to mortal vicissitudes might be expected to separate him from the common lot; on the other hand, even he (according to Theocritus) was subject to the same passion we mortals feel and can therefore be assimilated to the world of ordinary human experience. Heracles evidently shares in the common mortal failure to foresee the events of tomorrow, for he has lavished endless pains on the education of Hylas only to have the boy snatched from him before the process is complete or the fruits of his achievement can be enjoyed.[100] Heracles' violent, clumsy, and ineffectual search for Hylas brings out a comic incongruity between the traditional character of the hero, which Theocritus has retained, and the situation he finds himself in, an erotic impasse for which he is so ill suited. There is a grotesque (and ironic) disproportion between the superhuman vigor of his quest and its sentimental purpose, a disproportion which is heightened by Theocritus' comparison of Heracles, confused and bewildered by the faint, subaqueous cries of Hylas, to a hungry lion:

νεβροῦ φθεγξαμένας τις ἐν οὔρεσιν ὠμοφάγος λίς
ἐξ εὐνᾶς ἔσπευσεν ἑτοιμοτάταν ἐπὶ δαῖτα·
Ἡρακλέης τοιοῦτος ἐν ἀτρίπτοισιν ἀκάνθαις
παῖδα ποθῶν δεδόνητο, πολὺν δ' ἐπελάμβανε χῶρον.

[62–65]

At the cry of a fawn in the mountains a ravening lion hastens from his couch to enjoy a ready feast; so Heracles in his longing for the lad went raging through the untrodden thornbrake, and much country did he cover.

What we find here is an essentially *comic* strategy. Theocritus' practice of subverting traditional heroic figures by depicting them in postures of erotic discomfiture is calculated to appeal to his cultivated readers, who, however conscious they may be of their superiority to Heracles or Polyphemus, can nonetheless be expected to know from their own experience how an unlucky lover feels, and therefore be amused to see their own amorous absurdities reflected, at a safe distance, in his characters.[101]

The subversion of epic themes in Idyll 24, which is also devoted to Heracles, is effected not by involving the hero in erotic complications, as in Idylls 11 and 13, or by dwelling on Heracles' prodigious appetite or dimwittedness—a favorite topic of humor from the time of Aristophanes' *Birds* or Euripides' *Alcestis*—or on his drunkenness, a popular subject for artistic representation in the Hellenistic period; instead, Theocritus devotes his narrative to Heracles' exploits as a baby, concentrating on the charming absurdity of the episode. The story of Heracles and the serpents, teetering pre-

100. Effe (1978), 60. On Idyll 13.5–7, see Mastronarde (1968), 276–77; Effe (1978), 61.
101. Cf. Spofford (1969).

cariously as it does in any case on the brink of the ridiculous, could be imparted a lofty and serious tone only by a solemn evocation of the awesome mystery surrounding the infant's power and by careful suppression of all circumstantial details. Such indeed is the treatment accorded the myth in Pindar's First Nemean Ode, which Theocritus appears to be following, at least in its general outlines.[102] Theocritus' tactic, needless to say, is quite the reverse: his emphasis falls on the wildly improbable incongruities in the story and on all the homely domestic details of the royal household. Thus, Iphicles kicks at his woolen blanket in a terrified impulse to escape; Alcmena tells her husband not to bother with his slippers; the slaves are roused by a Phoenician woman who sleeps by the mill; and when the incident is over, everyone goes back to bed "as if they had been roused to turn a cat out of the house or to shut a window."[103] The comedy of the scene is heightened by the mock-heroic tone in which it is told. Similar features can be found in Idyll 22, the *Hymn to the Dioscuri,* and they have been glimpsed in Idylls 18 and 26 as well.[104]

Theocritus' purpose in these poems has been seen as a destructive and ironical critique of traditional heroic values (and their place in literature) mounted according to Alexandrian standards of good taste and contemporary moral sensibilities.[105] But the poet's irony is not merely destructive, nor is Theocritus concerned only with demonstrating how epic poetry should *not* be written. Theocritean irony serves a positive, constructive purpose insofar as it provides the device—here designated epic subversion—by which traditional subject matter can continue to be treated in heroic verse and treated, moreover, in a manner congenial to a modern—that is, Alexandrian—aesthetic. Theocritus can accordingly be viewed as a proper descendant of his venerable literary ancestors in that he transmits the deeds of legendary heroes in the metrical form consecrated to that end and in conformity with a fully conscious understanding of his social role as it is dictated by the function of art in contemporary culture. Theocritus' transformation of mythological epic in Idyll 13 therefore proves to be a matter of greater significance for Alexandrian poetics than does his contamination of genres in the poem. That the generic link between the Idylls and the earlier tradition of Greek epic poetry is so tenuous as to be almost indiscernible to modern readers, what with our increasingly thematic notions of genre, is a measure of Theocritus' thorough and penetrating reappraisal of the place

---

102. See Gow (1952), II, 415–37, generally, and Dover (1971), 251–53, for a discussion of Theocritus' manipulation of his sources.

103. Gow (1952), II, 415, paraphrasing Legrand.

104. Griffiths (1976); Horstmann (1976), 72–79; Effe (1978), 64–76.

105. Effe (1978), 61; cf. Mastronarde (1968), 288–90.

of *epos* in the Hellenistic literary predicament: genuine continuity with the past could be achieved only by the most radical of departures from tradition.

Theocritus, then, is employing two exactly opposite techniques in his adaptation of material conventionally associated with the genre of *epos*. On the one hand, he selects heroic subjects—particularly those liable to comic undermining—and sets them in a social context more closely approximating his own; heroic exploits are also restricted to the possible range of experiences available to Theocritus' audience, a limitation impinging in a variety of amusing ways on the fantastical adventures normally connected with legendary figures. The transferal of a traditional mythological subject to a mundane, anti-heroic situation creates through ironic juxtaposition a series of humorous incongruities which serve to undermine or abolish the ideal dimensions of the subject (as it had been conventionally represented) and to refashion it into a distant reflection of contemporary experience. This technique has been called epic subversion. On the other hand, Theocritus introduces into his poetry subjects drawn from contemporary society—often from its humblest strata—which by reason of their relatively subordinate social position had either been absent from traditional *epos* or had figured only in the background (in its rustic interludes or epic similes) as foils to the serious themes of the main action. The poet reverses this tactic, casting these low mimetic subjects in roles previously assigned to heroes and using heroic analogies as a foil to the humble, humorous, trivial, or unpretentious themes of his own work, surrounding his lowly characters with a literary dimension by citing mythological precedent for their humdrum, prosaic activities. This technique has been called epic inversion. The two complementary techniques are reflected alike by the fine points of Theocritean language. "Theocritus appears to be working in at least two different directions by using the same device: . . . [W]here he aims at getting the heroic saga into middle-class habits, he brings in, as a disruptive element, colloquialisms and realistic details; on the contrary in a [poem] which really works out a bourgeois [or low-life] theme . . . reality loses its contours by shading into a scene of enchantment . . . : the disruptive elements are in this case the epicisms. Only an inversion of ratios takes place, but the technique is still the same."[106] Each of Theocritus' two methods, then, of treating epic material (inversion and subversion) is ultimately designed to perform the same function: both enable the poet to preserve, renew, and extend the traditional range of the epic genre and adapt it to a modern (Alexandrian) sensibility.

106. Fabiano (1971), 536.

An examination of Theocritus' poetic technique as well as his choice
and treatment of themes reveals a pattern of contrasts or oppositions between bucolic *epos* and heroic *epos*—or perhaps it would be better to say,
between the heroic and non-heroic registers *within* the tradition of *epos*. For
Theocritus does not in general introduce totally alien material into the epic
genre; rather, he elaborates the non-heroic alternatives to the traditional
heroic mode which are already present, albeit inchoately, in early Greek
epic. Theocritus' handling of epic material, in other words, represents a
creative response to existing tensions or polarities within the tradition of
epos as it had come down to him. Some of these polarities have been
touched on in the course of surveying Theocritus' inversion and subversion
of heroic themes. Certain types of Homeric similes, for instance, can be
taken to indicate that the heroic world of the *Iliad* itself is built on a series of
juxtapositions between great and slight, between noble and ignoble, subjects; the resulting pattern of contrasts, which imparts greater complexity to
the meaning of heroism, even obtrudes upon the consciousness of the heroes, as when Achilles in furious indignation calls on Zeus to save him from
being drowned ignominiously like a swineherd-boy (21.282: ὡς παῖδα
συφορβόν). Through his use of similes and of *ecphrasis,* Homer manages to
include in an auxiliary role the very subjects which the requirements of his
theme, the Wrath of Achilles, oblige him to exclude from the main action:
namely, scenes of peace, productive nature, the activities of "little people,"
and life in a self-renewing society. The feat of Homer's narrative is to take
an incomplete world—the "inhabited battlefield" of the Trojan War—and
to make it appear complete: "through memory and anticipation, through
the shield [of Achilles] and especially through the similes the poem reaches
out to a wider world; by a trick of artistic inversion the wider world is
included in the narrower."[107] Theocritus responds to this ready-made thematic polarity within the heroic epic by reversing Homer's priorities, by
expanding upon what had traditionally been peripheral to the heroic action
and by reducing heroic subjects to a more modest, pedestrian scale. Similarly, in replacing scenes of battle with vignettes of frustrated love, Theocritus
capitalizes on another thematic polarity already implicit in the tradition of
epos. Erotic subjects are not foreign to the Greek epic (the Trojan War, after
all, was in a sense caused by love), but the poet of the *Iliad* treats love as a
less serious or absorbing subject than war and confines erotic material to a
relatively subsidiary place in his narrative—to a portrayal of Paris and Helen
and their lovemaking (at the end of book 3) or to the episode of the Διὸς

107. Redfield (1973), 142; cf. idem (1975), 186–87.

ἀπάτη (the seduction of Zeus by Hera in book 14). Theocritus, in according greater prominence to love, might be construed once again to have reversed the conventional thematic priorities of heroic epic.

A different set of alternatives within the epic tradition also proved useful to Theocritus in framing the design of bucolic poetry. Theocritus was able to exploit the contrasts between the *Iliad* and the *Odyssey* which ancient critics perceived, formulated, and eventually converted into the basis of a literary typology. Aristotle, for example, had appealed to the Homeric poems in order to illustrate the four types (εἴδη [1455b32, 1459b8]) of tragedy: καὶ γὰρ τῶν ποιημάτων ἑκάτερον συνέστηκεν ἡ μὲν Ἰλιὰς ἁπλοῦν καὶ παθητικόν, ἡ δὲ Ὀδύσσεια πεπλεγμένον (ἀναγνώρισις γὰρ διόλου) καὶ ἠθική (1459b13–15: "in fact each of his [Homer's] poems has a particular structure: the *Iliad* simple and fatal [*pathētikon*], the *Odyssey* complex—there being recognitions in it from beginning to end—and moral [*ēthikē*]"). Aristotle's distinction between the *Iliad* and the *Odyssey* in terms of *pathos* and *ēthos* became a commonplace of literary critical writing in antiquity—or, to put it more prudently, the *pathos/ēthos* distinction went on to acquire a life of its own. Later theorists, however, differ from Aristotle in regarding *ēthos,* which denotes both "character" or "manners" and a lack of emotional tension ("what you would expect of a normal, not-too-emotional, or irritable man"),[108] as inherently less serious than *pathos,* than a high pitch of emotion and intense suffering (cf. *Poetics* 1452b11–13). Thus, ps.-Longinus, who takes over Aristotle's distinction between the Homeric poems in terms of *pathos* and *ēthos,* suggests that *ēthos* in art represents a falling off from the grandeur of *pathos* and that the *Odyssey* was therefore composed by Homer in a state of decline. Homer's genius for depicting *pathos,* the human spirit *in extremis* (ps.-Longinus' example is Ajax's prayer, "Destroy us in the light!" at *Il.* 17.647), was at its height in the *Iliad,* but it later descended into "a mere ability to portray characters and scenes of everyday life"—as if there were "a positive correlation between realism and lack of seriousness or tension."[109] These assumptions lead to ps.-Longinus' famous judgment on the *Odyssey* (9.15): . . . ἡ ἀπακμὴ τοῦ πάθους ἐν τοῖς μεγάλοις συγγραφεῦσι καὶ ποιηταῖς εἰς ἦθος ἐκλύεται. τοιαῦτα γάρ που τὰ περὶ τὴν τοῦ Ὀδυσσέως ἠθικῶς αὐτῷ βιολογούμενα οἰκίαν οἱονεὶ κωμῳδία τίς ἐστιν ἠθολογουμένη ("the decline of emotional power [*pathos*] in great writers and

---

108. J. F. Lockwood, "ΗΘΙΚΗ ΛΕΞΙΣ and Dinarchus," *CQ,* 23 (1929), 184. Cicero *Or.* 37.128 defines ἠθικόν: "ad naturas et ad mores et ad omnem vitae consuetudinem accommodatum." See Longinus, *On Great Writing,* trans. G. M. A. Grube, Library of Liberal Arts, 79 (Indianapolis, 1957), 16n.

109. Russell (1964), 95, 99; cf. Trimpi (1973), 21n.

poets turns to a capacity for depicting manners [*ēthos*]. The realistic description of Odysseus' household, with its depiction of character, is of this kind. It
is a sort of comedy of manners" [trans. Russell]).

To be sure, the *Odyssey* could afford critics plentiful grounds for considering it a "comedy," above and beyond its occasional attentiveness to
matters of *ēthos:* Aristotle points out that the story of the *Odyssey,* in which
bad characters fail while good ones triumph, belongs to a species of plot that
produces in audiences the kind of pleasure proper to comedy (1453a30–
36).[110] If ps.-Longinus does not find comedy everywhere in the *Odyssey,*
but only in the scenes of domestic intrigue on Ithaca (the very scenes to
which Theocritus is so fond of alluding), perhaps it is because he represents
a well-established tendency of the ancient critics to associate comedy with
both *ēthos* and the depiction of everyday life. Quintilian, for example, de-
taches the Aristotelian distinction between *pathos* and *ēthos* from the context
of the various types of tragedy and makes it over into a criterion for differentiating tragedy from comedy instead: "ut proxime utriusque differentiam
signem, illud comoediae, hoc tragoediae magis simile" (6.2.20).[111] Furthermore, Quintilian connects *ēthos* with humble subjects: "non parum signifi-
canter etiam illa in scholis ἤθη dixerimus, quibus plerumque rusticos, su-

---

110. Moreover, Parry (1957), 20–28, views the *Odyssey* not only as a comedy but as a
romantic comedy; it is this aspect of the *Odyssey*—the removal of the action from immediate
experience to a fabulous or exotic setting—which anticipates the bucolic poetry of Theocritus.
"In the *Odyssey* . . . an alien setting is indispensable: for the Odysseus who is to return to clear
out the suitors and set things right must be defined by the natural world he passes
through. . . . This natural world . . . is nonhuman and static. . . . For in this poem it is,
curiously, only in the nonhuman world that heroic virtue can be expressed; or at least it must
first be expressed there. . . . Odysseus is a hero, but his society does not afford scope for heroic
action. As in Theocritus Daphnis must be in the pastoral, so in the *Odyssey* Odysseus must be
in the fabulous, world. . . . The price paid, in both the romantic comedy and the pastoral, for
this device whereby the poet has a fabulous-natural setting in which to place his hero and to
express himself without irony is, as Longinus objects, the element of unreality that must attend
it." Earlier (pp. 10–15), Parry had argued that "Daphnis, indeed, lives in a world where it is
possible to be a hero. But this world is no longer quite the poet's own—or the audience's. . . .
By a subtle device, it is the very magical unreality of the poetic landscape in the first Idyll that
prevails upon us to accept Daphnis' words as straightforward heroic speech, and to take
pleasure in them as spontaneous dramatic utterance." The distance intervening between the
poet and his subject, or between the subject and the audience, which is so necessary to
Theocritus' technique, can be seen as an inheritance from Homer's romantic comedy. See part
III, chapter 9 (pp. 164–67).

111. Cf. G. M. A. Grube, *The Greek and Roman Critics* (London, 1965), 292: ". . the *ēthos*
of a speech may refer to characterization or to speaking in character, to the character of the
speaker himself, to the less exalted emotional tone or the naturalness of his manner. And it is in
this last sense that *ēthos* was the proper tone of comedy while *pathos* was that of tragedy." For a
modern attempt to revive these ancient rhetorical terms, see H. Bloom, "Wallace Stevens:
Reduction to the First Idea," *Diacritics,* 6, no. 3 (Fall 1976), 48–57, who contrasts "the trope of
ethos" with "the trope of pathos."

perstitiosos, avaros, timidos secundum condicionem propositionum effingimus" (6.2.17: "There is also good reason for giving the name of *ethos* to those scholastic exercises in which we portray rustics, misers, cowards and superstitious persons according as our theme may require" [trans. H. E. Butler]). The same web of associations between *ēthos* or (in Latin) *mores*, comedy, rural figures, realism, and everyday life can be found in Cicero: ". . . certe ad rem nihil intersit utrum hunc ego comicum adulescentem an aliquem ex agro Veiente nominem. etenim haec conficta arbitror esse a poetis ut effictos nostros mores in alienis personis expressamque imaginem nostrae uitae cotidianae uideremus" (*pro Sex. Rosc.* 16.47: ". . . it surely does not matter for our purposes whether I mention [by way of example] the name of a youth from comedy or that of someone from the countryside around Veii. In fact, I think the poets made up such stories in order that we might see our own manners depicted through figures unfamiliar to us and behold a portrait of our daily life").[112] Similarly, in his treatise *On Types* Hermogenes defines "simplicity" (a subtype of *ēthos* common both to bucolic poetry and to comedy) in such a way as to include "infants, men of infantile mind, women, countrymen, and generally speaking simple, guileless folk of any kind"; because women, young men in love, cooks, and "all such personages (gluttons, countrymen, etc.) fall under the head of 'character' [*ēthos*], all or most of them must come under simplicity: they are what are strictly called 'character' elements."[113] As late as the fourth century A.D., Diomedes observes (I, 488 Keil): "comoedia a tragoedia differt, quod in tragoedia introducuntur heroes duces reges, in comoedia humiles atque privatae ⟨personae⟩; in illa luctus exilia caedes, in hac amores, virginum raptus" ("comedy differs from tragedy in that tragedy features heroes, chiefs, and kings, whereas comedy features lowly and private persons; the former includes lamentation, banishment, and slaughter, the latter love-affairs and abductions of maidens"). Ancient literature and literary criticism, as Erich Auerbach has argued, exhibits the presumption that "everything commonly realistic, everything pertaining to everyday life, must not be treated on any level except the comic. . . ."[114] The dedication of The-

---

112. Cf. Quintilian's judgment of Menander (10.1.69): "ita omnem vitae imaginem expressit, tanta in eo inveniendi copia et eloquendi facultas, ita est omnibus rebus, personis, adfectibus accommodatus"; also the famous remark of Aristophanes of Byzantium: ὦ Μένανδρε καὶ βίε, πότερος ἄρ' ὑμῶν πότερον ἀπεμιμήσατο; ("O Menander and Life, which of you imitated the other?"), aptly cited by Russell (1964), 99, in his helpful commentary on ps.-Longin. 9.15. Alcidamas, an older contemporary of Isocrates, called the *Odyssey* a "fair mirror of human life": see Curtius (1953), 336n., and Pfeiffer (1968), 50–51, for a discusion of this metaphor.

113. Hermogenes 2.306 (pp. 323–24 Rabe); trans. Russell and Winterbottom (1972), 573.

114. Auerbach (1953), 31.

ocritus to depicting the *ēthos* of humble folk and of everyday life imparts a
comic design to his work (when it is viewed from an ancient critical perspective) and signals its descent from a perhaps minor but nonetheless significant aspect of the epic tradition—namely, from the narrated κωμῳδία
ἠθολογουμένη, the comedy of manners, in Homer's *Odyssey*. Bucolic poetry is therefore associated with comedy in several branches of ancient literary
criticism.[115]

It should now be possible to identify the fundamental conception uni-
fying the seemingly disparate themes represented by the three tableaux on
the goatherd's ivy-cup in Idyll 1. Even after it had been shown that each of
these themes is present in a majority of the Idylls, it was still difficult to
comprehend why Theocritus had selected them instead of others to stand
for the distinctive subject matter of bucolic poetry—difficult to seize upon
the common element, shared by all three, that would allow them to be
combined into a unitary formulation of the thematic structure of bucolic
poetry. Now that we have considered some of the ways in which the heroic
and bucolic modes of *epos* are related, we should be in a better position to
grasp the underlying unity of the bucolic themes represented on the goatherd's ivy-cup. For, each of the scenes on the cup exemplifies one alternative to the traditional themes and manner of heroic *epos* and illustrates the
means Theocritus will employ in converting epic subjects to a new aesthetic
purpose. They help to articulate, in short, Theocritus' programme of epic
revisionism.

The first scene on the cup, the lovers' triangle, which is not directly
modeled on any passage in Homer or ps.-Hesiod but which seems to borrow language from the murder trial in the City at Peace on Achilles' shield,
serves as a figure for Theocritus' most startling reversal of epic themes: love
replaces war as the foremost subject of the new bucolic *epos;* an erotic theme
is substituted for the traditional heroic one. The struggles and frustrations
of love stand in for the mortal peril of heroic combat, and contests are no
longer waged by chieftains with swords on the battlefield (or by feuding
citizens in a court of law) but by rival lovers, with words, in the alternate
exchange typical of rustic singing matches: ἀμοιβαδὶς ἄλλοθεν ἄλλος/

115. Bucolic poetry was believed to have originated under the same conditions as those
which produced comedy, according to what may have been a Peripatetic tradition: see Cremonesi (1958)—Ławińska (1963) covers much of the same territory, though less helpfully—
and A. Pickard-Cambridge, *Dithyramb Tragedy and Comedy*, 2d ed., rev. T. B. L. Webster
(Oxford, 1962), 155–57, 159. In rhetorical theory, Hermogenes classed Theocritus together
with Anacreon and Menander as a practitioner of the "simple" style, drawing a plausible
stylistic analogy between bucolic poetry and comedy (περὶ ἰδεῶν 2.305–06, pp. 322–24 Rabe);
he was followed in the Renaissance by Minturno, who wrote that "this kind of speech is
appropriate to the Comic and Bucolic Poets": Patterson (1970), 59. Theon is also supposed to
have argued for the kinship of bucolic poetry and comedy, according to Rosenmeyer (1969),
36.

νεικείουσ' ἐπέεσσι (1.34–35). Even Theocritus' peculiar emphasis on erotic frustration can be seen as a corollary to the traditional emphasis on the agony of battle in heroic epic. Furthermore, erotic entanglements must be treated with neither awe nor wonder, as Homer is inclined to treat them, but only with distance, humor, and irony. Love is a great leveler among human beings—few of us can be heroes but we are all subject to the passion of love—and so the erotic theme serves Theocritus' purpose of scaling down the grandiose dimensions of legendary figures to the proportions of everyday life.

The second scene on the cup, the old fisherman, represents the new cast of characters which Theocritus will substitute for the gods, heroes, and kings of mythological epic poetry—a further insistence on the need for scaling down. In this case, emphasis falls on the social reversal of epic subjects, on the derivation of the actors in bucolic *epos* from the lowest social sector instead of the most exalted. Just as the physical strain of the old fisherman is clearly depicted in the sinews which stand out on his neck in the carving of the cup, so in bucolic poetry the traditional tendency to idealize heroic figures and suppress the mundane details of their lives will be abandoned in favor of an emphasis on *ēthos*, on a minute and veristic portrait of the manner and surroundings in which the little people of this world live.

The third scene on the cup, the boy outwitted by foxes, stands for the playful and humorous, not to say comic, treatment to be accorded bucolic themes—one thinks at once of the infant Heracles—and for the substitution of ironic detachment for tragic identification, pity and fear.[116] It also signifies Theocritus' modesty, the drastically reduced scale of his epic poetry, and his concomitant refusal to accept the roles of teacher, prophet, or sage which had previously attached themselves to the profession of poet in the Greek tradition. Theocritus does not claim to instruct; he writes poetry to gratify himself and others: like the boy absorbed in fashioning a cricket cage, the poet of the Idylls finds nothing so pleasant as the activity of pursuing his own hobby. It is now possible to understand why the herdsman, in comparison with other figures from the world of little people, was so important to Theocritus as a vehicle for poetic self-expression: because herdsmen can be observed to while away the time spent watching over their animals by singing and playing musical instruments (they have plenty of time and nothing better to do with it), the pastoral economy furnished Theocritus with a figure which could serve as the type of the Alexandrian poet who lavishes in a leisurely and playful fashion (ostensibly, at least) a

116. Cf. Berg (1974), 10–11: "Theocritus saw himself as the creator of miniatures, of diminuitive vignettes which portrayed in a charming, sometimes quaint, always humanizing manner the scenes and milieux which classical poets had taken much more seriously."

high degree of refinement upon a humble or even pedestrian craft. To sum up, the first scene on the cup represents a reversal of traditional epic subjects (the substitution of erotic for heroic themes), the second a reversal of traditional epic society (the replacement of princes with paupers), and the third a reversal of traditional epic tone and mode of presentation (comic irony is preferred to tragic sympathy).

The oppositional pattern characterizing the relation of bucolic poetry to traditional *epos* has been viewed hitherto as it conditions Theocritus' poetic technique and his manipulation of inherited themes. But in order to complete our inquiry into the ancient literary concept of bucolic poetry we must examine how the structure of bucolic *epos* (what Rossi calls "the dimensions and the disposition of the parts")[117] is defined vis-à-vis the structure of traditional epic. The clearest indication of how Theocritus conceived the literary genealogy of bucolic poetry, and in particular its derivation from a variety of possible sources within the earlier tradition of *epos*, can be found in the Seventh Idyll. Here Lycidas explicitly repudiates the attempt to compose lengthy epic poetry in rivalry of Homer:

> ὥς μοι καὶ τέκτων μέγ' ἀπέχθεται ὅστις ἐρευνῇ
> ἶσον ὄρευς κορυφᾷ τελέσαι δόμον Ὠρομέδοντος,
> καὶ Μοισᾶν ὄρνιχες ὅσοι ποτὶ Χῖον ἀοιδόν
> ἀντία κοκκύζοντες ἐτώσια μοχθίζοντι.

[45–48]

How much I hate the builder who seeks to raise a house high as the peak of Mount Oromedon—and the birds of the Muses who struggle wearily and to no purpose twittering against the bard of Chios!

The alternative to such foolish ambition is to sing the kind of songs Lycidas and Simichidas are about to perform: ἀλλ' ἄγε βουκολικᾶς ταχέως ἀρξ-ώμεθ' ἀοιδᾶς (49: "but come, let's begin our bucolic song right away"). By proclaiming his dislike of contemporary efforts to emulate Homer and by opposing to them the example of his own poetry, Theocritus places himself within the same faction of aesthetic politics as Callimachus—or, rather, he declares himself an adherent to the aesthetic creed whose tenets are most familiar to us from the literary polemics of Callimachus (it is not certain whether he or Theocritus had a greater share in formulating them). Both Theocritus and Callimachus define the character and limits of their poetry by contrast with the Homeric epic.[118] Callimachus enumerates quite unambiguously the defining features of *epos* which his own work lacks:

117. Rossi (1971a), 71.

118. On the "intense framework of pointed allusions existing between Theocritus and Callimachus," see the bibliography supplied by Giangrande (1970a), 7on., to which should now be added the metrical study of Bulloch (1970), especially 268: "Callimachus' attempt to

εἵνεκεν οὐχ ἓν ἄεισμα διηνεκὲς ἢ βασιλ [η
. . . . . .] ας ἐν πολλαῖς ἤνυσα χιλιάσιν
ἢ . . . . .] . ους ἥρωας, ἔπος δ᾽ ἐπὶ τυτθὸν ἑλ[ίσσω

[*Aetia*, fr. 1.3–5 Pfeiffer]

. . . because I did not accomplish one continuous poem [treating of] kings or heroes in many thousands of lines, but roll my *epos* a tiny distance. . . .

Theocritus is no less assiduous in avoiding such lofty enterprises. Like Callimachus, he is also seeking alternatives to traditional *epos;* unlike Callimachus, however, he is reticent about the options: he refuses to articulate his artistic ideology in so many words.[119] Thus, in Idyll 7 Lycidas gives no clearer account of his poetic ideals than whatever can be gauged from the bucolic song which he goes on to sing. But Lycidas does more than simply speak to Simichidas and sing an ode; he acts out a specific role prescribed for him by a narrative pattern in two earlier and authoritative examples of *epos*—and thereby imparts to his words an added programmatic dimension. Without entering into the controversy surrounding the extent, nature, and meaning of the literary symbolism in Idyll 7, I take it as established that the appearance of Lycidas represents in some sense a mock-epiphany of the bucolic muse and that his meeting with Simichidas is modeled on Hesiod's encounter with the Muses at the opening of the *Theogony* as well as on Melanthius' encounter with Eumaeus and Odysseus in the seventeenth book of the *Odyssey*. These two passages, then, represent prototypes of the kind of *epos* which Simichidas, a comic *persona* of Theocritus, is consecrated to compose (or to have composed and perfected already).[120]

Hesiod represented to the Alexandrians the originator of the literary tradition of which they considered themselves a part. As Pfeiffer remarks,

---

break away from the epic tradition found sympathy most with Theocritus amongst surviving Hellenistic poets."

119. See part III, chapter 9 (p. 161, n. 49).

120. Serrao (1971), 13–68, argues that Lycidas does not perform a ceremony of initiation but rather signals his approbation of a prior accomplishment, but this merely means that Simichidas is consecrated retrospectively. (References to the extensive literature on the meaning of Lycidas' behavior in Idyll 7 are conveniently listed in the preliminary notes to an article by Charles Segal, "Theocritus' Seventh Idyll and Lycidas," *WS*, n.s. 8 [1974], 20–76; an updated bibliography of recent work on the poem is provided by Arnott (1979), 99n. The latest conjecture about Lycidas' identity—he is really Pan—is by E. L. Brown, "The Lycidas of Theocritus' *Idyll* 7," *HSCP*, 85 [1981], 59–100.) Van Sickle (1975), 61, has concluded that "Theocritus classifies bucolic epic as a *sub-species*, if we may extend the taxonomic metaphor, of the non-Homeric (in this case defined as Hesiodic) *species* of the epic genus"; this overly schematic view must be modified in the light of the arguments advanced by Ott (1972), which Van Sickle (1976), 23, accepts: "Theocritus meant to demonstrate the proper restraint and elegance in use of Homer to set against the practice of making long Homeric poems, which Lycidas expressly condemns: again precept and example in one and the same work."

"His name was even a sort of programme for the new poetry."[121] In particular, Hesiod stood for the *formal* alternative to Homer within the epic genre itself, and the two poets came to represent the antithesis between slight and great in art. Callimachus' critical vocabulary with its polarizing evaluative terms could therefore be applied to the tradition of epic, in which Homer represented μέγεθος ("greatness"), as Aristotle had said, while Hesiod stood for "fineness" or λεπτότης.[122] The ancient story of a contest between Homer and Hesiod—encouraged perhaps by the possibility of interpreting *Theogony* 26–28 as an attack on the Homeric epics—can be traced back as far as the sixth century B.C., and it suggests that such an antithetical view of the two poets could claim the authority of a long-standing tradition.[123] In creating an alternative to the kind of *epos* distinguished by a heroic subject and a lengthy continuous narrative, which Theocritus and Callimachus alike renounce, Hesiod seemed to have anticipated Alexandrian aesthetic ideals.

First of all, Hesiod set a new and important standard for the permissible length of a work of *epos*. According to Aristotle, epic poetry is distinguished in part by the magnitude of its length: διαφέρει δὲ κατά τε τῆς συστάσεως τὸ μῆκος ἡ ἐποποιία καὶ τὸ μέτρον (1459b17–18). Callimachus' jibe at his opponents was even more specific on this point: a conventional epic comprised "many thousands of lines." The longest of Hesiod's hexameter poems, however, barely exceeds a thousand lines, and since Callimachus—to judge by his *Hecale,* by each book of the *Aetia,* and by his praise of Aratus—seems to have considered ὀλιγόστιχος ("a few verses long" [*Aetia,* fr. 1.9 Pfeiffer]) any poem shorter than a thousand lines, Hesiod might appear to have inaugurated Callimachean standards of brevity in the composition of epics.[124] But in this respect Theocritus was the truer disciple of Hesiod, for he went beyond Callimachus in curtailing the distance he would permit his *epos* to roll: the longest poem in the Theocritean corpus is Idyll 25, of uncertain authenticity, which runs to 281 lines; the normal length of a Theocritean poem is a hundred lines or less. Theocritus' success in composing miniature epics was pushed to an extreme by his imitators, such as the anonymous author of Idyll 19 who produced a

121. Pfeiffer (1968), 117.

122. Ibid., 137–38; *contra,* Koster (1970), 120–22; generally, 124–43. Cf. also Clausen (1964), 184–85. That this polarizing view of Homer and Hesiod represents something of a distorted perspective on both poets should require little emphasis.

123. Cf. Pfeiffer (1968), 11; also relevant is Giangrande's review of G. P. Edwards, *The Language of Hesiod in its Traditional Context,* Publications of the Philological Society, 22 (Oxford, 1971), in *JHS,* 92 (1972), 188–92, especially 191.

124. See, most recently, J. Van Sickle, "The Book-Roll and Some Conventions of the Poetic Book," *Arethusa,* 13 (1980), 8.

complete hexameter poem totaling eight lines! In devising a structure suitable to the aesthetic objectives of his poetry, then, Theocritus was able to appeal to Hesiod for an authoritative precedent within the epic tradition for reducing the magnitude of the form. The dimensions of bucolic *epos*, as a consequence, are distinguished by their drastically diminished scale.[125]

Second, Hesiod's poems, if not so brief as those of Theocritus, are discontinuous, moving from one topic to another or loosely connecting a series of mythological tales. They do not treat a single, continuous theme or narrate a lengthy story from beginning to end; like the *Aetia,* they diverge from the standard of ἓν ἄεισμα διηνεκές and thereby avoid comparison with the grand, sustained narratives of Homer. But the Idylls of Theocritus, though hardly grand, are frequently narrative in form. Not only in the so-called epyllia are narrative segments prominent (for example, in Idylls 13, 24, and 25) but in the canonical bucolic corpus as well (Idylls 6, 7, 8, and 11). To be sure, Hesiod had also manifested a deep concern for the lives of humble folk in the *Works and Days,* and Theocritus, who portrays rural laborers himself in Idyll 10, was doubtless attracted to Hesiod's treatment of the same topic. But the subject matter of Hesiod's poetry is in any case highly variable and so the example of Hesiod alone cannot have furnished Theocritus with an adequate thematic precedent; moreover, the Hesiodic allusion in Idyll 7 refers specifically to the *Theogony,* not to the *Works and Days.* It seems that the importance of Hesiod for Theocritus consists primarily in matters of form, style, and structure. Although Hesiod, then, may have provided a venerable model for the dimensions of the miniature epic which Theocritus undertook to compose, the bucolic poet still lacked a precedent within the epic tradition for continuous narrative poetry devoted to a non-heroic subject.

The obvious forerunner of bucolic poetry in this sense was the *Odyssey*. As we have seen, Theocritus' transformation of the encounter between Eumaeus and Melanthius in book 17 of the *Odyssey* into a scene of good-humored poetic rivalry in Idyll 7 encourages the reader to view bucolic poetry, in part, as an elaboration of the anti-heroic and comic material which had been included in the genre of *epos* from the very beginning by Homer himself and which could accordingly be considered legitimate stuff for an epic poet to treat. Whereas in the *Iliad* Homer had managed to accommodate herdsmen, laboring reapers, workmen, and even a youth singing the Linus-song on the shield of Achilles, and had provided occasional glimpses into the world of "little people" in the similes, it was only in

125. Schmidt (1972), 32–38, treats shortness as a distinguishing feature of the bucolic genre.

the *Odyssey* that he had devoted his full attention to such figures as the drunken Polyphemus, whom Theocritus evokes at the end of Idyll 7 (151–55), or the quarreling herdsmen Eumaeus and Melanthius. Homer's *Odyssey* therefore furnished an authoritative example of *continuous narrative poetry in hexameters* which could dignify humble characters (by portraying a noble swineherd, for example) and hence supply a precedent for Theocritean epic inversion, or depict a hero in circumstances more closely approximating those of an average man (shipwrecked, seduced, engrossed in the details of his domestic arrangements), an early precedent for epic subversion. The formal structure of bucolic poetry, in short, is constituted by a distinctive combination of elements derived from Homeric and Hesiodic *epos,* a combination implicit in Theocritus' fusion of two scenes from archaic Greek epic in the composition of the Seventh Idyll.

CONCLUSION

The Ancient Definition of Bucolic Poetry

Bucolic poetry, as it was conceived and composed by Theocritus and his followers, does not possess an autonomous identity or definition. It is a part of the genre of *epos* and is able to distinguish itself only in the context of the epic tradition as a whole through a delicate interplay of similarities and differences. It owes its genesis to a reaction against preexisting literary formulas, and its own identity is accordingly shaped and determined by the characteristics of the traditional *epos* in response to which it arose. The bucolic *epos* is therefore defined by opposition. The thematic diversity of bucolic poetry, like its fluctuating style, "is something more than a simple tribute paid to the Hellenistic ideal of ποικιλία, for it is a matter not so much of *variatio* as of meaningful *oppositio* reflecting all the polarities of Theocritus' poetry and mediating them in song."[1] The *oppositio* in question is nothing less than the conflict between the traditional and innovative aspects of Theocritean *epos* itself, between its ties to the literary past and its striving for freshness and originality within the bounds marked out by the generic definition of epic poetry. Scholars have used terms like *arte allusiva* and *oppositio in imitando* to describe the glancing, allusive art of the Alexandrian poets, their ζῆλος Ὁμηρικός, and have noted parallels with the Roman literary practices of *imitatio, aemulatio,* and *interpretatio*.[2] But the

1. Fabiano (1971), 536–37.
2. The term *arte allusiva* was coined by G. Pasquali in the title of a 1951 essay reprinted in *Pagine stravaganti* (Florence, 1968), II, 275–82; for a bibliography on the application of the concept of *arte allusiva* to the study of Hellenistic poetry, see Giangrande (1967), 85nn., and (1970a), 46–48, especially 46, n. 3. The term has been invoked more recently by G. B. Conte, "Memoria dei poeti e arte allusiva," *Strumenti critici*, 16 (1971), 325–33; Giangrande (1973a); and Pretagostini (1977). According to Giangrande (1967), 85n., the term *oppositio in imitando* originated with K. Kuiper, *Studia Callimachea, I: De Hymnorum I–IV dictione epica* (Leiden, 1896), 114; see also Conte, "Memoria dei poeti e arte allusiva" (cited above), 330–32, and Van Sickle (1978), 90, who attempt in different ways to redefine the meaning of *oppositio in imitando*.

rubric of *arte allusiva* is too broad: it cannot describe the specific set of opposing pressures (old versus new, great versus slight) within the tradition of Greek *epos*—and ultimately distinctive to it—that shaped bucolic poetry. By contrast, the term *oppositio in imitando,* as it has conventionally been applied, is too narrow: it refers to the characteristic method of literary allusion and reminiscence employed by Alexandrian poets who borrow phrases from Homer or from one another, altering and interpreting them in the process. Theocritus shares this practice with his contemporaries; it is not an identifying characteristic of his poetry. What is unique to Theocritus is the creation of an entire species of poetry—one might even call it a counter-genre—by the device of *oppositio in imitando.* This oppositional pattern informs the entire range of Theocritus' poetic technique, beginning with the mixture of dialects, the hybrid morphology of individual words,[3] the transposition (whether by inversion or subversion) of epic phrases and epithets, and the sequence of contrasting sentences. "This tension of opposite elements in words and sentences and also in two sentences in succession is the dynamic device of composition according to which almost every idyll is built up. It is a matter of well calculated distribution of complementary stylistic tones which through their functional opposition warrant the poetic unity of the poems."[4] But this oppositional pattern extends beyond matters of style, as we have seen: it controls the selection of themes, conditions the portrayal of characters, dominates the construction of plots. It is the distinguishing feature of bucolic poetry.

The oppositional nature of bucolic poetry complicates the task of defining it. One cannot say what bucolic is without also saying what it is not. A negative formulation of the "genre" is required by the basic sets of contrasts which distinguish it both from and within the more familiar tradition of *epos.* Thus, when the few ancient writers close enough to Theocritus to understand, at least in part, the nature of his invention attempt to describe it, they can do so only by means of a series of carefully articulated oppositions. The following epigram of unknown origin is ascribed to Theocritus in the *Palatine Anthology,*[5] probably because it purports to be a dramatic utterance spoken by Theocritus *in propria persona.*

Ἄλλος ὁ Χῖος, ἐγὼ δὲ Θεόκριτος ὃς τάδ' ἔγραψα
εἷς ἀπὸ τῶν πολλῶν εἰμὶ Συρακοσίων,

---

3. See Fabiano (1971), 529, and Dover (1971), xxxviii, on the form κομόωντι in Idyll 4.57.

4. Fabiano (1971), 530.

5. It is prefixed "to himself, since Theocritus was Syracusan" (εἰς ἑαυτόν, ὅτι Θεόκριτος Συρακούσιος ἦν) in the Anthology, but is also transmitted by the Calliergian edition with the lemma Θεοκρίτου εἰς τὴν ἑαυτοῦ βίβλον ("by Theocritus, to his own book") and is included among the prefatory material in the bucolic manuscripts KAET.

υἱὸς Πραξαγόραο περικλειτᾶς τε Φιλίννας·
Μοῦσαν δ' ὀθνείαν οὔτιν' ἐφελκυσάμαν.

[*A.P.*9.434]

The Chian is another, but I, Theocritus, the author of these works, am a Syracusan,
one among many, the son of Praxagoras and renowned Philinna, and I have taken to
myself no alien muse. [trans. Gow]

The testimony furnished by these lines is especially precious, since the
epigram, if not actually by Theocritus, was composed by someone familiar
with his poetry[6] and dates to a period before the mimetic conception of the
bucolic "genre" had taken over—or, at least, it is independent of the tradition which saw rusticity as the most typical feature of Theocritus' poetry.
Instead, the anonymous epigrammatist seems to have modeled his poem on
what he took to be Theocritus' own efforts at self-characterization in the
Idylls. Thus, the second line of the epigram reworks the language and
syntax of Theocritus' poetic confession in Idyll 16.101–03: εἷς μὲν ἐγώ,
πολλοὺς δὲ Διὸς φιλέοντι καὶ ἄλλους / θυγατέρες, τοῖς πᾶσι μέλοι
Σικελὴν Ἀρέθοισαν / ὑμνεῖν ("I am but one; many others beside do the
daughters of Zeus love. May they all be impelled to hymn Sicilian Arethusa. . . "). Similarly, the allusion to Homer ("the Chian") in the first line of
the epigram appears to glance at Lycidas' speech in Idyll 7, in which the
aesthetic ideals of bucolic poetry are set forth negatively, implicitly, by
contrast with the (undesirable but positively stated) qualities of the poetry
of Homer's rivals in heroic epic: "How much I hate the builder who seeks
to raise a house high as the peak of Mount Oromedon—and the birds of the
Muses who struggle wearily and to no purpose twittering against the bard
of Chios" (47: ποτὶ Χῖον ἀοιδόν). But the allusion to Homer may point
more directly to the end of Idyll 22, where Theocritus expands upon the
correspondences and oppositions between his own *epos* and Homer's.[7]

φίλοι δέ τε πάντες ἀοιδοί
Τυνδαρίδαις Ἑλένη τε καὶ ἄλλοις ἡρώεσσιν
Ἴλιον οἳ διέπερσαν ἀρήγοντες Μενελάῳ.
ὑμῖν κῦδος, ἄνακτες, ἐμήσατο Χῖος ἀοιδός,
ὑμνήσας Πριάμοιο πόλιν καὶ νῆας Ἀχαιῶν
Ἰλιάδας τε μάχας Ἀχιλῆά τε πύργον αὐτῆς·
ὑμῖν αὖ καὶ ἐγὼ λιγεῶν μειλίγματα Μουσέων,
οἷ' αὐταὶ παρέχουσι καὶ ὡς ἐμὸς οἶκος ὑπάρχει,
τοῖα φέρω.

[215–23]

6. See, generally, Wilamowitz (1906), 125–26, whose discussion of the epigram lays the
groundwork for the interpretation proposed here.

7. On the significance of these lines for Theocritean poetics, see C. Moulton, "Theocritus and the Dioscuri," *GRBS*, 14 (1973), 41–47; for a different interpretation, see Serrao
(1971), 49–55.

All bards are dear to the sons of Tyndareus, to Helen, and to the other heroes that aided Menelaus to sack Ilium. Glory for you, Princes, the bard of Chios fashioned when he hymned the town of Priam and the ships of the Achaeans, the battles round Ilium, and Achilles [of the great war-cry], that tower of strength in fight; and to you I too bear the soothing strains of the clear-voiced Muses such as they give me and my own store provides. [trans. Gow]

Although Theocritus claims to treat the same subjects as Homer and all the other epic poets (namely, the Dioscuri and the heroes generally) and to benefit no less than they from the munificence of the Muses—of the very Muses, perhaps, who lavished such splendid endowments on Homer—he admits that his poetic household is differently stocked: it affords slighter, more humble domestic offerings. In particular, the songs produced by Theocritus are gifts of the *clear-voiced* Muses, divinities whose inspiration is distilled in a small, sweet, piercing sound utterly unlike the hoarse cry of Achilles on the field of battle. The traditional epithet λιγύς ("clear-voiced")[8] seems to be a characteristic attribute of the slight style in poetry among the Alexandrians; it denotes the refined, even somewhat rarefied alternative to the purportedly foredoomed contemporary attempts to revive heroic epic which resulted in a noise (Callimachus maintained) akin to the braying of asses.

True to the authentic and original identity of bucolic poetry, then, our anonymous epigram defines the art of Theocritus negatively and by opposition. It is wholly free from the pastoral coloring which pervades the Byzantine epigrams contained in the Theocritean scholia. Rather, it places the poetry of Theocritus in the only proper, meaningful context it possesses: the tradition of Greek *epos*. Theocritus is seen to connect his poetry with the genre of *epos* in such a way as to highlight the individual differences distinguishing his original achievement from that of Homer, the founder and preeminent exponent of the epic tradition. The import of the allusion to Homer in the first line of the epigram was correctly understood by Wilamowitz, as his paraphrase indicates: "Homer ist ein anderer, ich bin zwar Epiker, aber nicht Homeriker, sondern habe meine eigne Muse."[9] That the allusion to Homer was similarly interpreted in antiquity is established by a passage in an ancient Life of Homer which includes among the authorities for Homer's Chian ancestry "Theocritus in his epigrams" (Θεόκριτος ἐν

8. Cf. Plato *Phaedrus* 237a and the Homeric passages cited by Gow (1952), II, 407, *ad* 22.221.
9. Wilamowitz (1906), 125; for a different identification of ὁ Χῖος in the epigram, see the forceful (but, I believe, mistaken) arguments of Gow (1952), II, 549–50, followed by Lesky (1966), 719n.

τοῖς ἐπιγράμμασιν [Vita 6.8–9, p. 250 Allen]). In the opinion of ancient critics, therefore, Theocritus could have identified himself and the nature of his individual artistic personality by saying, "I am he who is not Homer."

The oppositional relation of bucolic *epos* to heroic *epos* is most fully elaborated by the author of the *Lament for Bion*. The title character and subject of the *Lament* is clearly identified as a bucolic poet. He is urged to sing his odes to Persephone in language denoting their bucolic status (120: Σικελικόν τι λίγαινε καὶ ἁδύ τι βουκολιάζευ) and is called a *boukolos* (11: ὁ βουκόλος; 65: ὦ βούτα). His song is termed Dorian (12), not merely because of its dialect but also because of its local origin; it purports to belong to the same Sicilian tradition which produced the bucolic song of Thyrsis and the Idylls of Theocritus. The author of the *Lament* declares himself to be "no stranger to bucolic song" (94–95: οὐ ξένος ᾠδᾶς / βουκολικᾶς) inasmuch as he is a pupil of Bion. The longest stanza of the poem is given over to comparing and contrasting the poetry of Homer and Bion; only through a series of elaborate parallels and intricately balanced oppositions can the author of the *Lament* isolate and describe the distinguishing characteristics of Bion's bucolic contribution to Greek poetry.

> τοῦτό τοι, ὦ ποταμῶν λιγυρώτατε, δεύτερον ἄλγος,
> τοῦτο, Μέλη, νέον ἄλγος. ἀπώλετο πρᾶν τοι Ὅμηρος,
> τῆνο τὸ Καλλιόπας γλυκερὸν στόμα, καί σε λέγοντι
> μύρασθαι καλὸν υἷα πολυκλαύτοισι ῥεέθροις,
> πᾶσαν δ' ἔπλησας φωνᾶς ἅλα· νῦν πάλιν ἄλλον
> υἱέα δακρύεις καινῷ δ' ἐπὶ πένθεϊ τάκῃ.
> ἀμφότεροι παγαῖς πεφιλημένοι· ὃς μὲν ἔπινε
> Παγασίδος κράνας, ὃ δ' ἔχεν πόμα τᾶς Ἀρεθοίσας.
> χὠ μὲν Τυνδαρέοιο καλὰν ἄεισε θύγατρα
> καὶ Θέτιδος μέγαν υἷα καὶ Ἀτρείδαν Μενέλαον,
> κεῖνος δ' οὐ πολέμους, οὐ δάκρυα, Πᾶνα δ' ἔμελπε
> καὶ βούτας ἐλίγαινε καὶ ἀείδων ἐνόμευε
> καὶ σύριγγας ἔτευχε καὶ ἁδέα πόρτιν ἄμελγε
> καὶ παίδων ἐδίδασκε φιλήματα καὶ τὸν Ἔρωτα
> ἔτρεφεν ἐν κόλποισι καὶ ἤρεθε τὰν Ἀφροδίταν.

[70–84]

Here, o clearest-sounding of rivers, is a second grief—here, o Art of Song, is a new grief. Before this you lost Homer, that sweet mouthpiece of Calliope, and they say you let flow streams of great lamentation for your fair son and filled all the sea with the sound of your voice. Now once again you weep for your son and melt because of your fresh sorrow. They were both beloved of the sources [of inspiration]: one used to drink from the spring of Pegasus [on Helicon], the other would have a draught of Arethusa. One sang of the fair daughter of Tyndareus [Helen] and the great son of Thetis [Achilles] and Menelaus, son of Atreus; the other celebrated *not* wars, *not* tears, but Pan; he would sing of cowherds in a clear voice and, as he sang, would tend his herds and fashion syrinxes and milk the sweet heifer and teach the kisses of boys and rear Eros in his bosom and provoke Aphrodite.

(Note again the use of λιγύς ["clear-voiced"] and its derivatives.) This passage was analyzed with considerable thoroughness by van Groningen, who extracted from it in particular and from a survey of all the surviving Greek bucolic fragments and poems as a whole a historical definition of bucolic poetry which roughly coincides with the formulation offered here. " 'Bucolic' poetry can include pure pastorals, but it includes poems of another kind besides; these are most frequently love poems, light or pointed anecdotes concerning Eros or Aphrodite, poems whose matter and tone were clearly opposed to the grand tradition of classical epic which poets like Antimachus and Apollonius claimed to bring back to life."[10]

It is now possible to offer a definition of bucolic poetry as it was invented by Theocritus. Bucolic poetry should be viewed not as an autonomous genre but rather as a kind of *epos* that distinguished itself from the heroic and mythological narratives of Homer and Hesiod on the one hand as well as from the discontinuous and didactic epics of Hesiod and the Alexandrians on the other. Bucolic poetry is differentiated from these other varieties of *epos* first of all by its *themes,* which are selected in opposition to the major traditional heroic and mythological subjects of earlier Greek epic, and by the comic or ironic manner with which these themes are treated. Second, bucolic poetry is distinguished by its *form,* which consists either in narrative that is continuous but extremely brief or in alternating dialogue such as can be found in drama and in mime. Finally, bucolic poetry is distinguished by its *language,* which is opposed to the relatively stable dialectal system and evenly sustained stylistic level typical of the linguistic practice normally exhibited by the early Greek poets.[11] Each of these features in and of itself would not have been sufficiently distinctive to impart to bucolic poetry *quella particolare fisionomia,*[12] that characteristic literary profile which separates it from other poetic creations of the Hellenistic age. Taken together, however, they account for the uniqueness of the great majority of the hexameter Idylls and prevent them from being confused with the products of other generic experiments of the period.[13]

10. van Groningen (1958), 300.

11. To say this is not to deny that the language of the archaic Greek epic poets may have been thought to include occasional Doric forms; see Giangrande (1970b).

12. Rossi (1971a), 71.

13. The precise lineaments of bucolic poetry might be more clear to us if we had the benefit of comparing the *Hecale* of Callimachus in its entirety. Presumably, the length of that poem would have prohibited it from being considered an example of bucolic *epos*. Other examples of the widespread Hellenistic tendency to use the hexameter for novel and irreverent purposes (see Legrand [1898], 421) often betray an underlying traditionalism in that they seem

The identifying characteristics of bucolic poetry as a whole, then, are conditioned by the specific characteristics of the traditional genre of *epos* to which they are opposed—except for the meter, which establishes generic continuity. This oppositional tension arises from a carefully balanced set of similarities and differences between bucolic and conventional epic which determines the themes, form, language, and meter of this new species of poetry. It is therefore impossible to acquire a generic concept of bucolic poetry in isolation from an understanding of its oppositional relation to traditional Greek *epos*.

The most careful, able, and profound student of Theocritus known to us is Virgil. The strongest argument that can be advanced in support of the thesis proposed here is to claim that our new definition of bucolic poetry coincides with Virgil's understanding of it and even helps to eliminate an ancient difficulty in the interpretation of his *Bucolics:*

> Prima Syracosio dignata est ludere uersu
> nostra neque erubuit siluas habitare Thalea.
> cum canerem reges et proelia, Cynthius aurem
> uellit et admonuit: "pastorem, Tityre, pinguis
> pascere oportet ouis, deductum dicere carmen."
>
> [*Buc.* 6.1–5]

First in Syracusan verse did our Thalea deign to play, nor did she blush to dwell in woods. When I was about to sing of kings and battles, Cynthian Apollo pulled me by the ear and warned: "A shepherd, Tityrus, should pasture fat sheep and sing a slim song."

The passage is modeled on the famous and influential *recusatio* of Callimachus—his refusal to compose traditional epic poetry, announced in the prologue to the *Aetia:*

> καὶ γὰρ ὅτε πρώτιστον ἐμοῖς ἐπὶ δέλτον ἔθηκα
> γούνασιν, Ἀ[πό]λλων εἶπεν ὅ μοι Λύκιος·
> "........] .. ἀοιδέ, τὸ μὲν θύος ὅττι πάχιστον
> θρέψαι, τὴ]ν Μοῦσαν δ' ὠγαθὲ λεπταλέην·
> πρὸς δέ σε] καὶ τόδ' ἄνωγα, τὰ μὴ πατέουσιν ἅμαξαι
> τὰ στείβειν, ἑτέρων ἴχνια μὴ καθ' ὁμά
> δίφρον ἐλᾶν μηδ' οἷμον ἀνὰ πλατύν, ἀλλὰ κελεύθους
> ἀτρίπτο]υς, εἰ καὶ στειγοτέρην ἐλάσεις."
> τῷ πιθόμη]ν· ἐνὶ τοῖς γὰρ ἀείδομεν οἳ λιγὺν ἦχον
> τέττιγος, θ]όρυβον δ' οὐκ ἐφίλησαν ὄνων.
>
> [fr. 1.21–30 Pfeiffer]

---

to have been conceived as broad parodies or mock-heroic imitations of Homer: compare the poems of Euboeus mentioned in a fragmentary elegy of Alexander Aetolus (quoted by Athenaeus, 15.699bc).

For when I first set a writing-tablet on my knees, Lycian Apollo said to me: ". . . bard, rear your sacrificial victim to be as fat as possible but keep your Muse, my good fellow, fine. This too I bid you: direct your steps a way that wagons do not trample; do not drive your chariot over the same tracks as others, nor on a wide road, but over unworn paths, though your course be more narrow." Him did I obey. Therefore let us sing among those who love the clear-voiced sound of the cicada and not the noise of asses.

Once he had arrived at the second half of his *liber bucolicon,* Virgil might naturally pretend to cast a retrospective glance at the origins of his poetic enterprise,[14] but why should he ever think of appealing to Callimachus? How is Callimachus' manifesto of poetic ideals, and in particular his meditation on the foolishness of composing traditional epic, relevant to the creation of *pastoral* poetry or to the "discovery" of a spiritual landscape? And why is Thalea invoked as the muse who presided over Virgil's earlier experiments in the pastoral genre? These problems of interpretation rapidly disappear when bucolic poetry can be distinguished from pastoral. The *recusatio* of Callimachus can now be seen in its proper light as a necessary and highly pertinent literary precedent for Virgil's effort to differentiate between the various registers or levels (great and slight, high and low) within the genre of *epos,* for only on the basis of such a distinction can a declaration of bucolic poetics be successfully framed. Thus, the peculiar subject matter of bucolic poetry and the oppositional relation between bucolic and traditional *epos* is announced, as it is in the *Lament for Bion,* by the careful antithesis between "kings and battles" (a heroic or historical/ encomiastic theme) and "woods" (a rustic or humble theme). Moreover, Thalea is the muse of comedy, or at any rate of light and witty poetry;[15] as such, she is a fitting patron for what is a comic species of *epos.* By terming his poetry "play," Virgil recalls the bucolic poet's conventional guise of levity and unassuming modesty, which of course does not exclude artistic "labor" or "toil": *meditari* and *ludere* are constrasted in the Sixth Eclogue (lines 8 and 82), just as πόνος and παίγνιον are opposed in the second and third scenes on the goatherd's ivy-cup in Idyll 1. Finally, this slight, anti-heroic, comic, and playful variety of *epos,* as Virgil's backward glance seems to qualify it, is introduced by its Syracusan ancestry, under the auspices of Theocritus, who invented it. Although this bare summary cannot address

14. Cf. Clausen (1964), 193–95; on "mid-work proems" and Eclogue Six in particular, see G. B. Conte, "Proemi al mezzo," *Miscel. in memoria di Marino Barchiesi* (Rome, 1977 [1979]): *Riv. Cult. Clas. e Med.,* 1–3, 263–73, cited with commentary by J. Van Sickle, "Reading Virgil's Eclogue Book," *ANRW,* 2.31.1 (1981), 592, n. 47.

15. Cf. Ovid *A. A.* 1.263–64: "Hactenus, unde legas quod ames, ubi retia ponas, / praecipit imparibus uecta Thalea rotis." Horace's judgment on Virgil's *Bucolics*—"facetum"— is perhaps relevant in this connection.

the larger meaning of Virgil's *recusatio,* its place in the design of his *liber bucolicon,* or the judgment on Theocritus which it implies, the formulation of bucolic poetry which emerges from it—however sketchily—is the closest thing to an independent contemporary authentication of the definition of bucolic poetry proposed here that the ancient literary record is likely to yield.

The scholars of late antiquity, confronted with a bewildering variety of genres and subgenres, of literary conventions and *topoi,* reverted to the Platonic and Aristotelian scheme of classifying poetry according to its mode of representation; they even created further subdivisions by adding a number of dubious taxonomic refinements. With the consequent dissolution of the generic link between bucolic and other kinds of *epos,* the nature of the poetic discovery represented by Theocritus and his imitators slipped from the grasp of literary critics and went on to become—especially when later confused with the evolving breed of pastoral poetry—the intractable and elusive phantom it has ever since remained.

A few foredoomed attempts were made to recapture the ancient meaning of bucolic. In his *De Poeta* (1559), Antonio Sebastiano Minturno divided hexameter poets into the three classes of *Heroici* ("summi"), *Epici* ("mediocres"), and *Bucolici* ("infimi"). He has accordingly been taxed with pedantry and sterile formalism; indeed, his system of classification must have seemed an antiquarian curiosity, a narrowly imitative exercise in classicism, to the contemporary audience of Tasso's *Aminta* scant decades later.[16] Yet, even as late as the turn of the eighteenth century, Chetwood was still repeating Rapin's metrical classification of pastoral as a species of the genus *heroic.*[17] But such efforts were hopelessly outdated, and without the evidence on which to base a meaningful and convincing connection between bucolic poetry and the ancient genre of *epos,* they could not command respect. The future of critical theory belonged to such writers as Le Bossu, who in 1675 banished the *De rerum natura* of Lucretius and the *Georgics* of Virgil alike from the epic category; the classical genres were further fragmented by the modern literary definitions in the Dictionary of the French Academy (Paris, 1694).[18] The word *bucolic,* of course, continued to be current in the modern European languages, as it is in English today. But because ancient bucolic poetry was so closely tied to the literary context from which it arose, there is little cause for wonder that hardly any understanding of the category represented by Theocritus' term survived the death of antiquity.

16. Behrens (1940), 85–89, especially 87; Nichols (1969), 107–10; Rosenmeyer (1969), 5.
17. Congleton (1952), 257; on attempts to revive the hexameter, 255ff.
18. Behrens (1940), 142–45.

APPENDIX

Bucolic Diaeresis and Bucolic Genre

The most sophisticated of those recent critics who continue to regard the so-called bucolic diaeresis as a distinguishing feature of ancient bucolic poetry have tended to minimize its thematic significance and to view it instead as a purely formal determinant of the bucolic "genre." But the very concept of "bucolic diaeresis" is somewhat problematic, since the modern formulation of it (word-end coincident with end of the fourth foot of the hexameter) represents only one of the various criteria which ancient metricians used to identify the bucolic verse. Nonetheless, the earliest description of the bucolic hexameter, which can be found in the late second- or early third-century verse treatise of Terentianus Maurus, conforms roughly to modern notions:

> pastorale volet cum quis componere carmen,
> tetrametrum absolvat, cui portio demitur ima,
> quae solido a verbo poterit conectere versum,
> bucolicon siquidem talem voluere vocari.

[2123–26]

The commentary on Virgil attributed to Probus contains a similar formulation: "carmen bucolicum legem habere videtur, ut versus eius quartus pes partem orationis finiat" (p. 15.13–14 Wendel). This statement, which is actually an abbreviation of Servius' version, is perfectly in line with modern usage. But the fullest ancient definition of the bucolic hexameter appears in the "Life of Virgil" transmitted by Donatus: "cum tribus his probetur metrum: caesura scansione modificatione, non erit bucolicus versus, nisi in quo et primus pes partem orationis absolverit et tertius trochaeus fuerit in caesura et quartus pes dactylus magis quam spondeus partem orationis terminaverit, ⟨et⟩ quintus et sextus pes cum integris dictionibus fuerint" (pp. 18–19 Wendel). These requirements are reiterated by Servius: "adhibetur autem ad carmen bucolicum, quod debet quarto pede terminare partem orationis: qui pes si sit dactylus, meliorem efficit versum, ut ⟨I 3⟩ *nos patriae fines et dulcia*. primus etiam pes secundum Donatum et dactylus esse debet et terminare partem orationis, ut ⟨I 1⟩ *Tityre*" (Prooem., p. 2.5–9 Thilo). Servius regards the matter of diaeresis at the end of the fourth foot as established dogma; he cites Donatus as the authority for the rule requiring an independent dactyl at the start of the line, and he ignores what Donatus has to say about the trochaic caesura of the third foot and the syntactic unity of the words filling the last two feet of the line.

This difference of opinion about the nature of the bucolic verse takes on a special importance in the light of divergences, real or imagined, in the metrical practice of Theocritus and Virgil. Terentianus notes: "plurimus hoc pollet Siculae telluris alumnus, . . . noster rarus eo pastor Maro" (2127–32; quoted by Servius, p. 2.12–14 Thilo). Donatus, after laying out the requirements of the bucolic hexameter, adds: "quod tamen Vergilius a Theocrito saepe servatum victus operis difficultate neglexit" (p. 19.1–2 Wendel). Servius also emphasizes the contrast: "quam legem Theocritus vehementer observat, Vergilius non adeo; ille enim in paucis versibus ab ista ratione deviavit, hic eam in paucis secutus est" (p. 2.10–12 Thilo). More extreme still is pseudo-Probus: ". . . quod Theocritus custodivit. nam Vergilius in primo versu attendit, sequentis protinus aliam formam fecit" (p. 15.15–16 Wendel).[1] Under the influence of this ancient tradition, modern scholars have propounded the absurdity that Virgil "neglected this caesura,"[2] whereas in fact word-end coincident with the end of the fourth foot occurs in 62.5 percent of his bucolic verses, as Valckenaer showed in 1747.[3] E. A. Schmidt, who has undertaken a detailed study of the ancient evidence, suggests ingeniously that Servius arrived at his conclusion about Virgil's metrical deviation through a comparative study of the first three lines of Idyll 1 and Eclogue 1, to which he applied Donatus' metrical criteria for the bucolic hexameter— criteria which are derived in turn, perhaps, from the opening lines of Idyll 1; furthermore, while the frequency of word-end following the eighth position of the hexameter is indeed more pronounced in Theocritus than in Virgil, an even greater discrepancy between the two poets can be observed in the degrees of their adherence to the full set of metrical rules enunciated by Donatus: Theocritus conforms to Donatus' stipulations ten times more frequently than does Virgil.[4]

1. On this passage, see Schmidt (1972), 42.
2. Christ (1890), 446; repeated by Legrand (1898), 423.
3. O'Neill (1942), 167.
4. Schmidt (1972), 38–45; even so, the difference is between ten instances in Theocritus and one in Virgil. Schmidt's statistics (45n.) are not based on a sufficiently large survey of data to be reliable—merely on one hundred lines of Idyll 1—and his results may have been affected by his sample, for the First Idyll possesses some metrical properties which are unusual even by Theocritus' standards: see Van Sickle (1975), 55n.; Dover (1971), xxiii.

But before one can accept Schmidt's view that Donatus' understanding
of the laws of the bucolic hexameter is in fact the correct one, Terentianus'
earlier—and identical—comparative assessment of Theocritus and Virgil
must be explained. For unless Terentianus (whom Schmidt ignores) independently derived his notion about Virgil's abandonment of Theocritus'
metrical norms from Donatus' hypothetical source but at the same time
neglected, inexplicably, to borrow the metrical rules for the bucolic verse
form that Donatus is presumed to have found there (they are nowhere
attested in Terentianus), he would appear to be basing his judgment of the
two poets on the relative frequencies of diaeresis alone, and the high incidence of diaeresis in Virgil's *Bucolics* makes that seem unlikely. The solution
to this problem is to suppose that Terentianus included in his concept of the
bucolic verse not only word-end coincident with the end of the fourth foot
of the hexameter but also dactylic rhythm in the fourth foot. Such an
understanding of the bucolic hexameter is of course implicit in Terentianus'
decision to insert his commentary on bucolic meter into his larger discussion of the dactylic tetrameter rather than to include it in his earlier survey
of the various caesurae. Donatus, it will be recalled, similarly insists on the
presence of a dactyl in the fourth foot of the bucolic hexameter; this law is
also the only part of Donatus' elaborate formulation that Servius treats as if
it were a matter of factual description: the rest of Donatus' rules are either
left unmentioned by Servius or referred noncommittally to Donatus' authority. Moreover, all four of Terentianus' examples of the bucolic hexameter illustrate this doctrine. When Terentianus wishes to render the opening
lines of the First Idyll in Latin, he neither imitates the metrical pattern of the
corresponding verses in Theocritus nor does he make his translation conform to Donatus' specifications; he is careful, however, to precede the
bucolic diaeresis with a dactyl:

> dulce tibi pinus summūrmŭrăt, ⁝ ēn tĭbĭ, pāstŏr,
> proxima fonticulis; et tū quŏqŭe ⁝ dūlcĭă pāngĭs.
>
> [2129–30]

A similar metrical pattern can be found in the opening lines of the Third
Eclogue which Terentianus adduces as (rare) instances of Virgil's observance of the requirements of bucolic versification.

> "dic mihi, Damoeta, cuiūm pĕcŭs? ⁝ ān Mĕlĭbōeī?"
> "non, uerum Aegonis: nupēr mĭhĭ ⁝ trādĭdĭt Aēgōn."
>
> [2133–34]

The predominance of spondaic rhythms over dactylic ones in Latin makes
this coincidence all the more striking. Furthermore, whereas according to
Schmidt's own statistics Theocritus observes all of Donatus' rules in only 10
percent of his hexameters, he does place a dactyl before the bucolic diaeresis
in 78 percent of his lines (a survey of Idylls 1–7, 9–11, 15.1–83 produces the

more modest figure of 71 percent).[5] Thus Dover, in characterizing Theocritus' metrical practice, furnishes the following description: "The fourth
foot is very commonly a dactyl; its two short syllables belong both to the
same word, and there is word-end (the 'bucolic diaeresis') between the
fourth and fifth feet. . . . [E]very one of the first thirteen verses of poem I
follows this pattern and so do all but twenty of the 152 verses in the
poem."[6] Virgil, however, anticipates diaeresis with a dactyl in only 28
percent of his verses.[7] That is most likely the reason that ancient authorities
found the metrical practice of the two leading bucolic poets so much at
odds.

The ancient definition of the bucolic verse, however, was not based on
such statistics. Rather, it seems to have emerged, almost accidentally, from
the methodology employed by ancient grammarians in their attempt to
analyze the internal structure of the hexameter. When in the first century
A.D. students of Greek and Latin poetry began to discuss explicitly the
pattern of regular breaks within the hexameter line, they developed the
terms τομή and *caesura* to indicate that portion of the verse extending from
the beginning of the line up to the break; they did not use these words, as
we do, to designate the break itself (the only ancient authority to employ
the term *diaeresis* in its modern sense is Aristides Quintilianus).[8] It was
therefore reasonable for them to assume that the segment of the hexameter
which stretched from the start of the line to the end of the fourth foot had to
conclude with a dactyl rather than with a spondee, for if such a unit were to
stand by itself as a whole and independent verse, it would then "constitute a
dactylic tetrapody acatalectic. So long as this purely outer-metrical meaning
of Bucolic Caesura prevailed, the fourth foot in it necessarily remained
dactylic; if it had been spondaic it would have made the whole 'verse' a
tetrapody catalectic to two syllables; by this (Hephaestion's) terminology

5. The latter figure is based on the compilation made by Van Sickle (1978), 108n., and
corrected by me, of the statistical data furnished by O'Neill (1942), 138–50, using a sample of
one thousand lines.

6. Dover (1971), xxiii; cf. Rosenmeyer (1969), 14, who defines the term *bucolic diaeresis*
as "the frequent break between units of meaning after a trisyllabic fourth foot."

7. According to Valckenaer's statistics, cited by O'Neill (1942), 167; cf. Fritzsche-Hiller
(1881), 14–15. The scholiastic explanation—that Virgil disregarded the rules governing the
bucolic diaeresis because of their technical difficulty—is not convincing. Virgil's metrical
wizardry was not likely to have been defeated by such a requirement; so much can be surmised
from his willingness to adhere to it under certain extreme conditions: out of eighty-six instances in the *Bucolics* of diaeresis following the fourth foot of the verse and accompanied by
syntactical divisions so sharp as to require punctuation, seventy-four (or 86 percent) are preceded by dactyls: H. Holtorf, ed., *P. Vergilius Maro: Die grössere Gedichte* (Munich, 1959), 296.
As Legrand (1898), 423–24, remarked, "Virgile . . . n'aurait pas négligé une condition du
genre."

8. Bassett (1919), 348–49, who points out that Varro is credited by Aulus Gellius (18.15)
with having observed the frequency of word end following the fifth position in the hexameter;
Varro is thus the earliest known student of the inner metric of the hexameter: see O'Neill
(1942), 160–65.

the heroic hexameter is a hexapody catalectic to two syllables. When, however, the Bucolic Caesura came to mean merely the ending of a word with
the fourth foot, then it ceased to make any difference [to the grammarians]
whether that foot was dactylic or spondaic."[9] Hence, Terentianus is able to
treat the bucolic verse as if it were built around a segment of dactylic
tetrameter.

Before this ancient definition of the bucolic verse can be invoked as if it
were a legitimate means of distinguishing among the bucolic and non-
bucolic poems within the Theocritean corpus, the ancient testimony must
be placed in the context of current knowledge about the "inner metric" of
the Greek hexameter in general.[10] The statistical research undertaken by
Eugene G. O'Neill, Jr., makes it possible to measure the extent to which the
metrical practice of Theocritus differs from that of other Greek epic poets.
In particular, O'Neill's statistics indicate that whenever a word[11] coincides
with the end of the fourth foot of the hexameter, the ancient poets over-
whelmingly prefer to place a dactyl before the diaeresis. For over a hundred
years it has been known that diaeresis follows the fourth foot in approximately 60 percent of Homer's verses:[12] O'Neill's findings confirm this
figure for Homer, Hesiod, and Apollonius as well. In the poetry of Aratus
and Callimachus the incidence of diaeresis after position eight increases to
67 percent. Of those verses in which diaeresis occurs after the fourth foot,
80 percent contain a preceding dactyl in the *Iliad,* 84 percent in the *Odyssey,*
83 percent in Hesiod, 89.5 percent in Aratus, 96.7 percent in Apollonius,
and 98.3 percent in Callimachus.[13] The metrical principle embodied in the
so-called Bucolic Bridge, whereby verses containing a spondaic fourth foot
tend to include both the final syllable of that foot and the initial syllable of
the fifth foot within the same word, can be seen merely as a corollary to the
practice of anticipating diaeresis by a dactyl. Thus, the features which ancient scholiasts considered in some sense peculiar to the bucolic hexameter
are in fact displayed by a majority of the verses composed by Greek epic
poets, archaic and Hellenistic alike.

How, then, did this specific inner-metrical property of the Greek hexameter acquire the designation "bucolic"? The answer is not far to seek.

9. O'Neill (1942), 166.

10. Ibid., 165–70.

11. By "word" O'Neill (1942), 108–11, signifies every separately printed syllabic element
("monosyllables consisting of consonants and elided vowels are excluded" [106n.]), unlike
Maas (1962), 84, who states "we count as a 'word' not every part of a sentence that according
to our system of writing Greek is written separately, but the whole group formed by an
important part of the sentence (i.e., noun, verb, etc.) together with any prepositives (i.e.,
article, prepositions, monosyllabic conjunctions, and pronouns, etc.) and postpositives (i.e.,
monosyllabic enclitics, conjunctions, etc.) that go with it."

12. Cf. Kunst (1889), 854; Bassett (1919), 350.

13. These percentages are based on the totals of word-ends found at position eight by
O'Neill (1942), 138–50.

Certain poems of Theocritus exhibit this metrical feature so prominently as to make it appear a deliberate, even a characteristic, mannerism. To be sure, a survey of Theocritus' metrical practice overall does not show him to depart significantly from the norms of his contemporaries, at least in this one respect. Diaeresis after the fourth foot occurs in 74 percent of the lines in the "bucolic" (that is, pastoral) Idylls, 59 percent of the "mimic" Idylls, and 49.5 percent of the "epic" Idylls.[14] O'Neill's information about the ratio of dactyls to spondees in the fourth foot of those verses that do contain diaeresis covers only Idylls 1–7, 9–11, 15.1–83, but even in these poems (which might be expected to yield unusually high percentages of dactyls in this position) the results fall short of the record set by Callimachus and Apollonius: 93 percent. More surprisingly, a statistical survey of the so-called mimic and epic Idylls yields equally high percentages of dactyls in the fourth foot of verses containing diaeresis: 98 percent in Idyll 14; an average of 94 percent in Idylls 13, 16, 17, and 22.[15]

Moreover, there does not seem to be any strict correlation between metrics and subject matter in Theocritus, certainly no correlation between the incidence of diaeresis (whether preceded by a dactyl or spondee) and the portrayal of pastoral themes. True, the so-called bucolic caesura is unusually infrequent in Idyll 15 (30 percent or 45 percent, depending upon the method of calculation)[16] and the proportion of dactyls to spondees before the caesura is unusually low for Theocritus (only 80.6 percent dactyls); it is hard not to see this deviation as deliberate, especially given that all but one of the violations of the "Bucolic Bridge" occur within the dialogue portion of that Idyll (lines 1–99).[17] Similarly, the incidence of diaeresis after the fourth foot of the hexameter is extraordinarily high in Idylls 1–7, ranging from 74 percent in Idyll 7, to 78 percent in Idylls 2, 4, and 6, to 89 percent in Idyll 5; furthermore, the percentage of dactylic fourth feet in verses containing diaeresis averages 99.5.[18] In short, the first seven Idylls share a tendency to emphasize certain metrical patterns already present in Greek epic poetry and to exaggerate them to the point of extreme mannerism.[19] Since several

14. Kunst (1889), 854.

15. These figures are based on the statistics of Van Sickle (1978), 107n., who calculates word-end according to Maas's principles (see note 11, above). Consequently, there may be slight divergences between the results of Van Sickle's and O'Neill's statistics.

16. The first percentage is that of Kunst (1889), 854; the second is that of Van Sickle (1978), 107n.

17. Maas (1962), 94; cf. Lesky (1966), 725. Bulloch (1970) observes that in certain colloquial poems Theocritus is freer than his Alexandrian colleagues in violating metrical norms; this does not necessarily demonstrate that the poems in question are less "bucolic."

18. These figures are again based on Van Sickle's statistics, which yield results averaging two to four percentage points higher than O'Neill's for the incidence of diaeresis; Van Sickle's method of counting words also produces a percentage of dactylic fourth feet higher than O'Neill's by two-thirds of a percentage point.

19. Cf. Maas (1962), 94–95.

of these Idylls, particularly Idylls 1 and 5, explicitly identify themselves as bucolic poems, it would have been natural for the ancient grammarians, in describing the metrical technique of Homer or Callimachus, to isolate and dub "bucolic" those patterns of epic versification which stand out with especial clarity in certain poems of the Theocritean corpus. But it would be hazardous to make literary divisions among the Idylls on the basis of these calculations. The difference between the frequency of so-called bucolic diaeresis in Idylls 7 (74 percent) and 14 (67 percent) is seven percentage points—considerably less than the fifteen percentage points separating Idylls 7 and 5 (89 percent), for example, and the percentage of dactyls preceding diaeresis is equally high in Idylls 7 and 14; should we then include Idyll 14 among the group comprising Idylls 1–7 or detach Idyll 7 from the group and classify it with Idyll 14? Readers of Theocritus will find neither solution congenial, due to the great diversity between the two poems in subject matter, mode of representation, and setting. Idyll 14 most closely resembles Idyll 15, with which it is at considerable variance metrically. Similarly, the thematic connections between Idylls 6 and 11 are extensive and obvious, yet there is a 22 percent difference in the relative frequency of so-called bucolic diaeresis. The metrical patterning of Idyll 2 marks it as belonging to the group comprising the first seven poems in the Theocritean collection, but its anti-pastoral setting (unique within this group) and its cast of characters seem to associate it most intimately with Idyll 15, which from the standpoint of metrical technique it resembles least. This is not to deny the possible significance of inner-metrical patterning in the first seven Idylls but merely to point out the formidable obstacles which prevent us from interpreting that significance unambiguously and using it as the basis for dividing the hexameter Idylls into a variety of hypothetical subgenres.

The problem can perhaps be brought into sharper focus by analogy with the issues raised by another metrical peculiarity of Theocritus. A number of late antique and Byzantine metricians use the term *boukolikon* to refer to a hexameter verse in which a word ends with the *third* foot, thereby creating an unusual or "forbidden" caesura. A survey of two books each from the *Iliad* and the *Odyssey* yields an average occurrence for this phenomenon of 21 percent in Homer, with a maximum variation of only 2 percent from one book or poem to another. The "epic" Idylls of Theocritus contain this "forbidden" caesura in 17 percent of their verses, but the "bucolic" (that is, pastoral) Idylls exhibit an unusually high average of 38 percent. "Therefore—to continue the inference from numerical relations—if the use of a word-end after the fourth foot about one-fourth more frequently in the bucolic Idylls than in Homer justified the ancients in calling the τομή at this point βουκολική, *a fortiori* the verse in which a word ends with the third foot about four-fifths more frequently in the bucolic Idylls than in the Homeric poems might justly be termed βουκολικόν."[20] Yet no

20. Bassett (1920), 58.

one has suggested that this "forbidden" caesura be used to distinguish the bucolic from the non-bucolic Idylls of Theocritus or that it should constitute a formal determinant of the bucolic "genre." These subtleties of metrical texture are perhaps not without meaning, but it is far from evident that they provide a more stable or reliable indication of genre than other stylistic indices—with which they are often at odds: Van Sickle's metrical statistics cut across Di Benedetto's linguistic groupings of the Idylls.[21]

Theocritus' deviation from the structural norms of the hexameter verse form employed by Greek epic poets before him is for the most part statistically insignificant. According to O'Neill, "so far as the 'innermost' metric is concerned there is really no such thing as an 'Alexandrian hexameter,' in the sense of a body of peculiarities common to the Alexandrians and not found in the early texts."[22] Although Theocritus does make certain traditional features of epic versification the basis of a deliberate metrical patterning in several poems, he appears to have practiced this technique independently of his other experiments in theme, style, and dialect. Theocritus' manipulation of metrical possibilities, then, does not betray any immediately discernible principle of organization, much less an underlying literary programme or concept. The so-called bucolic diaeresis cannot be associated with any innately bucolic poetic qualities, nor can it serve as a reliable determinant of genre: Theocritus' practice of varying the inner metric of his hexameter verse within the limits imposed by tradition results in a whole series of continuous gradations in metrical properties among the Idylls at least as often as it admits of their division into distinct subcategories, and even in the latter case the metrical differences, though statistically significant, may be judged too minute to be perceptible—and hence incapable of alerting the reader to a shift in genre. An analysis of the inner metric of the Theocritean hexameter therefore cannot provide assistance in identifying the genuine bucolic poems or in classifying them according to genre.

21. Van Sickle (1978), 106–08, claims that the increased frequency of bucolic diaeresis in Idylls 1–7 is accompanied by the increased use of epic diction studied by Di Benedetto (1956), but this assertion is belied by his own statistics for Idyll 5 (which exhibits the highest incidence of bucolic diaeresis but is relatively poor in Homeric forms, according to Di Benedetto) and for Idylls 7 and 14 (roughly equivalent according to metrical criteria but totally diverse in their admittance of Homeric forms).

22. O'Neill (1942), 131.

Bibliography

This bibliography contains only items cited more than once in the notes.

Albright, W. F. "Primitivism in Ancient Western Asia (Mesopotamia and Israel)." In *Primitivism and Related Ideas in Antiquity*. Ed. A. O. Lovejoy and G. Boas. A Documentary History of Primitivism and Related Ideas, 1. Baltimore, 1935, pp. 421–32.

Alpers, P. "The Eclogue Tradition and the Nature of Pastoral." *College English*, 34 (1972), 352–71.

———. "What Is Pastoral?" *Critical Inquiry*, 8 (1981/82), 437–60.

Alster, B. "*Dumuzi's Dream*": *Aspects of Oral Poetry in a Sumerian Myth*. Mesopotamia (Copenhagen Studies in Assyriology), 1. Copenhagen, 1972.

Arnott, W. G. "The Mound of Brasilas in Theocritus' Seventh *Idyll*." *QUCC*, n.s. 3 (1979), 99–106.

Auerbach, E. *Mimesis: The Representation of Reality in Western Literature*. Trans. W. R. Trask. Princeton, 1953.

Barrell, J., and Bull, J., eds. *The Penguin Book of English Pastoral Verse*. London, 1974.

Bassett, S. E. "The Theory of the Homeric Caesura according to the Extant Remains of the Ancient Doctrine." *AJP*, 40 (1919), 343–72.

———. "ΒΟΥΚΟΛΙΚΟΝ." *CP*, 15 (1920), 54–60.

Behrens, I. *Die Lehre von der Einteilung der Dichtkunst vornehmlich vom 16. bis 19. Jahrhundert: Studien zur Geschichte der poetischen Gattungen*. Beihefte zur Zeitschrift für romanische Philologie, 92. Halle, 1940.

Berg, W. *Early Virgil*. London, 1974.

Bettini, M. "Corydon Corydon." *Studi classici e orientali*, 21 (1972), 261–76.

Brown, P. "The Rise and Function of the Holy Man in Late Antiquity." *JRS*, 61 (1971), 80–101.

Bulloch, A. W. "A Callimachean Refinement to the Greek Hexameter: A New 'Law' and Some Observations on Greek Proclitics." *CQ*, n.s. 20 (1970), 258–68.

Cairns, F. *Generic Composition in Greek and Roman Poetry*. Edinburgh, 1972.

Calame, C. "Réflexions sur les genres littéraires en Grèce archaïque." *QUCC*, 17 (1974), 113–28.

Chambers, E. K., ed. *English Pastorals*. London, 1895.

Cholmeley, R. J., ed. *The Idylls of Theocritus*. Rev. ed. London, 1919.

Christ, W. *Geschichte der griechischen Literatur bis auf die Zeit Justinians*. 2d ed. Handbuch der klassischen Altertums-Wissenschaft, 7. Munich, 1890.

Clausen, W. "Callimachus and Latin Poetry." *GRBS*, 5 (1964), 181–96.

Coleman, R. "Pastoral Poetry." In *Greek and Latin Literature: A Comparative Study*. Ed. J. Higginbotham. London, 1969, pp. 100–23.

―――. "Vergil's Pastoral Modes." *Ramus*, 4 (1975), 140–62.

―――. *Vergil: Eclogues*. Cambridge Greek and Latin Classics. Cambridge, 1977.

Congleton, J. E. *Theories of Pastoral Poetry in England 1684–1798*. Gainesville, Fla., 1952.

Cooper, H. *Pastoral: Medieval into Renaissance*. Ipswich, 1977.

Couat, A. *La Poésie alexandrine sous les trois premiers Ptolémées*. Paris, 1882.

Cremonesi, E. "Rapporti tra le origini della poesia bucolica e della poesia comica nella tradizione peripatetica." *Dioniso*, n.s. 21, nos. 1/4 (1958), 109–22.

Cunningham, I. C., ed. *Herodas: Mimiambi*. Oxford, 1971.

Curtius, E. R. *European Literature and the Latin Middle Ages*. Trans. W. R. Trask. Bollingen Series, 36. New York, 1953.

Dale, A. M. "κισσύβιον." *CR*, n.s. 2 (1952), 129–32.

Damon, P. "Modes of Analogy in Ancient and Medieval Verse." *UCalPublClPh*, 15 (1961), 261–334.

Della Valle, E. *Il canto bucolico in Sicilia e nella Magna Grecia*. Naples, 1927.

Deubner, L. "Ein Stilprinzip hellenistischer Dichtung." *NJbb. klass. Altert.* 47, (1921), 361–78.

Di Benedetto, V. "Omerismi e struttura metrica negli idilli dorici di Teocrito." *Annali della Scuola normale superiore di Pisa* (Classe di lettere e filosofia), 2d ser., 25 (1956), 48–60.

Dover, K. J., ed. *Theocritus: Select Poems*. London, 1971.

Duchemin, J. *La Houlette et la lyre: Recherche sur les origines pastorales de la poésie*. Vol. I. *Hermès et Apollon*. Paris, 1960.

Effe, B. "Die Destruktion der Tradition: Theokrits mythologische Gedichte." *RhM*, 121 (1978), 48–77.

Egger, É. "De la poésie pastorale avant les poëtes bucoliques." In *Mémoires de la littérature ancienne*. Paris, 1862, pp. 242–68.

Empson, W. *Some Versions of Pastoral*. Rev. ed. New York, 1974.

Fabiano, G. "Fluctuation in Theocritus' Style." *GRBS*, 12 (1971), 517–37.

Fraenkel, E. *Horace.* Oxford, 1957.

Friedländer, P. "Ueber die Beschreibung von Kunstwerken in der antiken Literatur." *Johannes von Gaza und Paulus Silentiarius: Kunstbeschreibungen justinianischer Zeit.* Leipzig, 1912, pp. 1–103.

Fritzsche, H. *Theokrits Gedichte.* 3rd ed. Rev. E. Hiller. Leipzig, 1881.

Frye, N. *Anatomy of Criticism: Four Essays.* Princeton, 1957.

Gallavotti, C. "Sulle classificazioni dei generi letterari nell' estetica antica." *Athenaeum,* n.s. 6 (1928), 356–66.

_____. "Le coppe istoriate di Teocrito e di Virgilio." *La Parola del Passato,* 111 (1966), 421–36.

_____. "Alcmane, Teocrito, e un' iscrizione laconica." *QUCC,* 27 (1978), 183–94.

_____, ed. *Theocritus quique feruntur bucolici graeci.* 2d ed. Rome, 1955.

Gerhardt, M. I. *Essai d'analyse littéraire de la pastorale dans les littératures italienne, espagnole et française.* Assen, 1950.

Giangrande, G. "'Arte Allusiva' and Alexandrian Epic Poetry." *CQ,* n.s. 17 (1967), 85–97.

_____. "Théocrite, Simichidas et les *Thalysies.*" *AC,* 37 (1968), 491–533.

_____. "Hellenistic Poetry and Homer." *AC,* 39 (1970a), 46–77.

_____. "Der stilistische Gebrauch der Dorismen im Epos." *Hermes,* 98 (1970b), 257–77.

_____. "Theocritus' Twelfth and Fourth Idylls: A Study in Hellenistic Irony." *QUCC,* 12 (1971), 95–113.

_____. "Gli epigrammi alessandrini come arte allusiva." *QUCC,* 15 (1973a), 7–31.

_____. "Two Theocritean Notes." *CR,* n.s. 23 (1973b), 7–8.

Gow, A. S. F., ed. *Theocritus.* 2 vols. 2d ed. Cambridge, 1952.

Grant, W. L. *Neo-Latin Literature and the Pastoral.* Chapel Hill, 1965.

Greg, W. W. *Pastoral Poetry and Pastoral Drama: A Literary Inquiry with Special Reference to the Pre-Restoration Stage in England.* 1906; rpt. New York, 1959.

Griffiths, F. T. "Theocritus' Silent Dioscuri." *GRBS,* 17 (1976), 353–67.

Hack, R. K. "The Doctrine of Literary Forms." *HSCP,* 27 (1916), 1–65.

Hallo, W. H., and Simpson, W. K. *The Ancient Near East: A History.* New York, 1971.

Harvey, A. E. "The Classification of Greek Lyric Poetry." *CQ,* n. s. 5 (1955), 157–75.

Hernadi, P. *Beyond Genre: New Directions in Literary Classification.* Ithaca, N. Y., 1972.

Hieatt, C. W. "The Integrity of Pastoral: A Basis for Definition." *Genre,* 5 (1972), 1–30.

Holden, A., trans. *Greek Pastoral Poetry.* Penguin Classics. Harmondsworth, 1974.

Horstmann, A. E.-A. *Ironie und Humor bei Theokrit.* Beiträge der klassischen Philologie, 67. Meisenheim am Glan, 1976.

Hunt, A. S., and Johnson, J. *Two Theocritus Papyri*. Egypt Exploration Society, Graeco-Roman Memoirs, 22. London, 1930.

Jacobsen, T. "Mesopotamia: The Cosmos as a State." In *Before Philosophy: The Intellectual Adventure of Ancient Man*. Ed. H. Frankfort et al. Harmondsworth, 1949.

———. *Toward the Image of Tammuz and Other Essays on Mesopotamian History and Culture*. Ed. W. L. Moran. Harvard Semitic Studies, 21. Cambridge, Mass., 1970.

———. *The Treasures of Darkness: A History of Mesopotamian Religion*. New Haven, 1976.

Kerlin, R. T. *Theocritus in English Literature*. Diss. Yale, 1906. Lynchburg, Va., 1910.

Kermode, F., ed. *English Pastoral Poetry from the Beginnings to Marvell*. 1952; rpt. New York, 1972.

Knaack, G. "Bukolik." *RE*, III. 1. Stuttgart, 1897, cols. 998–1012.

———. "Bukolik." *RE*, supp. 1. Stuttgart, 1903, cols. 260–61.

Koster, S. *Antike Epostheorien*. Palingenesia, 5. Wiesbaden, 1970.

Kramer, S. N. *The Sumerians: Their History, Culture, and Character*. Chicago, 1963a.

———. "Cuneiform Studies and the History of Literature: The Sumerian Sacred Marriage Texts." *Proceedings of the American Philosophical Society*, 107, no. 6 (1963b), 485–527.

———. *The Sacred Marriage Rite: Aspects of Faith, Myth, and Ritual in Ancient Sumer*. Bloomington, Ind., 1969.

Krauss, W. "Ueber die Stellung der Bukolik in der ästhetischen Theorie des Humanismus." In *Europäische Bukolik und Georgik*. Ed. K. Garber. Wege der Forschung, 355. 1938; rpt. Darmstadt, 1976.

Kroll, W. "Die Kreuzung der Gattungen." *Studien zum Verständnis der römischen Literatur*. Stuttgart, 1924, pp. 202–24.

Kühn, J.-H. "Die Thalysien Theokrits (id. 7)." *Hermes*, 86 (1958), 40–79.

Kunst, C. "Der Hexameter des Theokrit." In *Theorie der musischen Künste*. Ed. A. Rossbach and R. Westphal. Vol. 3, pt. 2. 3d ed. Leipzig, 1889, pp. 849–55.

Lattimore, R., trans. *The Iliad of Homer*. Chicago, 1951.

———. *The Odyssey of Homer*. New York, 1965.

Lawall, G. *Theocritus' Coan Pastorals: A Poetry Book*. Cambridge, Mass., 1967.

Ławińska, J. "Agon bukoliczny i komiczny." *Eos*, 53 (1963), 286–94.

Leach, E. W. *Vergil's Eclogues: Landscapes of Experience*. Ithaca, N. Y., 1974.

Legrand, Ph.-E. *Étude sur Théocrite*. Bibliothèque des Écoles françaises d'Athènes et de Rome, 79. Paris, 1898.

Lerner, L. *The Uses of Nostalgia: Studies in Pastoral Poetry*. New York, 1972.

Lesky, A. *A History of Greek Literature*. Trans. J. Willis and C. de Heer. New York, 1966.

Levrault, L. *Le Genre pastoral (son évolution)*. Les Genres littéraires. Paris, 1914.

Lincoln, E. T., ed. *Pastoral and Romance: Modern Essays in Criticism*. Englewood Cliffs, N.J., 1969.

Lindenberger, H. "The Idyllic Moment: On Pastoral and Romanticism." *College English*, 34 (1972), 335–51.

Maas, P. *Greek Metre*. Trans. H. Lloyd-Jones. Oxford, 1962.

Mair, A. W., trans. *Callimachus*. Loeb Classical Library. Cambridge, Mass., 1955.

Marinelli, P. V. *Pastoral*. The Critical Idiom, 15. London, 1971.

Marx, L. *The Machine in the Garden: Technology and the Pastoral Ideal in America*. New York, 1964.

———. "Technology and Classic American Literature." Lecture delivered at Stanford University, 6 October 1978.

Mastrelli, C. A. "Il κισσύβιον di Teocrito." *SIFC*, n. s. 23 (1948), 97–112.

Mastronarde, D. J. "Theocritus' Idyll 13: Love and the Hero." *TAPA*, 99 (1968), 273–90.

Maxwell, G. *The Ten Pains of Death*. New York, 1960.

May, H. G., and Metzger, B. M., eds. *The New Oxford Annotated Bible with the Apocrypha*. New York, 1977.

Mellaart, J. *Earliest Civilizations of the Near East*. The Library of Early Civilizations, ed. S. Piggott. London, 1965.

Muecke, F. "Virgil and the Genre of Pastoral." *AUMLA*, 44 (1975), 169–80.

Murley, C. "Plato's *Phaedrus* and Theocritean Pastoral." *TAPA*, 71 (1940), 281–95.

Nichols, F. J. "The Development of Neo-Latin Theory of the Pastoral in the Sixteenth Century." *Humanistica Lovaniensia*, 18 (1969), 95–114.

Nicosia, S. *Teocrito e l'arte figurata*. Quaderni dell' Istituto di Filologia Greca della Università di Palermo, 5. Palermo, 1968.

O'Neill, E. G., Jr. "The Localization of Metrical Word-Types in the Greek Hexameter: Homer, Hesiod, and the Alexandrians." *YCS*, 8 (1942), 105–78.

Oppenheim, A. L. *Ancient Mesopotamia: Portrait of a Dead Civilization*. Rev. E. Reiner. Chicago, 1977.

Ott, U. *Die Kunst des Gegensatzes in Theokrits Hirtengedichten*. Spudasmata, 22. Hildesheim, 1969.

———. "Theokrits 'Thalysien' und ihre literarischen Vorbilder." *RhM*, 115 (1972), 134–49.

Parry, A. "Landscape in Greek Poetry." *YCS*, 15 (1957), 3–29.

Patterson, A. M. *Hermogenes and the Renaissance: Seven Ideas of Style*. Princeton, 1970.

Perotta, G. "Arte e tecnica nell' epillio alessandrino." *Atene e Roma*, n.s. 4 (1923), 213–29.

Pfeiffer, R. *History of Classical Scholarship*. Vol. 1: *From the Beginnings to the End of the Hellenistic Age*. Oxford, 1968.

Poggioli, R. *The Oaten Flute: Essays on Pastoral Poetry and the Pastoral Ideal.* Cambridge, Mass., 1975.

Pretagostini, R. "Teocrito e Saffo: forme allusive e contenuti nuovi (Theocr. 2,82 sgg., 106 sgg. e Sapph. 31,7 sgg. L.-P.)." *QUCC*, 24 (1977), 107–18.

Pritchard, J. B., ed. *Ancient Near Eastern Texts Relating to the Old Testament.* 3d ed. with supp. Princeton, 1969.

Redfield, J. "The Making of the *Odyssey*." In *Parnassus Revisited: Modern Critical Essays on the Epic Tradition.* Ed. A. Yu. Chicago, 1973, pp. 141–54.

———. *Nature and Culture in the* Iliad: *The Tragedy of Hector.* Chicago, 1975.

Reitzenstein, R. *Epigramm und Skolion. Ein Beitrag zur Geschichte der alexandrinischen Dichtung.* Giessen, 1893.

Rohde, G. "Zur Geschichte der Bukolik." In *Studien und Interpretationen zur antiken Literatur, Religion und Geschichte.* 1932; rpt. Berlin, 1963.

Rosenmeyer, T. G. *The Green Cabinet: Theocritus and the European Pastoral Lyric.* Berkeley, 1969.

Rossi, L. E. "I generi letterari e le loro leggi scritte e non scritte nelle letterature classiche." *BICS*, 18 (1971a), 69–94.

———. "Mondo pastorale e poesia bucolica di maniera: l'idillio ottavo del *corpus* teocriteo." *SIFC*, 43 (1971b), 5–25.

———. "L' *Ila* di Teocrito: epistola poetica ed epillio." In *Studi classici in onore di Quintino Cataudella.* Vol. 2, Catania, 1972, pp. 279–93.

Rüdiger, H. "Schiller und das Pastorale." In *Schiller zum 10. November 1959,* edited by R. Alewyn. Festschrift des Euphorion. Heidelberg, 1959, pp. 7–29.

Russell, D. A., ed. *"Longinus": On the Sublime.* Oxford, 1964.

Russell, D. A., and Winterbottom, M., eds. *Ancient Literary Criticism: The Principal Texts in New Translations.* Oxford, 1972.

Sandars, N. K., trans. *The Epic of Gilgamesh.* Rev. ed. Harmondsworth, 1972.

Schadewaldt, W. "Der Schild des Achilleus." *Von Homers Welt und Werk.* 4th ed. Stuttgart, 1965, pp. 352–74.

Schiller, F. von. *Naive and Sentimental Poetry and On the Sublime: Two Essays.* Trans. J. A. Elias. New York, 1966.

Schmidt, E. A. "Hirtenhierarchie in der antiken Bukolik?" *Philologus,* 113 (1969), 183–200.

———. *Poetische Reflexion: Vergils Bukolik.* Munich, 1972.

Schmidt, E. G. "Bukolik." In *Der kleine Pauly.* Ed. K. Ziegler and W. Sontheimer. Vol. 1. Stuttgart, 1964, cols. 964–66.

Segal, C. P. "Nature and the World of Man in Greek Literature." *Arion,* 2, no. 1 (1963), 19–53.

———. "Simichidas' Modesty: Theocritus, *Idyll* 7.44." *AJP*, 95 (1974a), 128–36.

_____. "'Since Daphnis Dies': The Meaning of Theocritus' First Idyll."
MH, 31 (1974b), 1–22.

_____. "Landscape into Myth: Theocritus' Bucolic Poetry." *Ramus*, 4
(1975), 115–39.

Serrao, G. *Problemi di poesia alessandrina.* Vol. 1: *Studi su Teocrito.* Filologia e
critica, 8. Rome, 1971.

Shackford, M. H. "A Definition of the Pastoral Idyll." *PMLA*, 19 (1904),
583–92.

Smith, G. G., ed. *Elizabethan Critical Essays.* 2 vols. London, 1904.

Smith, H. *Elizabethan Poetry: A Study in Conventions, Meaning, and Expression.* Cambridge, Mass., 1952.

Snell, B. "Arcadia: The Discovery of a Spiritual Landscape." In *The Discovery of the Mind: The Greek Origins of European Thought.* Trans. T. G.
Rosenmeyer. Oxford, 1953, pp. 281–309.

Spingarn, J. E. *A History of Literary Criticism in the Renaissance.* 2d rev. ed.
New York, 1908.

Spofford, E. W. "Theocritus and Polyphemus." *AJP*, 90 (1969), 22–35.

Stark, R. "Theocritea." *Maia*, 15 (1963), 359–85.

Steinmetz, P. "Gattungen und Epochen der griechischen Literatur in der
Sicht Quintilians." *Hermes*, 92 (1964), 454–66.

Todorov, T. "The Origin of Genres." *NLH*, 8 (1976/77), 159–70.

Toliver, H. E. *Pastoral Forms and Attitudes.* Berkeley, 1971.

Trencsényi-Waldapfel, I. "Werden und Wesen der bukolischen Poesie."
Acta Antiqua, 14 (1966), 1–31.

Trimpi, W. "The Meaning of Horace's *ut pictura poesis*." *Journal of the
Warburg and Courtauld Institutes*, 36 (1973), 1–34.

Trypanis, C. A., ed. and trans. *Callimachus.* Loeb Classical Library.
Cambridge, Mass., 1975.

van Groningen, B. A. "Quelques problèmes de la poésie bucolique grecque." *Mnemosyne* (4th ser.), 11 (1958), 293–317.

Van Sickle, J. "Epic and Bucolic (Theocritus Id. vii; Virgil Ecl. i)." *QUCC*,
19 (1975), 45–72.

_____. "Theocritus and the Development of the Conception of Bucolic
Genre." *Ramus*, 5 (1976), 18–44.

_____. *The Design of Virgil's Bucolics.* Filologia e critica, 24. Rome, 1978.

Walker, S. F. *Theocritus.* Twayne's World Authors Series, 609. Boston,
1980.

Way, A. S., trans. *Theocritus, Bion, and Moschus,* Cambridge, 1913.

Webster, T. B. L. "Alexandrian Art and Alexandrian Poetry." In *Hellenistic
Poetry and Art.* New York, 1964, pp. 156–77.

Weingarth, G. *Zu Theokrits 7. Idyll.* Diss. Freiburg, 1967.

Welcker, F. G. "Ueber den Ursprung des Hirtenlieds." *Kleine Schriften.*
Vol. 1: *Zur griechischen Literaturgeschichte.* Bonn, 1844, pp. 402–11.

Wellek, R., and Warren, A. *Theory of Literature.* 3d ed. New York [1962?].

West, M. L. "A Note on Theocritus' Aeolic Poems." *CQ*, n.s. 17 (1967), 82–84.

———. *Studies in Greek Elegy and Iambus*. Untersuchungen zur antiken Literatur und Geschichte, 14. Berlin, 1974.

White, B., ed. *The Eclogues of Alexander Barclay*. Early English Text Society, 175. London, 1928.

Wilamowitz-Möllendorff, U. von. *Die Textgeschichte der griechischen Bukoliker*. Philologische Untersuchungen, 18. Berlin, 1906.

Williams, F. "Scenes of Encounter in Homer and Theocritus." *MPhL*, 3 (1978), 219–25.

Williams, R. *The Country and the City*. New York, 1973.

Index of Passages Cited

General Index

Achilles, shield of. *See* Shield
Adonis, 223
ἀδύς, 122, 130, 131, 164, 172, 186, 234, 253
ἀείδω, 163, 164, 174, 184, 232, 253, 255
ἄεισμα, 212, 245, 247
Aelian, 79, 81
aepolic, 79, 163, 182–86
Ageanax, 121–23
ἄγροικος, 149n., 150–51
Ahrens, H. L., 143n., 154
αἰπολικός, 163, 182–85
αἰπόλος, 128, 182–84, 226–27
Ajax, 220, 229, 231, 239
Akkadian, 86, 88, 100, 109, 116
Alcaeus, 146
Alcman, 152, 231
Alcuin, 36
Alexander Aetolus, 255n.
Alexandria, 157, 194–95, 222
Alexandrian: age, 231; aesthetics, 174–76, 181, 183–84, 203–05, 236, 246 (*see also* Callimachus); criticism (*see* Criticism, Alexandrian); poetry, 124, 132, 174, 177, 181, 183–84, 203–05, 207, 210, 212–14, 230, 250, 254, 266. *See also* Contamination; Hellenistic; Literature: classification of, by genre
Alpers, Paul, 6, 70
Amoeboean, 22, 145, 177–79, 243
Anaphora, 211
Anchises, 96
Anecdoton Estense, 149–51
Antinoe papyrus, 126, 127, 134–35, 155
ἀοιδή, 120–21, 144–45, 148, 165, 175, 244
ἀοιδός, 165, 212, 232, 244, 251, 255
ἀφελής, 19n., 150
Aphrodite, 96, 131, 220, 254

Apollo, 82, 130; (Cynthian), 255; (Lycian), 256; (Nomius), 16n., 148n.
Apollonius of Rhodes, 176, 210, 215–16, 231, 263–64
Aratus (in the Idylls), 123, 126, 178
Aratus (poet), 11, 173, 210, 212–13, 215, 216, 246, 263
Arcadia, 124, 129, 220
Archilochus, 227
Arethusa, 69, 129–30, 251, 253
Ariosto, 37
Aristarchus, 215
Aristides Quintilianus, 262
Aristophanes, 70, 152–53, 235
Aristophanes of Byzantium, 195, 198–99, 215
Aristotelian classification of poetry. *See* Literature: classification of, by mode of representation
Aristotle, 4, 30, 34, 39, 96, 201–02, 203, 208, 239–40, 245–46; on iambic, 197–98; *Poetics*, 197–98, 201–02; use of *epos*, 197; view of diction and meter, 201
arte allusiva, 249–50
Artemidorus of Tarsus, 10, 17, 77, 127–28, 147
Artemis, 80, 82
Asclepiades of Myrlea, 169, 172
Athena, 225
Athenaeus, 10, 16, 76–77, 81, 134, 142, 167–68
Auden, W. H., 68
Auerbach, Erich, 241

Bacchylides, 16, 199
Bacon, Francis, 68